To my father, William Weston,

who taught me that the past was full of drama,

to my grandfather, Dr. James Aubrey Little,

who taught me to look to the future,

and to my mother, Marybeth Weston Lobdell,

a fountain of encouragement and love.

Contents

Part Three   *History*

Foreword

by Walter F. Mondale

WHEN I SERVED as the United States ambassador to Japan, I wish I had had a book like *Giants of Japan* to hand out to visiting Americans, especially young people. By assembling profiles on some of Japan's greatest men and women into one volume, Mark Weston has made it easy for Westerners to learn about Japan's industry, history, and culture.

When first encountering Japan, so much on the surface seems familiar: modern buildings, nice cars, the latest consumer electronics, trendy western clothes—and lots of baseball. Not to mention a democratic parliament and a constitution that reads much like our own. But Japan, an ancient island kingdom that was long isolated from the rest of the world, remains a profoundly different nation in language, religion, values, law, the arts—in fact, in almost every way. Japan has a modern economy like our own, but its history and culture remain distinct—and these things matter.

It is important that Americans learn as much as we can about Japan. We have been called a "tongue-tied" nation because we are apt to be insular, lacking proficiency in other languages and with a tendency toward uninformed preconceptions about other cultures, their histories and values. Unfortunately, this is all too true when it comes to our knowledge and understanding of Japan. Even among educated Americans, I have too often found a shocking ignorance about the most basic matters concerning Japan.

Ignorance is always dangerous. But in international matters, it can lead to depression, cruelty, human hatred, and even war. One sees all of this in Asia—where the three great wars in my lifetime began and where we have, time and again, often for the noblest of purposes, tragically misunderstood these nations and their aspirations.

Even today, it is still too easy to get trapped in a prison of stock images and perceptions about Asia's very complex societies and cultures. More than ever, we need to develop a deeper, more nuanced understanding based on real experience and knowledge, not on caricature and stereotype.

As ambassador, I spent a great deal of time in Japan working and thinking about how we could narrow the dangerous ignorance that divides us from Japan and the rest of Asia. Much of our future will be deeply affected by what happens there and by how we seek to work with these nations. Yet it is almost as though Asia landed in our midst as a surprise and we have not yet adjusted our intellectual efforts to accommodate for its presence. We simply must be far better educated than we are about these matters.

That is why I welcome *Giants of Japan* as a valuable introduction to some of the key figures, past and present, in Japanese culture and society. In an age of information overload, Mark Weston has performed an admirable service. He has a gift for telling readers as much as they need, but not more than they will likely want to know.

I believe that *Giants of Japan* will be a useful aid to businesspeople, journalists, and students, among others, as well as a pleasure for the general reader. This introductory yet thoughtful work is a welcome new addition to the growing number of books about Japan.

Walter F. Mondale was the United States ambassador to Japan from 1993 to 1996. He also served as a United States senator, vice president, and the Democratic Party's nominee for president. He now practices law in Minneapolis.

Preface

WE DRIVE Japanese cars, watch Japanese television sets, and listen to Japanese stereos. We play Nintendo games, eat sushi, and admire haiku, Zen, and the martial arts. Yet in an age of global communication, how many Japanese people can most Westerners name? "Hirohito, um, and Kurosawa, and that baseball pitcher, Irabu? . . ."

Japan is the second most dynamic nation on earth. In some years it has been the world's number one manufacturing economy, having first surpassed the United States in 1993. Some experts predict that by the year 2025, it will be the leader in most high-tech industries. Japan now produces one eighth of the world's goods and services, more than twice as much as the rest of Asia put together. The trade deficit America runs with Japan often exceeds $1 billion a *week*. Japan is also home to nearly a quarter of the world's five hundred largest corporations—close to the total in Germany, France, and Britain combined. Abroad, the Japanese own almost $1 trillion worth of land, securities, and factories.

True, Japan's economy has recently been stagnant because of the inability of its leaders to deregulate inefficient industries that have long been overprotected, or to write off bad loans made during the speculative bubble of the 1980s. Japan's investments abroad are more than matched by these debts. Instability in Japan can depress trade, undermine markets, and reduce income around the world. But as Peter Drucker, the well-known management expert, cautions: "Don't underestimate the Japanese . . . once they reach a critical mass of consensus . . . they have an incredible ability to make brutal, 180-degree, radical changes overnight."

Today Americans and Europeans can no longer afford to limit their horizons to the West. For better or worse, Japan and the West are deeply interdependent. To succeed in the twenty-first century, Westerners need to know a little about the great men and women who have shaped Japan and given their society its unique emphasis on both achievement and serenity.

Westerners and Japanese need to "mutually teach and learn," as Fukuzawa Yukichi wrote in the nineteenth century. It is a rare Japanese businessman or student who doesn't know something about Abraham Lincoln, Mark Twain, and

Thomas Edison, not to mention current American leaders and entertainers. But relatively few Americans and Europeans are aware of the outstanding Japanese, past and present, who have made their nation great.

University professors write superb books about Japan, but often on subjects too narrow to interest many readers. Journalists focus on immediate issues of economics and trade. Somehow, despite good reporting and a wealth of scholarship, a basic knowledge of Japan is still rare even among educated Westerners.

Giants of Japan is meant to introduce Asia's powerhouse to the business reader, teacher, student, and traveler. Though fine histories of Japan exist, I believe readers will enjoy learning about Japan through the lives of its people. Each biography is independent of the others, and the book can be read in any order.

Giants of Japan covers men and women from the sixth century to the present, but it is not an encyclopedia and cannot include every Japanese of consequence. My choice of the men and women to include comes after years of reading, and many conversations with scholars on Japan as well as ordinary Japanese. It is based on both an individual's importance to Japan and my judgment of how interesting his or her life will be to the Western reader. Though the Japanese are reticent about their private lives, I have tried to include personal information in every chapter.

In the prologue to *Henry V,* Shakespeare says that he is "Turning the accomplishment of many years / Into an hour-glass." I have tried to convey centuries of history and decades of economic growth briefly through the stories—enterprising, adventurous, inspiring—of some remarkable men and women. As the hours of this century slip into the next, we need to cultivate mutual understanding and prepare for a new era of shared Japanese and Western leadership.

Acknowledgments

I WOULD FIRST like to thank Ambassador Walter Mondale for his kind words at the beginning of this book.

Many people helped me with *Giants of Japan*. Barbara Plumb encouraged me to write the book when it was only an idea, and introduced me to my agent, Regina Ryan. Regina Ryan edited my proposal and quickly found what every author wants most, a publisher.

I especially want to thank my editor, Deborah Baker, whose thoughtful comments helped make this a better and crisper book, and her hardworking assistant, Cicely Ignatowski. I also want to thank Johanna Tani for reading my manuscript and giving me her objective and valuable opinions, and finally Moriyasu Machiko and Noma Chikako for help with the photographs.

Mrs. Chungsoo Kim of the Oriental Division of the New York Public Library was a master at finding arcane but vital bits of personal information. I would also like to thank the staffs of the Starr East Asian Library at Columbia University, the Japan Society Library in New York, and the Manhattanville College Library in Purchase, New York.

I am deeply grateful for the lengthy hospitality shown to me by Takagi Shinji, his wife, Miyoko, and their children, Shinta, Koji, and Emi in Higashi Fuchu, near Tokyo. Their patience with my unfamiliarity with Japanese customs was remarkable. My thanks also go to Takemoto Manabu and his wife, Yoko, for showing me cities in western Honshu.

I could never have written this book without regular visits to quiet and supportive places to work. At the Hambidge Center in Rabun Gap, Georgia, I'm thankful for the warmth and encouragement of Ray Pierotti, Judy Barber, and Xenia Zed, directors, and Alice Watkins and Anne Warner, assistant directors. At the Dorset House in Dorset, Vermont, I'm grateful to director John Nassivera and manager Gene Sirotof.

My dear friend Suyama Misaho was invaluable in giving me a sense of the Japanese point of view toward various people, events, and issues, and in locating newspaper and magazine articles with hard-to-find personal information about individual "giants."

My stepfather, Leighton M. Lobdell, offered valuable insights and was always encouraging.

My deepest thanks go to my mother, Marybeth Weston Lobdell, a writer who nurtured a family of writers. She was enthusiastic about this book from the beginning.

A Note on Names and Pronunciation

In this book, as in Japan, family names come first, and given names second.

The Japanese language may be difficult to learn, but it is easy to pronounce. The vowels *O* and *U* sound the same as the long *O* and *U* in English, although at the end of a word the *U* is only whispered. The vowels *A*, *E*, and *I* are pronounced as they would be in the word "spaghetti."

The Japanese almost always pronounce syllables with equal force. For example, the proper pronounciation of Osaka is not oh-SOCK-ah, but OH-SOCK-AH.

JAPAN

N
W — E
S

SEA OF JAPAN

HOKKAIDO

HONSHU

• Niigata

• Nagaoka

• Nagano

Tokyo
(Edo)
Yokohama
Oiso
MT. FUJI △
Kamakura

• Fukui

*Battle of Sekigahara
in 1600*

+

LAKE
BIWA

Nagoya

Kyoto •
Ueno •
Kobe • • Nara
• Osaka
Sakai
Wakayama

Ise Shrine

Hamamatsu

Matsuzaka

Izumo Shrine

Tanabe

Onomichi •

Hiroshima •

SHIKOKU

• Hagi

Kochi •

Shimonoseki

Uchiko •

Nakatsu •
Fukuoka
(Hakata)

Kumamoto •

KYUSHU

Nagasaki •

Kagoshima •

TANEGA
*(first contact with
the Portuguese, 1543)*

PACIFIC OCEAN

*1 inch = 110 miles
1 cm = 70 km*

PART ONE
Industry

I

The House of Mitsui
Merchants for Four Centuries

IN 1616 a landless warrior, Mitsui Sokubei, and his thrifty wife gave up their samurai status and began brewing sake and soy sauce to make money. Three hundred years later their descendants were as rich as the Rockefellers, and controlled almost 15 percent of Japan's financial assets. The Mitsui family revolutionized retailing in Japan, and financed much of Japan's industrial growth.

Today the (Mitsui) Sakura Bank is one of the ten largest banks in the world, with assets of almost half a *trillion* dollars. The bank is also the largest stockholder of Toyota, with 5 percent of its shares, and owns similar chunks of Sony, Toshiba, and Fujitsu. A trading company, Mitsui Bussan, handles 4 percent of Japan's imports and exports—the largest trading firm in the world.

The corporations in the Mitsui group make everything from noodles to missiles, and generate yearly sales nearly equal to the gross domestic product of the Russian Federation. Of Japan's six major corporate groups (*keiretsu*), Mitsui is second only to Mitsubishi.

The name Mitsui means "three wells." The family's story begins in 1568, when the Mitsuis lost their land and wells as they fled the army of the ruthless Oda Nobunaga, the first of the three warlords who unified Japan. The Mitsuis settled in Matsuzaka, a town fifty miles (80 km) southeast of Kyoto. There Mitsui Sokubei realized that the unification of Japan could mean lasting peace and the permanent decline of the samurai warriors.

On a trip to Edo, now Tokyo, Sokubei marveled at the size and luxury of the homes of the supposedly low-caste merchants. Returning to his family, he took off his two samurai swords. "A great peace is at hand," he said, with "merchants being accepted in the highest position. . . . The Mitsuis must get money. . . . As a commoner, I shall brew sake and soy sauce, and we will prosper."

Business was slow at the sake shop, but fortunately his wife, Shuho, opened a pawnshop in the same cottage. The daughter of a merchant, she was good at the art of selling. She gossiped with customers in peasant dialect and served them tea, sake, and tobacco. Before long her pawnshop earned more money than the sake brewery.

Shuho worked long hours and had a reputation for thrift. She picked up strings off the street to use in her shop, collected worn-out straw sandals for use as fuel, and even found ways to cook the dregs at the bottom of her husband's soy and sake vats.

Her frugality served her well. Although Sokubei died young and left Shuho with eight children, she managed to save enough money to send her eldest son to Edo with sufficient funds to open a cloth shop.

It was Shuho's youngest son, Mitsui Hachirobei Takatoshi (1622–1694, pictured on page 3), who was the business genius behind the House of Mitsui. At fourteen he became his brother's apprentice; together they opened a second shop, and before long the hardworking Hachirobei was able to manage both stores by himself while his older brother made trips to buy cloth.

The two brothers got along well, but Hachirobei did not approve of his brother's selling silk and fine cotton on credit to the city's noblemen. He knew that lords often defaulted, and there was no legal way a merchant could force a lord to pay his bills.

Hachirobei wanted to ignore the aristocracy and cater instead to the growing middle class of clerks and craftsmen, but his dream had to wait. At twenty-eight Hachirobei had to go home to Matsuzaka and take care of his mother. For twenty-three years Hachirobei was a small-town banker, lending money to farmers and craftsmen.

Around 1651 his mother selected a bride for Hachirobei, an intelligent girl of fifteen named Jusan, the daughter of a local merchant. The couple eventually had sixteen children; eight sons lived to maturity.

When Shuho died in 1673, Hachirobei was finally free to move to Edo with his eight sons and open a cloth store. He also set up a cloth-buying firm in Kyoto.

Hachirobei hung a large wooden sign outside his store that said CASH PAYMENTS AND A SINGLE PRICE. Like his father, Sokubei, Hachirobei was choosing money over status, preferring to sell to commoners rather than extend credit to the aristocracy. Years later, when Hachirobei made an exception and supplied kimonos to the shogun, he was contemptuous of the accompanying honors. "Remember, we are merchants," he reminded his sons.

Because Hachirobei was paid cash right away and had no unpaid debts to collect, he could charge lower prices than any other cloth store. Business boomed. Within a year Hachirobei opened a new store, six times bigger, on the same street.

Charging a single price to everyone was revolutionary. Until Hachirobei opened his store, bargaining was universal in Japan, and no one ever knew if his neighbor bought the same goods at a cheaper price. The people of Edo appreciated the fairness of fixed prices, and also the time saved from not having to haggle.

Hachirobei's next change in retailing came from conversations his clerks overheard at a public bath. Women there were constantly looking for small bits of cloth to make hand bags, pouches, and dust covers. Until then, merchants sold cloth in only one length, about twelve yards, the amount necessary to make a kimono. They refused to cut into a bolt for small sales. Hachirobei, however, announced that he would sell cloth at any length his customers desired.

Sales increased so much that Hachirobei needed an even larger store. He had trouble finding a building because his competitors intimidated potential landlords. One angry rival even built an outhouse next to the Mitsui kitchen.

Eventually Hachirobei bought a building in another part of Edo. When a fire swept through his old district, Hachirobei opened his new store while most of his competitors were still clearing rubble. There has been a Mitsui store at this location ever since. Today it is the site of the Mitsukoshi department store in downtown Tokyo, the largest department store in Japan.

Hachirobei had a flair for publicity. He gave umbrellas with the Mitsui logo on them to customers when it rained, and soon the Mitsui symbol was seen all over Edo. The emblem grew so famous that, to Hachirobei's embarrassment, even brothels used it because everyone knew it stood for "cash payments at a single price."

Hachirobei also paid playwrights to mention his store in their plays, and artists to include it in their wood-block prints. Because of this, we have pictures that show us what the store looked like.

It was a huge open hall, almost as big as a football field, filled with lanterns, and with a raised wooden platform for people to sit on. Banners and kimonos hung from a high ceiling, and drawers were built into the walls. About forty clerks brought tea to their customers and made small talk while teenage apprentices brought cloth from a drawer or a nearby warehouse. Outside, on the street, there was a spectacular view of Mt. Fuji.

During the 1680s Hachirobei opened a second store in Kyoto, and in 1691, a third store in Osaka. Eventually Hachirobei had more than one thousand employees. He housed his apprentices in dormitories, and paid annual bonuses to his senior clerks and accountants.

For all his success at selling cloth, Hachirobei made even more money in banking. He opened his first bank next door to his cloth store in 1683. Quickly he developed such a reputation for accuracy and honesty that when the Mitsui seal was on a roll of coins, people did not even bother to count the coins inside. Hachirobei also established banks in Kyoto in 1686 and Osaka in 1691. At each bank he lent money to other merchants, but not to feudal lords.

Hachirobei warned his sons that the lords were like fishermen: baiting a merchant with the lure of samurai rank, then stopping the samurai's income of rice once a merchant had no more money to lend.

Throughout the 1680s Hachirobei shipped trunks full of gold and silver coins westward from Edo to Kyoto and Osaka in order to buy cloth, while at the same time the shogun collected taxes in Kyoto and Osaka and sent trunks of coins eastward to Edo, the capital city. It was a costly and time-consuming way to transfer money, and it was dangerous. There was always the risk of robbery.

In 1691 Hachirobei persuaded the government to let him collect the shogun's taxes in Kyoto and Osaka, where Hachirobei bought his cloth, and guarantee to repay the government 150 days later in Edo, where he made his sales. This saved the government the risk and expense of shipping money, and also allowed Hachirobei to have a huge sum of money, interest free, for five months. Hachirobei used some of this money to buy cloth, but lent most of it to other reputable merchants. Five months was plenty of time for him to sell his cloth, collect his loans, and repay the government.

When Hachirobei died in 1694, he was both Japan's most successful merchant and its most successful banker. During his last years he thought deeply about how to preserve the family fortune, and before he died he read a detailed will to his children. His eldest son codified the will into a family constitution in 1722. For the next two centuries, until 1945, every member of the Mitsui family, upon turning twenty, swore to obey its provisions.

Instead of dividing the banks and cloth stores among his sons, Hachirobei put the entire business under the control of a single family council. The council also had the power to approve individual debts before they could be incurred, and even marriages before they could take place.

Hachirobei urged his descendants to practice thrift and avoid luxury, and cautioned: "He who does not know, cannot lead. Make your sons begin with the mean tasks of the apprentice." He also recommended that the family "employ men of great abilities," advice that would prove crucial to the family's survival.

Hachirobei's plan to preserve his family's fortune worked. The Mitsui businesses ran smoothly, generation after generation, for 160 years after his death.

Then, in 1853, Commodore Matthew Perry of the United States Navy led his gunboats into Edo Bay, and Japan rushed into the modern world. The shogun tried to modernize the army, but because of corruption constantly ran out of money. Because the Mitsuis were still the shogun's leading bankers, they were expected occasionally to contribute large sums of money to the government. Between 1863 and 1866 the Mitsuis donated one million pounds of silver, yet later in 1866 the government demanded still more money. The family was suddenly on the verge of bankruptcy.

The Mitsui family council remembered Hachirobei's advice to "employ men of great abilities," and hired an outsider as its general manager, Minomura Rizaemon (1821–1877). He was the first of several salaried managers to lead the House of Mitsui; never again would a Mitsui family member hold this position.

Blunt, gap-toothed, illiterate, but highly shrewd, Minomura was an orphan who had worked as a sardine seller and a candy maker before becoming one of the leading gold and silver traders of Japan. Over the years he developed close ties to the government. Now he used them to negotiatate an 85 percent reduction in the amount of money the Mitsuis owed the shogun, saving the family from ruin.

Minomura also looked to the future and secretly sent money to the rebel armies that later overthrew the shogun in the name of the Emperor Meiji in 1868. The new government rewarded the Mitsuis by giving them the power to collect taxes and disburse public money.

For several years the Mitsuis were able to use the new government's money to make short-term loans and earn interest, always taking care to pay the principal back to the government. The income from these loans replenished the Mitsui treasury, and enabled the family to play a major role in the industrialization of Japan.

Minomura ruthlessly pushed the Mitsui businesses into the modern world. He separated the management of the banks from that of the cloth shops, tightened accounting procedures, prevented all but a few of the Mitsui family members from participating in decisions, and tied bonuses directly to performance.

Most important, in 1876, one year before he died, Minomura established the two companies that make up the core of the Mitsui group today, Mitsui Bank and Mitsui Bussan (trading company).

The man Minomura chose to lead Mitsui Bussan was Masuda Takashi (1848–1938). Masuda had learned English by working as an office boy for the first American consul in Japan, then traveled to France while still in his teens. By age twenty he started a trading firm in Yokohama. Masuda led Mitsui Bussan for twenty-five years, until in 1901 he became head of the entire House of Mitsui.

Masuda hated the fact that 99 percent of Japan's international trade was then handled by foreigners, and he began to work for the day when Japan would control its own trade again. He began by importing weapons and blankets for the Japanese army, and by exporting rice, silk, and, most important, coal. Masuda obtained the exclusive right to export coal from the government's mine on the island of Kyushu.

To advertise the high quality of this coal, Masuda sent some of it free of charge to foreign steamships. News of the excellent coal spread quickly, and soon ships and factories throughout Asia were buying their coal from Mitsui Bussan.

In 1888 Bussan bought the Kyushu mine outright. An M.I.T. graduate named Dan Takuma installed machines that made the coal mines much more productive, but for twenty years little was done for the miners. Men, women, and children of the outcast *burakumin* class worked twelve hours a day, seven days a week, in hot shafts choked with coal dust. They lived in shacks and had no holidays, not even the Emperor's Birthday. Many died from cave-ins.

Bussan used the profits from exporting coal to import spinning and weaving machines from Britain, and helped finance the building of electrically lit textile mills that ran day and night. By 1905 Asians were buying Japanese rather than British cloth, and at last Bussan spent money to improve the life of the miners.

Mitsui Bussan now handled one sixth of Japan's total trade, and generated enough revenue to buy oceangoing ships and open branch offices around the world. This enabled Bussan to become a full-service trading company. For a mere 2 percent commission, the firm helped thousands of Japanese manufacturers find and import raw materials, and then ship and sell their finished goods abroad. Mitsui Bussan also helped finance the building of paper, silk, glass, and many other kinds of factories in return for a percentage of each company's stock.

The Mitsui Bank also financed new companies, including the Tokyo Electric Company, which made lightbulbs, and the Shibaura Engineering Works, which built ship engines. Later, the two firms merged to form the *Tokyo Shibaura Electric Company*, known today as Toshiba, one of the world's largest manufacturers of color TVs, VCRs, and computers.

In 1900 the Mitsui family updated its constitution. The power of the family council was transferred to a holding company, run by a board of directors of salaried managers. Only five seats on the board were allotted to the Mitsui family. By then most of the Mitsuis were content just to receive dividends, play golf, collect art, and give the most elegant garden parties in Japan.

When World War I began in 1914, Mitsui factories, mills, mines, and ships worked feverishly to supply the European allies. Japan's industrial production quintupled between 1914 and 1919, and so did Mitsui's revenues and profits. Mitsui entered new industries such as shipbuilding, synthetic dyes, and insurance, and also helped finance Toyoda Automatic Loom, forerunner of the Toyota Motor Corporation.

By the 1920s the three arms of the Mitsui *zaibatsu* (a corporate group run by a single family)—Mitsui Bank, Mitsui Bussan, and Mitsui Mining—controlled over 130 companies and owned stock in many more. Bussan handled half of Japan's foreign trade, and retired Mitsui executives held top positions in government.

The Mitsuis were one of the richest families in the world, but little of their wealth trickled down to the people. When the depression arrived in 1930, Japan's farmers, poor to begin with, received almost nothing for their crops and sank deep into debt. Many began to hate the rich, especially the Mitsuis.

On March 5, 1932, a right-wing farm boy assassinated the leader of the House of Mitsui, Dan Takuma, the M.I.T. graduate who had modernized the Kyushu coal mines forty years before. In the wake of the killing, the Mitsuis decided to respond to frequent criticisms. For the first time, they sold some of their stock on the open market, releasing their companies to public ownership. They also gave large amounts of money to charity throughout the 1930s.

When Japan invaded China in 1937, Mitsui companies supplied the army with coal, explosives, armor plate, and electrical machinery, earning large profits in the process. Mitsui also followed the army into China, taking over mines, utilities, and textile mills. After Japan attacked the United States in 1941, the army forcibly brought more than 35,000 Chinese and Koreans to Japan to dig coal at Mitsui mines. About 5,000 died from harsh conditions.

Japan conquered most of Southeast Asia in 1942, and Mitsui absorbed dozens of companies in the East Indies. For the next three years the Mitsui *zaibatsu* was the largest private business in the world, employing about one million non-Japanese Asians, the vast majority at substandard wages.

In September 1945, one month after Japan surrendered to the Allies, President Harry Truman ordered the breakup of the *zaibatsu* in order to democratize Japan's economy. The American occupation authorities confiscated all the Mitsui family's stock and slowly sold it to the public. The family received some Japanese government bonds in compensation, but inflation was so high that the bonds were soon worth very little.

Because most Japanese barely had enough to eat, the Japanese government passed a graduated tax on personal assets in 1946. Many of the Mitsuis had to sell 90 percent of their art and real estate to pay the tax. This effectively ended the family fortune, and the younger Mitsuis began to work at a wide variety of white collar jobs.

The United States forced the highest Mitsui executives to retire, banned the commercial use of the name "Mitsui," split Mitsui Bussan into almost two hundred parts, and prohibited any of the new companies from hiring more than one hundred former Mitsui employees.

But the American antitrust reforms were too alien to the Japanese business tradition to last very long. Even without family ownership, the separated parts of the old companies slowly began to merge. As one executive described it: "[If] one's parents are dead . . . what could be more natural than the brothers and sisters of a family helping each other to keep going as a group?"

The American urge to modify the Japanese way of doing business cooled after the Communist revolution in China in 1949 and the start of the Korean War in 1950. From then on the United States saw Japan as a capitalist ally in the cold war, and building up the Japanese economy became more important than changing it.

The shares of Mitsui and other *zaibatsu* that the United States sold to the public were largely bought by Japanese banks and corporations, and in 1949 the United States recognized this and legalized the right of companies to own stock in each other. (Even today, when many firms are reducing the size of their outside shareholdings, half of the stock in companies traded on the Tokyo stock exchange is still owned by banks and other corporations.)

In 1950 the presidents of the old Mitsui companies started having lunch together every other Monday, a practice that has continued ever since. The following year the United States allowed Mitsui firms to use their old names again.

The Japanese corporate groups got back together because the services provided by the core companies were simply too valuable. Japanese companies needed loans, and the easiest way for a company to get one was to go back to the bank that it had previously done business with. Manufacturers also needed a trading company to secure imports and sell exports. One firm, Dai-ichi Bussan (First National Trading Company), started business in 1947, and by the time the American occupation ended in 1952, it had absorbed many of the small fragments of Mitsui Bussan. In 1958 Dai-ichi changed its name to the familiar Mitsui Bussan. In 1976, in a move symbolic of its central role in Japan's economy, Bussan built a twenty-four-story headquarters in the center of Tokyo, across the moat from the Imperial Palace.

Today Mitsui Bussan and the Sakura bank form the core of the group of seventy-three corporations that make up the Mitsui *keiretsu*, which in Japanese means "alignment." These "corporate blood brothers" own stock in one another and cooperate closely in matters of finance, trade, and technology. The *keiretsu* is "horizontal," spread across many industries. Mitsui companies produce 30 percent of Japan's cars, 40 percent of its nonferrous metals, 25 percent of its clothes and textiles, and 20 percent of its electrical machinery.

Within the Mitsui group there are also three "vertical" *keiretsu*, belonging to Toyota, Toshiba, and Oji Paper. Each of these corporations has its own network of over two hundred suppliers and distributors, with its own system of cross-shareholdings.

For all their enormous power, the *keiretsu* have no legal existence. They depend entirely on mutual trust. No written agreement exists among the companies, and in theory a company is free to leave a *keiretsu* at any time. A company is also free to do business with another *keiretsu*, and most do when the price is cheaper or the product is better. Often only 10 to 15 percent of a company's business is with other companies in its *keiretsu*.

Some Americans see the *keiretsu* as cartels, with manufacturers and retailers working together to stifle new companies, block imports, and keep prices high. Though true to a degree, the *keiretsu* also compete against one another vigorously, always seeking ways to expand their market share at their rival's expense.

Professor Chalmers Johnson, a specialist on the Japanese economy, has called the *keiretsu* "Japan's most important contribution to modern capitalism," because corporations in a *keiretsu* can raise large amounts of capital far more easily than corporations not aligned with other companies. First, companies in a *keiretsu* have a "sibling" relationship with a giant bank. Second, in a *keiretsu* the largest stockholders are corporations rather than individuals, and at least until recently Japanese corporations have been less concerned with short-term dividends than with long-term growth. Most companies in Japan pay dividends at an annual rate of less than one percent of the price of the stock, a low distribution that penalizes shareholders but leaves a company with extra money to invest in new plant and equipment. (If a company invests unwisely, however, cross-shareholding makes it almost impossible for an outside firm to take over an unprofitable company and hire new management.)

When Mitsui Sokubei opened his sake shop in 1616, he could not have forseen that dozens of Mitsui companies would influence the world economy well into the twenty-first century. But his wife, Shuho, his son Hachirobei, and men like Minomura Rizaemon and Masuda Takashi worked long and hard to make their businesses innovative, and they made detailed plans for the future. The Mitsui *keiretsu* evolved from the relentless drive of many generations of merchants, and that drive is still strong as the Mitsui group makes plans for its fifth century.

2

Iwasaki Yataro and the Growth of Mitsubishi

In 1870 a young businessman named Iwasaki Yataro took over the debts of his native island in return for three steamships, a half dozen sailboats, and some trading rights. Iwasaki (1834–1885) later named his shipping firm Mitsubishi, which means "three diamonds."

Today Mitsubishi is the world's largest corporate group, with thousands of companies. At the core of the Mitsubishi *keiretsu* (alignment), there are currently twenty-eight corporations that own stock in each other, and also own 10 percent or more of the stock of over one thousand smaller companies. Among these twenty-eight core companies are six of the world's hundred largest corporations:

❖ The Mitsubishi Corporation is one of the five or six largest companies in the world. Mitsubishi Shoji, as the trading company is known in Japan, imports raw materials such as iron, oil, and soybeans, and exports finished products such as steel, cars, and tofu for thousands of Japanese companies too small to import and export themselves. It handles these small firms' financing, insurance, warehousing, transportation, customs forms, and overseas marketing, in return for commissions and fees.

The Mitsubishi Corporation owns stock in hundreds of other firms, including 9 percent of Mitsubishi Motors and one percent of the Bank of Tokyo-Mitsubishi. In turn, the bank owns almost 10 percent of the giant trading company.

❖ The Bank of Tokyo-Mitsubishi is the world's largest bank and second largest financial services company (after Citigroup). Its assets total $700 billion, twice the size of America's Chase Manhattan Bank and almost as large as Canada's gross national product. Like the Mitsubishi Corporation, the Bank of Tokyo-Mitsubishi owns stock in hundreds of companies, including 3.6 percent of Mitsubishi Heavy Industries, which in turn owns 2 percent of the bank.

❖ Mitsubishi Heavy Industries (MHI) is both the world's largest manufacturer of industrial equipment and Japan's biggest defense contractor. Almost as large as Caterpillar and John Deere combined, it builds ships, aircraft, bulldozers, power stations, chemical plants, engines, and turbines. Mitsubishi Heavy Industries owns 24% of Mitsubishi Motors, which was a division of MHI until 1970.

❖ Mitsubishi Motors is perhaps the most famous Mitsubishi company, as it is the tenth largest car manufacturer and sixth largest truck producer in the world. The 1.5 million vehicles it makes annually include the Eclipse, Galant, and Diamante cars, the recreational Montero, and the Fuso line of trucks. Mitsubishi Motors is too new a firm to own blocks of stock in older Mitsubishi companies, but it has relationships with other Mitsubishi firms. Nearly all Mitsubishi vehicles, for example, use ignition systems made by Mitsubishi Electric.

❖ Mitsubishi Electric is the world's tenth largest manufacturer of semiconductors, the "chips" that make up a computer. It is a leading innovator in large-screen televisions and satellite design, and is Japan's second largest manufacturer of air conditioners and microwave ovens. The company also makes mobile telephones, locomotives, and many kinds of electrical devices.

❖ Meiji Mutual Life Insurance, the sixth Mitsubishi company among the world's hundred largest corporations, owns 4 percent of Mitsubishi Electric. It is the world's fifth largest life insurer. One of the oldest Mitsubishi firms, it owns between 3 and 8 percent of the stock of nearly all of the core Mitsubishi companies.

Other Mitsubishi core companies include the Nikon Corporation, one of the world's leading camera makers, Kirin Brewery, brewer of half the beer drunk in Japan, Nippon Yusen Kaisha (N.Y.K.), the world's largest shipping company, Tokio Marine and Fire Insurance, the largest casualty insurer in Asia, Asahi Glass, the world's largest maker of glass for car windows and television tubes, and Mitsubishi Estate, which owns $100 billion worth of office buildings in Tokyo, but lost over $1.5 billion in 1995 when New York's Rockefeller Center, of which it owned 80 percent, went bankrupt. Sixteen other core corporations share the Mitsubishi name: Mitsubishi -Aluminium, -Cable, -Chemical, -Construction, -Gas Chemical, -Kakoki (chemical engineering), -Logistics (warehousing), -Materials, -Oil, -Paper Mills, -Plastics, -Rayon, -Research Institute (management consulting), -Shindoh (copper), -Steel, and -Trust & Banking.

Almost all of these core corporations have dozens and even hundreds of affiliates and subsidiaries. The total number of Mitsubishi-affiliated companies around the world is unknown, but the figure is undoubtedly in the thousands.

The Founder

THE MAN WHO started it all, Iwasaki Yataro, was born on January 9, 1835, in the village of Inokuchi, near the southern coast of the island of Shikoku. His grandfather had spent the family savings on drink, and to raise money sold his family's samurai status in 1795. His son, Iwasaki's father, became a peasant, though with enough land to sublet to tenant farmers. Like his father, he also drank heavily.

Iwasaki's mother came from an unusually progressive and well-educated family. Not only was her father a doctor, both her brothers were doctors of "Dutch" (Western) medicine, and she had been taught to read and write. Under his mother's influence, the boy spent many days reading Japanese history and literature on a hill behind his home. At thirteen he went to school in Kochi, capital of Tosa, one of feudal Japan's most forward-looking provinces. There he studied the Chinese classics and was one of the best students in his class.

In 1854, the year after United States Commodore Matthew Perry's arrival, nineteen-year-old Iwasaki became an unpaid aide to a minor Tosa official in Edo, soon to be renamed Tokyo. After a year and a half, Iwasaki hurried home. His father had accused the village headman several times of cheating farmers, but this time the dispute came to blows and his father was severely injured. Iwasaki took the case to court. The suit was dismissed. In disgust, Iwasaki painted OUR LOCAL GOVERNMENT IS CORRUPT outside the magistrate's office. When it was whitewashed, he painted it again.

The magistrate charged Iwasaki with libeling the government and threw him in jail for seven months in 1856. In prison Iwasaki was fascinated by an abacus, a counting tool used by merchants but frowned upon as vulgar by farmers and samurai. Jail was no place for snobbery, and during his imprisonment Iwasaki mastered the art of high-speed calculation.

Upon leaving prison, Iwasaki taught school for a year in a neighboring village. A samurai named Yoshida Toyo also become a teacher. Yoshida had been in charge of Tosa's trade and industry until he lost a power struggle. Now he welcomed Iwasaki as a young colleague.

Unlike most Japanese in the mid-nineteenth century, Yoshida understood that military power was based on economics, and that Japan could not be equal to the West until it industrialized. He taught Iwasaki about the modern world, and in 1859 got him a job as a clerk at the province of Tosa's trading office in Nagasaki. There Iwasaki helped export camphor tree oil, a soothing liniment, and import modern weapons, but kept his job only two years because he failed to learn English.

Iwasaki did not return to his village in defeat. He had saved enough money to buy back his family's samurai status. Then on February 1, 1862, he married a seventeen-year-old named Kise.

Kise was a hard working and plain woman. Once when she put on makeup her husband laughed and said, "A crow covered with starch is still a crow." Later, when Iwasaki was rich, he often went to geisha houses. Kise forgave him for being unfaithful, and in her old age always told her grandchildren that their grandfather was a great man. The Iwasakis had nine children; five reached maturity.

Two months after Iwasaki married, his mentor Yoshida Toyo was murdered by extreme isolationists in Osaka. Iwasaki and a friend were obliged to go to Osaka to seek revenge, but Iwasaki saw the mission as old-fashioned and pointless and returned home to Tosa.

Coming home was the right decision, for Iwasaki's friend was killed. But colleagues thought Iwasaki had been cowardly and for three years it was impossible for him to get a decent job. To make ends meet, Iwasaki chopped trees and drained rice fields. Finally he became a clerk at the Tosa Industry Promotion Agency, but his rank was so low that he was not allowed even to express an opinion.

Fortunately, a superior at the agency noticed Iwasaki's hard work and brought Iwasaki with him to the Tosa government's trading office in Nagasaki in 1867. Because Tosa was in revolt against the shogun, it bought large amounts of rifles, cannon, and gunpowder from Dutch and English arms dealers, and ran up a huge debt.

Using champagne, geisha, and a bribe to an interpreter to smooth over negotiations, Iwasaki borrowed money from an American trading firm and refinanced Tosa's debt. In return he gave the Americans the right to sell Tosa's soothing camphor oil.

The next year the Tosa government transferred Iwasaki to Osaka. There he made more deals with foreign merchants, exporting crops and importing weapons. But Tosa's business dealings were coming to an end. The new central government that overthrew the shogun in 1868 was privatizing the businesses owned by the old feudal provinces. Tosa's government had to decide what to do with its assets and debts.

In a meeting with senior Tosa officials in 1870, Iwasaki agreed to take over Tosa's debts in return for three steamships, some sailboats, and the exclusive rights to sell Tosa's lumber, tea, silk, and coal.

After a year Iwasaki bought more steamships and began passenger and freight service between Tokyo and Osaka, and between Kobe and Shikoku. Using inside information, Iwasaki also made money by trading in provincial currencies during the transition from feudal domains to modern prefectures, and paid off part of his debt.

Iwasaki drove competitors out of business by undercutting their prices while offering more courteous service. He recruited "bold and honest" young men from the best universities, paid them well, and gave them responsiblity quickly. Iwasaki told them to "worship the customers," but because many of them were samurai, they found this hard to do. Iwasaki explained: "If you feel ashamed at bowing to the clerk . . . you will be angry and offended, but if you are aware that you are bowing to money, you will have patience."

In 1873 Iwasaki named his company Mitsubishi. The logo, a leaflike arrangement of three diamonds, was inspired by three oak leaves in the lord of Tosa's family crest and three water chestnuts in his own crest. It soon became famous because Mitsubishi defeated three separate competitors during the next three years.

Mitsubishi's first major competitor was the Japan National Mail Steamship Company (Y.J.K. in Japanese), a heavily regulated firm that received modern steamships and a generous subsidy from the government. Its managers, however, were inept and its crews were arrogant to passengers. In contrast, Iwasaki told his crews to "worship the passengers."

Y.J.K.'s biggest mistake was to refuse to help the government send troops to Taiwan during a military expedition in 1874. It feared losing shipping business back home. When the government asked Mitsubishi, Iwasaki was "honored" to help his country.

Mitsubishi ships made twenty-four voyages to and from Taiwan that summer, carrying soldiers, rice, and weapons. As a reward, the government sold Mitsubishi thirteen steamships cheaply, and gave the company a large annual subsidy to handle the day-to-day mail business. By 1875 Y.J.K. was almost bankrupt, and sold its ships to Mitsubishi, which now owned thirty-seven steamships and was the undisputed leader in Japanese coastal shipping.

On ocean routes, however, foreign ships still carried all of Japan's imports and exports. A government subsidy allowed Mitsubishi to cut fares to Shanghai again and again, and by the end of 1875 the rival American Pacific Mail Steamship Company gave up and sold its ships to Mitsubishi.

The next year a British firm, the Peninsular and Oriental Steam Navigation Company (P&O) sent ships to compete on the same route. In response, Mitsubishi began accepting cargo as security for the cost of shipping. This was a huge help to commodities brokers, who could pay shipping fees at their convenience instead of before each voyage. The P&O withdrew from competition in less than a year.

Mitsubishi opened new shipping routes to the island of Hokkaido, to Pusan, Korea, and to Vladivostok. Iwasaki told his employees that one day he wanted his ships to "encircle the earth." He also bought 18 percent of the Tokio Marine Insurance Company, letting Mitsubishi clerks across Japan act as agents for the firm. With no competitors, Mitsubishi raised fares and made big profits in the late 1870s. Newspapers called Mitsubishi "the Sea Monster," and sometimes crowds at political rallies burned a papier mâché sea dragon. The public resented Mitsubishi's subsidized monopoly, and the fact that Iwasaki spent his profits not to buy new steamships, but to diversify his business. Iwasaki purchased coal and copper mines and later bought stock in railroads and in the Meiji Mutual Life Insurance Company.

By 1881 Iwasaki's enemies had ousted his allies from the government. They set up a rival shipping firm, the Cooperative Transport Company (K.U.K. in Japanese) and leased steamships to it. Mitsubishi and K.U.K. began a brutal rate war in 1883, with Mitsubishi cutting some passenger fares 90 percent. Both companies lost money, and by the end of 1884 they feared that if they went bankrupt, foreigners would once again dominate coastal shipping. On February 5, 1885, the two firms began talks that led to a merger.

Two days later Iwasaki Yataro died of stomach cancer. He was only fifty. On his deathbed Iwasaki regretted that he had achieved only one third of his ambitions, and asked his brother Iwasaki Yanosuke (1851–1908) to lead Mitsubishi until his eldest son, Hisaya, was ready to run the company.

The Brother

YANOSUKE WAS sixteen years younger than his brother Yataro, less powerfully built, and more inclined to seek the opinions of advisers. He spent a year learning English in New York City in 1872–1873, then returned home to become Mitsubishi's vice president.

Yanosuke was the chief architect of Mitsubishi's diversification. In 1881 he had urged his brother to buy the badly managed Takashima coal mine on the island of Kyushu. Three years later Mitsubishi engineers doubled the production of the mine, making more money than all the company's other enterprises put together. These profits came at a terrible cost. Miners worked twelve hours a day, were clubbed if they took unauthorized rests, and were beaten if they tried to escape. The brutality eased after newspapers publicized these abuses in 1887.

Yanosuke leased the Nagasaki shipyard from the government in 1884. Mitsubishi engineers made the enterprise profitable, and steamships no longer had to be towed to Shanghai for major repairs. Mitsubishi began building ships when it purchased the shipyard three years later.

In the fall of 1885 Mitsubishi finalized its merger with K.U.K. Each firm contributed twenty-nine ships to a new company called Nippon Yusen Kaisha (Japan Mail Steamship Company), or N.Y.K. The Iwasaki family received 45 percent of the stock, but Yanosuke gave almost half of these shares to 590 employees as a reward for their hard work. Slowly, he sold most of the remaining shares to pay for new Mitsubishi acquisitions. By 1889 the company had bought more coal and copper mines, and also a bank, 50 percent of a paper mill, some gold mines, and more stock in railroad companies.

Mitsubishi made its most profitable purchase in 1890, when it bought a sixty-eight-acre (twenty-eight-hectare) parade ground in the center of Tokyo from the army. Four years later Mitsubishi completed Japan's first office building. Since then, Mitsubishi companies have built dozens of buildings nearby. Today, even allowing for inflation, the Marunouchi district in Tokyo is worth over *three million* times what Mitsubishi paid for it.

The Son

IN 1893 Yanosuke resigned as president of Mitsubishi in favor of his nephew, Yataro's eldest son, Iwasaki Hisaya (1865–1955). Hisaya had gone to high school in Philadelphia and earned a bachelor of science degree from the University of Pennsylvania in 1891. Perhaps because his father was so forceful, Hisaya was quiet, humble, and indecisive. He was only twenty-eight when he became president of Mitsubishi Limited, and for the next fifteen years he relied on Yanosuke in almost every decision he made.

Hisaya started a sales department to market coal. Mitsubishi exported over one third of its coal, mostly to foreign shipping firms. The exports paid for imported machinery. The sales department also marketed the products of Asahi Glass, cofounded by Yanosuke's second son, Toshiya, a British-educated chemist.

In 1895 N.Y.K. ordered a six-thousand-ton steamship from Mitsubishi's Nagasaki shipyard. Using British designs, British materials, and a government subsidy originally paid to N.Y.K., Mitsubishi completed the first Japanese-built oceangoing steamship, the *Hitachi-maru*, in 1898. By 1905 the Nagasaki shipyard had eight construction berths and a turbine factory. Two years later Mitsubishi was making ships equal to any in the West, including destroyers for the Japanese navy, cargo transports, and passenger ships.

The Nephew

IN 1906 Yanosuke's eldest son, Iwasaki Koyata (1879–1945), became vice president of Mitsubishi Ltd. Koyata had just earned a degree in history from Cambridge University, and was so unusually bright and aggressive that many people at Mitsubishi said he was a reincarnation of his uncle Yataro. When his father, Yanosuke, died in 1908, Koyata became the most powerful man at Mitsubishi. Hisaya retired in 1916, and Koyata succeeded him as president, staying in office twenty-nine years, until 1945.

When World War I began in 1914, many countries that had always bought their goods from Europe turned to Japan. As demand increased for ships, ore, glass, and chemicals, Mitsubishi spent large sums building new factories. To ease financing, Koyata spun off Mitsubishi's divisions as separate companies. This way if a company needed money, it could simply sell stock to the public. As late as 1931, however, the Iwasakis' holding company, Mitsubishi Ltd., still owned an average of 52 percent of each Mitsubishi company.

The global demand for Japanese goods during World War I induced Mitsubishi's sales division to export non-Mitsubishi products in return for commissions. Between 1915 and 1920 it opened eighteen offices worldwide. When the sales division incorporated in 1918, Koyata became the trading firm's first chairman. Skillfully, he used loans to small companies to secure many exclusive distribution agreements. He also helped other Mitsubishi firms acquire patent rights to machine parts such as carburetors, turbine rotors, and boiler cylinders.

By 1921 the engine works at Mitsubishi's shipyard in Kobe had split into Mitsubishi Electric and Mitsubishi Internal Combustion Engines. Engineers at the shipyard had built an automobile based on a design by Fiat in 1917, and a complete airplane engine in 1919. But in 1921 the executives at Mitsubishi Internal Combustion Engines had to choose between cars and airplanes; they could not afford to make both. They chose airplanes. Few Japanese could afford cars in 1921, and the competition with America was severe. By contrast, the Japanese military could provide a steady demand for domestic aircraft. The new company renamed itself Mitsubishi Aircraft Manufacturing in 1928.

The 1920s were a difficult time for the Japanese economy, with a postwar slump in 1919 and 1920, a banking crisis in 1922, an earthquake in 1923, another financial crisis in 1927, and, finally, the worldwide depression that began in 1929. Mitsubishi companies were relatively unaffected by the downturns because the Mitsubishi Bank had funds to lend to its sister firms. But thousands of small companies were ruined, then purchased cheaply by Mitsubishi, Mitsui, Sumitomo, and others. By the end of the 1920s, *zaibatsu* (family-owned conglomerates) were more powerful than ever.

In 1931 the Japanese army began occupying Manchuria. At first the army officers, many of whom were poor farm boys suspicious of big business, wanted to ban Mitsubishi and Mitsui from Manchuria. But they quickly changed their minds when they discovered they needed money for things as basic as underwriting a new currency. Before long, Mitsubishi investments in Manchuria included an oil refinery, a magnesium mine, a pulp mill, and a glass factory.

Industry boomed as Japan built up its military. Between 1931 and 1936 chemical production more than doubled and the manufacture of machinery more than tripled. Yet in spite of an increase in orders from the Japanese navy, Mitsubishi Shipbuilding remained in a slump because of a lack of foreign demand during the Depression. Many of its engineers began working at Mitsubishi Aircraft because the technologies were similar. By 1934 the two companies merged into a single corporation, Mitsubishi Heavy Industries (MHI).

After Japan invaded the rest of China in 1937, the military took full control of Japan's economy. Mitsubishi Heavy Industries received orders for airplanes, ships, tanks, trucks, and torpedoes, and grew to twenty times its original size by 1945. Even Nikon made fewer cameras and began manufacturing range finders, binoculars, and periscopes.

In China the army assigned twenty-three companies to Mitsubishi firms. Mitsubishi executives took charge of factories, mines, docks, textile mills, and tens of thousands of sullen and badly paid Chinese workers. Some were forced against their will to work in coal mines in Japan. In 1942, when Japan conquered Southeast Asia, Mitsubishi companies again took over mines, docks, sawmills, jute mills, small boatyards, and thousands more ill-paid laborers.

To raise money for expansion during wartime, the Iwasakis sold half the stock in their holding company in 1940 in a private offering to employees and Mitsubishi stockholders. The family's ownership of their holding company dropped to 48 percent, but now they had the funds to control a much larger industrial empire.

In the Pacific war, American pilots encountered the "Zero" carrier-based fighter plane, which Mitsubishi Heavy Industries began making in 1939. The planes were famous for their maneuverability. MHI also manufactured bombers, attack planes, and reconnaisance craft. During the war MHI made more than 16,000 airplanes and 114 ships, including the 69,000-ton battleship *Musashi*. The massive *Musashi* had a crew of 2,500 men, yet moved at a speed of thirty miles (50 km) per hour. The United States Navy needed seventeen bombs and twenty torpedoes to sink the giant ship off the Philippines on October 24, 1944.

When Japan surrendered in August 1945, Koyata expected the Mitsubishi companies to lead Japan's postwar reconstruction, so he was shocked when President Truman ordered the breakup of Mitsubishi and other industrial combines just one month later. Japan's finance minister asked each of the *zaibatsu* to submit a plan for dissolution, and Mitsui, Sumitomo, and Yasuda did so.

Koyata refused to end his life's work so easily. Mitsubishi has "nothing to be ashamed of," he said. "We have only followed national policies. . . . If it's an order, we have no choice. But we will not disband voluntarily." But Koyata became ill, and while he was in the hospital his deputies joined the other *zaibatsu* in a voluntary dissolution. A month later, on December 2, 1945, Koyata died of a ruptured aneurysm of the sinuses.

An allied occupation agency called the Holding Company Liquidation Commission confiscated all the shares of the Mitsubishi holding company and gradually sold them to the Japanese public. Later the commission also seized the personal assets of the Iwasaki family. Though the Iwasakis were eventually compensated with Japanese government bonds, the bonds lost most of their value during the postwar inflation.

Hisaya, who was eighty, moved into a caretaker's cottage while ten United

States Army officers occupied his Tokyo mansion. Every morning the soldiers held target practice in his garden, but what really angered Hisaya were the late night parties. "We have lived in this house for seventy years without any scandal," he complained, "and look! It is now a house of prostitutes."

Mitsubishi Since the War

IN A SWEEPING purge, the Allied occupation authorities ordered the Iwasakis and the top Mitsubishi executives to retire. This marked the end of the Iwasaki family's power. In 1947 the occupation officials also dissolved Mitsubishi Shoji, the trading company, barring any new company from hiring more than one hundred of Shoji's former employees. By 1948 Shoji had splintered into 163 separate firms. The Allied powers were more merciful to Mitsubishi Heavy Industries, which they split three ways into Eastern, Central, and Western Japan Heavy Industries.

Allied military authorities also banned the use of the Mitsubishi name and logo, but when the occupation ended in 1952, the Japanese government legalized them again. By 1954 Mitsubishi Bank and Mitsubishi Shoji were back in business, and about thirty of the Mitsubishi companies began exchanging directors and buying stock in each other. Before long an average of 25 percent of each Mitsubishi company was owned by other Mitsubishi firms.

Unlike the prewar *zaibatsu*, the postwar *keiretsu* are not controlled by a family-owned holding company or any other central authority. Mitsubishi's twenty-eight corporations are equals. If a company does not like a proposed deal, it is free to do business with a competitor, and in fact this often happens. (For more on *keiretsu*, see chapter one, "The House of Mitsui.")

In 1953 the presidents and chairmen of the core Mitsubishi companies resumed their prewar habit of having lunch together on the second Friday of every month, surely the world's most awesome "power lunch." The food is simple, often just curried rice and tea. The CEOs share their opinions about dealing with governments or entering a new industry. They will also rescue a firm if it is in trouble, and mediate a dispute between companies if one arises.

The lunch is often led by the head of Mitsubishi Shoji, which anglicized its name to the Mitsubishi Corporation in 1971. During the 1950s and 1960s Shoji helped other Mitsubishi firms buy thousands of patent licenses from American and European companies in return for over $2.5 billion in royalties. Mitsubishi Chemical, for example, worked closely with Monsanto, while Mitsubishi Electric had so many ties to Westinghouse that for a while the American company was its biggest shareholder.

In the 1950s Mitsubishi Electric had to import American technology to help manufacture "the three gods" of the postwar era: washing machines, refrigerators, and television sets. A generation later, in 1983, it exported its technology when it built one of the largest semiconductor factories in the world in Durham, North Carolina.

After World War II the three remnants of Mitsubishi Heavy Industries—Eastern, Central, and Western—were in such dire straits that for a time they just made pots, pans, and bicycles. It took years to rebuild the Nagasaki shipyard, but by 1955 Western-MHI had developed a ship engine 40 percent lighter than European models, but just as powerful. The closing of the Suez Canal in 1956 created a huge demand for oceangoing oil tankers, and to coordinate the shipbuilding the three regional divisions of MHI reunited.

During the 1950s MHI also made three-wheel trucks and tiny cars with two-cylinder engines that had to struggle up hills slowly. By 1962 the Minica car was more powerful, and in 1967 MHI manufactured a modest 75,000 cars a year.

The time had come to compete with Toyota. In 1970 MHI spun off its automotive division as a new company: Mitsubishi Motors, 85 percent owned by other Mitsubishi companies and 15 percent owned by the Chrysler Corporation. In return for its 15 percent share, Chrysler agreed to sell Mitsubishi's cars in America as Dodge Colts and Plymouth Arrows.

The two companies also started a joint venture, Diamond-Star Motors, and built an automobile factory in 1988 in Normal, Illinois, which today produces over 150,000 cars a year. Mitsubishi Motors still makes its engines in Japan, and often transports them to the United States on N.Y.K. ships, but the air conditioners in a Mitsubishi car are made by MHI in California, the windows are built by Asahi Glass in Ohio and Kentucky, and the springs are made by Mitsubishi Steel in Ontario. Mitsubishi Motors also persuaded dozens of smaller Japanese suppliers to build parts factories in or near Illinois. The ball bearings in Mitsubishi vehicles, for example, are made by United Globe Nippon at a factory in Chicago Heights. Some of these plants are financed by the Bank of Tokyo-Mitsubishi, others are insured by Tokio Marine and Fire Insurance.

In the early 1990s Chrysler needed cash and slowly sold both its 15 percent share of Mitsubishi Motors and its 50 percent interest in Diamond-Star. Mitsubishi Motors still exports an estimated 400,000 V-6 engines a year to Chrysler and tens of thousands of smaller engines to Hyundai in Korea and Proton in Malaysia. Mitsubishi is unique among car companies in offering a full range of vehicles, from 600 cc. minicars to heavy-duty trucks.

The Mitsubishi corporate group is not without problems. It is strong in industries such as cars, ships, and chemicals but weak in information technologies such as computers, software, and telecommunications. In addition, many Japanese companies such as Sony and Honda have their own global sales networks and do not need the help of a trading firm. Since 1974 the share of Japan's exports handled by the Mitsubishi Corporation has dropped from 8 percent to 4 percent.

During the prolonged recession of the 1990s, some corporations such as Mitsubishi Oil and Mitsubishi Motors have suffered heavy losses, but most Mitsubishi companies remain well positioned for the future. The list of technologies in which Mitsubishi firms lead the world is long, partly because the structure of a *keiretsu* has promoted long-term investment. Corporate stockholders have usually been more patient than individual investors. A Japanese company that is 25-percent-owned by other members of its *keiretsu* has been freer than other firms to keep dividends flat and invest more of its earnings in factories and equipment, though this is less true today. It is also easier for a firm to raise money when its sister corporation is the largest bank in the world.

Even when a Mitsubishi company seeks money from an outside bank, it has an easier time than most firms do in securing a loan. A loan officer knows that even a troubled Mitsubishi company can probably still get a loan from the Bank of Tokyo-Mitsubishi, save payroll costs by contracting surplus workers out to another Mitsubishi firm, or, as a last resort, merge with a friendly company. The firm's cost of capital is reduced because having the Mitsubishi name has long been considered "a guarantee of nonbankruptcy." Today, however, when even the Bank of Tokyo-Mitsubishi struggles with a mountain of bad loans, smaller Mitsubishi companies know that help from a larger Mitsubishi firm is no longer a sure thing.

More than 125 years have passed since Iwasaki Yataro began building one of the greatest family fortunes the world has ever seen. After World War II, Allied occupation officials confiscated the Iwasaki family's assets and did everything they could to shatter this empire.

Yet today Mitsubishi companies share their technology, markets, and even ownership, and do it with few and often no lawyers. Relationships between Mitsubishi executives are personal and long-standing. Deals are made with one's word. Even without the Iwasakis, the enormous Mitsubishi *keiretsu* is still a family enterprise.

3
Matsushita Konosuke
Founder of Matsushita Electric (Panasonic)

I N 1917 a twenty-two-year-old named Matsushita Konosuke quit his job as an electrician and started making adapter plugs at home. This first product was a failure, but it was followed by thousands of successes. Today his company, Matsushita Electric, is the world's largest manufacturer of consumer electronics products.

Under the brand names Panasonic, Technics, Quasar, and National, Matsushita Electric's 250,000 employees make color TVs, VCRs, video camcorders, satellite dishes, compact disc players, stereo equipment, tape recorders, car radios, cordless phones, cellular phones, fax machines, copiers, industrial robots, integrated circuits, refrigerators, air conditioners, microwave ovens, rice cookers, vacuum cleaners, irons, fans, washing machines (one every eight seconds), toasters (one every three seconds), batteries (137 kinds), lamps (12,000 kinds), and personal computers and laser printers, including the ones used to write most of this book.

Matsushita Konosuke (1894–1989) did not understand his life's purpose, however, until a summer day in 1932, when he saw a vagrant drink water from a homeowner's outdoor faucet—and realized that no one minded because the water was so available and cheap. Matsushita decided that he wanted "to make electric appliances as abundant as tap water." He worked steadily to cut costs, lower prices, and expand the markets for his products. In the process he freed millions from household drudgery.

As his company grew, Matsushita sought to share his sense of mission with his thousands of employees. His corporation became the first in Japan to have a spiritual philosophy, a company song, financially independent divisions, employee groups devoted to quality control, a five-day workweek, equal pay for women, and wages as high as those in the West. By the end of his life Matsushita was regarded as a genius at business management.

Matsushita Konosuke was born on November 27, 1894, in Wasamura, a village thirty-five miles (55 km) south of Osaka. He was the youngest of eight children. His father owned 150 acres of land, worked by seven tenant farmers, but speculated wildly in the rice market and lost everything, even his home, when Matsushita was four. The family moved to a tenement in a nearby town and sold wooden sandals to make ends meet. Soon three of Matsushita's brothers and sisters died of tuberculosis. Matsushita was the only surviving son, the embodiment of all of his family's hopes, and even he suffered from lung problems for the rest of his life. (By 1921 all seven of Matsushita's siblings had died of illnesses.)

Just before his tenth birthday Matsushita left elementary school and began work as an apprentice. For six years he worked eighty hours a week in a bicycle shop in Osaka. He scrubbed floors and cleaned tools, but also repaired bicycles and used a lathe to make bicycle parts. He had only five days off a year, and meals were just rice and vegetables. But the shop owner was kind, and the owner's wife taught him good manners and proper grammar.

Before long Matsushita's family moved to Osaka, where his father had begun work as a clerk. His mother found Matsushita a job as an office boy at the postal savings bureau and hoped he could continue school at night. His father vetoed the idea. He wanted Matsushita to start his own business, and felt an apprenticeship was the best preparation. Shortly before he died, he told his son: "If you succeed in business, you can employ people to make up for the skills you lack."

By custom Matsushita might have stayed in the bicycle industry for the rest of his life, but he began to have doubts about the future of bicycles when Osaka installed an electric trolley system. Fascinated by electricity, he left the bicycle shop in 1910 to begin work as a wiring technician for the Osaka Electric Light Company. He was sixteen.

The electric light company did all the wiring in the city at that time, so Matsushita worked in homes, stores, and factories throughout Osaka. He also attended a technical night school briefly, but because of his limited education he couldn't take notes fast enough to keep up with the professors and had to drop out.

In September 1915, at age twenty, the short, big-eared electrician married Iue Mumeno, an attractive, cheerful, and ambitious woman of nineteen. Mumeno had an eighth-grade education, slightly more than most young women at the time, and worked as a servant for a rich merchant. Matsushita's sister arranged the marriage. Before the engagement Matsushita had only a brief glimpse of Mumeno one night outside a movie theater.

During the early years of the Matsushita Electric company, Mumeno kept the accounts and cooked meals for the employees. Matsushita also brought appliances home and asked her opinion. The young couple shared a love for the Japanese tea ceremony, and had one daughter, Sachiko, and a son, Koichi, who died in infancy.

Two years after his marriage Matsushita was promoted to the job of wiring inspector. He found that he could finish his daily rounds in less than three hours. "I was left with a great deal of idle time to be whiled away chatting with co-workers ... it was dispiriting and empty." To keep busy, he designed improvements to an adapter plug, a plug that screwed into a light socket, which at that time was the only electric outlet in most Japanese homes. Matsushita's supervisor was not impressed by the plug.

Bored and restless, the energetic Matsushita quit his job in 1917, an action he later called "the boldest decision I ever made." With the help of his wife and her younger brother, Iue Toshio, Matsushita began making adapter plugs on a clay floor at home. His workshop was so primitive that he mixed his insulation materials in a stone mortar with a wooden pestle, molded them under a screw press, and dried them over a charcoal grill.

Unfortunately the plugs did not turn out to be better or cheaper than other plugs on the market, and Matsushita sold so few that his wife had to pawn her best kimono to pay their bills. Then an electric parts wholesaler ordered one thousand insulator plates for use in electric fans. Matsushita and Iue Toshio worked eighteen hours a day to fill the order, and more and larger orders followed. Matsushita's next plug was a much greater success. It screwed into a light socket and had two branches, one for a lightbulb, the other for an appliance. This allowed Japanese families to use an appliance and an electric light at the same time.

Matsushita visited hundreds of wholesalers throughout Japan to increase sales, and always impressed them with his combination of humility and determination. Over the decades he built a network of 25,000 wholesale and retail stores that sold his products exclusively. (In contrast, Sony's network has just 1,000 stores.)

By 1922 demand for the cheap two-pronged plugs grew so high that Matsushita had thirty employees, including live-in apprentices. There was not room for all of them to work at his home, so he built a factory nearby, the first of many. Until then, insulation makers kept their ingredients secret, but Matsushita realized that if he was going to mass-produce his plugs he would have to trust his workers. He hoped his employees would respond to his trust with loyalty, and they did. His secrets remained within the company.

Once, at the end of 1923, Matsushita saw that his factory's toilets were filthy. No one had cleaned them. Quietly Matsushita grabbed a brush and a bucket and scrubbed them himself. Only when he was finished did he ask his shame-faced employees to keep the bathrooms clean.

That same year Matsushita started manufacturing a bicycle lamp. Even in the 1920s the Japanese still bicycled after dark by candlelight, and on a windy night they had to relight candles constantly. Few cyclists used battery-powered lamps because a new battery was required every three hours, and this was expensive.

Matsushita designed a miniature bulb that could shine forty hours before it needed a new battery, but could not sell the lamp because store owners did not believe it. Finally, Matsushita told his salesmen to deliver three lamps each to shops throughout Osaka, and turn one lamp on at each store. When the retailers saw that the lamp really did shine for forty hours, they worked hard to sell them. By 1925 Matsushita was making 10,000 bicycle lamps a month at a new factory devoted entirely to the lamps. The higher volume enabled him to reduce prices, which stimulated demand and increased profits.

In 1927 Matsushita produced an even better lamp for roughly the same price. He marketed this lamp under the brand name National, a foreign word that stuck out, unlike the ordinary name Matsushita. Eventually the National brand became as widely known in Japan as GE is in the United States.

By 1928 Matsushita was manufacturing irons, heaters, wires, batteries, and radio parts, but in the fall of 1929, when the Depression hit, sales fell over 50 percent. Matsushita had just built another factory, financed partly by a loan from Sumitomo Bank, and had no cash reserves. Firing some of his 477 employees seemed the only alternative to bankruptcy.

Matsushita refused to do this. Instead, he cut production in half and told his employees to work half-days for full pay. He asked them to devote the other half-day to increasing sales, and because they were grateful to keep their jobs, they worked hard to sell his products. By the spring of 1930 sales were back to normal, and the practice of turning factory workers into salesmen during economic downturns quickly spread to other companies.

Matsushita's wholesalers urged him to make radios, and the entrepreneur responded in 1930 by buying a radio factory. To his horror, customers began returning broken radios by the hundreds. It turned out that the factory made good radios, but the store owners did not know how to adjust them before delivery.

Matsushita asked his engineers to design a new radio that would not need adjustments. When they protested that they had no experience with radios, he replied that if amateur radio hams could build them, so could the engineers of Matsushita Electric. A few months later the company won a national contest for building the best radio. Later Matsushita would advise businessmen that "it is necessary to approach a project with the conviction that it *can* be done, and not waste energy worrying about its difficulty." He also said that "failure comes only when one stops making an effort."

In 1932 a friend invited Matsushita to visit a Buddhist temple complex where everyone contributed work free. Matsushita did not convert to that particular sect, but he did leave convinced that his company needed spiritual as well as commercial motivation. Remembering the vagrant he had seen drinking water, Matsushita gathered his office employees and told them that "the mission of a manufacturer is to overcome poverty . . . to make all products as inexhaustible and as cheap as tap water." He felt it would take 250 years, but that each generation should do its part.

The following year Matsushita set forth five guidelines for the company, and in 1937 he added two more. The seven principles of Matsushita Electric are:

1. Service to the public by making quality goods at reasonable prices

2. Fairness and honesty in all business dealings

3. Teamwork for the common cause

4. Untiring effort for improvement

5. Courtesy and humility

6. Accord with natural laws and adjustment to change

7. Gratitude for blessings

For over half a century Matsushita employees have recited these principles every morning in every factory around the world. Yamashita Toshihiko, who was president of Matsushita Electric from 1977 to 1986, once confessed:

> When I joined Matsushita in 1937, I hated the daily ritual of morning assemblies—everyone reciting the company creed, and singing the company song. I suspect many of our young employees today feel the same way. But by daily repetition of these laudable ideas about service, honesty and teamwork, you gradually take them to heart.

Ironically, during the same year that Matsushita first publicized his lofty ideals, he also made one of his shrewdest business decisons. With 1,100 employees by 1933, he divided Matsushita Electric into four divisions—radios, lights and batteries, wiring, and heating appliances—and gave each division the unprecedented opportunity to retain and reinvest 40 percent of its pre-tax profits. Matsushita was one of the first companies in the world to create financially autonomous divisions. The new system encouraged executives to develop an entrepreneurial spirit, because as one of them said, "You can't imagine how hard managers will work when they know they're responsible for their own destiny."

Today each of Matsushita's many divisions is in charge of its own product development, manufacturing, and sales. The managers of the divisions make the major decisions at Matsushita, but their performance is evaluated every six months by accountants from the head office. They look at sales statistics particularly closely for clues as to consumer trends. Over time, if a division is not doing well, its manager will not be fired, but he will be asked where his talents might better help the corporation.

As his company grew, Matsushita made fewer decisions, but he never stopped asking questions. He telephoned executives around the world, day and night, and asked them about everything from financial reports to worker morale.

After Japan invaded China in 1937, there were many shortages of materials.

The government ordered Matsushita Electric to stop making heaters and fans, which were now considered luxury items. In 1942, when Japan conquered Southeast Asia, the government also asked Matsushita to reduce its production of batteries and civilian radios. By then the company had become Japan's number one manufacturer of both products. To stay in business, Matsushita made weapon parts for the military.

One by one young men at factories were drafted and replaced by women and teenagers. Matsushita later said he knew the war was lost in 1943, when the navy asked him to build wooden airplanes. Having no experience in aviation, the company managed to eke out three planes by 1945.

The period after the war was the most frustrating of Matsushita's life. With many of his factories in ruins, the ever-optimistic entrepreneur wanted desperately to rebuild his company, but the American occupation authorities prohibited him from doing so. The United States sought to break up the *zaibatsu*, the great family-owned industrial conglomerates such as Mitsubishi, Mitsui, and Sumitomo. To Matsushita's astonishment, the United States listed Matsushita Electric as one of them, and scheduled it for dissolution. The occupation authorities had mistaken Matsushita's network of wholesalers and parts subsidiaries for a full-blown industrial combine. They prohibited Matsushita from setting foot on company property, and even froze his personal assets.

For several weeks Matsushita just stayed home and drank sake. Then he raised money and started a foundation, the Peace and Happiness through Prosperity Institute, to help prevent a "suicidal" war from ever happening again. The PHP Institute publishes books, sponsors management seminars, and puts out a monthly magazine, *Asia 21*, which is full of inspirational human interest stories. Today the magazine has a circulation of 1.5 million, one of the largest Japanese monthlies.

Between 1946 and 1949 Matsushita made over fifty trips to Tokyo to contest the American classification of his company as a *zaibatsu*, and had over five thousand pages of documents translated into English. Even the new electrical workers union sent a petition with fifteen thousand signatures asking for Matsushita's return to the company. Occupation officials granted the petition in May 1947, although the company itself was still marked for dissolution.

Matsushita was back in charge, but unrealistic government price controls made it impossible to make a profit. Losses in 1949 and early 1950 were so massive that Matsushita was forced to lay off one eighth of his employees, an action he called "heartbreaking," and limit the rest of his workers to half-days.

One employee who left the company voluntarily was his brother-in-law, Iue Toshio. When the Americans listed Matsushita Electric as a *zaibatsu*, he resigned and started his own company, Sanyo Electric. Today Sanyo is Japan's fifth largest electronics company, and the second largest producer of color TVs.

At last, in December 1949, the American occupation authorities removed

Matsushita Electric from the list of companies to be dissolved. "Never before or since," Matsushita wrote, "have I felt so acutely the joy of being free to work and to produce."

By the autumn of 1950 the American war effort in Korea was pumping jobs and money into Japan. Soon Japanese families had money to buy appliances again, and the three items they wanted most were refrigerators, washing machines, and black and white TV sets. By 1954 Matsushita Electric was manufacturing all of them. Because it repeatedly cut prices as volume grew, by the end of the decade the company became Japan's leading producer of "the three treasures." To expand markets further, Matsushita had to export.

As early as 1951 Matsushita traveled to the United States and Europe to buy licenses to use foreign technology. The following year Matsushita started a joint venture with Philips, a giant Dutch electronics company it had done business with before the war. Matsushita Electric contributed most of the money, paid Philips a 1.5 percent fee for services, and, most important, provided access to its network of 25,000 dealers. In return, Philips supplied advanced European technology that made Matsushita's products competitive around the world. The first factory the two firms built together in Osaka in 1954 manufactured picture tubes and vacuum tubes (and, soon, transistors) for use in television sets and radios.

Matsushita also acquired new technology in 1953 by buying 51 percent of the Victor Company of Japan. The phonograph manufacturer had been a subsidiary of RCA before the war, but was now on the verge of bankruptcy. Matsushita reorganized Japan Victor and made it profitable, and today "JVC" is the world's second largest maker of VCRs. (Matsushita Electric is number one.)

Armed with new technology, Matsushita began exporting stereo speakers to America in the late 1950s. The National name was already in use and registered in America, so Matsushita chose the name Panasonic instead. Soon the Panasonic label was on radios, tape recorders, and many other Matsushita exports, and later the company used the brand name Technics as well.

Matsushita Electric's sales quadrupled in the late 1950s, and exports grew even faster. In some years Matsushita was the number one taxpayer in Japan, surrendering 77 percent of his income. Despite his wealth, Matsushita flew commercial rather than private jets, and slept on a futon instead of a Western-style bed.

Matsushita also tried to make life pleasant for his employees. He provided generous bonuses, low-cost home mortgages, discounts on appliances, health clinics, libraries, recreation centers, and fresh flowers along the assembly lines. The company could easily afford this in the 1950s, when salaries were low, but even since the mid-1970s, when its wages became equal to those of comparable American corporations, Matsushita has still maintained these benefits.

In 1961, at age sixty-six, Matsushita Konosuke resigned as president of Matsushita Electric and took the post of chairman of the board. He appointed his son-in-law (and adopted son), Matsushita Masaharu, as the new president. A Tokyo University law graduate, Masaharu had worked for the company almost twenty years.

In most Japanese corporations the president runs the business and the chairman's powers are advisory, but when Matsushita felt it necessary, he left his traditional Japanese-style estate outside Kyoto and took over the company's day-to-day affairs. He did this, for example, during the recession of 1964–1965, when among other cost-cutting measures he pulled the company out of the expensive business of making computers. The withdrawal from the computer industry was one of the few shortsighted decisions of Matsushita's career, and the company reentered the field thirteen years later.

Despite the recession, in 1965 Matsushita Electric became the first large company in Japan to reduce the work week from six days to five. Attendance rose, and Mondays were far more productive than before. The following year Matsushita also gave women equal pay for equal work.

In the 1970s Matsushita Electric began building factories around the world to achieve its goal of making 30 percent of its products outside Japan by the year 2000. The company set up training schools to teach foreign employees its technical and managerial methods, and in poor nations such as Indonesia and Tanzania it serves breakfast before the morning shifts. Matsushita's greatest foreign success has been in Malaysia, which is now the world's leading manufacturer of room air conditioners.

In 1973 Matsushita resigned as chairman and retained only the honorary title of executive adviser. He then let his son-in-law Masaharu run the company without interference. Masaharu's greatest success was his purchase of Motorola's aging Quasar color TV factories in 1974. The quality of Motorola's TVs was so low that the American company was losing $16 million annually in warranty repair costs. After six years of Matsushita management and quality control, the same group of Quasar factory workers doubled their output, with forty times fewer defects.

This triumph was overshadowed by a greater struggle. In 1975 the Sony corporation introduced the first videocassette recorder priced and designed for ordinary consumers. It used the Betamax taping system, which had a recording capacity of one hour at standard speed. Matsushita gambled that Sony would not be able to produce enough VCRs in its first year to meet the demand, and delayed production for a year so that Matsushita and JVC could develop their own VCR using the VHS (Video Home System) taping format in 1976. The VHS system did not record quite as well or as long as the Betamax, but it was cheaper.

A multibillion-dollar market in VCRs was up for grabs, and the winner would be the manufacturer that could induce American television and movie studios to adopt its taping format. Consumers would buy whatever kind of videotape the studios used.

With so much at stake Matsushita persuaded his son-in-law to resign after sixteen years as president of Matsushita Electric in 1977. The company needed a hungrier, more aggressive leader. Matsushita chose Yamashita Toshihiko. Yamashita had taken the troubled air-conditioner division and made it highly profitable. He was the second youngest of Matsushita's twenty-six directors, so the press called the appointment "the Yamashita leap."

Matsushita laughed at the publicity and returned to the pleasures of retirement. He wrote articles on management for *PHP Intersect;* an autobiographical memoir, *Quest for Prosperity;* and a book, *A Vision for Japan in the Twenty-first Century,* that proposes the use of annual government budget surpluses to create a tax-free state by the year 2100. (Even then, Matsushita believed, the rich should continue to pay high taxes.)

Meanwhile, Yamashita promised American companies that Matsushita Electric would build VHS systems with a two-hour recording capacity by late 1977. Matsushita did not even have blueprints for the improvements at the time, but the company devoted all of its resources to the task and delivered the new units on time. It also signed profitable license agreements with other electronics companies to allow them to make VCRs using the VHS format as well.

Sony was frozen out. As more companies adopted the VHS format, more American studios recorded their movies on the cheaper and longer VHS tapes, and more consumers bought the Panasonic, JVC, Sharp, and Hitachi VCRs that played them. Sony's founder, Morita Akio, went to see Matsushita personally to ask for a compromise, but the gesture was about a year too late and Matsushita refused. Sony finally gave up and withdrew its Betamax VCRs from the market in 1988.

Throughout the 1980s, while the aging Matsushita opened the Matsushita School of Government and Management near Yokohama, his successors at Matsushita Electric worked to cut costs, trim the corporate bureaucracy, and increase spending for research and development. They wanted to rid Matsushita of its embarrassing nickname, "Maneshita" (copied), which arose because Sony had been the first company to manufacture the VCR, the compact disc player, the Walkman, and other products.

Yet Matsushita was destined to copy Sony once more. Burned by its losses from the Betamax, Sony was determined never to lose another technological battle because of a lack of entertainment to go with its machines. Sony bought CBS Records in 1987 (signing up Michael Jackson) and bought Columbia Pictures in 1989.

Matsushita executives, worried that they might lose the market for high-definition television and other future products, responded by buying MCA for $6.59 billion in 1990. MCA owns Geffen Records, one of rock music's leading labels, and Universal Studios, which makes about 10 percent of America's movies. But executives at Matsushita and MCA quickly disagreed over how much money to spend on alliances with other communications companies, and Matsushita finally sold 80 percent of the movie company for $5.7 billion in 1995. Matsushita lost well over a billion dollars on the deal, counting lost interest, but its 20 percent stake in MCA should insure the company the continued access to MCA products that it needs to compete with Sony in any future battles over entertainment technology.

Matsushita Konosuke did not live long enough to see his company buy a Hollywood studio, but he understood the relationship between electronics and entertainment, and the need to enter new fields to stay competitive. Always suffering from bad lungs, Matsushita died of pneumonia on April 27, 1989, at age ninety-four. Over twenty thousand people attended his funeral.

In the last ten years of his life, Matsushita gave $340 million to a variety of charities. At his death his wife of seventy-four years received $940 million, and his daughter $687 million. In a legal settlement three illegitimate sons and a daughter, children of an Osaka geisha thirty years younger than Matsushita, also received $63 million each.

Despite his wealth, Matsushita was basically a hardworking and modest man. He once said, "All I did [was] devote my best to the job at hand from day to day." But Matsushita was not modest about the importance of management. "A superbly run company," he wrote, "is itself a work of art, comparable even to a masterpiece of literature or a great symphony."

Whether Matsushita Electric is comparable to Beethoven's Ninth is open to debate. What is not is that few of us could even listen to a symphony if men like Matsushita had not made the machines that play them nearly as commonplace as tap water.

4
Tashima Kazuo
Founder of Minolta

W HEN Tashima Kazuo left his father's silk-trading firm to start a camera business in 1928, his craftsmen took four months to build a prototype. Since then, the Minolta Company has manufactured and sold over eighty million cameras around the world, twenty-five million interchangeable lenses, four million copiers, and millions of binoculars, fax machines, laser printers, color copiers, microfilm readers, and medical scanners.

Tashima (1899–1985) came up with the brand name Minolta in 1933. It is an acronym for (m)achinery and (in)struments (o)ptica(l) by (Ta)shima. The Japanese pronunciation, *Minoru-ta*, has the pleasant meaning of "ripening rice."

Only three Japanese companies make both a full line of sophisticated cameras and a variety of copiers and other business machines: Konica, Canon, and Minolta. Konica's founder died in the 1920s. Canon's founder, Mitarai Takeshi (1901–1984), ran Canon in the morning, practiced medicine in the afternoon, and retired as Canon's president in 1974, when the giant company was only beginning to make its successful entry into copier manufacturing.

By contrast, Tashima Kazuo ran Minolta from 1928 until 1982. An account of his life best tells the story of the spectacular rise of Japan's camera and copier industries.

Tashima was born on November 20, 1899, in Kainan, a hillside town on the Pacific coast forty miles (65 km) southwest of Osaka. He was the eldest of three sons. His grandfather had been a prosperous wholesaler of lacquerware. Tashima's father entrusted the firm to his chief clerk and started an export company instead. From the city of Kobe he shipped silk and cotton cloth to his two brothers, who lived in Australia.

When Tashima was four, he and his mother rode in a rickshaw that turned over in an accident. Instinctively she shielded him from the fall, but she never recovered from her injuries, and died six years later. Tashima, just ten, cried for weeks.

Tashima's mother had urged her sons to be humble, because "the branches that bear most hang lowest." Tashima, who never forgot that his mother had sacrificed her life for his, took her advice to heart and remained unassuming even when he was rich.

As a boy Tashima led his friends in mock sword fights on a hill overlooking a Buddhist temple. When he was twelve he enrolled in a business-oriented public school whose motto was "Make Japan the number-one trading country in the world." He worked hardest at English because he had a crush on his teacher, a pretty young American named Miss Piper. He also joined the wrestling club.

At seventeen Tashima began studying economics at Keio University in Tokyo. He was short and serious, but warm, friendly, and well liked by his classmates. Like most Japanese students who have worked hard in high school, Tashima slacked off in college. He spent time rowing and playing baseball, but during his senior year he wrote a long, detailed thesis on the economic history of Russia.

After graduating in 1923, Tashima began work as a bookkeeper for an advertising agency in Tokyo. Six months later, when the great Tokyo earthquake killed 200,000 people and destroyed his office, Tashima returned to Kobe to work for his father. For four years Tashima helped ship silk and cotton fabrics to Australia. He did not get along with his uncles because they speculated in textile commodities markets, which Tashima thought too dangerous.

In 1927 Tashima's father suggested that his son represent Japan's silk merchants in a government-sponsored trade mission to the Middle East and Eastern Europe. In Egypt Tashima presented his finest silk to Prince Mahomed Ali Pasha, who in spite of his royal blood immediately began bargaining over the price of the fabric. Tashima felt humiliated. "I no longer wanted to stay in the textile business where prices could be so easily negotiated by others," Tashima wrote later. He wanted instead to make highly processed goods that could be sold at a fixed price.

Tashima took his silk to Beirut, Istanbul, Bucharest, and Belgrade before finishing his trip by visiting a friend in Paris in May 1928. The friend, a banker, showed Tashima an optics factory that was manufacturing binoculars and range finders for the Japanese army. "They were just the kind of goods I wanted to make," Tashima realized. "I vowed that I would enter this field."

When Tashima returned home in June he learned to his dismay that his uncles opposed expanding the silk trade beyond Australia. This made him even more determined to start his own optics business.

One day two Germans came to visit him, Willy Heilemann, an importer of cameras who was an acquaintance of his father's, and Billy Neumann, an optical engineer. Together they urged Tashima to make cameras. If he could raise enough money, they said, they would import parts from Germany and assemble them cheaply in Japan. Tashima knew immediately that this was what he wanted to do.

He hoped his new enterprise could be a part of his father's trading company, but his father vetoed the idea as too risky. "You must do it yourself," he said. Tashima then turned to the manager of his family's lacquerware business, Moriwake Sasuke, an old friend who owed much to the Tashima family. Tashima asked him for a loan of 150,000 yen to pay for a factory site near Osaka, machines from Germany and Switzerland, and several months worth of wages. It was over a million dollars in today's money; Moriwake lent it to him without hesitation.

Tashima, Heilemann, and Neumann hired two dozen craftsmen and began operations on November 11, 1928. Tashima, not yet twenty-nine, named his new business the Japan-German Camera Company. There would be several name changes before the firm was called the Minolta Company, Limited. Tashima watched each worker closely, gradually learned some of their jobs, and occasionally filled in.

Subcontractors were nonexistent in Japan at that time; craftsmen even had to make their own screws. But after four months, in March 1929, the first camera was completed. The lens, shutter, and folding bellows were imported, but most of the rest of the camera was homemade. The accordionlike camera was made of sheepskin. It was small, stylish, and much cheaper than the cameras made by German companies such as Leitz and Zeiss Ikon. By May the factory was making one hundred a month.

Tashima went door-to-door selling his cameras to stores in Osaka, and refunded money whenever the sheepskin covering was defective and leaked light. He also went to Tokyo carrying one hundred cameras packed into two suitcases, but did not sell a single one because he refused to let the merchants there bargain down his price. To pay his employees, Tashima secured an additional loan from Moriwake Sasuke. He returned to Tokyo in November. When the store owners realized they could not take advantage of him because he was no longer short of capital, they paid the price he asked and began to sell his cameras.

While Tashima was in Tokyo a labor organizer exploited the resentment his employees felt about having to work for foreigners. Some of the craftsmen called a strike, demanding an increase in wages and the dismissal of Willy Heilemann. Heilemann, who was a stubborn, severe man, brought in replacement workers.

By the time Tashima arrived in Osaka, compromise was impossible. Heilemann threatened to resign unless all the strikers were dismissed, and reluctantly Tashima complied. He needed Heilemann's expertise more than he needed the craftsmen.

Two years later, however, Heilemann and Neumann left without warning to start a camera parts business of their own. By then Tashima's employees were more knowledgeable about optics, and Tashima reorganized the factory so that a specialist was in charge of each function. With Heilemann gone, the craftsmen stopped importing shutters from Germany and began making them themselves. Tashima also made long-term plans to build a lens factory. His style of management was to give complete responsibility for a project to a single individual, but also to stay fully informed.

Despite the Great Depression that began in 1929, Tashima's cameras sold well. The Nifcadox, introduced in 1930, was the first camera in Japan that could be focused with a simple lever in the front of the camera. By 1931 Tashima had seventy employees and was secure enough to borrow money from a bank and repay Moriwake.

The next year Tashima met his wife, Kamiyama Mutsuko, the daughter of a minor landowner and a friend of one of his mother's relatives. She was intelligent, gentle, and shy. They married in November 1933. She was a traditional Japanese housewife, who enjoyed knitting and rarely accompanied her husband on business trips. They had one daughter and five sons, four of whom have had careers at Minolta.

Shortly before Tashima married, it became difficult to import the sheepskin used in the camera bellows. One of his employees proposed using a plastic called Bakelite instead, but others feared that it would break too easily. Tashima saw an opportunity to reduce costs and ordered several employees to research the matter.

They discovered that by mixing bits of cloth into the plastic, the bellows became stronger, and easier to fold in and out. In 1934 Tashima introduced the Minolta Vest, modeled after Kodak's Vestpocket camera, which folded up so neatly that it almost fit into a large pocket. The Minolta Vest was the world's first camera to have a plastic bellows, but no one knew whether anyone would buy it. Tashima gambled and ordered full-scale production. His risk paid off handsomely. The camera was easier to focus and less expensive than any other camera in Japan.

Tashima poured all the profits from the Minolta Vest into the expansion of his business, and introduced a new camera model every few months. By 1937 he had over one thousand employees. Many were low-paid young women with nimble fingers, out of school but not yet married. The lens-crafting factory that Tashima had dreamed of building finally began production; Minolta no longer had to import parts.

The year 1937 was also the year Japan started a war with China. Materials became scarce, and Tashima knew that to stay in business, he would have to make military equipment. He paid several visits to the Imperial Navy's headquarters in Tokyo, and finally won orders for binoculars, range finders, and aerial photography equipment.

In 1942 the navy asked Tashima to build an optical glass melting factory in a suburb of Osaka. It took two years to build. When it opened in June 1944, eight hundred of its workers were schoolboys and girls. Despite the high heat of the molten glass, every window had to be covered to avoid being seen at night by American bombers.

When World War II ended in August 1945, all three of Minolta's factories lay severely damaged from bombing. A final payment by the navy allowed

Tashima to keep four hundred employees, and they spent their time repairing machines and growing sweet potatoes on the factory lawns.

Fortunately United States General Douglas MacArthur did all he could to revive the Japanese camera industry. He felt that every dollar an American soldier spent on a camera would be one less dollar spent on liquor and women, so he authorized special licenses that allowed Japanese camera companies to import precision tools from Switzerland. In return, the Japanese firms agreed to sell 80 percent of their cameras to the post exchanges at American military bases.

By April 1946 Minolta had built a new camera factory a few miles southeast of Nagoya. Within months the Semi III was not only Japan's first postwar camera, it was the nation's first with coated lenses to protect against unwanted glare. In 1948 Tashima's engineers introduced the Minolta 35, a copy of the German Leica but with a hinged back cover that opened for easy film loading.

During the Korean War (1950–1953) more American soldiers than ever came through Japan. Many bought Minolta, Canon, and other Japanese cameras, and this brought in badly needed foreign currency. *Life* magazine photographer David Duncan began using lenses made by Nikon, a rival Japanese manufacturer, for his combat photography, and this boosted the prestige of all Japanese cameras.

Tashima decided it was time to export cameras to America. He sent a twenty-six-year-old employee, Kusumoto Sadahei, to be his sales representative. Sadahei, who spoke English and soon shortened his name to Sam, arrived in New York with two blue aluminium suitcases, each containing twenty-four Minolta cameras.

For seven months in 1954 Kusumoto went from one dealer to the next, but could not sell a single camera. Americans regarded Japanese goods as inferior, and dealers did not think his cameras would sell. Finally, in September, Tashima flew to New York to help jump-start the process. Kusumoto arranged several meetings, including one with Lawrence Fink, president of the FR Corporation, a photochemical company that was diversifying into camera sales.

Fink suggested that he sell Minolta's cameras under his own FR label, but Tashima refused. After more negotiation the two men agreed to a joint "FR-Minolta" brand name and warranty. Fink also insisted that Minolta make new cameras with an electronic flash powered by transistors instead of the troublesome and soon-to-be-obsolete flashbulbs. Tashima agreed, and by 1955 his engineers had produced two cameras with this feature. One, the Minolta A, allowed a user to cock the shutter and advance the film in one motion.

Exports increased in 1955 but were not high enough to cover expenses. One Minolta shareholder criticized Tashima's American venture as "an expensive hobby." Tashima and Kusumoto persevered, attending trade shows, placing advertisements in *Life* and *Playboy*, and entertaining American dealers at nightclubs when they visited Tokyo. Tashima always left the clubs at ten-thirty P.M. and let the younger Kusumoto continue to entertain his clients.

Gradually Minolta found its niche as the camera company for the serious amateur. Nikon catered to professionals. Canon specialized in inexpensive cameras. In 1957 Minolta's reputation grew when Peerless, a major New York camera store, ran full-page ads in *The New York Times* declaring that Minolta cameras were as good as German cameras and cheaper.

The biggest boost to the company's prestige came when astronaut John Glenn used a Minolta Hi-Matic to take pictures of the earth during his three-orbit space flight on February 20, 1962. After buying and comparing seven cameras, Glenn chose the Hi-Matic because its automatic adjustment of the exposure made it the easiest camera to use in a space suit. The following year Glenn visited the Minolta factory near Osaka, where the Hi-Matic was made, and Tashima himself, then sixty-three, proudly gave him a tour of the plant.

If Tashima had wanted to retire, this might have been a good time. But two new inventions challenged the optics industry: the single-lens-reflex camera and the plain paper copier. Minolta could not afford to stand still.

From 1937 onward Minolta had manufactured a variety of twin-lens-reflex cameras, where one lens was used to view the image and the other to throw light on the film. In the 1950s, when interchangeable lenses became popular, twin-lens cameras presented a problem: No matter how powerful a lens a photographer put on his camera, he or she still saw the same unmagnified image through the viewing lens. Focusing therefore had to be done by measurement, not by sight.

The solution to this problem was the single-lens-reflex camera (SLR) invented by the German company Zeiss Ikon in the late 1940s. In an SLR, a five-sided mirror called a pentaprism reflects light through a complicated path from the front of the lens to the rear viewfinder window. The photographer sees exactly what is encompassed through the lens he has chosen, whether it is a zoom lens or a wide-angle.

Although Minolta built an SLR in 1958, the pentaprism made the camera heavy and expensive, so the company was slow to pursue the concept. The Nikon F, introduced in 1959, became the camera of choice for professionals, and by 1964 it had also cut deeply into Minolta's share of the amateur market.

Tashima suspended dividend payments in 1965 and 1966 and increased spending on research and development. Finally, late in 1966, Minolta introduced the SR-T 101, an SLR with interchangeable lenses and a through-the-lens exposure meter that allows additional light into the bottom half of a lens to compensate for the bright sky that is usually in the top half of outdoor pictures.

The SR-T 101 was lighter and cheaper than the Nikon F, and became the best-selling SLR in America during the 1970s. By then Minolta had set up its own sales force of sixty men and women to sell cameras directly to over 12,000

American retailers. It was the first Japanese camera company in America to do so. By 1974 Minolta's exports accounted for 80 percent of its sales, and sales of Japanese cameras had far surpassed those of Germany. To meet the global demand for SLRs and other cameras, Minolta built a new camera factory in Malaysia that same year. Today this factory makes nearly three million cameras a year—two thirds of Minolta's total production.

The success of the SR-T 101 was gratifying, but as early as the 1950s Tashima knew that almost everyone in America and Japan who wanted a camera already owned one. Prospects for growth were limited. Minolta began making microfilm reader-printers for libraries in 1962, but Tashima knew the great opportunity for expansion was in the manufacture of copiers.

The pioneer in copying was Xerox, which in 1959 produced the first machine that could make copies on plain paper. Minolta was years behind. It did not build its first copier factory until 1964, and even then its first product, the Minoltafax 41, used chemically coated rather than plain paper. Coating prevented a customer from making notes on the copies, but the copier did have the world's first size-reduction capability.

Until 1977 Xerox enjoyed 80 percent of the world market share in copiers. Yet Xerox rented rather than sold its machines, and it ignored small businesses that needed to make only a few copies at a time. As in other industries, Japanese companies carved their first niche in the low end of the market.

In 1970 both Canon and Konica introduced plain-paper copiers that were free of Xerox patents. Neither machine worked well, however, and the copier that Minolta's engineers built was so poor that Tashima never even bothered to market it.

By the mid-1970s the Japanese were more proficient. Minolta's EG 101, introduced in 1975, used paper with such a thin coating that note-taking was easy. At $3,000 a machine, the EG 101 was eight times cheaper than a plain-paper copier, and sold very well. Minolta built up a nationwide network of five hundred copier dealers.

The EG 101 was a profitable machine, but it was the last Minolta copier to use coated paper. In 1973 the Ricoh Corporation, which had fallen behind in the field of cameras, introduced the DT series of plain-paper copiers that were half the size of a Xerox machine and required 40 percent less maintenance. They contained fewer custom-made parts than Xerox's copiers, and sold at a price equal to just one year of a Xerox rental. By 1977 Ricoh was sending jumbo jets full of copiers to America, and outsold Xerox all over the world.

Tashima was determined to catch up. He loved a challenge, and sometimes recited a samurai motto to his employees: "Difficulty is here. I give thanks." To match the reliability of Ricoh's DT copiers, Tashima encouraged his engineers to adopt Toyota's "just-in-time" production system, which is designed to eliminate defects. With this in mind, a new copier plant built in 1980 was surrounded by the factories of dozens of Minolta suppliers. This increased the cooperation between Minolta and its vendors, and made parts deliveries almost instantaneous.

By the end of the 1970s Minolta had become the first copier manufacturer to use fiber optics, eliminating the need for bulky lenses and mirrors, and the first to use "micro-toning," where smaller particles of toner make for cleaner and more detailed copies. In 1980 Minolta introduced the EP 710, the world's first copier with both enlargement and reduction capability.

The EP 710 was Minolta's first best-selling plain-paper copier, yet within two years it was overshadowed by Canon's PC-10, the world's first personal copier with a replaceable, service-free cartridge. Ironically, it was Minolta's advances in micro-toning that made a replaceable cartridge possible, but because no one at Minolta saw the potential of the technology, it was licensed free to Canon in a patent trade. Actor Jack Klugman, half of TV's *The Odd Couple*, advertised the PC-10s on American television, and Canon sold two million of these copiers during the 1980s. It still leads in personal copier sales today.

Canon also leapt ahead of Minolta in camera sales in 1976 when it introduced the AE-1, the first SLR camera to use integrated circuits to set the proper aperture and shutter speed. The use of integrated circuits meant that there were fewer parts in the camera, so the "point and shoot" camera was lighter, cheaper, and more reliable than comparable SLRs made by Minolta.

Minolta responded with several cameras the following year, including the XG series, where the current in the integrated circuits starts with the touch of a finger. Other companies also computerized their cameras, and sales of SLRs tripled by 1982. But Canon's AE-1 remained the leader, with sales exceeding five million.

Amid such brutal competition, Tashima, who was eighty-two, retired as Minolta's president in August 1982. His eldest son, Hideo, became president, and Tashima assumed the new post of chairman. Tashima continued to go to work every day, but also found time to take his wife to Hawaii—her first trip abroad—and to build a memorial tower for deceased Minolta employees.

Minolta did not stay behind Canon for long. In 1983 it introduced the EP 450Z, the world's first copier with "stepless" enlargement and reduction capabilities that allow a user to select a level of magnification or reduction in one percent increments. It was also the first copier with automatic paper size selection.

Actor Tony Randall, the other half of TV's "odd couple," advertised a faster model of this copier, the EP 650Z, on television. He called it a "neat copier," and closed with the line, "I'm not really a neat freak, but then, I'm not a slob like . . ." This of course reminded everyone that it was Canon's spokesman who was the slob in *The Odd Couple.*

The popular EP copiers pushed Minolta's sales of business equipment ahead of its sales of cameras for the first time. The company also began making laser printers in 1984, and management-information systems in 1985. These systems, widely used in offices, coordinate the activities of a computer, printer, telephone, fax, optical scanner, and electronic mail and filing unit.

In cameras, Minolta bounced back in 1985, when it introduced the camera known as the Maxxum in America and the Alpha in Japan. With integrated circuits equivalent to 150,000 transistors, the Maxxum 7000 was the first SLR camera with a computerized automatic focus, which works even when the subject is moving.

Tashima took a risk when he authorized the development of the Maxxum in 1981, because it uses a different set of interchangeable lenses than those used by previous Minolta cameras. There was a real possiblity that longtime Minolta customers would revolt and refuse to buy a new camera incompatible with their lenses.

The fears proved groundless. Hundreds of thousands of customers bought the camera, and eighteen months passed before competitors could offer a computerized autofocus camera of their own. By then the Maxxum (Alpha) 7000 had replaced Canon's AE-1 as the best-selling SLR camera in the United States, Europe, and Japan. Maxxum cameras remained number one for a decade.

Tashima lived to see the success of the "stepless" copier, the management-information system, and the Maxxum 7000 camera before he died on November 19, 1985, one day shy of his eighty-sixth birthday. Shortly before his death he compared himself to the driver of a carriage. "I took the reins," he said, "and made the horse run."

Today Minolta makes color copiers with an image resolution of 400 dots per inch, and 256 gradations of color for each dot. It also makes over 170 camera lenses, including "stepper" lenses that focus integrated circuits onto computer chips.

Minolta is constantly competing with Canon, Xerox, Ricoh, and Nikon, among others. Half of Minolta's research and development today is in the field of digital products, including cameras where the film is a computer disk rather than a negative, and scanners that transmit three-dimensional images on to a computer screen.

Tashima Kazuo may have been less colorful than some other industrialists written about in this book, but he single-mindedly pursued his dream of making optical goods—at a fixed price. He got only half his wish. Minolta makes products he could not have dreamed of when he started his company in 1928, but to stay competitive their prices drop just as quickly as the price of his silk did when he dealt with hard bargainers long ago.

5
Honda Soichiro
Founder of Honda

Wᴴᴇɴ he was sixteen, Honda Soichiro (1906–1991) dropped out of school to become a garage mechanic. When he retired a half century later, his name could be seen on cars and motorcycles around the world. Everywhere, Honda products have earned a reputation for being reliable, fuel-efficient, and stylish. In the United States today, the Honda Accord is often the number one selling car. In underdeveloped nations, Honda motorcycles have transformed daily life because even the poor can afford them.

Honda Soichiro was born on November 17, 1906, in Tenryu, a small town outside Hamamatsu, a coastal city one hundred thirty miles (210 km) southwest of Tokyo. The eldest of nine children, Honda was the son of a blacksmith who also repaired and improved bicycles and avidly read trade magazines to keep up with the latest in bicycle technology. His mother, a strict woman, did her husband's accounting.

As a boy, Honda helped his father chop slabs of charcoal. Coal dust on his nose led to a nickname, "Weasel," because the animal has a black nose too. When he was seven Honda saw his first car, a Ford Model T. "I smeared my hands with the oil and deeply inhaled the smell," he once told a reporter. "It was then that I dreamed of manufacturing a car someday."

Honda began work as an apprentice in an automobile repair shop in Tokyo. For months all he did was sweep and clean; he was forbidden even to touch a car. After six years he became a master mechanic and opened his own branch in Hamamatsu. He quickly gained a reputation for excellence, and within three years he was employing fifty men.

For a while Honda spent much of his profits on geishas, sake, and a home-made motorboat. Once he got so drunk he drove off the side of a bridge. Honda also enjoyed building and driving race cars, setting a Japanese speed record in one race, suffering a severe head wound in another. He continued to design race cars all his life, but stopped driving them after he married a schoolteacher, Isobe Sachi, in 1935. They had two sons and two daughters.

In 1937 Honda built a small factory to manufacture piston rings. At night he studied metallurgy at a local technical school to learn more about making them, but never earned a diploma, which he brashly felt was "worth less than a movie ticket." His first piston rings lacked flexibility and were useless. Quickly he learned from his mistakes and by 1940 was selling piston rings to Toyota.

During World War II Honda built parts for aircraft engines. He also designed machinery that cut down the time needed to make an airplane propeller from a week to just thirty minutes. Toward the end of the war, an earthquake reduced his factory to rubble.

After the war Honda once again repaired engines. In 1948 he bought five hundred tiny one-cylinder military surplus engines. Tired of riding crowded trains, he attached an engine to a bicycle one day with a second chain belt. This was the beginning of the Honda Motor Company.

When the postwar supply of motors ran out, Honda decided to make his own motorcycle engines. First he had to raise the money, and this was not easy. Bankers didn't care for Honda. Not only had he not gone to the right college, he had not gone to college at all. Fortunately a businessman named Fujisawa Takeo invested money in Honda Motor and became Honda's business partner. Fujisawa managed to keep the company one step ahead of its creditors, and also freed Honda from administrative duties, enabling him to devote himself entirely to engineering.

During the early years of struggle, Honda carried motorcycle parts inside his clothing because he could not afford to pay the excess baggage charges on an airplane. Once, in 1952, Honda and Fujisawa asked the Mitsubishi Bank for a loan of one million dollars to buy high-quality manufacturing machinery from the United States and West Germany. They entertained the bankers, got drunk, told jokes, and sang geisha songs. The bankers had a great time but denied the loan the next day. "We cannot trust a company run by two clowns."

Fortunately another bank approved the loan, and during the next several years Honda doubled the horsepower of the standard four-stroke engine and sold hundreds of thousands of motorcycles. Few Japanese at that time could afford to buy a car, but almost everyone could afford to buy a motorcycle. By the end of the 1950s, 40 percent of them had bought Hondas. Better built than competing brands, they were not any more expensive. What the Honda Motor Company did was to combine the best motorcycle technology with the best manufacturing technique in order to sell good machines as cheaply as possible.

Some of the features of a Honda motorcycle were strong power, good mileage, an automatic clutch, an electric starter, direction lights, and the fact that it didn't leak oil. The engine also had an easy "clamshell" assembly. The parts were set in one half of a case and the assembly closed with the other. In addition, the controls to a Honda motorcycle could be operated with one hand, allowing a driver to carry a package with ease. Honda's method of work was to set the goal first, whether it was increasing power or reducing weight, then try one technical approach after another, not giving up until the task was complete.

Honda began exporting as early as 1953. The first motorcycles shipped were very small, but they were cheap and sold well throughout Asia. In 1958 the company introduced the more durable "Super Cub" for the American market. By 1960 Honda was selling 60,000 Super Cubs a month, a rate it still maintains today, having sold more than 20 million of them around the world.

Honda knew that most Americans associated motorcycles with gangs, leather, chains, and noise. But the Super Cub, with an engine just fifty cubic centimeters, seemed too small to be threatening. Honda's advertising theme was "You meet the nicest people on a Honda." (An advertising major at UCLA created the slogan.) Motorcycle sales soared as Americans who had never considered riding motorcycles began buying them. Honda started by selling Super Cubs on the West Coast, then gradually moved eastward over the next five years.

Honda Motor also began exporting larger models, and by the early 1960s was the number one manufacturer of motorcycles in the world, eventually producing 50 percent of the world's motorcycles. Many competitors went out of business, both in America and in Japan.

In 1961 Honda set up the Honda Research and Development Company, which automatically receives 2.5 percent of Honda Motor revenues. Honda also encouraged innovation by letting workers with new ideas take out patents in their own names and keep the royalties. "I have always had a stronger interest in the work itself than the money," Honda explained. He held 470 patents himself.

Honda was a stickler for quality, and adopted the "just-in-time" production system pioneered by Toyota to reduce defects and inventory. He spent a lot of time on the factory floor and watched his assembly line workers closely. Because he often screamed at them over small mistakes, they called him "Mr. Thunder." If it were an engineer rather than an assembly line worker who was careless, Honda became even angrier, sometimes throwing pencils, rulers, and even wrenches at the unfortunate technician. "I have been very severe," Honda admitted. "We are not selling clothing or apparel. . . . If a small thing like a bolt or a nut goes wrong, the customer's life is in jeopardy."

Employees (Honda called them "associates") also remember Honda's wide smile, frequent laughter, and sincere concern for the work at hand. Despite his temper, workers have been very content at "Mr. Thunder's" company. In the United States, for example, the employee turnover rate at Honda is only two percent per year. One reason for this is that Honda associates, like employees in many Japanese companies, receive benefits such as housing loans, access to a gym and swimming pool, and, most important, new jobs if sales are down or if machines make their old jobs obsolete. Honda employees also put in less overtime than workers do at Toyota and Nissan.

Another reason for Honda's low turnover is an informal style not typical of Japanese companies. Everyone, even a top executive, wears a white jacket. This encourages cleanliness as well as equality. Regardless of their educational background, young workers are trained to become experts and are given increased responsibilities quickly without having to move up an administrative hierarchy. Many foremen are in their early thirties and help design the factories they work in.

At the top level, senior executives act as a group and only a few have their own offices. Until 1991 even the chairman, president, and senior vice presidents worked together in one enormous room. At lunch senior executives eat in the same cafeteria as associates on the assembly line. There is no executive dining room. But what Honda Motor executives have lacked in luxury they have made up in power. To encourage independent thinking on the part of his directors, Honda stopped attending their meetings after 1963.

This was also the year the Honda Motor Company began manufacturing cars. "I am not satisfied with being number one only in the motorcycle world," Honda told his employees. "Progress is when you go forward, when you keep graduating from one stage to another."

Once again it was difficult getting started. The Japanese Ministry of International Trade and Industry (MITI) wanted there to be fewer car manufacturers, not more. MITI didn't think small companies would compete well against an anticipated wave of American exports. The MITI economists proposed a law to limit the number of Japanese automobile companies, and Honda had to wage a fight in the Japanese Diet to stop the legislation.

Honda's first cars were really just overgrown motorcycles. They looked sporty but had little power. By 1969, however, Honda made cars with good-sized (1,300 cc.) engines, and had a network of dealers throughout Japan. Even so, Toyota and Nissan had such huge shares of the Japanese market that Honda, with a market share of just 9 percent, calculated that its opportunities for expansion were better in the United States.

A major debate took place within the Honda Motor Company. Should the car it planned to export to America have air-cooled or water-cooled engines? Honda admired the air-cooled Volkswagens, and finally decided that his company's engines should also be air cooled. "Who wants pumps and hoses and things that leak?" he asked.

But several young engineers, led by Kume Tadashi (b. 1932), were convinced that Honda was wrong and refused to go along with his decision. Water-cooled engines are more powerful and quieter. Kume and his colleagues knew that if Honda wanted to build bigger cars in the future, the company would have to switch to water-cooled engines. When his protests were ignored, Kume left work in 1969 to go fishing on a remote island, a "one-month strike" as he later put it.

Honda had created within his company an environment where a young engineer could feel bold enough to challenge a "final" decision by the president. Now Honda showed his wisdom by changing his mind even though he lost face as an engineer. The engine that Kume helped design was the four-cylinder

1,500 cc. CVCC (compound vortex controlled combustion) engine from which the Civic model gets its name. In 1983 Kume became Honda's president.

The Civic could not have arrived in the United States at a better time. The energy crisis of 1973 permanently changed the habits of the American people. They began buying cars with good gas mileage, and the Civic got forty-four miles to the gallon.

The Civic was also rated the lowest-polluting car in the mid-1970s by the United States Environmental Protection Agency, much to the chagrin of American auto executives, who were still trying to get emissions standards postponed. Using a newly designed cylinder with two combustion chambers, the CVCC engine reduced the emissions of nitrogen oxides, carbon monoxides, and hydrocarbons simultaneously, whereas previous engines had reduced only one pollutant while increasing the output of the other two. Soon Ford, Chrysler, and even Toyota were paying Honda license fees to use CVCC engine technology.

In 1973, at the moment of his greatest victory, the conquest of the American automobile market, Honda Soichiro retired as president of the company at the age of sixty-six. He also declined the post of chairman of the board. The successor he picked, Kawashima Kiyoshi, was forty-five at the time, young enough to be the child of most other Japanese corporate presidents. Honda still kept the title of supreme adviser, but he did not interfere. He even refused to let his relatives work at Honda. The publicly owned company, he explained, "does not belong to the Honda family."

The Honda Accord arrived in the United States in 1976. A little more expensive than the Civic, the Accord was a lot more stylish. Sales surged. Almost instantly there was a six-month backlog of orders. The success of the Accord led to the introduction of the larger Prelude in 1978, and the Acura Integra in 1980. Today Honda sells over 700,000 cars a year in the United States, making it roughly the fourth largest seller of cars in America, about even with Toyota and Chrysler.

Less than 20 percent of these Hondas are imported from Japan. Honda has built factories that make cars, motorcycles, outboard motors, and lawn mowers in forty countries around the world. From Brazil to Nigeria, the quality of the vehicles that Honda makes locally is just as high as the quality of the vehicles it makes in Japan.

In 1979 Honda built a motorcycle factory in Marysville, Ohio, thirty miles (50 km) northwest of Columbus. Three years later at the same site, it built the first Japanese automobile plant in the United States. At the time many people doubted whether American workers could build cars of the same high standard as the Hondas produced in Japan. But largely because of the top priority that Honda's management gives to technical quality, the men and women at Marysville soon proved doubters wrong. By 1991 the Marysville plant, and a second Honda factory in nearby East Liberty, Ohio, were assembling over 450,000 cars a year, with three fourths of the parts and all the steel in them made in the United States.

Honda helped many American auto parts companies adopt the "just-in-time" production system, and by 1989 it was rejecting less than one part in a thousand delivered by its suppliers. Nevertheless, the more sophisticated components in a Honda are often made by Japanese suppliers in newly built factories in western Ohio, or are imported directly from Japan.

During the 1980s six other Japanese companies followed Honda and opened factories in the United States. Honda Motor also became the first Japanese company to make a luxury car, the Acura Legend, in 1985, and the first Japanese firm to export American-made cars to Japan, beginning with the two-door Accord in 1988.

Although Honda retired as the president of his company early, his passion for innovation continued. He set up foundations to sponsor traffic safety and environmental causes, and continued to talk regularly with Honda's young engineers. Recently Honda Motor has built a car with computer-controlled piston valves, the Civic VX, that mixes more air with gasoline and achieves forty-eight miles a gallon in the city and fifty-five miles a gallon on the highway.

In the early 1990s Honda Motor faced a recession in Japan and increased competition in the United States from the Ford Taurus and other cars. To keep its prices competitive, it was vital for the company to cut expenses, and Honda reluctantly agreed with his new president, Kawamoto Nobuhiko, that an individual could slash budgets more easily than a group. "I rejected Mr. Honda's way [of consensus]," the cost-cutting president said, "but that is the Honda spirit." Kawamoto also jettisoned Honda's seniority system; today employees are paid and promoted on merit alone.

In his old age Honda painted, played golf, and even took up hang gliding. He enjoyed his large home and garden in the middle of Tokyo, and watched a television set built into his bedroom ceiling. He stayed healthy until he was eighty-four, dying of liver failure on August 5, 1991.

Honda once said that there are three requirements for making cars and motorcycles. The first is that workers feel pleasure in making the product. The second is that dealers feel pleasure in selling the product. And the third is that customers feel pleasure in buying the product. In the days following Honda Soichiro's death, thousands of Honda employees, dealers, and car owners left flowers and gifts outside his home.

6

Kobayashi Koji
*The Man Who Turned NEC
into a Global Computer Giant*

Kobayashi Koji was one of the first men to foresee the "information super-highway" that would arise from the merger of communications and computer technologies. He transformed the Nippon Electric Company, a medium-sized maker of telephone and broadcast equipment, into NEC, a global computer giant. During the years he led the company, NEC became the eighth largest industrial corporation in Japan and one of the fifty largest in the world, with annual sales exceeding those of Coca-Cola and Xerox combined.

From the 1960s onward Kobayashi (1907–1996) concentrated NEC's efforts on three industries: NEC is the world's fifth largest maker of telecommunications equipment, the fourth largest manufacturer of computers, and the second largest producer (after Intel) of the integrated circuits inside a computer. No other company is a leader in all three of the fields crucial to an information society.

Kobayashi Koji was born February 17, 1907, in Hatsukari, a village fifty miles (80 km) west of Tokyo and just north of Mt. Fuji. He was the fourth son in a family of nine children. His father was an elementary-school principal; his mother, the daughter of a landowner and silk broker.

Kobayashi spent much of his boyhood fishing. He also had to clean a kerosene lamp every evening, and was delighted when the arrival of electric lights made this unnecessary. Kobayashi was an excellent student, but being stocky, was poor at gymnastics in an elementary school where this was the leading sport. His high school was far from home; he walked ten miles a day, rain or shine. He often studied an English reader on the way to and from school, and eventually became fluent, although he had a heavy accent.

Kobayashi won a scholarship to the junior college in Matsumoto, a town in the Japanese Alps near Nagano. He struggled with chemistry and disliked the smells of the laboratory. He preferred physics and calculus.

Kobayashi spent most of his third year at Matsumoto preparing for the difficult entrance examination given by the Department of Electrical Engineering at Tokyo Imperial University. He passed, and entered the prestigious university in 1926.

Kobayashi spent long hours studying radio-wave and high-voltage engineering, though on Sundays he liked to row with friends on the Sumida River through downtown Tokyo. He also studied power transmission and worked as a trainee at a power station in the mountains in the fall of 1928. When he returned to school he wrote a thesis on the remote control systems of unattended power stations. Because Japan's leading authority on the subject worked for NEC, in 1929 Kobayashi applied for a job there after graduating.

When NEC was incorporated in 1899, it was 54 percent owned by Western Electric, the telephone-making subsidiary of AT&T. At first NEC imported telephones and switchboards, but gradually it made its own. By the time Kobayashi joined the firm, NEC made many kinds of telephone and broadcast equipment, including long distance lines, radio transmitters, and the glass vacuum tubes that glowed inside radios as they amplified or inhibited electric current.

During the 1930s Kobayashi taught workers at relay stations how to fine-tune and repair their equipment, and also helped modify power lines in Manchuria to carry telephone calls. Kobayashi often visited Manchuria's Lushun Institute of Technology, where he became friends with Noda Kazuko, the daughter of the president of the institute and a recent graduate of Shoin Women's College in Osaka. The couple married on March 10, 1935, and had three daughters.

After his wedding Kobayashi began writing a dissertation on the negative-feedback amplifier, a device that stabilizes electric current. His thesis was accepted in 1938, and won him a Ph.D. in electrical engineering from Tokyo Imperial University.

That same year NEC sent Kobayashi on a study tour of technical laboratories in Germany and the United States. Kobayashi was astonished that in America it took only a few minutes to place a long distance call. In Japan, reserving a long distance line between Tokyo and Osaka usually took an entire day. Overseas calls were even harder to make because they were sent by shortwave radio signals, which faded in and out. When he returned home, Kobayashi helped install vacuum tubes to amplify voices along an underwater telegraph cable between Japan and Korea.

Kobayashi was then put in charge of building a 1,900-mile telephone line running the length of southern Japan and up the Korean peninsula. Completed in 1939, it connected Tokyo and Osaka with the major cities of Korea, and with Shenyang, Manchuria. At the time it was one of the longest telephone lines in the world.

By then Japan was at war with China, and the Japanese government disapproved of the fact that Americans still owned 54 percent of NEC. AT&T had sold its interest in NEC to International Telephone and Telegraph (ITT); now ITT reduced its holdings to 37 percent. The Japanese government seized ITT's stock after the attack on Pearl Harbor, and did not return it until 1950.

The Sumitomo industrial group bought 46 percent of the company, and even today the twenty largest Sumitomo firms collectively own over 20 percent of NEC's stock. NEC's real master during World War II was the Japanese military, which ordered thousands of radio transmitters, telephones, switchboards, radar systems, echo sounders, and many other kinds of communications equipment. In 1939 Kobayashi became assistant manager of NEC's production of torpedoes and sonar equipment in Kawasaki, a suburb of Tokyo. Here the studious young executive began a lifelong habit of reading books on the art of management.

Kobayashi reorganized the factory floor, but union leaders resented his interference. He avoided a walkout by visiting the homes of each of the most senior workers at night and appealing to them, and especially to their wives, not to strike.

By 1944, because so many men were in battle, many of the workers at Kobayashi's factory were teenagers. Bullies began stealing the students' pocket money, but Kobayashi, who was now the manager of the factory, took a sword and one by one challenged nine of them to a duel. Taken aback, all nine of the thugs promised to stop stealing immediately.

By the end of the war, food was so scarce that Kobayashi lost seventy pounds and could not even climb stairs without holding on to a handrail. His eldest daughter, who was living at a camp in the mountains with her schoolmates, almost starved. At the factory, work stopped because of shortages of materials and because other NEC plants had been bombed. On May 23, 1945, an American B-29 dropped a hundred-pound bomb in the garden at Kobayashi's home in Tokyo. The bomb was a dud; otherwise Kobayashi, his wife, and two of his daughters would have been killed instantly.

After the war, with no military production, NEC was forced to lay off 12,000 workers. Kobayashi had to fire 300 people from his own factory but found jobs for most of them in smaller plants nearby that were not suffering as badly as NEC. Funds were so limited that when Kobayashi had cash, he left his factory through a side exit, walked along back roads, and paid his employees at home before the company's creditors could find him.

Layoffs continued for several years, and occasionally led to strikes. Before a tense forty-five-day walkout in 1947, Kobayashi installed a trapdoor behind his desk in case things got violent. Fortunately he never had to use it.

In the late 1940s NEC received orders for hundreds of thousands of telephones from Japan's Ministry of Communications. The ministry formed the Nippon Telegraph and Telephone Public Corporation in 1952, and NTT has remained NEC's biggest customer to this day.

By the early 1950s NEC was on its feet again, and Kobayashi was the youngest member of the company's board of directors. The United States Army ordered huge amounts of communications equipment during the Korean War, and in Japan commercial broadcasting resumed. NEC built radio transmitters throughout the nation, and also made a large percentage of the vacuum tubes inside radios.

Radio waves are often distorted by storms and industrial activity. Microwaves, only a few inches long, are less subject to distortion because they can easily be focused by dish-shaped antennas. Towers must be built every thirty miles (50 km), but it is worthwhile because microwaves, once focused, can carry thousands of phone calls and television and radio programs simultaneously.

In 1952 Kobayashi talked the president of a rural utility into buying a microwave system, so long as the utility did not have to pay for it until it was up and running. Kobayashi urged his bosses to build the towers, taking full responsibility. A year later he and his staff successfully completed Japan's first civilian microwave system.

By the early 1960s NEC had built microwave towers all over Japan, making direct telephone dialing possible in most of Japan's cities. NEC also built a microwave system linking the islands of Indonesia. Today NEC has built microwave systems in over eighty countries, and its microwave technology is generally considered the best in the world.

Japan's first television stations used equipment imported from America, but Kobayashi found a broadcasting executive willing to gamble on Japanese technology. In 1956 NEC built the first two Japanese-made TV stations in Osaka and Nagoya. Kobayashi also became NEC's senior vice president in charge of technology.

In the late 1950s transistors began to replace vacuum tubes because they were smaller, cheaper, and did not overheat. Taking up less size than a pencil eraser, a transistor is usually made of silicon, which does not conduct electricity as well as copper and thus is called a "semiconductor." The advantage of a semiconductor is that it can be treated chemically to make it a good conductor of electricity in one spot and a poor conductor in another. Electric circuits created this way can fit into a very tiny space.

The world's first hand-sized transistor radio was introduced by Sony in 1957, and this spurred NEC to build a transistor factory. Production began in 1958, and within three years NEC's transistors were outselling its vacuum tubes.

Before the invention of transistors, computers used thousands of vacuum tubes, filled huge rooms, and often overheated. Only governments could afford them. Transistors made computers economical. NEC built the world's first transistorized computer in 1959, and installed a computer reservation system for a railroad in 1960.

NEC was still far behind the United States in computer technology, so at Kobayshi's urging NEC entered into a technical agreement with Honeywell in 1962. In return for license fees, NEC used Honeywell technology to build better computers. NEC soon became Japan's second largest maker of small and moderate-sized computers, surpassed only by IBM-Japan.

That same year the satellite *Telstar 1* began to relay live transatlantic television broadcasts, and Kobayashi realized immediately that NEC's microwave technology could be useful to satellite manufacturers. He flew to Los Angeles to talk with executives at Hughes Aircraft, and they showed him plans for their own satellite above the Pacific. They asked Kobayashi if NEC could build an earth station to receive its signals.

NEC completed Japan's first earth station in 1963. President John Kennedy was scheduled to give a short speech on November 22 to commemorate the first live TV broadcast across the Pacific; instead, the tragic news of his assassination was televised to Japan. The following year NEC's earth station beamed television coverage of the 1964 Summer Olympics from Tokyo up to the satellite *Syncom 3*, which then relayed the broadcasts live to the United States. Today NEC has built more than half of the world's earth stations.

Kobayashi became president of NEC on November 30, 1964. His predecessor picked him for the post because he had always been more open to innovation and change than had his fellow board members.

In most Japanese corporations the president runs the day-to-day affairs and the chairman makes long-term decisions. But NEC's chairman died in 1966, and Kobayashi left the office vacant for ten years. When Kobayashi finally assumed the post himself in 1976, he became a highly active chairman, limiting the authority of the new president. In effect, Kobayashi's power at NEC was unchallenged until he retired in 1988.

Kobayashi began his presidency by increasing quality control and reducing layers of management. He delegated more authority to his vice presidents, and made each division of the company responsible for its own marketing so that employees could respond to consumer trends more quickly. He also started building factories overseas.

Kobayashi's most important decision of the 1960s was to start making integrated circuits. An integrated circuit has no wires. Instead, transistors, which amplify or retard current, are printed on a small board known as a "chip." Chips are the DNA of modern industry. They are used not only in computers, but in ordinary measuring devices inside everything from robots to fuel pumps.

In 1965 NEC built a computer using chips made in the United States. Four percent of the integrated circuits were defective. Kobayashi decided that NEC should make its own integrated circuits, but this was expensive. The slightest speck of dust can spoil a miniature circuit, so chips have to be made in highly automated, dust-free "clean rooms."

Kobayashi created a new Integrated Circuit Division in 1966 and filled it with young engineers. By 1968 NEC built Japan's first computer with domestically made integrated circuits.

Kobayashi also decided not to make NEC's computers compatible with IBM's. He felt it would be impossible to retool NEC's factories every time IBM came out with a new model. He reached this decision after RCA, which made computers compatible with the IBM 360, dropped out of computer manufacturing when IBM introduced the 370. Although NEC's incompatibility with IBM hurt its sales in the United States and Europe, its focus on Asian-language computers with Asian-language keyboards kept sales high in the Far East.

To concentrate on telecommunications, computers, and integrated circuits, Kobayashi sold NEC's Nuclear Energy Research Laboratory in 1966. By contrast, General Electric did the opposite four years later, when it sold its computer division to focus on building nuclear power plants. NEC's major stockholder, International Telephone and Telegraph (ITT), was equally short-sighted. Not only did ITT shun the computer business itself as too expensive and too long-term an investment, it also continuously sold its shares of NEC. ITT used the proceeds to buy hotels, food companies, and rent-a-car firms and transform itself into a "conglomerate," a corporate strategy that was popular in the 1960s and 1970s but has since been discredited. The effect of ITT's frequent sale of NEC stock was to keep the price of NEC shares low until 1978, when ITT finally sold its last shares of the company.

Like many Japanese businessmen, Kobayashi has not been afraid to make a long-term investment. He once compared management to gardening, his favorite hobby. "Cultivate the strong points of an individual or an enterprise," he wrote, "and nurture them like a gardener. It may take ten or twenty years for them to mature."

In 1969, when Apollo 11 landed on the moon, its small computers used LSIs (large-scale integrated circuits.) In an LSI, thousands of electric circuits are photographed, reduced, and printed onto a thin wafer of silicon, as if the street map of a large city were etched on a rectangular coin. By 1971 the Intel corporation produced an LSI chip that was a computer all by itself. The "microprocessor" made the pocket electronic calculator possible, and NEC began manufacturing calculator chips in 1972.

Production of large-scale integrated circuits required investment in new factories and equipment, but in 1973 the price of oil quadrupled and sent Japan's economy reeling. Orders declined, and NEC cut back working hours, slashed executive salaries, and stopped hiring temporary workers. Kobayashi gambled that the economy would recover quickly, and he increased NEC's investment in semiconductor production even when other Japanese firms cut back.

The gamble paid off. In 1974 NEC became Japan's number one seller of semiconductors, a position it still holds today. During the next few years NEC built nine factories to make integrated circuits and LSIs in Japan. To avoid tariffs, it also built plants in Malaysia, Singapore, Mexico, Brazil, Ireland, and California.

By 1977 computer and communications technologies were merging. NEC made computers that linked to form networks, and microwave systems that transmitted data "digitally"—in binary code. In October Kobayashi gave a speech to the International Telecommunications Exposition in Atlanta. He predicted a future where computers and communications would be intertwined in the course of their development, a vision he called "C&C." Well ahead of his time, Kobayashi made the merger of computers and communications the core of NEC's corporate identity.

That same year NEC also installed the no-inventory, "just-in-time" production system pioneered by Toyota, and in 1980 NEC opened new laboratories for software and optical electronics. NEC's investment in research and development has been a whopping 10 percent of sales, but Kobayashi said that research and development is vital not just to a company's growth, but to its survival.

Kobayashi was chairman of NEC for twelve years, from 1976 to 1988, a time of great technical progress for NEC in many fields. NEC became the world's number one manufacturer of telephone digital switching systems. It also became a leader in fiber-optic technology, where thousands of telephone calls are carried on light waves traveling through just a few fiberglass wires. Each phone call remains distinct because each beam of light zigzags through a glass wire in its own separate way.

After a decade of research NEC built the world's first optical telephone circuit in Florida in 1978. It then built a complete fiber-optic system in Buenos Aires in 1981. Telephone service there immediately became much more reliable, and by 1987 NEC was installing fiber-optic telephone systems in over forty countries. NEC also became Japan's third leading producer of fax machines.

In semiconductors, the next advance was the VLSI (very-large-scale integrated circuit), where electron beams are used to print hundreds of thousands of circuits on a single silicon chip. The VLSI was developed jointly by Japan's five largest computer manufacturers (Fujitsu, NEC, Hitachi, Toshiba, and Mitsubishi Electric), with 43 percent of the funding coming from a Japanese government loan. The firms succeeded in making a 256-kilobit memory chip in 1980, with a tiny nine-chip pack capable of processing one hundred typed pages.

The use of VLSIs enabled NEC to take the lead in creating a new generation of "supercomputers" in the early 1980s, faster and more powerful than any previous computer. The tables had turned. By 1984 NEC was licensing technology to Honeywell, its one-time mentor.

Until the mid-1970s, Japanese tariffs had protected companies like NEC by limiting the number of imported semiconductors. In the 1980s, the newly powerful Japanese companies began flooding the market with *exports* of semiconductors. When world demand declined in 1985, Japanese corporations started selling chips at prices below cost until they briefly accounted for 90 percent of the world market share. To avoid American tariffs that would have penalized this "dumping," the Japanese agreed in 1986 to charge fair prices for semiconductors in the future, and also let American chip makers have a 20 percent share of the Japanese market by 1992. Since then NEC and Intel have competed to be the world's number one manufacturer of semiconductors, with Toshiba, Hitachi, and Motorola close behind.

Occasionally VLSI and other chips were defective because of errors in the software used in their manufacture. While these defects were a minor nuisance, they showed the need for a more systematic approach to the writing of software.

Kobayashi felt that 90 percent of NEC's software could be written using factorylike methods. With his encouragement, software writers began dividing their work into sections that could be reused in other programs. They also started using computers that could automatically translate their instructions into computer languages, saving time and reducing errors. By the late 1980s NEC's software had become significantly cheaper and more reliable than before.

In 1976 NEC introduced a do-it-yourself personal computer assembly kit for just $400. It was an immediate success with students and computer buffs, and they offered many suggestions for improvement. Kobayashi then gave the green light to build Japan's first personal computer, the PC-8001, which NEC completed in 1979. NEC sold more than 50 percent of the personal computers in Japan between 1980 and 1995, and today its market share is still dominant. NEC is also Japan's leading seller of mid-range computers. (Fujitsu leads Japan in large computers.)

At eighty-one, Kobayashi retired and became chairman emeritus, an honorary position, in 1988. Although he spent time reading, gardening, and seeing his grandchildren, he still went to work twice a week and often traveled to attend NEC functions. He also wrote several books about computers and communications.

It was fortunate for Kobayashi that he retired when he did. The Japanese stock and real estate markets crashed in 1990, and orders for nearly all NEC products declined. Worse, the American company Compaq began selling inexpensive Japanese-language computers in 1992, forcing NEC to slash its personal computer prices in half to stay competitive. NEC lost $393 million in 1992, but bounced back and made a small profit in 1993. NEC is currently selling hundreds of thousands of personal computers to elementary and secondary schools throughout Japan, but whether it can continue to hold its dominant share of the Japanese market in the face of so much competition is questionable.

Abroad, NEC merged its international personal computer division with Packard Bell Electronics, one of America's leading manufacturers of PCs, in 1996. By 1998, despite investments by NEC of over $1.8 billion that gave it a majority stake in the new company, Packard Bell–NEC nevertheless slipped to number three in American PC sales, behind Compaq and Dell.

NEC's personal computers now use a Japanese-language version of Microsoft Windows, and a new notebook-sized PC comes with a color screen. (NEC is a leader in liquid crystal display technology.) NEC has also built a supercomputer that performs *one trillion* operations a second. In addition, NEC recently became the world's first company to make a four-billion-bit memory chip. This chip has sixteen thousand times the capacity of the most advanced computer chip made in 1980, and can store two copies of all the information in the *Encyclopaedia Britannica*. Yet it is the size of a thumbnail.

Kobayashi took great pride in these innovations, but he did not live to see his dream machine, which has yet to be manufactured. He died at eighty-nine from a hemorrhage of the esophagus on November 30, 1996. For his one hundredth birthday (in 2007) Kobayashi had asked NEC's scientists to build a telephone that automatically interprets Japanese into English and vice versa. The machine must recognize speech from any speaker (no matter what the regional accent), have a wide vocabulary, be able to translate idioms, and assemble speech in another language quickly enough for conversation to flow.

This is a tall order that will require a major breakthrough in software writing, among other technologies. Many scientists believe that even childlike language is beyond the capability of the most sophisticated computers.

But every year and a half computers have doubled in power. Machines now perform telephone banking, convert digital transmissions into natural voices, and do basic English-to-Japanese translation for reservations at Tokyo hotels.

The automatic interpretation telephone may not be ready by 2007, or even 2057, but if it does come, it will be the greatest communications advance of all. Kobayashi could be remembered as a pioneer who helped break down the language barriers that separate nation from nation.

Even if automatic translation proves impossible, Kobayashi's farsighted leadership at NEC provided millions of people with direct telephone dialing, clear radio and TV signals, satellite reception, electronic calculating, business computing, personal computing, and easy access to the information superhighway. It is a stunning achievement for someone whose first daily chore was cleaning a kerosene lamp.

7
Toyoda Eiji
The Man Behind Toyota's
Spectacular Growth

In 1950 an engineer named Toyoda Eiji spent six weeks wandering through every corner of the Ford Motors assembly plant in Detroit. He asked factory workers hundreds of questions and learned as much as he could. At the time Ford produced more than 8,000 cars a day, while in Japan, his company, Toyota, made just 32. Yet Eiji concluded that there were ways to improve Ford's mass production methods. When he returned home he helped create a remarkable production system that is as revolutionary today as Henry Ford's assembly line was in the 1910s.

Thirty years after Eiji's trip to Detroit, Toyota had become the third biggest automobile manufacturer in the world, making more cars per employee, more cheaply, and with fewer defects, than any other company. Ford, in turn, had lost much of its market share to Toyota and to other Japanese car makers, and was suffering huge losses. In desperation, Ford sent hundreds of engineers to Japan to learn the secrets of Toyota's "just-in-time" production system. Toyoda Eiji, the student at Ford thirty years before, had become the teacher.

The lessons of Toyota's production system apply to every manufacturing industry, not just the automobiles. In the twenty-first century, factories that adopt "just-in-time" production may or may not prosper—but those that don't may very likely fail.

But Toyoda Eiji (b. 1913) is only one of several men responsible for Toyota Motors's outstanding success. Eiji's uncle, Toyoda Sakichi (1867–1930), founded the family fortune by inventing and manufacturing automatic looms. Eiji's first cousin, Toyoda Kiichiro (1894–1952), started the Toyota Motor Company in 1937 and ran it for thirteen years. And Eiji's engineering colleague, Ohno Taiichi (1912–1990), perfected the details of "just-in-time" production. But of the four men it is Eiji whose life most closely parallels the struggles and triumphs of the Toyota Motor Corporation, the giant company he helped to build.

In Japanese, the name Toyoda means "plentiful rice field." When the Toyoda family began making automobiles in 1937, they felt this would be a poor name for a car. So they changed the D in their name to a T. To the Japanese ear, "Toyota" has a much crisper sound.

Toyoda Eiji was born on September 12, 1913, in Nagoya, the fourth largest city in Japan. His father worked for a while selling the looms that his older brother had invented, but had started his own small textile mill by the time Eiji was born.

As a boy Eiji begged to help operate the steam engines that powered the looms, but usually he just answered the telephone and wrote down the day's quotation of the price of cotton and other commodities. Because his mother died when he was only six, Eiji also spent a lot of time at the home of his wealthy and kindly uncle, Toyoda Sakichi.

Sakichi had spent much of his childhood watching his grandmother operate a loom, and slowly acquired a thorough knowledge of how a loom works. When he grew up and became a carpenter, Sakichi built his first wooden loom in the 1890s, as a gift for his mother. Not content with foot-powered looms, in 1897 Sakichi added steam engines to the machines. Twenty years later the Toyoda Spinning and Weaving Company had over a thousand employees operating a thousand steel looms. When Sakichi added a device that stopped a loom automatically if a thread snapped or ran out, his looms were suddenly in demand around the world, because they reduced the amount of defective cloth to almost zero.

In 1926 the Toyoda Automatic Loom Works began mass production of these machines. Three years later a British firm bought patent rights to the loom outside East Asia for over $10 million in today's money. Sakichi gave this money to his son Kiichiro, an engineer who specialized in metals casting, and before he died in 1930, urged Kiichiro to make automobiles. The ambitious Sakichi still remembered a trip to America he had taken in the 1910s, and told his son that someday 10 percent of the Japanese would drive cars.

While the Toyoda Loom Works grew and prospered, young Eiji, Kiichiro's cousin, was still a student. In middle school he joined the kendo club, where he learned to fence with bamboo swords. In high school he took many science courses, but found time for gymnastics and skiing. From his house he could see Mt. Ibuki, and in the winter if there was enough snow on a Sunday, he hiked up the mountain and skied down.

In 1933 Eiji began studying mechanical engineering at Tokyo Imperial University. He worked long hours at the drafting table and won a prize for his high grades. He graduated in 1936 after completing his thesis: a design for a diesel automobile engine.

During summers Eiji helped his cousin study engines. Kiichiro was convinced that the Japanese could build cars as well as the Americans. "It is not a matter of whether it can be done," he said, "but who will do it." In 1933 Kiichiro and his staff took apart a tiny American two-cylinder motorcycle engine, examined its parts, modified them slightly to avoid patent infringements, and put them back together. The next year they did the same thing with a Chevrolet engine, a Chrysler body, and a Ford frame and rear axle.

One by one Kiichiro and Eiji also found Japanese suppliers for pistons, gaskets, spark plugs, wheels, tires, brakes, radiators, and many other components. Toyota finally built an assembly plant in 1936, and the following year it made 577 cars.

Kiichiro did not want to waste money producing more cars than he could sell. Instead of mass-producing cars and paying the expenses of inventory, warehousing, and the excessive use of materials, parts, and labor, Kiichiro wanted Toyota to "just make what is needed in time, but not too much." He let the amount of sales orders determine the number and kind of cars Toyota would assemble, a policy Toyota continues to this day. He also asked his machine shops to make only enough parts to fill the assembly plant's needs. With Eiji's help, Kiichiro even arranged for Toyota's suppliers to deliver just one day's worth of parts to the factory each day.

This was the beginning of the Toyota's "just-in-time" production system, but almost as soon as Kiichiro outlined it he had to abandon it. In 1937 Japan started a war with China, so Toyota stopped making cars and began building trucks for the military. As steel, rubber, and other commodities grew scarce during wartime, inventories became necessary. And with orders from the army guaranteed, Toyota simply built as many trucks as it could.

Eiji was drafted in 1937, but two months later the army decided engineers should continue their work as civilians, so Eiji returned to Toyota. In 1938 Toyota built a new factory in the town of Koromo, a suburb of Nagoya. For several months Eiji trained new workers to operate the many machines that build a truck, and by 1939 the plant was producing about a thousand trucks a month. In 1959 Koromo was renamed Toyota City. Today it is home to eight Toyota plants, dozens of auto parts factories, and 325,000 people.

Kiichiro put Eiji in charge of the production of engine accessories. Unlike Kiichiro, who was something of a scholar, Eiji always devoted his full attention to the task at hand. A taciturn and demanding boss, he rarely complimented his employees, although he often criticized things that needed improvement. He was curious and flexible and listened carefully to the advice of his subordinates, trying when possible to manage by consensus. He was also modest about taking credit for successes.

In April 1939 Eiji met Takahashi Kazuko, the daughter of a financial trader. They were married six months later. He was twenty-six, she was nineteen. They had three sons and one daughter; Eiji was a gentle and devoted father. Today all three of his sons are senior executives at different Toyota subsidiaries. His wife, Kazuko, has worked many years to help the blind and retarded, and also to maintain a recreation center for young Toyota employees.

During World War II, Eiji often ran the company because Kiichiro, foreseeing Japan's defeat, retreated to the world of books. Factory workers during the war included women, schoolchildren, geishas, and even criminals. By 1945

Japan was so short of materials that the army ordered trucks with just one head-light, and with brakes on the rear wheels only.

Toyota's factory was not bombed until the last day of the war, when a stray bomb destroyed a fourth of the plant. The United States Air Force had sched-uled a full bombing run over the plant only one week later. After the war Amer-ican occupation authorities fired the top executives of all Japanese companies where the face value of stock was 100 million yen or more. Because by chance Toyota had been capitalized at 97 million yen, Kiichiro and Eiji were allowed to continue working.

Almost no one in Japan had the money to buy a car in the late 1940s, so to stay in business Toyota repaired trucks and even opened up several dry cleaning businesses. Toyota sold several thousand trucks to the United States Army, but by 1949 the struggling company had fallen a month behind in paying wages.

In 1950 several banks lent money to Toyota, including the Sakura (Mitsui), Tokai, and Sanwa banks, each of which own about 5 percent of Toyota's stock today. (By contrast, the Toyoda family owns just one percent.) The banks insisted that Toyota cut costs by firing 2,000 employees, one fourth of its work force. The auto workers union protested the cuts with several brief strikes, but accepted them in the end because Kiichiro took personal responsibility for the layoffs by resigning himself. He died two years later.

Soon after this, Eiji, just thirty-seven, became Toyota's executive vice presi-dent for technical affairs. The new management gave the company's remaining 4,000 employees a guarantee of lifetime employment, and a promise of pay and bonuses based on seniority rather than job classification. In return, the workers, now represented by a more docile union, agreed to be flexible about their job assignments and to work at whatever jobs needed doing. Workers also put in long hours for many years, because Toyota cut costs by paying for overtime rather than by hiring new workers.

In the summer of 1950, Ford invited foreign engineers, including Eiji, to come to Detroit to study its plant. At the time, no one at Ford ever dreamed that for-eign car-makers would one day become serious competitors. Eiji also visited machine tool makers in Cleveland, Cincinnati, Rochester, and Providence.

Eiji left the United States convinced that traditional mass-production meth-ods with their large inventories and many defects were far too wasteful for a small company like Toyota. He felt many jobs done at Ford by specialists, such as quality checking and tool repair, could be done better by the assembly line workers themselves.

When Eiji returned to Japan in October he immediately began working with his chief production engineer, Ohno Taiichi, who had visited Detroit with him. Together the two men spent the next twenty years relentlessly instilling quality control, and reestablishing Kiichiro's "just-in-time" production system not only at Toyota Motors, but at each of Toyota's subsidiaries and even among Toyota's hundreds of suppliers.

Ohno, who studied engineering at an industrial high school but never went to college, was inspired by supermarket procedure. Consumers do not pile up inventories of food at home, but buy food when they need it, and grocers replace items only as they are sold.

Eiji and Ohno trained assembly-line workers to take parts only when they needed them. They limited the storage space for headlights, for example, to just ten units. Similarly, workers making parts took only the materials necessary to make a new batch of parts, and only at the moment they began making the new parts.

Toyota discovered it was cheaper to assemble cars in small quantities rather than large quantities for two reasons. First, it eliminated the cost of inventory. Second, in small batches, defects could be seen and corrected immediately.

But inventories could stay low only if suppliers made deliveries every day, or, even better, every several hours. This has been easier for Toyota to implement than for other companies, because most of Toyota's suppliers are in the Nagoya metropolitan area, at most an hour's drive from a factory. In Tokyo, where heavy traffic makes hourly deliveries impossible, some suppliers did not convert to the "just-in-time" system until the 1970s, and then only after they formed car pools with other suppliers.

At most factories around the world, suppliers deliver parts with an acceptable percentage of defects. But with inventories at Toyota as low as ten units, a faulty delivery could stop production completely. With consequences this severe, Toyota's suppliers were forced to improve their quality during the 1950s and 1960s. By 1965 the delivery of a defective part was a rare occurrence.

Toyota is a demanding company, but it also works closely with its suppliers from the moment it begins designing a car, and saves them money by giving them advance notice of a rise, fall, or change in consumer demand.

To make the "just-in-time" system work smoothly, Eiji and Ohno created a record-keeping system, using 3½-by-8-inch (9-by-20 cm) signs called *kanban* (pronounced kahn-bahn). As parts move forward in the assembly process, *kanban* signs move backward with the empty containers. No worker can withdraw automobile parts without leaving a numbered *kanban* to order new parts. Machine shops and suppliers, in turn, do not produce more parts than the number requested on the *kanban*.

A cardinal rule of "just-in-time" production is Do not send defective products to the subsequent process. A worker who sees a defect should immediately show it to his supervisor, who must go back as many steps in the manufacturing process as is necessary to trace the cause. Perhaps a piece of metal was not lined up properly. Or a worker was inattentive. Or instructions were hard to understand. Or a machine took more time to operate than was previously thought. Whatever the cause, it would be corrected promptly so the defect would not reoccur.

Eiji and Ohno instituted the most dramatic feature of the Toyota production system in 1955. They gave every worker on a Toyota assembly line the power to pull a rope and stop the factory's production. By contrast, at most plants around the world, only senior managers have this power.

When a worker finds a defect, he first turns on a yellow light and tries to correct it quickly, replacing it with another part if necessary. But if he cannot correct the defect before the next component comes down the assembly line, then he must pull the rope and stop the assembly line. The policy is that it is better to stop production than to knowingly pass on a defect.

Ohno got the idea for letting workers stop the line from Sakichi's automatic looms, which stopped before a broken thread could lead to defects. At first Toyota's assembly lines stopped often and workers grew discouraged. But they rarely stopped for the same reason twice, and soon the lines almost never stopped at all.

In most factories workers correct any defects in a rework area at the end. Even in a Mercedes-Benz factory 25 percent of labor time is devoted to reworking at the end of assembly. At Toyota, by contrast, there is almost no reworking.

Toyota's use of quality control and "just-in-time" methods worked so well that by 1959 Toyota's production of vehicles per employee was equal to Ford's and 50 percent higher than that of General Motors. By 1970, even allowing for differences in the amount of work sent out to suppliers, Toyota produced over three times as many vehicles per employee as Ford and GM.

But in the first half of the 1950s Toyota made only 11,500 cars. Called Toyopets, they were really just Volkswagen Beetle–style bodies put on truck chassis, and were used mainly as taxis.

Toyota did not introduce its first true passenger car until New Year's Day, 1955, when Eiji, dressed in a tuxedo, drove the first "Crown" off the assembly line. It was not suitable for export because it could not run for long hours at high speeds. But it was fine for Japanese roads and cheaper than American and European imports.

Since then many Toyota models have taken up the "Crown" theme. "Corona," for example, is Latin for crown. "Corolla" is Latin for small crown. And "Camry" (from *kanmuri*) is Japanese for crown.

In the late 1950s Eiji realized that ordinary Japanese would soon be able to afford cars. He persuaded his colleagues to build a new factory that could produce 10,000 cars a month, twice the output of Toyota's old plant. The factory was a gamble because it had to be financed by loans, but only four months after its opening in 1959, it was producing cars at full capacity. Toyota's older factory was now devoted exclusively to trucks, and by 1961 the company was the fourth biggest producer of trucks in the world.

Toyota was greatly helped by a government tariff throughout the 1950s and 1960s of 34 percent on all but the smallest imported cars. The tariff helped reduce the American share of the Japanese car market from a high of 60 percent in 1953 to just one percent by 1960. The government cut the tariff in half in 1969, but did not eliminate it entirely until 1978. By then less than 8 percent of Japanese dealer showrooms even bothered to display foreign cars.

In 1966 Toyota introduced the Corolla. It had a slightly bigger engine than the Nissan Sunny, and soon became Japan's most popular family car. By 1986 Toyota had sold twelve million Corollas, and for over three decades Toyota's market share in Japan has continued to be around 40 percent.

As Japanese competitors lost out to Toyota, they worked hard during the 1960s and 1970s to convert to the "just-in-time" system, as American car manufacturers have done in the 1990s. But no company has yet matched Toyota's high level of productivity or low rate of defects. Toyota's huge savings allow it to set prices consistently below those of its direct competitors.

The year 1966 marked several turning points for Toyota. It finally sold more cars than trucks. Its suppliers were just completing their conversion to the "just-in-time" system. Most important, Toyota began its exponential growth in exports.

Toyota's market research showed that what American consumers, especially housewives, wanted most was low maintenance and high reliability. The company designed its cars accordingly. The Corolla was Toyota's first car comparable in quality to small European cars, and it was cheaper. Toyota's exports, mostly to the United States, rose from 4000 cars in 1957, to 158,000 cars in 1967, to 1,413,000 cars in 1977. Car sales were always highest in California, and in some years Californians bought more Toyotas than Fords.

In 1967 Toyota's board of directors chose Eiji, now fifty-four, to be president of Toyota. In a Japanese firm it is the president who typically exercises real power; the chairman's duties are usually advisory. Eiji served as president of Toyota until 1982—fifteen years of what he later described as "smooth sailing."

It didn't seem so smooth at the time. In the early 1970s, when Japan adopted stringent pollution controls, Eiji spent half his time attending hearings in Tokyo to explain that it is a difficult technical problem to clean exhaust without sacrificing performance. But no one was interested in the mechanics of the problem. Politicians and newspaper editors simply said, in effect: Cut the grousing and clean up the air. Eiji, a quiet man who hates publicity, was horrified by the avalanche of criticism.

Toyota swallowed its pride, borrowed some features from Honda's low-emissions CVCC (Civic) engine, and managed to reduce exhaust without sacrificing fuel economy. When the second world oil crisis struck in 1979, Toyota was already offering many inexpensive models with low exhaust, high performance, and high mileage, including Coronas, Corollas, Celicas, Carinas, Starlets, and Tercels.

In the 1970s Eiji also authorized the building of five new engine and assembly plants, all of which have hummed for years at 100 percent of their capacity.

Toyota's vehicle production quadrupled during Eiji's presidency, rising to 3.14 million in 1982—8 percent of the world's output. Today Toyota's global market share of cars (not including trucks) is 10 percent, behind General Motors and Ford, just ahead of Volkswagen, and far ahead of Fiat, Nissan, and Honda.

Eiji became chairman of Toyota on July 1, 1982, when Kiichiro's eldest son, Toyoda Shoichiro, replaced him as president. Eiji rarely interfered while Shoichiro ran the company, and for the first time in decades he had time to read for pleasure and to swim daily in his own pool.

With Eiji's full backing, Toyota followed Honda's example and built factories around the world in the 1980s. At one factory in Fremont, California, Toyota and General Motors jointly produce over 350,000 Corollas, Tacoma pickup trucks, and Chevy Geo Prizms annually. Toyota also built a plant in George-town, Kentucky, where American workers make over 300,000 Camrys a year. Only one percent of the five thousand employees at this plant are Japanese, and 75 percent of the parts used at the factory are American made.

Today 60 percent of the Toyota cars and trucks sold in the United States and Canada are built in the United States and Canada, and their quality is equal to that of cars made in Japan. Toyota has also built automobile factories using "just-in-time" methods in Britain, Taiwan, Thailand, the Philippines, and Indonesia. By 2000 it will also be making 500,000 engines a year in Buffalo, West Virginia, and 150,000 trucks and sport utility vehicles a year in Princeton, Indiana.

Factories abroad give Toyota protection against trade barriers and sudden rises in the yen. But even without such protection a "just-in-time" factory where workers earn high wages can still outcompete a mass-production factory where workers earn low wages. This became clear when sales of Korean Hyundais collapsed in 1990. The public realized that Toyotas and other Japan-ese cars were far superior to Hyundais, at prices only slightly higher. Despite Toyota's rising costs after the yen doubled in value in 1985, the efficiency of the Toyota production system proved to be a greater competitive advantage than the low wages Hyundai paid its workers in Korea.

Since 1981 Toyota and other Japanese car makers, facing American resent-ment, have voluntarily agreed to limit the number of cars they export to the United States. Rather than sell more small cars, Japanese companies have expanded by selling bigger and more luxurious cars. In 1989 Toyota introduced the Lexus. A lifelong dream of Eiji's, the Lexus was the first Toyota designed to compete directly with Mercedes and BMW. Within months it outsold every other luxury car in the United States, as consumer magazines agreed that the Lexus offered nearly all the advantages of a Mercedes at a much cheaper price.

This is one of the latest triumphs of the "just-in-time" production system. A Lexus is cheaper than a Mercedes because Toyota makes luxury cars using only *one fourth* the labor it takes to make a Mercedes. The Lexus has also had fewer defects than any other car, according to J. D. Power surveys. (Even the inexpensive Corolla is usually among the ten cars with the fewest defects.)

Eiji finally retired in 1992, just as one of the most severe economic recessions in Japan's history began to deepen. With cash reserves of over $25 billion, Toyota weathered the downturn and refused to cut costs by laying off workers. Five years later Toyota had fully recovered and profits were higher than ever.

Eiji remains honorary chairman of Toyota and still sits on the company's board of directors, commuting to his office several times a week. He helped Toyota grow from a small workshop into a global corporation, and with Toyoda Kiichiro and Ohno Taiichi, Toyoda Eiji ranks with Henry Ford as one of the giants in the history of industry.

Today only one fourth of the world's adults drive cars. There is plenty of room for Toyota and other companies to grow, and it is the "just-in-time" production system that can make cars affordable to the poorer three quarters of the world.

8

Morita Akio
Co-founder of Sony

N<small>O ONE HAS</small> done more to establish Japan's reputation for high technology than Morita Akio. His company, Sony, has been the world's most innovative consumer electronics firm for half a century. It was the first to mass-produce the pocket-sized transistor radio, the Trinitron color TV, the VCR, the Walkman, the compact disc player, and the video camcorder.

Starting with a few shacks with roofs so leaky that engineers had to keep umbrellas over their desks, Sony has grown into a giant corporation with over 170,000 employees and $1 billion in sales every week. Sony products bring music and entertainment to hundreds of millions of homes around the world, and its name ranks just behind Coca-Cola as the most widely recognized brand name on earth.

Two men started Sony in 1946: Ibuka Masaru (1908–1997) and Morita Akio (b. 1921), and they remained the best of friends. Ibuka was an engineering genius who led Sony to many technical breakthroughs, but it is Morita who transformed the company from a small workshop into a multinational corporation.

Morita Akio was born on January 26, 1921, in the city of Nagoya, and was the eldest of four children. His father was a rich businessman. For over three hundred years the Morita family has run a regional sake brewery, and also made miso (soy) paste and soy sauce. Morita grew up in a large house with a tennis court, six servants, and a chauffeur.

When Morita turned eleven, his father began taking him to business meetings. He expected his son to succeed him when he retired, and showed him how to read financial reports. He also taught Morita the importance of motivating employees and the uselessness of scolding them when they made mistakes.

As a teenager Morita was more interested in physics than in business. His enthusiasm began when his father brought home an electric record player to replace the hand-cranked, big-horned Victrola his mother had previously used to listen to European classical music. It fascinated him that vacuum tubes inside the record player could improve sound quality so much. He began to buy books

and magazines about electronics, and visited a relative who had built a phonograph of his own as a hobby.

Morita tried unsuccessfully to build a wire sound recorder, and almost
flunked out of high school before he finally found the time to study English and
the Chinese classics. Excelling at physics and math, he enrolled in Osaka Imperial University in 1940 because it had Japan's youngest and brightest science
professors.

As a student Morita did scientific research for the navy during World War II.
After he graduated in 1944, Lieutenant Morita worked in an optics laboratory,
then headed a small unit trying to develop a heat-seeking torpedo. As food
became scarce toward the end of the war, Morita asked his family to send him
two barrels of soy sauce and soybean paste and bartered them for fish to keep
his men well fed.

One of the civilians in the torpedo unit was an electrical engineer named
Ibuka Masaru. He was thirteen years older than Morita, but because both men
dreamed of starting their own engineering company, they quickly became close
friends.

The son of a mining engineer who died young, Ibuka had been a ham radio
operator as a teenager before earning a science degree from Waseda University
in 1933. After college he failed to pass the Toshiba corporation's entrance exam,
but found jobs with a radio equipment firm and a film processing laboratory. In
1940 he helped start the Japan Measurement Instruments Company, working as
its chief engineer. He made voltmeters and radar parts for the Japanese navy,
and began working with Morita in the torpedo unit in 1944.

Ibuka was not content with making electrical components. After the war
ended in August 1945, he (and soon, Morita) moved to Tokyo to start a new
enterprise, Tokyo Tsushin Kogyo (Tokyo Telecommunications Engineering
Company), or "Totsuko" for short. It was renamed Sony in 1958.

Ibuka and Morita had no interest in manufacturing anything already made
by giant electric companies such as Matsushita or Toshiba. They wanted to
make completely new products, but in postwar Japan their first concern was to
make enough money and find enough food to feed Totsuko's twenty employees.
They repaired radios and stitched electric heating pads, and tried and failed to
make a reliable electric rice cooker.

In April 1946 Ibuka and his father-in-law, a former minister of education,
took a train to Nagoya to meet Morita's father. They asked him to release his
eldest son from the obligation to carry on the family sake business, and to allow
the second son to run the firm instead. The elder Morita agreed, and over time
invested in his son's new company. Today the Morita brewery remains the
largest stockholder of Sony, owning about 9 percent of the corporation.

The first Totsuko products to earn a steady income were voltmeters, which
Ibuka had made for years, and adaptors that gave AM radios the capacity to

receive shortwave broadcasts. Totsuko also made broadcast consoles for Japanese radio stations.

Despite these successes, Ibuka and Morita were frustrated because they had not yet made a new product. In 1948 they almost decided to make a wire sound recorder, when by chance they met an American soldier with a new kind of recorder that used magnetic tape.

Ibuka and Morita had never seen tape before, but they realized immediately that unlike wire, it could give clear sound, splice easily, and fit on a small reel. They decided that Totsuko would be the first Japanese company to make tape recorders.

It was not hard for them to build a recording machine, but it was very difficult to make tape. There was no plastic in Japan during the postwar years, and regulations discouraged imports. Ibuka and Morita tried to use cellophane, but it stretched too easily. Thicker cellophane didn't work either. Finally, the two men used long strips of calendar paper and coated them with a lacquer mixed with an iron oxide powder that they had ground from magnets.

By 1950 Totsuko had made fifty tape recorders, each weighing seventy-five pounds and costing roughly five thousand dollars in today's money. Morita and Ibuka naively assumed that there would be a big demand for their technological innovation. Instead, three months passed before they sold a single tape recorder. People liked hearing their own voice, but nobody wanted to buy a machine. Morita realized that he would have to become his company's salesman and set up his own distribution network.

His first customer was a Tokyo pub that used the tape recorder to entertain its customers. The next twenty machines were bought by the Supreme Court of Japan, to help their stenographers. Morita also sold tape recorders to police officers for use during interrogations, and to junior high school language departments.

The engineers at Totsuko also gave a tape recorder as a wedding present to Kamei Yoshiko, whom Morita married in 1951. Like her husband, Yoshiko is attractive, outgoing, and vivacious, and grew up in a rich and sophisticated family. (The Kamei family publishes dictionaries.) During the 1950s the Moritas had two sons and one daughter, and in later years Yoshiko hosted a television show on international fashion.

Another person who impressed Morita at this time was a singing student, a young man named Ohga Norio. A perfectionist with an interest in electronics as well as music, Ohga made many detailed criticisms of the early tape recorder. Morita liked his ideas and candor, and when Ohga went to West Germany to study opera in 1954, Morita paid him a salary to keep up with developments in German electronics. Five years later he finally talked Ohga into joining Sony; Ohga became chairman of the corporation in 1994.

Morita and Ibuka knew their first tape recorders were too heavy and expensive. In 1951 they produced a new machine that was 50 percent lighter and 50 percent cheaper. Morita traveled throughout Japan to demonstrate the new tape recorders to music and language teachers; within two years nearly a third of all the primary schools in Japan had purchased a Totsuko tape recorder.

In 1952 Ibuka learned that Western Electric wanted to license its rights to the transistor, which its scientists had recently invented. (A transistor is no bigger than a pill and usually made of silicon. It can amplify or retard waves of energy or flows of current, and is smaller, cheaper, and more durable than the glass vacuum tubes used inside most electronic equipment before 1960.)

Western Electric's transistor only amplified sound, and was used only in hearing aids. Ibuka was certain that transistors could be modified to amplify radio waves as well, which would make it possible to build small radios that were portable and battery powered. Morita agreed with Ibuka, but suggested a more ambitious goal. Not just portable, he said, but "pocketable." They should make a radio small enough to fit into a shirt pocket.

Morita traveled to the United States in 1953 to negotiate a deal with Western Electric, and agreed to pay about $200,000 in today's money as an advance against royalties. He also brought back a two-volume textbook, *Transistor Technology*, which four engineers at Totsuko studied closely for months.

The following year Ibuka and Iwama Kazuo went to the United States to visit the laboratories and factories of Western Electric. Iwama was Morita's brother-in-law, and a hardworking physicist. Every few nights, with Ibuka's help, Iwama wrote eight- and nine-page letters containing detailed diagrams of equipment that their engineers would need to duplicate back home.

The scientists at Totsuko added new metals to the transistor to make it more heat-resistant, and reversed its positive-negative polarity. By the end of 1954 they succeeded in making a transistor that amplified radio frequencies—but they were beaten to the punch. In December Texas Instruments made the world's first transistor radio for a company named Regency, which ultimately decided not to mass-produce the item. Totsuko's jade-green radio was smaller and more reliable than Regency's, but it was not ready for sale until the following August.

Morita knew that Totsuko was too hard a brand name for most foreigners to remember, and considered many possible names as replacements. He thought about TTK, but there was already a Japanese company called TKK. He poured through dictionaries, and eventually found the Latin word *sonus*, meaning "sound." The word itself seemed to have sound in it, and his company was in the business of sound.

Morita wanted a name that would be easy to pronounce but have no meaning in any language. Sony was ideal because it was similar to the optimistic words "sonny" and "sunny," but short enough so the four letters themselves could be the company logo, even in Japan. Morita marketed all of the transistor radios under the brand name Sony, and by 1958 the entire company adopted the new name.

Sony's first radio was "coat-pocket-sized." The company had difficulty finding subcontractors willing to make tiny speakers and transformers, and could not produce a "shirt-pocket-sized" radio until 1957. Even then Morita had to buy his salesmen custom-made shirts with extra-large pockets, because the new radio still couldn't quite fit into an ordinary shirt pocket.

Sony sold 1.5 million "pocket" radios in the 1950s, a third of them in the United States. Morita followed a strategy of "succeed first in the U.S. market, bring back the reputation to Japan, then spread out to Europe and other countries." It worked. Before long Morita was flying around the world setting up sales networks in one country after another.

Some of Sony's dealers urged Morita to cut costs and lower prices, but Morita refused to sacrifice quality, and consumers responded by paying a little extra for "the radio that works."

Sony stayed ahead of its competitors by making an FM transistor radio in 1958, a transistorized television in 1960, and a transistorized videotape recorder in 1961 that became popular with American football teams. Sony made each of these products without doing any market research, a bold practice that it still continues today. Morita explained: "Our plan is to lead the public with new products rather than ask them what kind of products they want. The public does not know what is possible, but we do."

To maintain its position as an electronics pioneer, Sony spurs even junior employees to develop new ideas and display them at an annual fair open only to Sony personnel. If management decides to pursue a particular idea, the employee who developed the concept will lead the team from the drawing board to the assembly line.

In typically Japanese fashion, the titles and salaries of most Sony employees advance slowly, according to seniority. The Japanese think that a feeling of equality is better for employee morale. Responsibility, by contrast, varies widely from one department to the next, depending on the ambition of its members.

To help aggressive employees find challenging work, Morita began a weekly company newspaper that advertises job openings and allows employees to apply for new company jobs confidentially. Until the person finds a new job, the boss never knows he or she is looking.

Morita also ordered his personnel department to ignore the school records of all Sony employees once they had been on the job for two years. He wrote a book, *Never Mind School Records*, that criticized Japan's overemphasis on university credentials. It struck a chord with the Japanese public and sold 250,000 copies.

In 1963 Morita and his family moved into a twelve-room apartment on Fifth Avenue in New York. For several years he had been commuting between Tokyo and New York, setting up showrooms, launching a TV advertising campaign, and working with lawyers to offer Sony stock to American investors. (Today over 40 percent of Sony's shares are owned by non-Japanese.) Morita found that his high school English was better than he thought, and he and Yoshiko hosted lavish parties to entertain celebrities in the worlds of music and finance. The family returned to Tokyo only when Morita's father died in 1964.

In the mid-1960s Sony was selling millions of portable black and white TV sets just when color television began to make black and white television obsolete. It would have been easy enough for Sony to make the kind of television sets with three electron guns (emitting red, blue, and green beams) that RCA made, but Ibuka and Morita refused to simply copy another product, particularly because they were not impressed with the picture quality of the RCA product to begin with. For a year Sony's engineers experimented with a "chromatron" tube, then dropped it. By 1967 Sony still had not made a reliable color TV.

Sony's dealers were furious because they were losing a big market to their competitors. During a series of speeches that Morita gave every January to dealers throughout Japan, Morita asked for patience—and promised that in the long run they would all make *more* money because Sony would create a superior product.

Meanwhile Ibuka spent long hours working with his engineers. "Once Ibuka focuses his interest, he *never* gives up," a colleague observed. Eventually Ibuka and his staff attached three emitters to just one electron gun. When they finished in April 1968, the Trinitron was twice as bright as other color TV sets and used much less power. Soon Sony was selling almost two million TV sets annually. Years later, it also became the leading supplier of color monitors for Apple Computer, and since 1995 Sony has been the world's number one manufacturer of color television sets.

In the late 1960s Sony began to make stereo equipment, and to advertise its new products it formed a joint venture with CBS Records in 1968 to handle CBS's sales in Japan. CBS had spent years negotiating with other, more cautious Japanese companies, but one lunch with Morita was sufficient to close the deal. Morita put Ohga in charge of CBS-Sony, and it became Japan's top record company.

In 1972 Sony opened its first American factory, a Trinitron television plant in San Diego, California. At first the employees merely assembled parts made in Japan, but once quality control at the factory met Japanese standards, the American workers made all the Trinitron's major components except the electron gun. Ironically, Sony television sets are more "American" than many U.S. brands made in Asia.

Sony also built a television factory in Bridgend, Wales, in 1974, an audio- and videotape factory in Dothan, Alabama, in 1977, and a variety of plants in the 1980s in Tijuana, Stuttgart, Singapore, Bangkok, and Penang (Malaysia), among other places. When Morita visited a factory he tried to meet as many of the employees as he could and ate meals with them in the company cafeterias.

Today over 50 percent of all Sony products are made outside Japan. This is not just to protect the company against a rise in the yen. It is part of a policy Morita calls "global localization," where factory managers, working arrangements, and marketing ideas all come from the local country that buys the Sony products.

As Sony grew more international, Morita became an unofficial ambassador for Japanese business, giving interviews and writing articles for many publications. In an interview in *Playboy*, for example, Morita said, "We are not invading, we just make things you like." He also commented on why technological borrowing is not two-way: "We subscribe to all your technical publications . . . do you think many Americans read ours?"

Morita at times has been a vocal critic of American business. Too many corporate chiefs, he says, are lawyers or accountants who don't understand the manufacturing process of their own companies, and therefore don't take the technical risks necessary for long-term growth. Looking only to the next quarter's statement, they busy themselves with mergers and acquisitions, and fire thousands of workers at the slightest downturn.

Layoffs are a "disgrace," Morita says, and terrible for morale. It is better, he feels, to sacrifice profits and keep workers, as Sony did at the San Diego Trinitron factory during the 1973–1974 recession, because grateful employees will reciprocate a company's loyalty and work more productively.

Morita has also criticized Japanese businessmen. They compete too aggressively for market shares abroad, and import too few goods back home. Japan's corporate wealth, Morita says, has not translated into shorter working hours for employees or higher dividends for stockholders. Morita would like Japan to become a "lifestyle superpower," but even at Sony, working hours are often long, and dividends are still less than 20 percent of net earnings.

Morita is at home all over the world. In addition to a twenty-four-room mansion with an indoor swimming pool in suburban Tokyo and a country home near Mt. Fuji, Morita has apartments in New York and Hawaii, and until recently often traveled to London, Los Angeles, and Munich. From Munich he and his wife often drove two hours to hear a Mozart concert in Salzburg, or a Wagner opera in Bayreuth.

Before he retired, the flamboyant Morita had a corporate jet, two helicopters, four attractive secretaries (two domestic, two international), and five telephone lines at home and two more in his car. He talked from dawn to dusk to high- and low-level Sony executives around the world, usually doing more listening than speaking. He also found time to play tennis and golf, and to ski.

In the early 1970s Sony revolutionized television news with a portable videotape recorder called the U-Matic. Its ¾-inch videotape was easy to edit, and eliminated the cost of developing film. But Ibuka and Morita were not satisfied. They had brought audiotape recorders into ordinary homes in the 1950s and

1960s, and now they wanted to bring videotape recorders into the home too. They told their engineers to make a home videocassette the size of a paperback book with one hour of playing time.

Until then, every other band on a videotape was blank. This prevented spillover from one band to the next, but also made videotape bulky. A Sony engineer named Kihara Nobutoshi eliminated spillover another way by placing two recording heads at a 90-degree angle from each other, so that neither head could interfere with the band next to it. This ended the need for alternating blank bands, and made possible smaller videotape, and a smaller recorder.

Sony called its new video cassette recorder (VCR) the Betamax, because in Japanese "beta" means a full brushstroke without blank spaces. Sony released the Betamax in 1975, and it sold especially well among night workers who wanted to record prime-time television.

For nearly two years Sony had little competition, but because it neglected to license its technology to other electronics companies, it failed to establish the Betamax system as the industry standard. In 1976 Matsushita Electric's subsidiary, JVC, introduced its own VHS (video home system) recording format that was cheaper than the Betamax and played for *two hours*. Unlike Sony, Matsushita quickly licensed the use of its system to other corporations such as Sharp and Hitachi, and suddenly most of the Japanese electronics industry was competing against Sony. Morita stubbornly refused to lower the price of the Betamax, expecting that as usual consumers would pay a little extra for a machine of superior quality.

But the public did not care as much about picture quality as it did about playing time. A two-hour tape made it possible to record movies on television, a one-hour tape did not. The VHS recorders quickly outsold the Betamax, and movie studios followed the public by issuing videos in the VHS format. This caused even more people to buy VHS machines, and finally Sony gave up and began making VHS recorders itself.

Sony missed out on the VCR boom of the 1980s even though it invented the VCR in the 1970s. Morita had misjudged the importance of video playing time, and it was the biggest mistake of his life. Sony profits fell sharply in the early 1980s, and Morita was heavily criticized at stockholders' meetings.

The bad times did not last long. By 1984 Sony profits had rebounded thanks to a series of new products. First came the Walkman in 1979. Ibuka had asked his engineers to make a smaller stereo tape recorder, but Morita suggested the miniature headphones, and later convinced skeptical colleagues that if a tape cassette player was small enough, the public would buy it even if it lacked a recording capability. During the 1980s over fifty million people proved Morita right.

Sony also introduced the 3.5-inch plastic-encased computer disk, which soon became the standard-sized disk everywhere. And it began making a variety of computer components for other companies.

In 1982 Morita, who had become chairman after Ibuka had retired, picked Ohga to be Sony's new president. That same year Sony, in association with Philips, the Dutch electronics giant, began making compact discs (CDs) and compact disc players. A CD player reproduces sound with a laser beam instead of a needle. Because nothing ever touches a disc, there is no pop, scratch, or hiss. The sound is flawless. The disc's playing time is seventy-four minutes; Ohga wanted it to be long enough for Beethoven's Ninth Symphony.

Sony promoted its technology in Japan by releasing hundreds of CDs on the CBS-Sony record label, but American record companies were cool to the CD. They saw no need to switch from records and tapes. Always the salesman, Morita bypassed record executives and took his CDs directly to rock stars, pop singers, and symphony conductors. They loved the CD, and pressured their record companies to issue new releases in the CD format.

Sales of CD players earned huge profits for Sony, but it was sobering for Morita and Ohga to realize that the CD player would have been as big a failure as the Betamax if they had not persuaded record companies to issue CDs. In the future Sony could no longer simply introduce new technology. It would have to make sure that there was a supply of music and movie software to accompany its new products, otherwise no one would buy them. Morita and Ohga concluded that in order to protect Sony's huge investment in future technologies such as high-definition television, Sony had no choice but to enter the entertainment business.

In 1988 Sony paid $2 billion to buy CBS Records. The world's largest record company has a roster of stars that includes Michael Jackson, Barbra Streisand, and Bruce Springsteen, and a library holding the music of Billie Holiday, Benny Goodman, and *My Fair Lady*. Sony renamed the company Sony Music Entertainment, and profits since the purchase have been high.

Emboldened by its success in the music industry, Sony paid $3.4 billion in 1989 for Columbia Pictures Entertainment, a major Hollywood studio that now has a library of over 3,500 films and 40,000 television episodes. Journalists wrote stories about Japan's "invasion" of Hollywood, and unfortunately this coincided with the Japanese-language publication of a book co-authored by Morita called *The Japan That Can Say No*. Morita wrote that Japanese officials must learn to be frank and say no to America's trade demands, many of which he said were "outrageous."

His co-author, a politician named Ishihara Shintaro, suggested that if Japan wanted, it could cripple the United States nuclear capability by refusing to sell computer chips to the Pentagon. In fact, the low-end chips the United States buys from Japan are easily replaceable, but the outrage that the book caused was enormous. Morita, whose comments were far milder than Ishihara's, was deeply embarrassed, and refused to authorize an English translation of his half of the book for fear that it might hurt Sony's sales.

Ironically, because of the uproar over the book, Morita hesitated to interfere and say no to the excesses of Walter Yetnikoff, the chief of Sony Music Entertainment who arranged the purchase of Columbia Pictures. As part of the deal, Yetnikoff put his friends Jon Peters and Peter Guber, the producers of the movie *Batman*, in charge of Sony's new studio. But the two men still had a contract to make movies for Warner, and because they had not asked for Warner's permission to get out of the contract beforehand, Warner refused to grant permission afterward. Warner sued, and Sony had to pay $400 million to settle the case. In addition, Sony paid Peters and Guber over $200 million for their production company, and another $100 million to refurbish Columbia's production facilities. Sony also incurred $1.5 billion in debt to pay for the acquisition, so the true cost of Sony's purchase of Columbia Pictures was $5.6 billion.

For all the money that it took to hire Peters and Guber, Sony was soon disappointed by their performance. Peters was forced to resign in 1991 after he had put both his girlfriend and his ex-wife on the Sony payroll. Guber stayed longer, but after a string of flops that lost well over $100 million, including the movies *Hook, Geronimo, Last Action Hero*, and *I'll Do Anything*, he too resigned in 1994. Since then Sony has installed a Japanese as executive vice president of Sony Pictures. As the studio's number three man, he is the "eyes and ears" for his superiors in Tokyo.

Later in 1994 Sony bit the bullet and wrote off $2.7 billion in losses at Sony Pictures, which meant that the studio was worth only half of what Sony paid for it in 1989, at least on paper. But Sony executives have not yet given up on the basic idea of combining electronics and entertainment into one company. "Business has to continue a long, long time," Morita has said, "I'm very patient."

Despite Sony's success, conservative Japanese businessmen had long regarded Morita with disdain as too blunt, too flamboyant, and too Western. By the early 1990s, however, many executives had become as internationally minded as Morita, and he had won enough respect among them to be next in line as chairman of *Keidanren*, Japan's most powerful business organization.

This highest honor never came. At age seventy-two, in November, 1993, Morita suffered a cerebral hemorrhage. He had brain surgery and spent six months in a Tokyo hospital. Though able to write messages and enjoy the company of his grandchildren, he was confined to a wheelchair and resigned as chairman of Sony. His interest in Sony and its many new technologies remains undiminished.

PART TWO
Traditional Culture

9
Lady Murasaki
Author of The Tale of Genji, *the World's First Great Novel*

ONE THOUSAND years ago a noblewoman named Murasaki Shikibu wrote *The Tale of Genji*, the novel many Japanese think is the all-time classic of their nation's literature. Longer than *War and Peace*, with over fifty important characters, Lady Murasaki's vivid book describes the life and many loves of Genji, a lord who lacks a royal title but is nevertheless a "shining prince." *The Tale of Genji* was the first work of fiction to have lifelike characters with complex states of mind. Written six hundred years before Miguel de Cervantes's *Don Quixote*, it is the first great novel in the history of the world.

In the twentieth century, several of Japan's greatest writers spent years of their lives translating *The Tale of Genji* from archaic into modern Japanese. Most notably, the poet Yosano Akiko's appeared in 1912, novelist Tanizaki Jun'ichiro's in 1941, and the novelist Setouchi Jakucho's in 1998. They did so because they wanted to share their love of *The Tale of Genji* with new generations of readers.

Murasaki (c.975–c.1025) was born in Kyoto sometime between 973 and 978 to a minor branch of the Fujiwara family, at that time the most powerful family in Japan. Her girlhood name is unknown. Shikibu is a reference to her father's government office. She did not receive the nickname Murasaki until she was an adult. Probably it was a humorous reference to a character in her novel, for Murasaki is the name of Genji's favorite wife and greatest love.

The era during which Murasaki lived is known as the Heian period (794–1185). Heian Kyo, later called Kyoto, was a brilliant capital, one of the four largest cities in the world at the time, along with Chang'an in China, Cordoba in Spain, and Baghdad, now in Iraq.

For the aristocracy it was an era of great refinement. Men and women exchanged beautifully painted fans upon meeting. Guests thanked their hosts by giving them decorative boxes with intricate carvings. Royal ceremonies lasted late into the night as men and women danced, played zithers and lutes, and recited Chinese and Japanese poetry.

Although women owned property and received income from it, they spent much of their lives behind screens and blinds, sheltered from public view. They wore layers of long-sleeved kimonos of different colors, even different scents, and many grew their hair down past their feet. Their kimonos were so long, they often flowed under screens, or sleeves dangled through blinds, so that a man on the other side of a screen could recognize a woman just from a glimpse of her kimono.

In his best penmanship, a man might write a woman two lines of poetry that usually had a double meaning. She would reply on scented paper with a couplet of her own. If the two became serious and started a correspondence, eventually the man could step behind the blinds. Their first night of love would be sleepless—lovers embraced and talked until the light of dawn, according to accounts of the time. Then the man left quickly, but always, without fail, sent her a poem later in the morning.

The best Japanese writers during the Heian era were women. While men struggled to write Chinese characters, which were used in royal decrees, women learned to write clearly in *kana*, the phonetic alphabet of their native language. Murasaki was unusual because she wrote well in Chinese too. Her father was a scholar of the Chinese classics, and had allowed her to sit in on her brother's lessons. Murasaki proved to be a much better student than her brother, prompting her father to sigh, "If only you were a boy, how happy I should be."

Only the bare outlines of Murasaki's life are known. Her mother died while she was still a child. In 996, when Murasaki was about twenty, her father became the governor of Echizen (today, Fukui prefecture), a province north of Kyoto on the rough shore of the Sea of Japan. There, Murasaki keenly felt the absence of society but loved the beauty of the sea. These themes are dominant in the two chapters of *The Tale of Genji* when Genji, after being caught in an illicit affair, lives in temporary exile on the coast.

After two years in Echizen, Murasaki returned to Kyoto to marry Fujiwara no Nobutaka, a fourth cousin who, like her father, was also a provincial governor. He was a flamboyant man in his mid-forties who already had three wives and concubines, and grown children. She was in her early twenties, gentle, intellectual, and shy.

By tradition Murasaki's marriage was a happy one. Scholars believe that her love poems, not her best work, were directed to her husband and not to a lover. Three years after their wedding, in 1001, Nobutaka died in an epidemic. They had one daughter, Daini no Sanmi, who grew up to be a wet nurse to the crown prince, a minor poet, and a powerful figure at court.

During the next several years the newly widowed Murasaki wrote the first and most famous chapters of *The Tale of Genji*, probably receiving her support from her late husband's family.

❖

Genji is the son of the emperor by a beautiful but low-ranking concubine who died when Genji was three. In contrast to noblemen in real life, Genji has so many virtues as to be almost perfect. He is "so handsome that a smile from him can make you think that all the world's problems have been solved." He has "a gentle sense of humor," dances with exquisite grace, and plays the lute and the zither with such talent that "the heavens echo." He is a wise statesman, a sensitive lover, and writes Chinese and Japanese poetry so well that "professors are deeply moved."

The characters in *The Tale of Genji* write almost eight hundred two-line poems to each other. In most of them, someone uses an image from nature to skillfully convey the emotion he or she is feeling. Here is the couplet Genji writes after he first meets his true love.

> *Having come upon an evening blossom,*
> *the mist is loath to go with the morning sun.*

And the reply sent back by her attendant.

> *Can we believe the mist to be so reluctant?*
> *We shall watch the morning sky for signs of truth.*

Genji is irresistible to young women, yet also appeals to their ambitious fathers. He is the emperor's favorite son, but because his mother was a concubine, he is within reach of any woman at court.

Genji enters a political marriage to an older woman of good family whom he does not care for, has many affairs, and is a good father to a handsome, studious son and a beautiful illegitimate daughter. His deepest love, however, is reserved for two women.

The first is Fujitsubo, a woman of "sublime beauty." Genji cannot have her because she is the consort of his father, the emperor. He can only play the flute, while on the other side of a curtain she plays the strings of the koto. Yet one night they succumb to their passions, and nine months later Fujitsubo gives birth to a boy who closely resembles Genji. Genji and Fujitsubo are racked with worry that the truth about this child will come out, and from then on Fujitsubo refuses even to see Genji. "Ninefold mists have risen and come between us," she writes Genji, "I am left to imagine the moon beyond the clouds."

For Genji, no woman ever compares to Fujitsubo until one day, while he is on a pilgrimage, he meets a child called Murasaki at the home of a priest. Murasaki is young, but she is graceful, clever, and looks remarkably like Fujitsubo, her aunt. Genji realizes that Murasaki will soon be his special love, "standing in place of the one whom she so resembles." He asks the nurse who takes care of her if he can take her home to Kyoto and bring her up at court. The nurse refuses his request as outrageously premature.

When the nurse dies, Genji brings Murasaki to court and spends a great deal of time with her. They play games such as *go* and *hentsugi*, a game where you guess the hidden part of a Chinese character. Genji wins Murasaki's complete trust and patiently waits for her to mature. He pays special attention to her education, hoping to create the perfect companion. When his first wife dies of an illness, Genji is able to bring Murasaki home not as a concubine, but as his one and only wife.

❖

Why did Murasaki Shikibu spend more than a decade of her life writing about the loves of an imaginary lord? As Genji himself put it when he found a niece reading a novel: "I have been rude and unfair to your romances, haven't I? . . . *The Chronicles of Japan* and the rest are a mere fragment of the whole truth. It is your romances that fill in the details." Genji continues: "But I have a theory of my own about what this art of the novel is . . . something in [the writer's] own life, or in that around him, will seem so important that he cannot bear to let it pass into oblivion."

After five years of writing, Murasaki finished a good portion of her book. Friends copied individual chapters, or hired calligraphers for the task, then passed them on. Soon even the royal family read many of her chapters, and thought so highly of them that around the year 1006 they invited her to come to court and be a lady-in-waiting to Empress Shoshi, an intellectual young woman in her late teens. Shoshi was also the patron of the century's best poet, Izumi Shikibu (c. 974–1030), who wrote almost 250 poems of mourning for her deceased lover, Prince Atsumichi. Just one example:

> *Again daylight*
> *and I haven't joined him.*
> *What should I do*
> *with this body*
> *that lives stubbornly on?*

Not only was it a high honor for Murasaki to be part of such an illustrious court, she also had access to an unlimited supply of paper, which in the eleventh century was very expensive. One of her few duties at court was to teach the empress enough Chinese for her to be able to read the works of China's great ninth-century poet, Po Chu-i. Murasaki probably tutored the empress in other subjects as well, but still had sufficient time to finish *The Tale of Genji*.

For several years Murasaki also kept a diary. The portions that survive were written in the years 1008 to 1010. The diary is a bit sour; perhaps Murasaki used it as an outlet for emotions she could not express openly, or possibly it was a book of observations for her daughter. In one entry she expresses contempt for a literary rival, Sei Shonagon, the woman who wrote *The Pillow Book*, a series of witty essays about personal likes and dislikes that is also a classic of this era.

Murasaki complains that "Sei Shonagon's chief trait is her extraordinary conceit. She pretentiously fills her work with Chinese writing, but examine it closely and it is full of errors."

In another passage Murasaki reveals how tiresome a royal banquet could be:

> Lord Kinto [who was drunk] shouted: "Little Murasaki is still on her best behavior!"
>
> "None of you are in the least like Genji," I thought to myself, "so what should Murasaki be doing here?" . . . Then the Vice Councillor began bothering poor Lady Hyobu, and the Prime Minister made comic noises that were terribly vulgar . . .

Murasaki sometimes wished that she were waiting upon the easygoing high priestess of Kamo instead of on the more serious Empress Shoshi, who regarded flirting of any kind as "frivolous." The high priestess and her ladies often went on walks to see the cherry blossoms at dawn, or to listen to the mating call of the wood thrush. "Rarely are they ever in the rush we are," Murasaki lamented, "in constantly preparing for the presence of the emperor and his retainers."

Murasaki served Shoshi for many years, at least until the year 1013, and possibly until her death. A list of ladies-in-waiting from the year 1031 does not include Murasaki. We know from another woman's diary that Murasaki completed the last of the fifty-four chapters of *The Tale of Genji* by or before the year 1022.

In the second half of the novel, beginning with chapter thirty-four, Genji becomes a less ideal, more realistic figure. He is the most powerful statesman at court, and his daughter marries the crown prince and gives birth to a boy. In his forties and graying slightly, Genji is increasingly aware of how brief and transient life is. He also sounds like a middle-aged man in our own era when he observes that

> Today, people dabble at music and pick up mannerisms, and what passes for music is very shallow stuff indeed.

At the request of the retired emperor, Genji marries the monarch's third daughter, a girl still in her teens. He is more of a teacher to the girl than a husband. The elegant and childless Murasaki, who soon suffers a long illness, remains Genji's favorite. The new wife becomes pregnant after an affair with Genji's nephew, but Genji absorbs the news calmly. He slept with a married princess himself when he was young, and now accepts his karma and raises his wife's child, Kaoru, as if the boy were his own.

One year after Murasaki dies, Genji retires from court and spends a year, possibly two, away from the capital, meditating and praying in seclusion. At the beginning of chapter forty-two, we learn that Genji has died; he was fifty-one. In the novel's last ten chapters the story shifts to Uji, a small temple town in the mountains south of Kyoto, and focuses on Genji's adopted son, Kaoru.

Kaoru moves to Uji to seek enlightenment, but becomes sidetracked when he falls in love with three sisters in succession. The first sister dies, the second marries his best friend, and the third sister betrays him, attempts suicide, and finally becomes a Buddhist nun. The flawed characters in these final chapters reflect a darker, more resigned view of life and people that may have come with Murasaki's advancing years.

In the Middle Ages some Confucian scholars who loved *The Tale of Genji* were chagrined that a woman had written such a towering classic, and suggested that Murasaki's father had outlined the work and that a top official had written the final chapters. But in the last two hundred years the overwhelming majority of scholars have agreed with the point of view expressed by Edward G. Seidensticker, who wrote: "To suggest that, at some point in the process of composition, a second talent took over, maintained the narrative at its high level, and pushed it to yet higher levels, is to suggest the unbelievable."

Hardly any of the characters in *The Tale of Genji* are common laborers, and the book is silent on the hard work of growing food and maintaining an army. What Murasaki portrays is love, ambition, and friendship at the Imperial Court, because the life she knew there was so important to her that she could "not bear to let it pass into oblivion." Largely thanks to her work, the refinement of the Heian court at its best continues to live in the minds of the Japanese people. Stories from *The Tale of Genji* have been adapted into *no* plays, kabuki dramas, movies, and television shows, and excerpts from the book have been assigned to schoolchildren for centuries.

One hundred fifty years after Murasaki Shikibu wrote *The Tale of Genji*, the Heian aristocrats lost their power to samurai warriors. Yet they passed on their love of art, literature, and refined manners. A samurai could not be just a brave warrior—to win respect he also had to be a gentleman. And for a thousand years the model of the refined gentleman has been Genji, Lady Murasaki's "shining prince."

10

Sen no Rikyu

Grand Master of the Japanese Tea Ceremony

T EA—"the drink that cheers but does not inebriate"—is part of life around the world. The British pause at four in the afternoon to drink it. Russians offer tea to a guest even before conversation begins. So do Indians and Pakistanis. But only the Japanese have turned the serving of tea into a performing art, a spiritual discipline, and a microcosm of their nation's culture.

The Japanese tea ceremony evolved during the fifteenth and sixteenth centuries and today is practiced more widely than ever. It combines elements of architecture, interior design, Zen Buddhism, landscape gardening, flower arranging, calligraphy, ceramics, lacquerware, metalwork, and woodwork. The ceremony has deeply influenced the Japanese concept of beauty, finding art in simple, everyday objects.

The greatest tea master of all time, the man who perfected the tea ceremony, was Sen no Rikyu (1522–1591). He had a genius for combining the rustic and the refined, and in a time of extravagance he was a force for restraint.

Rikyu understood that the step-by-step procedure for serving tea was also an ideal way to practice Zen. The ceremony enabled his guests to focus on the present moment and the beauty of ordinary miracles: a charcoal fire, a whistling kettle, a handmade bowl, and the warmth and taste of tea.

Today the tea ceremony is much the same as it was at the end of Rikyu's lifetime. If a host has enough land, four or five guests open a gate and enter a garden path. They walk on stepping-stones rising gently above moss or pine needles until they reach a stone water basin, where they use a bamboo scoop to wash their hands and mouths. Rikyu built the water basins because he wanted his guests to wash "the dust of impurity" from their hearts before they began the tea ceremony. He also set the basins close to the ground to force even the most powerful guests to crouch as they washed their hands.

A typical tea hut is made of unpainted clay walls, with paper windows that let in light but offer no view. Thatched roofs were common in Rikyu's time, but tile roofs are more frequent today.

Guests enter a hut through a "crawling-in door" only 26½ inches (66 cm) square. Tea huts once had a separate entrance for lords, but Rikyu did away with this and obliged nobleman to crawl into his tea rooms on their hands and knees. There would be no class distinctions here; all guests were equal.

In the tea hut, guests kneel in front of a wooden alcove, where they admire the beauty of a hanging scroll of Zen Buddhist calligraphy, and underneath, a single flower or branch. Rikyu carved his vases out of bamboo, and always chose a flower in harmony with the season.

Like most rooms in Japan, tea rooms are covered with mats of rice straw called tatami. Tatami mats are three feet by six feet (one meter by two meters) in size. A typical tea hut holds 4½ mats, an area about 9 feet (2.8 m) square. Rikyu liked small tea rooms because they made for more intimate gatherings.

A kettle is already boiling as the guests seat themselves on the floor, making a sound the Japanese compare to a wind whistling through the pines. The guests admire the charcoal fire; since Rikyu's time the host has ignited the charcoal beforehand so that the fire will burn more quickly when the guests arrive. The host also rakes the ashes to improve the ventilation of the fire. In autumn and winter the fire is set in a sunken hearth in the middle of the floor. This helps warm the room. In spring and summer the host uses a portable brazier which he removes once tea is served.

The host begins the tea ceremony by serving something sweet, typically a thin cookie. Then he brings in tea utensils from a tiny (2-by-4-foot) adjoining preparation room, and lines them up before his guests. The utensils include a ceramic tea bowl, a laquered jar of powdered green tea, a ceramic jar of cold water, a waste water container, a bamboo tea scoop, a wooden ladle, and a bamboo whisk for mixing the tea.

Although the utensils are already clean, the host carefully wipes the tea scoop and the rim of the tea jar with a silk napkin before ladling hot water from the kettle into the tea bowl. Then the host rinses the whisk in the hot water before pouring the water in the waste water container and drying the tea bowl with linen.

Finally the host scoops tea from the jar into the tea bowl, and ladles hot water from the kettle. Using the bamboo whisk, he whips the green tea until it has the texture of a heavy soup. Depending on the size and style of the tea ceremony, guests either take 3½ sips each before wiping the rim and passing the bowl, or they receive a bowl of their own.

The host asks the first guest if the tea is satisfactory. Later, when everyone has finished drinking, the first guest asks the host to see the tea jar and bamboo scoop. While the host cleans up, the guests admire and discuss the objects. The best tea jars are coated with over seventy layers of lacquer and are worth thousands of dollars, but the bamboo scoops are personally carved by the host. It was Rikyu who began the custom of carving tea scoops.

When the host has finished cleaning, he answers any questions the guests might have about the tea utensils. Then he takes the utensils to the door of the small preparation room, kneels, and bows to his guests, who bow in return. Finally, he escorts the guests out to the garden, ending the tea ceremony.

❖

Sen no Rikyu, the grand master of the tea ceremony, was born in 1522 in the city of Sakai, which today is a surburb of Osaka. For most of his life his name was Sen no Soeki. He did not receive his priestly name Rikyu, which means "old needle" but signifies enlightenment, until he served tea to the emperor in 1585.

Unlike most Japanese cities, Sakai was a self-governing port run by merchants rather than warriors. Many grew wealthy making swords (and later guns) or by importing art and tea utensils from China.

The tea ceremony was popular in Sakai because it brought men of different regions and classes together on a basis of equality. It also enabled merchants to show off their wealth by displaying ancient Chinese scrolls and tea bowls during a ceremony.

As a boy Sen no Rikyu studied the Chinese classics and probably did clerical work at one of his father's fish warehouses. He also learned about art from his grandfather, who had once been an appraiser for Shogun Yoshimasa.

Rikyu also studied the tea ceremony. By age fifteen he was an accomplished host. At sixteen Rikyu became the pupil of a tea master named Dochin, who taught him how to serve formal "lord's teas" in large rooms, and how to handle and appreciate Chinese art and tea utensils. Rikyu also practiced Zen at a local temple.

In 1540 Rikyu's father died. Rikyu inherited his warehouses, and at age eighteen he was a rich man in a free city, which no doubt encouraged his independence of spirit. Later that year Dochin recommended his star pupil to Takeno Jo-o, a Zen priest who was the leading tea master of his time.

Jo-o taught Rikyu a very different kind of tea, the *wabi* or "poverty" tea ceremony. Followers of *wabi* value simplicity, and find beauty in the imperfect and unadorned. Jo-o removed the paper from the walls of his tea hut, leaving only clay underneath. He also replaced silver utensil shelves with plain slabs of wood, and wooden lattice with cheaper bamboo.

In the winter Jo-o once put a bucket of water in the alcove instead of the customary flower. The water was to remind guests of the fleeting beauty of the snow outside.

Rikyu took the ideals of *wabi* to heart, and later recited a twelfth century poem to explain the concept of *wabi* to his pupils:

> *If I could only show the man*
> *Who seems to wait for nothing*
> *But the cherry blossoms,*
> *The springtime in a mountain village*
> *With grasses sprouting from amidst the snow.*

Rikyu was thus the heir to three traditions: the elegant "lord's tea" taught to him by Dochin, the simple *wabi* tea that he learned from Jo-o, and finally, Zen. The history of tea and Zen are deeply intertwined.

❖

Zen is a movement away from Buddhist ritual. It focuses instead on the awareness that the Buddha-heart, or the Mind of God, is present in all things, from the highest mountain to the smallest cup of tea. This heightened awareness may come like a flash of lightning, or it may be the result of years of meditation and self-discipline.

The word *Zen* comes from the Chinese word *Ch'an*, which in turn comes from the Sanskrit *dhyana*, meaning "meditation." According to legend, Daruma, the monk who brought *dhyana* from India to China in the sixth century, once cut off his eyelids to keep from falling asleep during meditation. The eyelids fell to the ground and sprouted into tea bushes, and their leaves made a drink that warded off sleep. The Chinese started growing tea as early as the third century. By the eleventh century China's monks ceremoniously honored Daruma by passing around a large bowl of whipped green tea beneath his portrait.

In Japan, tea was rare until 1191, when a monk named Eisai (1141–1215) came back from China to plant tea and teach Zen. Eisai began the Rinzai school of Zen, which emphasizes sudden, intuitive enlightenment. To encourage such leaps of spirit, Eisai assigned his students koan, illogical problems to think about during meditation. The most famous is "the sound of one hand clapping."

Eisai planted tea seeds on the island of Kyushu and also gave seeds to friends near Kyoto. Twenty years later, in 1211, he completed *The Book of Tea and Mulberries*, which praised the medicinal properties of both plants. "Tea is the most wonderful medicine," Eisai wrote, "the secret of long life."

In 1214 Eisai sent his book to Shogun Sanetomo who found tea helpful during hangovers. The drink became popular among warriors, partly because of the teachings of another monk named Dogen.

Dogen (1200–1253) founded the Soto school of Zen, which seeks gradual enlightenment through meditation and good conduct. Like Eisai, Dogen used tea as a stimulant to stay awake during meditation. But he rejected the use of koans and emphasized "sitting straight, without any thought of gain" as the best way to let go of the mind. For hours, students of Soto Zen sit cross-legged, with backs straight, shoulders relaxed, breathing even, and eyes half shut. The discipline and anti-intellectualism of Soto Zen appealed to Japan's often illiterate warriors, who also liked the fact that calming the mind improved their swordsmanship.

By the early 1300s warriors held contests to test their powers of taste. Competitors drank several cups of tea and tried to guess which parts of Japan the brews came from. They also gambled on which tea would lose its foam first. (Some tea is quite thick.)

Shoguns served tea at banquets and entertained guests with dancers and courtesans. Local lords held smaller teas to show off their Chinese bowls and tea jars; wealthier lords paid fortunes for ancient or famous utensils.

A Zen monk, Murata Shuko (1422–1502), hated this ostentation. He created *wabi* tea and returned the tea ceremony to its Zen roots. Shuko was the first to realize that serving tea could be a means to enlightenment, that the Way of Tea was also a way of Zen.

Shuko reduced the size of the tea room to 4½ mats, about the size of a hermit's hut, and removed all decoration from the walls. He displayed only one variety of flower at a time, and sometimes it was just a batch of bamboo grass. He also limited the number of hanging scrolls in an alcove to two, and nearly always chose Zen calligraphy rather than Chinese landscapes.

Most important, Shuko used Japanese rather than Chinese tea utensils. He loved the rough, unglazed earthenware made by Japanese potters, and thought simple utensils such as scoops and ladles should be made of bamboo or wood rather than ivory or silver. Occasionally Shuko did use an ancient Chinese bowl or jar. He said a beautiful bowl looked its best in a simple tea room.

One of Shuko's pupils, Soju, was the first man to build an outdoor tea hut rather than an indoor tea room. The hut resembled a mountain shed, but he built it in the middle of Kyoto.

Huts were cheaper to build than formal rooms, and *wabi* tea was cheaper to serve than "lord's tea." This allowed the tea ceremony to be enjoyed by a wider variety of people, especially merchants. Soju's best student was a leather dealer from Sakai, Takeno Jo-o. Jo-o, of course, became Rikyu's teacher.

❖

Under Jo-o's influence, Rikyu became a deep admirer of Shuko's. At great expense he bought one of Shuko's bowls in 1544 and used it in many tea ceremonies.

Rikyu married a woman named Myoju around this time. They had a son named Doan and several daughters, one of whom grew up to be unusually beautiful.

By the 1560s Rikyu had hosted countless tea ceremonies for all the leading men of Sakai and firmly established himself as one of the three leading tea masters of the city. He also began to train his teenage son in the Way of Tea. Once he ordered him to sweep a garden path twice until it was immaculate. Then Rikyu gently shook a branch until only about a dozen leaves fell on the stones.

On another occasion a guest asked Rikyu to tell him the secret of tea. Rikyu replied:

Suggest coolness in the summer and warmth in the winter. Set the charcoal so that the water will boil. Arrange the flowers as if they were still in the field.

"Anyone can do that," the guest said. To which Rikyu responded, "Then I will become your student and you will be my teacher."

In 1569 Lord Oda Nobunaga conquered Sakai without a fight and put the arms-manufacturing city under his direct control. The fierce warrior chose Rikyu and two others to be his tea masters, and took lessons from Rikyu on the fine points of serving tea.

Because Nobunaga was at war with several (non-Zen) Buddhist fortresses, he was unusually friendly to Jesuit missionaries who arrived from Portugal. The Jesuits enjoyed the tea ceremony because it did not involve any "pagan" ritual, despite its roots in Zen.

The priests were amazed at the value of tea utensils. Allesandro Valignano reported that a regional lord paid 9,000 silver coins for a small tea jar, "although in all truth I myself would not have given one or two farthings for it." Today a bowl made by Honami Koetsu (1558–1637) would sell for over a million dollars.

Rikyu's wife Myoju died in 1577, and the tea master married a woman named So-on a year or two later. She is remembered for designing the slit in the silk bags that cover tea jars, and also the silk napkin used to wipe them.

In 1582 Oda Nobunaga was ambushed and killed by the army of a disloyal general. His successor, Hideyoshi, defeated the rebel army, unified Japan, and also began a golden age of tea. Hideyoshi and Rikyu had become close friends during their years together serving Nobunaga. (Both Nobunaga and Hideyoshi are the subjects of chapters in this book.) Now Japan's new ruler appointed Rikyu as his supreme tea master. The job came with a large salary equal to the rice crop of 400 acres (160 hectares).

Hideyoshi entertained constantly, so Rikyu hosted a tea ceremony almost every day. Guests included regional lords, rich merchants, and other leading tea masters. Rikyu also hosted tea for generals in portable huts near the battlefield.

Rikyu strove for an atmosphere of equality in his tea rooms. He asked warriors to leave their swords on a rack outside, and had all of his guests sip tea from the same bowl.

Rikyu also commissioned a roof-tile maker named Chojiro to make tea bowls for him, because tile-based bowls stayed cool even when tea was boiling hot. Later Hideyoshi gave the tile maker a new name, Raku, which means "enjoyment." Today the fifteenth generation of the Raku family still makes Japan's finest tea bowls in traditional charcoal-fed kilns. Raku bowls are usually red or black, to provide the best contrast to bright green tea.

Guests liked Rikyu's tea ceremonies better than those of other tea masters, and rich merchants and powerful lords came from all over Japan to receive his instruction in matters of tea and taste.

Sometimes Hideyoshi tried to fluster Rikyu. "Arrange this!" he commanded Rikyu one day, though there was nothing in a golden bowl but water and a single branch of red plum blossoms. Without hesitation Rikyu pulled the petals off the flowers and let them fall in the water. The floating petals were a beautiful sight, and Hideyoshi laughed at his failure to perplex his friend.

Another time Rikyu planted an entire garden of morning glories. Everyone in Kyoto admired them. Hideyoshi wanted to see the flowers too, so Rikyu invited him to tea. When Hideyoshi arrived, however, there was not one morning glory in the garden. Rikyu had cut them all. Visibly annoyed, Hideyoshi burst into Rikyu's tea room, and in the alcove saw a single, flawless morning glory, the most beautiful one in the garden. Hideyoshi smiled in admiration.

In 1585 Hideyoshi served tea to the emperor at the Imperial Palace. Rikyu assisted Hideyoshi, but as a commoner he could not enter the palace until he was declared a priest and given a new name. This is when he received the ecclesiastical name Rikyu.

The following year Hideyoshi hosted another tea for the emperor, this time in a portable golden tea room that was carried to the palace. Everything in the room was gold: walls, ceiling, doors, bowl, jar, and kettle. Only the whisk, ladle, cloth, and carpet were made of ordinary materials.

The golden tea room was such a departure from the principles of *wabi* that some writers have criticized Rikyu for helping Hideyoshi to build it. The golden room was used only twice, once for the emperor in 1586, and once during peace talks with a Chinese envoy in 1592. The rest of the time Rikyu and Hideyoshi usually served *wabi* tea rather than formal tea. Even the size of the golden room, three mats, was the size of a *wabi* hut, not a formal parlor.

Hideyoshi invited the public to see his golden room and his most valuable tea utensils at the Great Kitano Tea Party of 1587. Rikyu and Hideyoshi encouraged tea lovers from every region and all social classes to bring "kettle, ladle, and cup" to the Kitano grove in Kyoto and serve each other tea. More than eight hundred people set up tea huts; the most striking was just a lacquered red parasol.

Hideyoshi and Rikyu each personally served two hundred people chosen by lottery. Their portable two-mat *wabi* hut had walls papered with old calendars, but in the alcove there was an ancient painting by the Chinese artist Yu-chien. Afterward Hideyoshi and Rikyu visited dozens of other huts, admiring utensils and sipping tea.

The following year Hideyoshi banished Kokei, one of Rikyu's best friends, to the island of Kyushu for reasons unknown today. Kokei was both Rikyu's teacher in matters of Zen and Rikyu's pupil in matters of tea. Before Kokei departed, Rikyu hosted a farewell tea ceremony for him, a mild act of defiance that Hideyoshi ignored.

A year later Rikyu convinced Hideyoshi to pardon Kokei. When the Zen master returned to Kyoto, Rikyu donated a great sum of money to enlarge the gate at Kokei's temple as a way to commemorate the fiftieth anniversary of the death of Rikyu's father. In gratitude for the money and for the pardon, Kokei built a statue of Rikyu on the second story of the gate, which was finished in 1590.

Unfortunately, the statue showed Rikyu standing up. This meant that every time Hideyoshi entered the temple he walked directly under Rikyu's feet. When Hideyoshi noticed this early in 1591, he was furious and banished Rikyu to his home city of Sakai. (Some say Hideyoshi was also angry because he desired Rikyu's most beautiful and widowed daughter as a concubine and Rikyu had refused him.)

Rikyu's friends urged him to apologize to Hideyoshi, but pride may have prevented the tea master from acknowledging that he was Hideyoshi's servant. It is also possible that Rikyu was afraid that if he did win a pardon, the vengeful Hideyoshi would destroy the temple instead.

After twelve days of Rikyu's silence, Hideyoshi ordered his tea master to return to the capital and commit seppuku (ritual suicide), which unlike execution was an honorable death. To prevent Rikyu's friends from attempting a rescue, Hideyoshi ordered three thousand soldiers to surround Rikyu's house.

Rikyu hosted a farewell tea for his best friends and pupils, and composed a final poem.

> *Holding this sword of mine*
> *Now is the time*
> *To throw myself to the heavens.*

Rikyu's suicide was dramatically accompanied by thunder and hail. A Shinto priest measured the hailstones in Kyoto that day at $\%_0$ of an inch (1.5 cm) in diameter. The next day Hideyoshi ordered the offending statue of Rikyu taken down from the temple gate, beheaded, and publicly displayed on a busy bridge.

Rikyu's children left for Sakai and other parts of Japan, but by 1594 Hideyoshi regretted his death sentence and allowed Rikyu's stepson Shoan to return to Kyoto and teach *wabi* tea. Shoan and his son avoided politics entirely, but in the next generation three of Rikyu's great-grandsons served powerful lords and started schools of tea that still exist today. The most famous is the Urasenke school, which has branches around the world.

Much of what we know about Rikyu comes from a book published ninety-six years after his death, *Namboroku*. It is a summary of Rikyu's thoughts and styles, and urges a return to the simplicity of *wabi* tea. The book was supposedly written by a pupil of Rikyu's, Nambo, in 1593 and "discovered" a century later by a samurai named Jitsuzan. It is more likely that Jitsuzan wrote most of the book himself and claimed the discovery in order to generate publicity. In any case, the book preserved the *wabi* tradition at a time when most tea masters had again become class conscious, treating guests according to their rank.

Two hundred years later, during the industrialization of the 1890s, the government introduced the tea ceremony into women's schools as a way to preserve Japanese tradition. Ever since, more than two thirds of the tea masters and pupils in Japan have been female, and the ceremony is performed today more widely than ever before.

Although the best tea masters vary their ceremonies according to the occasion, deviations from Rikyu's service are small. One master, Rand Castile, has written that Rikyu's ceremony is "too smooth, too logical, too comfortable to be much improved upon."

With a Zen-heightened awareness that transcended his time, Rikyu understood that the Japanese needed a break from hierarchy, that even Japan's most powerful lords enjoyed the informality of a small tea room where men could sit together as equals. Rikyu calmed his guests by focusing their minds on the beauty of simple tasks and everyday objects. Four hundred years later his tea ceremony continues to refresh new generations.

11

Izumo no Okuni

The Actress and Dancer Who Created Kabuki Theater

UNTIL THE arrival of movies in the twentieth century, kabuki theater was Japan's most popular form of entertainment. People loved to see the exaggerated movements and flamboyant costumes of their favorite actors, all of whom were men. The actors who played women were especially popular. They were more feminine in their walk and manner than women themselves, and set trends in ladies' fashion. Geishas and even young noblewomen copied the latest styles worn by kabuki actors.

Ironically, the creator of kabuki theater was an actress and dancer who often dressed like a man, Izumo no Okuni (c.1571–c.1615). At her peak she led her own troupe of dancers, and sang, danced, and acted before tens of thousands of people.

Okuni was born in the early 1570s, the daughter of a blacksmith (some say an iron miner) who worked for the great Shinto shrine at Izumo, a town near the Sea of Japan, seventy miles (115 km) north of modern-day Hiroshima. At that time the shrine also held Buddhist services, and as a girl Okuni learned to perform a variety of devotional dances. In her teens she joined a group of dancers who traveled throughout Japan raising money for the Izumo shrine. This is a song that Okuni often danced to:

> *The light of Buddha's mercy*
> *Brightens the ten directions—*
> *Buddha's prayer includes everyone—*
> *Praise Amida Buddha*
> *Praise Amida Buddha's name.*

Little is known about Okuni's early years as a traveling performer, or, for that matter, her life. At some point she began dancing to songs without religious themes. She learned to sing the popular songs of the day, to change costumes at lightning speed, and to improvise when a colleague made a mistake. She impressed everyone with her clear singing voice and with the lightness of her movements.

During the late 1590s Okuni began living and performing in Kyoto, then the capital of Japan. With over 500,000 people, Kyoto was one of the largest cities in the world. It had a thriving middle class that liked to be entertained, and on the banks of the Kamo River there were always dozens of musicians, dance groups, ballad chanters, puppeteers, acrobats, swordsmen, and animal acts.

Around the year 1600, at roughly the same time Shakespeare was writing *Hamlet* in London, Okuni started performing with her own all-female troupe of dancers. Usually they appeared at a makeshift theater on the riverbank, but sometimes they danced in the mansions of lords. They sang popular songs, put on humorous skits imitating people from all walks of life, and performed sacred dances in an erotic, suggestive manner. She managed to combine the refined gestures of the *no* plays still enjoyed by the aristocracy with the light, fast-paced steps popular among Kyoto's street dancers. She was soon considered the most graceful dancer in Kyoto.

Paintings and folding screens from the time give us some idea of Okuni's flamboyant appearance. Tall and pretty, she wore short-sleeved kimonos that only loosely covered her ample breasts, and sported many bracelets on her long, bare arms. Sometimes instead of wearing kimonos made of local silk, Okuni wore green- or orange-colored robes of velvet or Chinese silk, bought from the Portuguese. Often she also wore pants, a sleeveless cape, bells on her wrists, and a white headband or a hat made of beaver fur. She also wore a crucifix and coral rosary beads that hung around her neck or sometimes swung from her waist. The crucifix was simply a fashion accessory.

Okuni was equally noticed for what she did not wear—a mask. Masks were a central part of the *no* theater, where the ghost of a hero performs a dance while telling the story of the hero's death. The actor expresses deep emotions through subtle movements of his mask and fan, and much is left to the imagination of a sophisticated audience.

Okuni's sketches and dances, by contrast, were bold, sensual, and offbeat, or, as the Japanese described them, kabuki. The word *kabuki* comes from the Japanese verb *kabuku*, which means to deviate or behave deviantly. At first the word was used to describe the strange clothes sold by Portuguese traders, but like the English word *deviant*, *kabuku* also has a strong sexual connotation.

Okuni reached the height of her popularity when she began dressing like a man in the spring of 1603. Like a samurai, she cut her hair and wore two swords. She delighted her audiences by satirizing a young warrior flirting with and then making love to a courtesan. Other women in her troupe also dressed like men.

Okuni drew thousands of shopkeepers, craftsmen, and traders. Often they clapped in unison as she danced, and sometimes they tossed coins onto the stage even though they had already paid admission. Okuni also had the high honor of performing before the ladies of the Imperial Palace in July 1603.

In 1604, as Okuni's company grew, she built a theater of her own, with dressing rooms, living quarters, and banners that flapped in the wind. The stage had a thatched roof, but the audience sat outdoors on mats. Much of Okuni's time was spent supervising carpenters, bookkeepers, seamstresses, flute players, drummers, and the other dancers.

Accounts conflict, but Okuni may have received both financial and creative help from a rich, brave, and unusually handsome warrior named Nagoya Sanzaburo. The grandnephew of Lord Oda Nobunaga, Sanzaburo was known for his charm and wit, and for wearing outlandish Portuguese clothes. He also had a deep knowledge of *kyogen*, the short, funny skits that were performed in between the longer and more serious *no* plays. Sanzaburo had laughed at *kyogen* since childhood, and may have helped Okuni incorporate their comic elements into her skits. He is also said to have originated the exaggerated entrances so characteristic of kabuki theater.

On a narrow, elevated walkway through the middle of an audience, a kabuki actor pauses when he is precisely 70 percent of the way to the stage and strikes a pose—he may glare, grimace, cross his eyes, even stick out his tongue—to vocal audience approval.

Many lovers of kabuki say that Okuni and Sanzaburo were lovers. Others say this was just a rumor that swept Kyoto. Whatever the truth, Sanzaburo was stabbed to death at this time by a rival samurai in a petty but fatal quarrel concerning the building of a provincial castle.

A few months later, in the middle of a performance, a handsome young man wearing fashionable Portuguese clothes leapt onto Okuni's stage and demanded to see her, claiming to be Sanzaburo's ghost. The audience quickly realized that the actor playing the ghost was none other than Okuni herself, and erupted in cheers. For several minutes "Sanzaburo" danced sensuously with the actress playing Okuni, until finally an angry hunchback drove "Sanzaburo" back to the underworld.

Around 1606 Okuni began performing in Edo (Tokyo), a rough new city that would soon eclipse Kyoto because it was the home of the shogun and his government. During the three-hundred-mile (500 km) journey between Kyoto and Edo, it is likely that Okuni danced in provincial towns and cheerfully introduced kabuki theater to appreciative small-town audiences. Her performances usually ended with the entire company dancing together, a custom that has endured in kabuki ever since.

In March 1607 Okuni and her troupe performed at the castle of Shogun Tokugawa Hidetada, son of the great Ieyasu, although Hidetada himself may not have been in attendance. For this performance Okuni probably dressed more conservatively than usual.

In her late thirties, at the peak of her fame, Okuni decided to retire while she was still fairly young. She may have paused in Kyoto to give some final performances, but around 1609 she returned home to Izumo, where for several years she lived in a small but comfortable cottage. Perhaps she danced occasionally in one of the same shrine festivals in which she had participated as a girl, and tutored the shrine's most promising young dancers. The exact date of her death is not known, it was probably between 1610 and 1620.

Many dancers imitated Okuni even before she retired. The vast majority of them performed merely to advertise their availability as prostitutes. In 1629 a fight over a dancer-courtesan injured many people in a theater, and caused Shogun Tokugawa Iemitsu, grandson of Ieyasu, to ban all women from the stage. The prohibition remained in force for nearly two and a half centuries.

Young boys in their teens replaced the women. They dressed in women's kimonos onstage and sold sexual favors offstage. Shogun Iemitsu was a great fan of their performances, but in 1652, a year after he died, his successor issued new laws that put an end to boy's kabuki.

From then on, by law, a kabuki performance had to be a play, not just an erotic dance. The new actors were grown men who rarely sang and who could not rely merely on charm to entertain an audience. They had to act.

In the late 1600s kabuki theater progressed in many ways. Competition from puppet theaters made kabuki actors realize that good stories were as important as sexy performers. New plays had complicated plots that took several acts to unfold, though actors always remained free to improvise. The use of puns increased, and many speeches were written in rhythmic five- and seven-syllable meter. Sound effects improved. So did swordplay. Curtains made changes of scenery possible, and actors often wore several costumes during a play and shed them one at a time.

Ichikawa Danjuro I (1660–1704) developed the *aragoto*, or "wild" style of acting, playing warriors or supermen who ripped off the heads of their enemies, pulled trees up from their roots, and tore tigers to pieces. Danjuro is said to have stamped his foot on the stage so hard that vibrations were felt in pottery shops a quarter of a mile away.

By contrast, Sakata Tojuro (1647–1709) created the *wagoto*, or "gentle" style of acting. A consummate professional who could play any role, Tojuro's performances were widely admired for their subtlety and realism.

Perhaps the most important kabuki actor of the time was Yoshizawa Ayame (1673–1729), the great female impersonator, or *onnagata*, who developed his profession into a fine art that required years of apprenticeship. Ayame's admirers collected his thoughts on acting into a book, *The Words of Ayame*, that is still a big influence on those aspiring to be an *onnagata* today.

When he was five, Ayame was sold by his poverty-stricken mother to a brothel in Osaka that specialized in male prostitution. At first he did household chores for the brothel and lived with a family of kabuki musicians. Upon reaching puberty, Ayame was lucky enough to acquire a patron, a wealthy lord who paid for the boy's lessons in acting, dance, music, and female impersonation. By the time he was seventeen his patron had bought him his freedom, and Ayame began performing as an *onnagata* in small roles.

Ayame soon got bigger parts because he was widely admired for his tearful expressions of grief. "He never weeps alone," a contemporary critic wrote, "but always with a crowd of 100 or 200. The tissue sellers love him."

By 1698 Ayame had earned the reputation as "the best *onnagata* in kabuki" because he could make an audience feel even the most subtle feminine emotions. Whether he played a lover, wife, mother, or servant, "it's as if real people come alive when he plays them," one critic wrote.

At home Ayame was a married man with four sons. Away from home, even when offstage, Ayame dressed, moved, spoke, and ate like a woman until well into his fifties. He did this not only to refine his art, but also so that the male actors he worked with would have an easier time falling in love with him onstage.

By the late 1700s the most popular *onnagata* had become such a deep influence on fashion that they made a great deal of money endorsing cosmetics, tea, and lines of clothing.

In the twentieth century an *onnagata* no longer felt compelled to act like a woman offstage, but the best *onnagata* of our own era, Bando Tamasaburo (b. 1950), dances with ballet companies and plays women's roles in movies and in Japanese productions of Shakespeare's plays.

More than three hundred plays are in the kabuki repertory today. Some of the most popular dramas are based on stories told elsewhere in this book. *The Subscription List* is about Benkei, the legendary servant of Yoshitsune. *Chushingura* tells the story of Oishi Kuranosuke and the Forty-Seven Ronin. And *The Love Suicides at Sonezaki* and *The Love Suicides at Amijima* are two of the many puppet plays written by Chikamatsu that have been adapted to the kabuki theater.

If Okuni were alive today, it would be almost impossible for her to continue the kabuki tradition that she began. When the shogun fell in 1868 and the new government let women return to the stage, several kabuki theaters hired actresses to play the parts of women. But audiences did not like them. They had grown to love *onnagata*, and real women were not the same. As the actor Nakamura Utaemon V drolly asked in the 1920s, "Why should women appear when I am here? There is no woman in all Japan who acts as feminine as I do."

I 2

Matsuo Basho
Japan's Great Haiku Poet

U NLIKE MOST Americans, many Japanese adore poetry. Newspapers publish poems every day, and in the spring young women write romantic verses and attach them to stalks of bamboo as prayers that their love will be returned. The most popular Japanese poems are haiku, and the supreme master of the haiku was a teacher of poetry named Matsuo Basho (1644–1694). Basho transformed the haiku from being the focus of a drunken evening's wordplay into one of the world's most subtle and moving forms of literature. He is generally considered Japan's greatest poet.

The haiku is the shortest form of poetry. Traditionally it has just seventeen syllables. (Why seventeen? One theory is that this is the average number of syllables a person can pronounce in one breath.) It first appeared in Japan in the 1400s, but in the twentieth century it spread around the world. The brevity and discipline of the form influenced such noted poets as Wallace Stevens, Amy Lowell, Ezra Pound, and William Carlos Williams.

Before Basho was born, the most common form of poetry in Japan was the *renga*, or linked verse. In an age without movies or television, people spent many evenings drinking sake and taking turns creating poetry. One man would make up a three-line poem of 5, 7, and 5 syllables, and the next person would counter with a two-line poem of 7 and 7 syllables. The second poem would be linked in some way to the first, and each poem that followed would be linked to the poem before.

Many aristocrats composed verses of stylized refinement, recombining well-known phrases from poems centuries old. By contrast, the merchants and traders in the cities created poems of humor and originality, though often the subjects were quite coarse, as in this sixteenth-century poem by Sokan:

Even when
My father lay dying
I went on farting
(translated by Ryusaku Tsunoda, William Theodore de Bary, and Donald Keene)

Basho sought to combine the freedom and vigor of popular verse with the elegance and subtlety of traditional poetry. Because he became the best composer of linked verse of his time, he was a welcome guest in homes throughout Japan.

In quiet moments, however, Basho made his most important contribution. Isolating the opening lines of the linked verse (the triplet of 5, 7, and 5 syllables), Basho turned the haiku into a new and separate art form. During his life he wrote over one thousand haiku.

A haiku's two essential components are a word or a phrase that sets the season (such as ice, blossom, sun, or harvest) and a "cutting word" (in translation often followed by a dash) that provides a pause before the beginning of a new idea. Possessing a definite time and creating a specific impression, the haiku becomes a concise way, as Basho put it, to reveal "an eternal truth in fleeting form."

Basho was born with the name Matsuo Kinsaku in 1644 in the city of Ueno, about thirty miles (50 km) southeast of Kyoto. He was the fourth of seven children. His father was a low-ranking samurai who made his living farming and teaching writing to nearby children. He died when Basho was twelve. Nothing is known about Basho's mother.

Basho must have been one of his father's best pupils, because at age nine he became the study mate of eleven-year-old Todo Yoshitada, the eldest son of the lord of Ueno. The two boys became close friends. They shared a love for composing linked verse, and in their early twenties even published some verse together. They probably also discovered the charms of women at this time, for Basho may have had a mistress named Jutei, who later became a nun. A poem Basho wrote later in life recalls this period,

In my new robe
this morning—
someone else.
(translated by Lucien Stryk)

Unfortunately Yoshitada died, and his younger brother did not care for Basho. At twenty-three Basho left the service of the Todo family, thereby giving up his samurai status, and moved to a Buddhist temple in Kyoto to further his education.

For five years Basho studied both Chinese and Japanese classics, poetry, and calligraphy. He published some more linked verse, and tried and failed to get a government post. Years later he wrote that he also experimented with homosexuality "for a time."

At twenty-eight Basho published an anthology of haiku, *The Seashell Game*. Like children sorting and comparing seashells, Basho matched and compared thirty pairs of haiku written by other poets. Witty and erudite, the work established Basho's reputation as a poetry critic, and gave him the courage to move to Edo (Tokyo), which had become Japan's largest and most dynamic city.

For several years Basho worked for the Edo waterworks department, but gradually, as his reputation as a poet spread, he became a full-time teacher of poetry. His students regarded him as a perceptive, constructive, and gentle critic, and kept his "gourd filled with rice," and his "bottle filled with sake."

In 1675 Basho had the opportunity to compose some linked verse with Soin, a great poet forty years his senior. Soin taught Basho to appreciate the beauty of the homely things of ordinary life, a lesson reinforced several years later when Basho undertook the study of Zen Buddhism. Before long Basho composed one of his greatest haiku.

> *On a bare branch*
> *A crow is perched—*
> *Autumn evening.*
> (translated by Makoto Ueda)

Basho also judged poetry in the Rustic Haiku Contest and the Evergreen Haiku Contest, and in the summer of 1680 published an anthology of his pupils' best poems.

Later that year one of Basho's admirers, a fish wholesaler named Sampu, built a cottage for him by the Sumida River, just outside Edo. Another friend planted a banana tree, and the house became known as Banana Cottage. From this, the great poet took his pen name, Basho, which is Japanese for "banana."

The cottage burned down in a neighborhood fire in 1682, but friends rebuilt the hut and replanted the tree the next year. Although the banana tree was too far north to bear any fruit, Basho loved it all the same, especially the leaves, "They remind me of a green fan ripped by the wind. . . . I sit underneath, and enjoy the wind and rain that blow against them."

Because an unusually wise priest named Butcho lived at a temple near his cottage, Basho began a serious study of Zen. He even dressed in the robes of a monk, although he never actually became one. He compared himself to a bat: "Neither priest nor layman, bird nor rat, but something in between." Possibly Basho was too familiar with the different branches of Buddhism to wholly commit himself to one,

> *Four temple gates—*
> *under one moon,*
> *four sects.*
> (translated by Lucien Stryk)

Even so, Basho was deeply influenced by Zen. His later haiku are firmly rooted in nature and in the present moment. Only rarely did he use a haiku to be witty or to make a literary reference.

Zen also influenced the way Basho taught his pupils. "Do not simply follow the footsteps of the men of old," he told them, but "seek what they sought." He also urged that they "learn about pine from a pine tree, and about bamboo from a bamboo stalk."

Once a student showed Basho the following haiku:

> *Take a pair of wings*
> *from a dragonfly, you would*
> *make a pepper pod.*

"No," Basho said, "You kill the dragonfly. If you want to compose a haiku and give life to it, you must say:

> *Add a pair of wings*
> *to a pepper pod, you would*
> *make a dragonfly."*
> (translated by Kenneth Yasuda)

Working closely with his best pupils, Basho published six major anthologies of poetry. A seventh was published after his death. The second anthology, *A Spring Day*, includes only three haiku by Basho, but one of them is his most famous:

> *An ancient pond*
> *a frog jumps in—*
> *the sound of water.*
> (translated by Misuzu Bergman)

Many scholars say this haiku not only brilliantly captures a moment in a pond, but that it may also be an allegory for the smallness of man's works in the sight of God.

Basho's fifth anthology contains over four hundred poems, many by Basho himself. Its title, *The Monkey's Coat*, comes from this haiku:

> *Cold winter rain—*
> *even the monkey needs*
> *a tiny raincoat.*
> (translated by Misuzu Bergman)

Two other vivid haiku of winter were also written in this period:

How harsh it sounds!
The splattering of hail
on my traveling hat.

The sound of a water jar
cracking on this icy night
as I lie awake.
(translated by Makoto Ueda)

Pupils flocked to Basho; over his lifetime the poet may have had as many as two thousand. Not surprisingly, he sometimes wondered whether he would ever have any time alone for his own work. In frustration he once referred to his less talented pupils as "rhyming imitators"—as identical as "the halves of a cantaloupe cut in two."

In 1684 Basho decided to leave Edo and travel; he made three major trips during the next five years. The travel journals he produced make up his finest work. He wrote short, crisp prose about the rigors of the road, the beauty of a region, what ancient poets said about a particular place, and, finally, some haiku that distilled his personal experience.

Sometimes Basho stayed at temples and rustic inns, but more often he was the guest of a rich merchant or a local poet. He probably spent countless evenings politely listening to the bad poetry of his hosts, but he was always thrilled when he found "a genius hidden among weeds."

Basho's first trip, recounted in *The Records of a Weather-Exposed Skeleton*, was a roundabout trek from Edo to Kyoto and back, made during 1684–1685. Upon leaving Edo, Basho realized that "after ten autumns," the city had become his "native place."

Along the way a young woman named Butterfly gave Basho a piece of silk and asked him to create a poem that included her name. Basho wrote:

Orchid—breathing
incense into
butterfly's wings.
(translated by Lucien Stryk)

Three years later Basho traveled along roughly the same route as before. But his new journal, *The Records of a Travel-Worn Satchel*, is a more interesting work than his first. Writing that an appreciation of nature is what distinguishes a civilized man from a barbarian, Basho made his goal "to be one with nature throughout the four seasons of the year."

The poet rejoiced that "every sunrise gives me fresh emotions." This, in spite of the fact that on his back he carried "a raincoat, an overcoat, an inkstone, a brush, writing paper, medicine, and a lunch basket,"

I took a kimono off
to feel lighter,
only putting it in the load
on my back.
(translated by Yuasa Nobuyuki)

Basho climbed several mountains, and saw the hardship of life at high altitudes:

Tell me the loneliness
of this deserted mountain,
the aged farmer
digging wild potatoes.
(translated by Yuasa Nobuyuki)

He also took every opportunity to see cherry trees in bloom, but was intimidated by the many famous poets who had praised cherry blossoms in the past. Basho confessed, "I was not able to compose a single poem [about cherry trees]. . . . I thus found the present journey utterly devoid of poetic success."

Basho returned to Edo late in 1688, but wrote that "I barely had time to sweep the cobwebs from my broken house . . . [before] I wanted to be on the road again." This time Basho wished to see the northern half of Honshu (the main island of Japan), an area still quite remote in the seventeenth century. He wanted to introduce his readers to the region's stark beauty and simple, virtuous people.

Basho put his affairs in order and sold his house, for he had become indifferent to possessions. On his hat he wrote a pilgrim's motto: Homeless I wander, in company with the Buddha.

On May 16, 1689, Basho began a five-month trip north along the Pacific coast, west across the island of Honshu, and south along the Sea of Japan. Many of his friends came the night before to see him off, and they joined him on a riverboat for the first few miles. Probably there were many toasts of sake, for on another occasion Basho wrote:

Firefly-viewing—
drunken steersman,
drunken boat.
(translated by Lucien Stryk)

Basho's traveling companion was a young, newly ordained Buddhist priest named Sora. Together they walked over one thousand miles.

Five years later Basho's pupils published the poet's greatest work, a journal, *Oku no Hosomichi* (*Narrow Road to a Far Province*, also translated as *Narrow Road to the Interior*). Because Sora also kept a journal, we suspect that Basho's account is not always factual. But the few changes he made always add drama to an event, or intensify a feeling.

Basho's opening lines are particularly beautiful:

The moon and sun are travellers through eternity. Even the years wander on. Whether drifting through life on a boat or climbing toward old age leading a horse, each day is a journey, and the journey itself is home.
(translated by Sam Hamill)

The poet's journey was not just a trip north, it was also a journey backward in time. "We visited places made famous by poetry," Basho wrote, including a celebrated pine tree at Takekuma and a battlefield where Basho expressed the futility of war in one of his most moving haiku:

Summer grass
hides all that remains
of soldiers' dreams.
(translated by Misuzu Bergman)

Sometimes the traveling was hard. Basho forded streams, braved thickets of bamboo, and stumbled over hidden rocks. One set of cliffs was so treacherous that each turn had names like "Dogs Turn Back" and "Send Back Your Horse." After such a trek, it was demoralizing if an inn lacked comfort.

Fleas and lice did bite;
and I'd hear the horse pass water
near my bed at night.
(translated by Dorothy Britton)

Fortunately Basho also encountered people such as the painter Kaemon, who showed him a hillside full of blooming rhododendrons and gave him sandals with laces dyed the blue of an iris.

Basho could not stop and pull out his brush and inkstone every time he was inspired, so he kept an

Old fan scribbled
with poems—
shredded by summer's end.
(translated by Lucien Stryk)

Basho was especially pleased when a farmer asked him for a poem, but once, when yet another Buddhist monk made such a request,

My straw sandals were already tied on, so I did not even
take the time to read over my hurried lines.
(translated by Dorothy Britton)

On another occasion Basho told a local poet,

For verse, it did suffice,
to hear the peasants sing
as they planted rice.
(translated by Dorothy Britton)

The most beautiful place in all Japan, Basho felt, was the bay at Matsushima on the Pacific coast, with its hundreds of tiny islands. Basho admired the bay both by sunlight and moonlight, but as with the cherry trees on his previous journey, he could not then compose a single haiku.

Basho had a similar writer's block at the celebrated Pines of Shiogoshi, where he finally concluded that to write any more about them "would be like trying to add a sixth finger to the hand."

In October 1689 Basho arrived at the town of Ogaki, roughly halfway between Kyoto and Nagoya. Dozens of friends came from every direction to see him, "as if I had returned from the dead." But Basho lingered only a few days. He wanted to see a ceremony at the Shinto shrine at Ise that took place only once every twenty-one years. Before he left, he recited the final haiku of his great journal:

Sadly, I part from you;
like a clam torn from its shell,
I go, and autumn too.
(translated by Dorothy Britton)

His trip was over, but Basho could not bring himself to return to the city of Edo. He described his body as "an old tree that bears bitter peaches," and said he was "like a sick man weary of people." He visited a few friends in Kyoto and in his native city of Ueno, then spent the summer and autumn of 1690 at a cottage on Lake Biwa, just east of Kyoto. Amid wisteria vines and cuckoos, the poet had a view of two mountains that "would not have blushed before the loveliest scenes in China." He gathered firewood, dipped for spring water, talked with local farmers, and worked on poetry with his best pupils.

Early in 1691 Basho finally returned to Edo after an absence of almost three years. His followers soon built him a new cottage, and this time they planted five banana trees. But as he had foreseen, he had little time to himself. An invalid nephew came to live with him, and so did his old mistress Jutei and at least one of her children. The great poet was also inundated with visitors, with whom, he said, "I have to waste my words in vain."

Approaching fifty, Basho was feeling old. Possibly a spiritual struggle added to his weariness. He knew his literary ambition and his Buddhist desire for serenity were in direct conflict. He even began to call his love of poetry "a sinful attachment." But he could not stop writing haiku. Among his most pessimistic haiku at this time is one in which he anticipates how impersonal urban life was becoming as cities like Edo grew ever larger and neighbors no longer knew one another.

Autumn deepens —
The man next door, what
Does he do for a living?
(translated by Makoto Ueda)

Basho left Edo to travel again, but in Osaka he contracted dysentery and died on October 12, 1694. Three centuries later, many Japanese say that great haiku "began and ended with Basho." When challenged, they may agree that three other poets can also be counted as masters of the haiku: Buson Yosa (1716–1784), Kobayashi Issa (1763–1827), and Masaoka Shiki (1867–1902). But without question it is still Basho's haiku that the Japanese most admire and love.

13
Chikamatsu Monzaemon
Japan's Great Playwright

C HIKAMATSU MONZAEMON (1653–1725) is considered Japan's greatest playwright. He was one of the first dramatists in the world to make tragic heroes of ordinary men and women. His characters include merchants, courtesans, farmers, smugglers. He wrote 160 plays, mostly for the *bunraku* (puppet) theater.

His mastery of the Japanese language made his fame endure. Chikamatsu mixed classical poetry with popular slang, and delighted his audiences with puns, metaphors, and alliteration. Only a fraction of this can be translated into English, but the plays are still easy and interesting to read, and provide an excellent look at Japanese city life in the eighteenth century.

Born with the name Sugimori Nobumori in 1653 in what is today Fukui prefecture, on the Sea of Japan, Chikamatsu was the second of three sons of a low-ranking samurai. (He adopted his pen name when he was in his twenties.) When he was a teenager his family moved to Kyoto, where he became a servant in the household of the emperor's ninth-eldest son. He watched the nobility closely, and later in life was able to write upper class dialogue with authenticity. He had access to many books during this period, and probably saw his first puppet plays.

Chikamatsu's family loved literature, and published a collection of haiku in 1671. Here is Chikamatsu's poem:

> *Clouds*
> *Cover the shame*
> *Of the flowerless mountain*

When the emperor's son, Chikamatsu's master, died, the young servant began several years of study at the Chikamatsu Buddhist monastery, just northeast of Kyoto. It is likely that he took his pen name, Chikamatsu Monzaemon, from this temple. He read Buddhist scriptures and Chinese classics, and probably also read more than a hundred *no* plays, the restrained dance-dramas of medieval Japan. Chikamatsu quoted lines from eighty-two of them in his own plays.

In the mid-1670s Chikamatsu returned to Kyoto to work as a scene-changer at a theater. He liked the theater world immediately, and began to assist others in writing plays.

The 1600s were a time of peace and prosperity in Japan. Merchants in Kyoto, Edo, and especially Osaka (home of the rice exchange) were wealthy enough to support a dozen theaters. Each theater held hundreds of people, and vendors sold programs, cushions, matches, and jam buns. Audiences saw two performances, staying from eleven in the morning until ten at night. Theaters almost never performed *no* plays, which were popular only among the aristocracy. Common people preferred kabuki, where actors use exaggerated language and movements, and bunraku, puppet theater.

Puppet theater began as an art form around the year 1600, when a three-stringed banjo called the samisen came to Japan from China. The samisen player sets the tempo of a puppet play and heightens the emotion of a scene. He also produces sound effects resembling laughter and tears, or wind and rain.

The most important performer in a puppet play is the chanter. He sits next to the samisen player on a platform to the right of the stage, and acts all the parts of the play. Narrating, shouting, whispering, and sobbing with hardly a pause for breath, he mimics emperors and laborers, warriors and courtesans, grandmothers and children. In Chikamatsu's time the chanter was also the leader of his puppet troupe, and the theater was named for him.

Despite the chanter's importance, an audience pays the most attention to the puppets. They are about three-fifths lifesize, from 2½ to 4 feet tall. They can move their eyes from side to side, open their mouths, raise their eyebrows, lift their arms, wave their hands, and even curl their fingers.

During Chikamatsu's lifetime a play had only one puppeteer. Dressed in black, he stood partly below the stage and operated each puppet with his hand, pulling strings inside.

Since then, three puppeteers dressed in black kimonos and hoods work together in full view onstage. The strings of the chief puppeteer control a puppet's face and right arm. A second puppeteer controls the left arm and handles props such as towels, mirrors, and fans. The third puppeteer moves the feet if a puppet is male, or tugs at a kimono (to suggest moving legs) if a puppet is female. The coordination among the three makes the puppets come alive.

Puppeteers use forty-five kinds of doll's heads. There are heads for old villains and young warriors, for wicked stepmothers and beautiful courtesans. Often a puppet's face is exaggerated to be more scary or more alluring than most actors' faces could ever be. Puppeteers also use tricks to astonish an audience, such as tearing off a mask in the middle of a fight to show a bloody face.

In an age before movies and television, the combined effect of the puppets' gestures, chanter's dialogue, and samisen's sound effects was powerful enough to make Japanese audiences laugh and weep. While in Europe puppets merely amused children, in Japan the prestige of the puppet theater was equal to that of the kabuki. In fact, half of all kabuki plays were originally performed in the puppet theater.

Chikamatsu began his writing career by adapting *no* plays to the kabuki stage. It was a frustrating time for him because a kabuki playwright had no status. Kabuki actors were lionized by the public, and Chikamatsu was expected to tailor each play to particular individuals. The pampered actors were also free to add, drop, and change lines at will.

One kabuki actor who noticed Chikamatsu's talent was the great Sakata Tojuro, whom Chikamatsu admired for his unusually realistic and subtle performances. Chikamatsu wrote ten kabuki plays for Tojuro, and also incorporated Tojuro's *wagoto* (gentle) style of acting when he wrote plays for the puppet theater.

In the late 1670s Chikamatsu began helping a well-known chanter, Uji Kaganojo, write puppet plays. Chikamatsu was twenty years younger than Kaganojo, so the relationship was strictly one of master and pupil. Playwriting credit went solely to Kaganojo. Not until 1683 was Chikamatsu acknowledged as the author of a play, a historical drama called *The Soga Successors*.

A year later *The Soga Successors* was performed in Osaka by a young chanter named Takemoto Gidayu, who had just started a theater of his own. Gidayu was about the same age as Chikamatsu, and had also been a student of Uji Kaganojo's. Gidayu had a powerful voice and an excellent sense of timing, and combined chanting styles from folk songs, *no* plays, and older chanters.

Gidayu's performance of Chikamatsu's play was a huge success, and in 1685 Chikamatsu accepted Gidayu's invitation to join his puppet theater in Osaka. It was the beginning of a thirty-year collaboration between two geniuses.

Uji Kaganojo was furious with these upstart pupils and moved his theater to Osaka to compete directly with them. But the public preferred the puppet plays of the younger men, especially a 1686 play about jealousy, *Kagekiyo Victorious*. Kaganojo returned to Kyoto with his fame permanently eclipsed by his former students.

For the next twenty years Chikamatsu alternated between writing puppet plays in Osaka for Gidayu and kabuki plays in Kyoto for Tojuro. Chikamatsu also married, but little is known about his wife except that she outlived him. The couple had two sons; one became a painter, the other a theater manager.

None of Chikamatsu's greatest work was written during this period. Four fifths of Chikamatsu's 129 puppet plays are histories, and to the modern reader many of them are a jumble of legends and scrambled facts, with gods and goddesses intervening to save the day. Nevertheless, Chikamatsu brought many periods of Japanese history to life, and sometimes used the past to camouflage a satire of the present. He also tightened the structure of the history play by reducing the number of its acts from twelve to five.

Even in the most escapist, spectacle-oriented history play, Chikamatsu's dialogue is still witty. And his narration is always in meter, with alternating lines of seven and five syllables.

Chikamatsu wrote one of his greatest plays, *The Love Suicides at Sonezaki*, in just four weeks in 1703. The play is based on actual love suicides that took place only one month before the show opened. The drama is the first of twenty-four "domestic" puppet plays that Chikamatsu wrote about illicit love—the plays for which he is most famous.

Illicit love was common in Japan because marriages were arranged, and often loveless. If men had money, they visited prostitutes in the "licensed quarters" of the larger cities. Wives tolerated infidelity because they were powerless to stop it, and because they were taught from childhood that jealousy was a great evil.

In contrast to the rest of Japan, where merchants were considered lower class and prohibited from building mansions or buying fine clothes, in the licensed quarters all classes were equal. Merchants could spend as much money as they liked. The quarters were full of brightly decorated restaurants, tea houses, bath houses, and, of course, brothels.

Roughly speaking, there were two groups of prostitutes in Japan: courtesans and whores. The whores were uneducated farm girls whose poverty-stricken fathers had sold them to a brothel. The courtesans, by contrast, spent years learning the arts of singing, dancing, poetry, the tea ceremony, and, most important, conversation. They were better educated than the wives of most merchants and samurai, and unlike the less fortunate whores, they had the right to refuse customers.

Within these two general groups there was an elaborate hierarchy with dozens of ranks. The ranks differed from city to city, and from decade to decade, so today the Japanese language has over 450 words for prostitute.

The most beautiful and accomplished courtesans belonged to the highest rank of "pines." They had servants and influenced fashion, and required a long and expensive courtship before they accepted a lover.

Occasionally a prostitute and her customer fell in love. If the customer was rich, he could buy his lover's contract from the owner of the brothel and make her his wife or his concubine. If not, then the only way he could see his love was to pay for her services, for prostitutes were forbidden to leave the licensed quarters. Some lovesick merchants spent so much money in brothels that they drove their businesses into bankruptcy. Others watched helplessly as a richer rival bought their beloved's contract.

Sometimes a young man who no longer had the money to see his lover would commit suicide with her. The Japanese called such a love suicide *shinjushi*, "sincerity death"—and it was always sensational news.

The women involved in love suicides were invariably uneducated girls rather than cultivated courtesans, and Chikamatsu probably thought that only the emotional high points of these tragedies would interest his audience. His domestic plays are therefore shorter than his history plays, three acts rather than five.

The Love Suicides at Sonezaki, Chikamatsu's first domestic play, has just one act. It features Chikamatsu's most innocent, blameless characters. Tokubei, a clerk for a soy sauce dealer, is engaged to his master's niece but loves Ohatsu, a young courtesan. He manages to break his engagement, but before he returns the dowry money to his master, he lends it to a friend for a single day. The friend betrays Tokubei and keeps the money, and presents documents that imply that Tokubei has forged the proof of his loan.

Unless Tokubei can return the money to his master, he will have to marry his master's niece. In a climactic scene, Tokubei takes Ohatsu's foot and slides it against his throat—a sign that like her, he too is resolved to commit suicide. Before dawn they walk together to the Sonezaki shrine. There, as "the Big Dipper's bright reflection shines in the water," Tokubei asks Ohatsu for a "vow to be husband and wife stars for eternity." Ohatsu promises, "I'll be your wife forever." "Their strings of tears unite like entwining branches," and Ohatsu prays, "May we be reborn on the same lotus!"

The Love Suicides at Sonezaki was a brilliant success. It made so much money for Gidayu's theater that Chikamatsu decided to move to Osaka permanently. He preferred writing puppet plays because, unlike kabuki actors, puppets did not change his lines. Also his friend Tojuro, the kabuki actor, was retiring.

Chikamatsu wrote a dozen love suicide plays during his career, and helped make these deaths so fashionable that eventually the shogun outlawed plays with "love suicide" in the title. Even as late as the 1950s, before the decline in arranged marriages, young couples attempted love suicides in Japan almost every day.

Chikamatsu's next great play was *The Drums of the Waves of Horikawa*, first performed in 1706. Based on a true story, the play is about a lonely woman named Otane who drinks too much because her husband is away for months at a time. One night she shares too many cups of sake with her son's drum teacher, and the two make love. They are horrified when they wake up in the morning, but it is too late. Otane becomes pregnant, and is unable to induce an abortion. When her husband returns she apologizes, then stabs herself. The play ends when the husband finds and kills the drum teacher.

Without saying so directly, Chikamatsu was criticizing the double standard in Japan that let men seek sex in the licensed quarters while their wives suffered lonely nights at home. In Chikamatsu's plays women are nearly always strong and sympathetic characters, even if they are adulterous wives or low-ranking prostitutes. Chikamatsu once said that his plays showed a woman's true feelings because his puppets were free to express things that a woman could never say in real life.

Chikamatsu wrote several plays a year for Gidayu, but in 1714 the great chanter died, leaving the theater without a star performer. In his will, Gidayu chose twenty-three-year-old Takemoto Masatayu as his successor, angering

Gidayu's older assistants. Most of them joined other theaters immediately, and news of their exits caused audiences to dwindle.

Masatayu's voice was weak in volume, but conveyed a wide variety of subtle emotions. Chikamatsu, then sixty-one, liked the earnest young chanter, and wrote a play for him entitled *The Battles of Coxinga*. It is his finest history play, and it broke attendance records by running for seventeen months, from November 1715 until April 1717; the puppeteers ran through three sets of costumes.

The play is based on Kokusen'ya (a.k.a. Guoxingye), a half-Japanese, half-Chinese general who fought for the Ming dynasty against the Manchus in southern China. The drama has little to do with historical reality—Coxinga ultimately lost to the Manchus, but this did not trouble Chikamatsu. He once said, "Art lies in the shadowy frontiers between reality and unreality."

The Battles of Coxinga is an all-day spectacle with events ideally suited to a puppet play. Coxinga fights a tiger, a young man grows old in an instant, a villain gouges out his eye to prove his loyalty to the Manchus, and a hero cuts open a pregnant but dying empress to rescue the heir to China's throne.

The turning point of the play comes in act three, when a general's wife kills herself so that her husband will be free to join Coxinga and fight the Manchus. In the following act Coxinga and the general spend five years conquering dozens of fortresses, but the action is beautifully telescoped through two old men who play the game of *go* on top of a sacred mountain. The *go* board is the center of the universe, and as one man moves stones about, he asks, "Does not the good or bad fortune of mankind depend on the chance of the moment?"

The Battles of Coxinga appeals to Japanese patriotism. Coxinga's father is an exiled Chinese official, but his Japanese mother is a simple woman among fishermen, and from her humble island her son rises to become the conqueror of China. "Have you learned now the meaning of Japanese prowess," Coxinga asks a defeated enemy, "before which even tigers tremble?"

Theaters have performed *The Battles of Coxinga* for almost three hundred years. The play gave Chikamatsu and his young chanter financial security, and marked the beginning of a collaboration that lasted for the rest of Chikamatsu's life.

Chikamatsu had been a pupil under the chanter Kaganojo, and then an equal to the great Gidayu. Now Chikamatsu was Masatayu's senior partner, free to write whatever he pleased.

During the winter of 1718–1719, Chikamatsu wrote *The Girl from Hakata, or Love at Sea*. In this play, Soshichi, a merchant, and Kezori, a seaside smuggler, both desire the same courtesan, Kojoro. Eventually the smuggler offers Soshichi an agonizing choice: He can marry the girl if he joins the smugglers and thus disgrace his father, or he can refuse, be killed, and die knowing that the smuggler will possess his true love.

Soshichi joins the smugglers and prospers for several months. But when his father learns of the smuggling, he disinherits him and auctions off all his loot for a pittance.

The father refuses even to see his son, but cannot ignore him completely. He talks to Soshichi from the other side of a wall. All that Soshichi and the audience can see is his father's hand coming through a hole, offering a cup of tea. Soshichi and his wife, Kojoro, drink from the teacup, then, sobbing, cling to his hand, which itself trembles with emotion.

Soshichi kills himself to avoid the disgrace of capture and execution, but Kojoro is pardoned because courtesans are "birds of passage" and therefore not guilty of the crimes of the men who purchase them. She vows to spend the rest of her life serving her father-in-law, to atone for the disgrace that she and her husband brought upon him.

Two years later, in 1720, Chikamatsu wrote one of his finest plays, *The Love Suicides at Amijima*. Its main characters are known to every educated Japanese: Jihei, a paper merchant; Osan, his wife; Koharu, a courtesan whom Jihei loves; and Tahei, a rich but vulgar man who is about to buy Koharu's contract.

Osan fears that her husband and Koharu are planning a love suicide, and requests and receives a promise from both of them that they will not see each other anymore. But soon Osan realizes that her husband has lost face before his boasting rival Tahei, and more important, that Koharu will commit suicide alone.

To save her husband's face and Koharu's life, Osan, a model wife, pawns her own clothes and those of her children and tells her husband, "It doesn't matter if the children and I have nothing to wear. My husband's reputation concerns me more. Ransom Koharu. Save her. Assert your honor before Tahei."

Only when she fulfills her duty does she finally consider her own loss of status should Koharu become her husband's new wife. "What shall I do?" she grieves. "Shall I become the children's nurse, or the cook?"

Unfortunately the money Osan raises is insufficient. Tahei buys Koharu's contract and intends to make her his concubine. Jihei and Koharu resume their plans for suicide, and the description of their nighttime journey past twelve Osaka bridges to the temple at Amijima is full of homonyms and other wordplay.

When dawn finally arrives, Koharu insists that she and Jihei die separately. She has made a promise to Osan, and does not want to dishonor it by dying next to Jihei. She pleads:

Kill me here, then choose another spot, far away, for yourself. . . .We may die in different places, our bodies may be pecked by kites and crows, but what does it matter as long as our souls are twined together? Take me with you, to heaven or to hell!

Jihei abandons a wife and two children, and Koharu leaves behind an impoverished mother. Yet they both have faith in Buddha's salvation. In Japanese the *ami* in *Amijima* means "heaven's net." The play's title therefore suggests that the lovers can expect mercy as well as retribution.

Chikamatsu wrote his last play, *The Tethered Steed,* in 1724. It includes a scene with a large bonfire, and two months after the play opened, much of Osaka went up in flames. Afterward a superstitious public refused to see the play. It closed immediately, never to be revived. Chikamatsu was ill at the time, and this unfortunate coincidence did not help matters. He died at seventy-one on January 6, 1725.

"I have used care in my writing," Chikamatsu once told a friend, "which was not true of the old plays. As a result the medium has been raised one level."

Chikamatsu's supreme gift was to create unforgettable moments of the most intense and conflicting emotions. Centuries after his death, his plays remain the core of both the bunraku and kabuki repertories.

14
Katsushika Hokusai
Master of the Wood-block Print

H OKUSAI (1760–1849) is probably the most well-known Asian artist in the West. One print, *The Great Wave off Kanagawa*, is among the most famous works of art in the world. His detailed wood-block prints astonished European admirers in the nineteenth century, and his bold use of color and broad choice of subjects were a great influence on the French Impressionists, especially Monet, who kept dozens of Hokusai prints in his home.

Hokusai worked from dawn to dusk for more than seventy years. In his lifetime he produced over thirty thousand prints, drawings, paintings, illustrations, and New Year's cards, ranging in subject from goddesses to chickens.

If only one word could be used to describe Hokusai it would have to be *restless*. He studied one style of art after another, and signed his works with a different name each time he used a different style. It was customary for a Japanese artist to use four or five names in a lifetime, but Hokusai used thirty, among them Gakyo-jin, "Art-Crazy Man," and, of course, Hokusai, which means "north studio." He also lived in ninety different dwellings during his life, moving an average of once a year.

Hokusai was born in the Katsushika district just east of Tokyo, then called Edo. He was proud of his home district, and often signed his paintings "Katsushika Hokusai." His father (possibly a stepfather) was a mirror maker for the shogun, though he never accepted Hokusai as an heir, so his mother may have been a concubine.

Hokusai was called Tokitaro as a child, and began to paint when he was about six. Probably he learned to paint from his father, who in all likelihood not only polished mirrors but also painted the designs that surrounded them.

The cities in Japan enjoyed handcrafted manufacturing as specialized and well developed as that of Renaissance Europe. The craftsmen and merchants formed a large and literate middle class that read books for pleasure. The books were not printed from movable type, as books were in Europe, but from woodblocks. This is why they contained such beautiful illustrations; from a woodblock it is as easy to print an illustration as to print a text.

When Hokusai was twelve his father sent him to work in a bookshop and lending library. He was fascinated by the many illustrations in the books in the shop and studied them closely. Some of the volumes were akin to modern-day comic books, with ghosts, superhuman warriors, and evil foxes who could change into beautiful women.

By 1776 Hokusai was an apprentice to a wood-block engraver, whom he served for three years. An engraver's job is to make an exact copy of the illustration or painting provided to him. Hokusai explored the limits of the wood engraver's craft, then stretched those limits for the rest of his life.

Hokusai also began to paint illustrations of his own. He must have been talented, for when he was eighteen he was accepted as a pupil by Shunsho, one of the great *ukiyo-e* artists of his time. *Ukiyo-e* means "floating world," and refers to the courtesans and kabuki actors who were almost always the subjects of the artists' wood-block prints.

After a year Shunsho gave the name Shunro to his pupil, and under this name Hokusai published his first prints in 1779—pictures of kabuki actors. He worked for Shunsho for a decade, making prints of actors and courtesans and illustrating inexpensive novels.

Hokusai married during these years, but nothing is known about his first wife except that she died in the early 1790s. He remarried in 1797, but his new wife also did not live long. By his two wives Hokusai had three daughters and two sons. One son died as a young man; the other son became a minor government official. Oyei, his youngest daughter, became a talented artist in her own right. Eventually, she divorced her husband and came back to live with Hokusai when he was in his seventies, and was a great comfort to him.

After Shunsho died in 1793, Hokusai studied many different styles of Japanese and Chinese art. He also obtained some copper plates of Dutch and French landscapes and studied European perspective and shading. Under this widening influence, and perhaps because he was now the father of young children, Hokusai drew fewer actors and courtesans. He began instead to draw *surimono* (New Year's cards and announcements) and, more important, to draw landscapes and scenes from daily life.

Hokusai was one of the first and by far the best of the wood-block artists to do landscapes and street scenes. This was his great contribution to Japanese art. Before Hokusai, wood-block printing had focused mainly on the "floating world." Hokusai freed *ukiyo-e* from its limitations and made prints of everything from barrel makers to insects.

In 1800 Hokusai published *Famous Sights of the Eastern Capital* and *Eight Views of Edo*. He began to use the name Hokusai but continued using other names too. About this time he also began to attract pupils, taking in fifty during his lifetime.

Hokusai's fame as an artist and his reputation as an eccentric spread rapidly in 1804 when, at a crowded festival in Tokyo, he painted a 600-foot-long portrait of the ancient Zen priest Daruma. He used a broom as a brush and dipped it into buckets full of ink, to the delight of the crowd.

Soon after this, Hokusai was summoned to paint before Shogun Iyenari, an unusually high honor for an artist of "the floating world." The shogun commanded him to compete against a well-known brushstroke artist of the traditional Chinese style. Each artist had to make a painting before the shogun. Hokusai started by painting blue curves on a long sheet of paper. Then he pulled out a chicken, dipped its feet in red ink, and chased it down the length of the paper. Hokusai held up the sheet and described it as the Tatsuta River in autumn, with maple leaves floating downstream. The shogun laughed and declared him the winner.

In 1807 Hokusai illustrated three books by Takizawa Bakin, one of Japan's most popular novelists. It was a stormy collaboration. Bakin accused Hokusai of departing from his text and Hokusai complained to Bakin about his story's lack of visual opportunities. On their fourth book together their quarrel became irreparable. Each man refused to work with the other any longer. The publisher had to choose between finishing the book with either a new illustrator or a new writer. He kept Hokusai and found a new writer, and demonstrated the tremendous importance of illustrations in Japanese literature at this time.

Finances were tight for Hokusai in 1812. To win new pupils he published *Quick Lessons in Simplified Drawing*. He also sought to spread his reputation by traveling to Kyoto and Nagoya. Hokusai was coolly received in traditional Kyoto, but in Nagoya he won new pupils and admirers, who encouraged him to publish his many sketches.

In 1814 Hokusai published the first of fifteen volumes of sketches. Eleven more volumes followed by 1820 and three final volumes were published after his death. These volumes were called *manga*, or "caricatures," and they are among his most important works. In thousands of sketches Hokusai drew everything that interested him: carpenters, wrestlers, porters, Buddhas, animals, fish. Often his works are humorous, portraying a dancer blowing bubbles or a fat man bathing. The *manga* were extremely popular. Copies sold until the blocks wore out.

A sign in Hokusai's studio at this time indicated his popularity and also his testy nature. It said: IT IS NO USE BOWING AND SCRAPING, AND IT IS NO USE BRINGING ME BRIBES. Occasionally Hokusai delighted in humiliating callers. Once, when a servant of the shogun came by, Hokusai told him that he was too busy removing fleas from his clothes to see him.

In the late 1820s Hokusai was at the height of his genius. He published *Thirty-Six Views of Mount Fuji*, the prints that eventually made him world famous. They proved so popular that he had to add ten extra prints, so there are actually forty-six views of Fuji. Most of them show ordinary activities in settings where Mt. Fuji is in the background, for example, at a timber yard, in a tea house, or on a ferry boat.

The most dramatic of the prints is also Hokusai's most famous single work, *The Great Wave off Kanagawa*. In this print a towering wave is about to crash down on three small fishing boats. On the horizon, snow-covered Mt. Fuji stands in silence, indifferent to but dwarfed by the huge wave with its falling, fingerlike foam.

The range of color and wealth of detail in *Thirty-Six Views of Mount Fuji* was beyond anything that had been done in wood-block prints before. Some of the prints were made from as many as twelve separate blocks. Equally striking was the grandeur of the theme. In forty-six portaits Hokusai captured the daily life of his people and set it all within sight of Fuji, as if the mountain were watching like some detached god.

Hokusai also published *Views of Famous Bridges*, with its especially beautiful print, *Evening of the Festival of Lanterns*. In this print a long, curved bridge in Osaka is bedecked with Japanese lanterns, as are the ships in the wide river below. In *A Tour of Famous Waterfalls*, which Hokusai also published at this time, the waterfalls are not the misty veils found in traditional Chinese paintings, but powerful, roaring rivers that crash down at the feet of tiny people gazing up in awe.

Hokusai was expanding the art of the wood-block print, but he was also responding to market demand. Craftsmen, shopkeepers, and teachers could not afford paintings, but they still wanted pictures of the places they visited.

Around 1830 Hokusai published some prints of flowers and birds. In one masterpiece, *Poppies*, every curve of leaf and petal mimics nature. In another, *Flock of Chickens*, the fowl are portrayed so minutely—down to the smallest feather—that it is a wonder it could ever have been engraved at all.

Hokusai knew the importance of using an expert wood-engraver, having been one once himself. In 1834, when Hokusai had to flee Tokyo to avoid the creditors of a spendthrift grandson, he wrote anxious letters to his publishers to make sure they employed only Egawa Tomekiti to engrave his books. "What I ask for is the sharpness of his execution," he pleaded, "and this would be a satisfaction to a poor old man who hasn't much further to go." Hokusai also gave precise instructions on how to print his work, describing one ink tone as having the thickness of shellfish soup, and another as having the thickness of bean soup.

In this same year Hokusai published *One Hundred Views of Fuji*. These prints did not have the full breadth of color contained in *Thirty-Six Views*, but Hokusai made up for this deficiency by the imaginativeness of his designs. Mt. Fuji, half hidden, is seen through a summer shower, a bamboo grove, and in the reflection of a cup of sake. One print in this set, *Fuji Seen from the Sea*, is reminiscent of *The Great Wave Off Kanagawa*. But as this wave curls upward, the drops of foam at the crest seem to turn into small birds, giving a hint of the prints the artist M. C. Escher would make a century later.

Hokusai's last years were not prosperous. A fire destroyed much of his work in 1839 and his fame was eclipsed by a younger wood-block artist, Ando Hiroshige. (Hiroshige's prints are less vigorous but more atmospheric than Hokusai's.) Still, Hokusai never stopped painting. One of his last works was *Ducks in a Stream*, a brush painting of great beauty which he composed when he was eighty-seven.

Hokusai died at the age of eighty-nine in 1849. During his life he had been so completely devoted to his art that he never found the time to build a home, dine well, or be sociable. When he died he was still dissatisfied with his craft, begging heaven for another ten, even five more years to improve his painting. In his seventies he wrote:

> At seventy-three I have at last caught every aspect of nature—birds, fish, animals, insects, trees, grasses, all. When I am eighty I shall have developed still further, and I will really master the secrets of art at ninety. When I reach a hundred my work will be truly sublime, and my final goal will be attained around the age of one hundred and ten, when every line and dot I draw will be imbued with life.

Only four years after Hokusai's death the U.S. Navy steamed into Tokyo Bay, changing Japanese life completely. Wood-block printing was replaced by photography and movable type, and younger artists who might have looked to Hokusai for inspiration followed Western styles instead. Hokusai is as solitary a figure in the history of art as he was in life.

The Japan of Hokusai's lifetime was one of the most physically exquisite societies the world has ever seen. Some of this was portrayed by others in brushstroke landscapes or block prints of kabuki actors, but it was Hokusai more than anyone who caught the day-to-day life of Japan before it changed forever.

PART THREE
History

15

Early Japan

*Shinto Myths, the Imperial Lineage, and
Shotoku, the Prince Who Spread Buddhism*

JAPAN HAD a late start. A thousand years after Moses led the Jews out of Egypt, the people of Japan were still living largely as hunters and gatherers. They hunted, fished, picked fruit and herbs, and often starved during the winter because they could not store enough food. Then around 200 B.C., immigrants from China and Korea taught the Japanese how to forge iron and to grow rice.

In spring, when these early Japanese farmers transplanted their rice shoots into paddies, they held a ceremony to pray for a good crop. During summer they held another ceremony to ward off insects. In fall, when they harvested their rice, they gave thanks. And in winter the farmers prayed for the renewal of their fields. Gradually, these seasonal rites took an established form, and this was the beginning of Shinto, which means "the way of the spirits." In time, Shinto also provided a genealogy for the first emperor.

Unlike most religions, Shinto has no founder, no scripture, and no central deity. The Japanese believe that *kami*, or spirit, dwells in any object that inspires awe or mystery—a mountain or a rock, a forest or a tree, a hero or an animal—and that the spirit will respond to the prayer of a true heart. This is why the Japanese prize sincerity above all other virtues. The importance of sincerity also helps explain why the Japanese often perform even the most menial tasks so well.

When the Japanese build a Shinto shrine by a forest grove or a hero's grave, the entrance is marked by a *torii*, the typical Japanese gate of two horizontal beams supported by two vertical columns. The *torii* indicates that the area beyond is sacred.

Many of the over 85,000 Shinto shrines in Japan are not much bigger than voting booths, but at the larger shrines people celebrate births, marriages, and certain birthdays. The third, fifth, seventh, twentieth, sixtieth, seventy-seventh, and eighty-eighth birthdays are considered most significant. Priests recite prayers and offer the *kami* rice, sake, vegetables, and fish.

In 1945, during the Allied occupation, the Japanese government cut its ancient tie to the Shinto religion. Nevertheless, the emperor, worshiping as a private citizen, is still Shinto's leading figure. He leads purification ceremonies twice a year, and at midnight on November 23, during the Festival of First Fruits, the emperor offers rice grown in a special field tended by virgins.

The emperor presents the rice to the sun goddess, Amaterasu Omikami, whom pious Japanese believe to be his direct ancestor. The genealogy supporting this claim comes from two books, *Kojiki* (The Record of Ancient Matters), written in 712, and *Nihon Shoki* (The Chronicles of Japan), written in 720. The books preserve an oral tradition that had been passed down for centuries.

The Shinto creation myths begin with a dark, oily mass. Out of this chaos several generations of gods and goddesses came into being and vanished. Finally, two gods remained, Izana-gi, "Male Who Invites," and Izana-mi, "Female Who Invites." On a rainbow bridge they thrust a jeweled spear into the oily mass, and stirred. The brine dripping from the point of the spear coagulated and became an island, and the divine couple floated down to live there.

Izana-mi looked at Izana-gi and exclaimed, "What a beautiful man you are!" But Izana-gi said, "It was not proper for you to speak first." Their first child was deformed and wormlike, and they put it out to sea in a tiny boat.

Later Izana-gi said to Izana-mi, "What a beautiful woman you are!" This time, according to the myths, they gave birth to Honshu, Kyushu, and six other Japanese islands, as well as to mountains, waterfalls, trees, and the wind. The wind blew away the primordial mist and revealed to everyone the beauty of creation.

The divine couple's last child was fire, but in giving birth to fire Izana-mi suffered a burning fever and died. Izana-gi was grief-stricken. He followed his wife to the underworld and begged her to come back, but when he lit a torch he saw that she was rotting and covered with maggots.

Horrified, Izana-gi returned to the earth's surface and bathed in the ocean to wash away the demons that had left the underworld with him. These evil spirits still lurk about the earth, and cause trouble everywhere they go. While scrubbing his right eye, Izana-gi gave life to the moon god. Washing his left eye, he gave birth to Amaterasu, the sun goddess.

Amaterasu was beautiful and gave light to all the world. She built irrigation canals to help farmers grow rice, then chose her grandson, Ninigi no Mikoto, to rule the earth.

Ninigi married a beautiful goddess who caused flowers to blossom, but he had refused to marry her ugly older sister, who was named Long-as-the-Rocks. The homely sister and her father were offended by Ninigi's refusal, and put a curse on his descendants. Instead of living as long as the rocks, their offspring would bloom and fade quickly like blossoms. The blossom goddess's mortal children became the world's first human beings.

Ninigi's great-grandson was a boy named Jimmu, and he became Japan's first emperor. It is not certain whether Jimmu actually existed, but by tradition he was born on the island of Kyushu in 711 B.C., conquered western Honshu, and reigned as emperor from 660 to 585 B.C., when he died at age 126. But not only is his life span unbelievably long, the dates are impossibly early.

Most Japanese believe that someone, perhaps Jimmu, conquered western

Japan and started the Imperial dynasty about one thousand years later than the traditional date of origin, during the first half of the fourth century A.D. Starting in Kyushu, this warrior fought his way east along the coast of the Inland Sea, and finally led troops inland from modern-day Osaka. There he founded the state of Yamato, which is the name of the surrounding area and also an ancient name for Japan. This first emperor was not only a warrior chief but also the high priest of the Shinto religion. His right to rule Japan came from the claim that he was a direct descendant of Amaterasu.

The people whom the first emperor defeated were the Ainu, an aboriginal, part-Caucasian race that the Japanese continued to push north for centuries. Today, the only Ainu left in Japan live in remote areas of the northern island of Hokkaido.

At first the Japanese state was weak. Except for a handful of Korean immigrants familiar with Chinese, no one could read or write. The emperor's authority over the warrior clans was limited, and he had little influence beyond the Yamato region and the coast of the Inland Sea. Much of the rest of Japan was ruled by outlaws, pirates, and the Ainu.

Nevertheless, by A.D. 369 the new kingdom was strong enough to conquer the southern tip of Korea. Possibly the Japanese were looking for iron, which was in short supply back home.

Japan's toehold in Korea led to two major changes. The first was the discovery of horses. When Japanese soldiers encountered northern Korean warriors on horseback around the year 400, they fled in terror. But within a few years Japanese warriors were riding horses themselves, and for the next 1,400 years they fought their wars on horseback.

The second change came in 538, when the ruler of southwest Korea sought Japan's help against the army of southeast Korea. To win Japan's favor, the southwestern chief sent two presents to the emperor: a bronze statue of Buddha and several scrolls of Buddhist scriptures. They were small gifts, but they changed Japan forever.

❖

It took fifty years for Japan's rulers to accept Buddhism because the religion was a threat to their legitimacy. Not only was the emperor's power based on his descent from Amaterasu, the authority of regional chiefs came from local Shinto deities. When disease spread soon after the arrival of the Korean statue, Shinto chiefs threw the stone Buddha into a canal.

In Korea, by contrast, Buddhism thrived. Thousands of people were reading Buddhist scriptures in Chinese and also keeping up with Chinese advances in carpentry, weaving, and metallurgy. The Japanese were behind the Koreans in almost every field.

In Japan, the Soga family and a few other clans offered protection to Korean immigrants, and grew wealthy buying and selling their excellent cloth and metalwork. The source of power for these clans came not from their Shinto ancestry, but from their tolerance of Buddhism.

Buddhism offered the Japanese a worldview wider than anything they had encountered before. Ideas such as reincarnation, karma, and salvation had no counterparts in Shinto, and many Japanese were fascinated by the prospect of an eternal and blissful existence.

In 585 a Buddhist prince named Yomei became emperor. Yomei's faith was grudgingly tolerated by Shinto chiefs during his brief two-year reign, but when he died in 587, the Buddhist and Shinto clans went to war.

In battle a Buddhist archer killed the chief of the strongest Shinto clan, and the Soga family's warriors took advantage of their enemy's confusion and decimated them. The Sogas were now the most powerful family in Japan, but their leader, Umako, did not make himself emperor. Instead, he began the long Japanese tradition of ruling behind the throne. He knew that even those Shinto clans that had stayed neutral during the war would never accept him as the high priest of their religion.

Umako installed the dead monarch's younger brother Sujun as emperor in 588, and for the first time the Japanese state was openly tolerant of Buddhism. But after four years the new emperor resented his powerful patron. When a hunter gave him a wild boar, Sujun asked, "When shall those to whom we have an aversion be cut off as this boar's throat has been cut?"

Umako faced a stark choice: kill the emperor or be killed himself like a wild boar. Secretly, he ordered Sujun's assassination. Then in 593 he nominated his niece, Suiko, to be Japan's first empress since legendary times. Suiko was acceptable to the Shinto clans because she was the widow of a recent emperor. To make sure she would be only a figurehead, Umako appointed a regent, Shotoku Taishi (574–622), to run the government. Just nineteen years old when he took office, Prince Shotoku became one of the greatest rulers in Japan's history.

Records from Shotoku's time are scarce, so the story of his life is an educated guess. His name, Shotoku Taishi, means "wise virtue—saint," and was given to the prince after his death. During his life his name was Umayado, or "stable door," for reasons unknown.

Shotoku was the son of Yomei, the Buddhist emperor who died in 587 after a two-year reign. Umako, the Soga clan leader, chose Shotoku as regent for several reasons. First, *both* of Shotoku's grandmothers were sisters of Umako's. Second, at thirteen Shotoku had fought bravely with Umako in the war between the Buddhist and Shinto clans that followed the death of his father. Third, Shotoku was unusually well educated and could read and write Chinese. Finally, because Shotoku was a devout Buddhist, his goals were the same as Umako's: to open Japan to the Buddhist civilization of China and Korea, to strengthen the Imperial government, and to reduce the power of the Shinto clans. Umako might have turned a less skillful leader into a puppet, but he recognized Shotoku's ability from the start and simply let him do his job.

In 594, at Shotoku's request, Empress Suiko ordered the aristocracy to be tolerant of Buddhism. From then on, they had to regard the monarch not only as the high priest of Shinto, but also as Buddha's agent in Japan. Shotoku discouraged local ancestral cults, but he respected Shinto's agricultural rites and did not see them as being in conflict with Buddhism. Many years later, when China's influence in Japan was much stronger, Shotoku was said to have compared Japanese religion to a tree, with Shinto as the roots of national tradition, Confucianism as the trunk and branches of an ethical code, and Buddhism as the fruit of spiritual life.

Once the Shinto clans realized that Buddhism was not a threat to the majority of their rituals, many of them began building small Buddhist temples themselves for added divine protection. Larger temples were financed by the monarchy, including the famous Horyu-ji compound outside Osaka, which was rebuilt after a fire in 670 and still stands—the oldest wooden buildings in the world.

Nearby is a nunnery with a tapestry embroidered by Shotoku's wife, Iratsume, who was Umako's daughter. Like her husband, Iratsume was a devout Buddhist. Her tapestry displays a Buddhist heaven, and also contains an embroidered picture of her husband saying, "The world is impermanent; Buddha alone is real."

Not yet thirty, Shotoku continued his education under the guidance of a Korean priest. He read works on Buddhism, Taoism, Confucianism, astronomy, and geography. Later he gave lectures on Buddha's final teaching, the Lotus Sutra, and compared Buddha's salvation to the rain, which is the same everywhere yet nourishes each plant in its own way.

A manuscript of one of the lectures still exists and is thought to have been written in Shotoku's own hand. Shotoku may have been Japan's first writer, although he wrote in Chinese. The Japanese did not develop a system of writing until the ninth century.

In 603 Shotoku adopted the Chinese administrative system of "caps and ranks." Court rank would be based on achievement rather than heredity, and granted at the pleasure of the monarch. Shotoku divided his officials into twelve grades. A man's level was indicated by the color of the feathers in his purple silk cap. The purpose of this new, merit-based bureaucracy was to reduce the number of offices held by clan members.

The following year Shotoku issued seventeen moral instructions. Drawing upon a dozen works of Chinese philosophy, literature, and history, Shotoku ordered his officials to obey the emperor, worship Buddha, work late, and consult advisers. He also told them to avoid sycophants, bribes, anger, and excessive taxation and punishments. The directive is Japan's first legal document, synthesizing three ideals: Buddhist faith, Confucian behavior, and Imperial authority.

Shotoku's most important action was to bypass Korea and send diplomats directly to China. Japan's mission in 607 is especially famous because of the written greeting given to China's emperor: "The ruler of the land of the rising sun addresses the ruler of the land of the setting sun." The Chinese monarch was angered by the tone of the message and told his foreign minister, "If memorials from barbarians are written by persons who lack propriety, do not accept them." The Japanese ambassador hastened to explain that Empress Suiko had heard that China was ruled by a bodhisattva, a Buddhist saint who returns to earth to help others, and that she wished to pay her respects. This satisfied the emperor somewhat, and in any case he needed the country named Jih-pen (Chinese for "source of the sun") as an ally against northern Korea.

The real significance of the missions to China was cultural. Accompanying the diplomats, with Shotoku's encouragement, were ambitious monks and scholars hungry to learn everything they could about China. Many of these young men stayed there for twenty years, then returned home to Japan to become leaders in their fields.

During the next few decades the Japanese adopted Chinese writing, law, philosophy, medicine, astronomy, calendars, architecture, painting, styles of dress, and varieties of Buddhism. The speed of Japan's cultural growth in the seventh century was equaled only by the swiftness of its industrialization in the late nineteenth and twentieth centuries. In each case the brightest young Japanese studied abroad and returned home to modernize their country. In both eras Japan came from behind and quickly caught up with the world's most advanced nations.

Little is known about the last dozen years of Shotoku's life. His government built roads, bridges, reservoirs, and irrigation canals, and also planted orchards and encouraged silk production. Shotoku moved to a villa near the Horyu-ji temple, and spent hours meditating in front of a statue of Kannon, the Buddhist goddess of mercy. After his death, some Buddhists claimed that Shotoku had been an incarnation of Kannon. In 620 Shotoku wrote two books of history about Japan and its emperors, but a fire destroyed the manuscripts twenty-five years later.

In March 622 the forty-eight-year-old Shotoku became ill. While attending him, his wife became sick too, and they both died in April. On his deathbed, Shotoku's last words to his children were "Avoid every kind of evil and practice every kind of good."

In *Nihon Shoki* (The Chronicles of Japan), it is written that when ordinary people heard that Prince Shotoku had died, "The farmer ceased from his plough, and the pounding woman laid down her pestle." The old mourned "as if they had lost a dear child, the young as if they had lost a beloved parent."

The sons of Shotoku and Umako did not get along as well as their fathers did. When Empress Suiko died in 628, Shotoku's eldest son, Yamashiro, was in line for the throne, but Umako's son, Iruka, opposed him. Iruka was afraid that Yamashiro would use his father's immense prestige to become a strong emperor, and that the Soga family would no longer be the power behind the throne.

Many warriors wanted to fight for Yamashiro's right to be emperor, but the prince was too good a Buddhist to plunge his nation into civil war, and gave up his chance at power. When a second succession crisis occurred in 643, Yamashiro had less power than before, and this time he and his family were forced to commit suicide.

Although Shotoku's family line came to an end, his policies triumphed. When China's T'ang dynasty invaded northern Korea, all three Korean states armed rapidly in self-defense, and this alarmed even the most conservative Japanese. Suddenly everyone in Japan wanted a stronger and more efficient government to protect them in an increasingly dangerous world.

In 645 several aristocrats stabbed the unpopular Iruka to death, installed a new emperor, and took over the government. With the help of scholars that Shotoku had sent to China, they initiated a "great reform" and reorganized Japan's government along more modern Chinese lines.

Japan's new rulers confiscated the swords and armor of the local clans and built up the arsenal of their own Imperial Army. The emperor's appointees took control of taxation, local government, and the adjudication of land titles, and also sent Buddhist missionaries to northern Honshu and the island of Okinawa.

With the Soga and local clans powerless, Buddhist temples looked to the monarchy for money. To win favor, monks began to glorify past emperors and regents, especially Prince Shotoku. By the year 700 the father of Japanese Buddhism was worshiped, and legends arose about his miraculous powers and his mother's virgin birth.

Worship is hardly necessary to appreciate Prince Shotoku Taishi's crucial role in Japan's history. When he became regent in 593, the Japanese were isolated and illiterate. Fifty years later they were a part of the great civilization of East Asia. With Shotoku's encouragement, the Japanese absorbed centuries of Buddhist faith and Chinese knowledge in just a few decades, and still managed to preserve their monarchy and their native religion. In spite of Shotoku's belief that the world is impermanent, this is a lasting achievement.

16

Yoritomo, Hojo Masako, and Yoshitsune

The First Shogun, His Wife, and His Legendary Brother

THE CIVIL WAR of the 1180s that brought Yoritomo, Hojo Masako, and Yoshitsune to prominence is Japan's equivalent of the Trojan War. The struggle between the Minamoto and Taira families has been the source of so many myths, plays, books, and films that over time the legends have probably become as important as the events.

Minamoto no Yoritomo (1147–1199) became Japan's first permanent shogun in 1192. Three generals had previously held the title during wartime, but Yoritomo was the first to pass the office on to his sons. He did not simply influence the Imperial court, he formed an entirely new government.

Yoritomo created military, feudal, and judicial systems that lasted almost seven hundred years, yet most Japanese ignore his achievements and remember him for his ingratitude and ruthlessness toward his youngest half brother, Yoshitsune (1159–1189). Although Yoshitsune won three quick battles against steep odds, his lasting influence on Japan's history is nil; even so it is the young Yoshitsune who is the dashing hero of countless stories.

The shogun's cunning wife, Hojo Masako (1157–1225), maneuvered her way through a maze of intrigue after her husband's death and kept his government strong. In spite of this, many Japanese remember her chiefly for a single outburst of jealousy.

Yoritomo was born in or near Kyoto in 1147, the third son in a family of eight children. His mother died young. His father led a branch of the Minamoto clan and married again, producing three more sons, including Yoshitsune, the hero of many myths and plays.

During the eleventh and twelfth centuries the Imperial government was too weak to keep order in the countryside. Landowners looked to local warriors to protect them, and warriors formed alliances to increase their strength. Gradually the rival Minamoto and Taira families had extended branches throughout Japan, and were known as the "teeth and claws" of the Imperial court.

In 1156 an emperor's death led to a war, and noblemen used branches of the Minamoto and Taira clans to fight for their claims. It was a turning point. Power in Japan had shifted from the graceful aristocrats of Kyoto to the local warrior chiefs who could raise armies on short notice. Yoritomo was only nine. He had learned to ride a horse and shoot a bow and arrow, but was too young to accompany his father, Yoshitomo, when he led two hundred horsemen into war. Although the father was victorious, the court gave the most land and best titles to the rival Taira family.

The victorious Yoshitomo resented the court's ill treatment of his men and, in 1160, rebelled. Yoritomo was then twelve, old enough to join his father and two older brothers in battle. Like other warriors, he wore silk, armor made of metal and leather plates, and a helmet with a small flag in the back. At the start of a battle, warriors shouted out the brave deeds of their ancestors before fighting an enemy one-on-one.

The more numerous Taira clan completely defeated the Minamoto horsemen, dispersing them in every direction. Yoshitomo fled Kyoto with just seven men, including his three sons. One of Yoritomo's brothers was so badly wounded that at his own request his father killed him to prevent his capture by the enemy. Another soldier turned traitor and killed Yoshitomo while he was taking a bath. The oldest brother rode back to Kyoto to kill a Taira leader in revenge, and died fighting a horde of warriors.

Young Yoritomo lost his way in the mountains, and rode alone until he was captured by a Taira warrior. The chief of the Taira family, Kiyomori, spared Yoritomo's life because he reminded the chief's stepmother of a son who had died young, and she begged Kiyomori not to kill him. Kiyomori exiled Yoritomo to the Izu peninsula instead. His mercy proved to be a fatal mistake.

Yoritomo's young half brother, Yoshitsune, was an infant at this time; his mother, the beautiful Lady Tokiwa, had three sons. It is part of Japanese lore that after her husband's defeat she fled Kyoto through moonlit snow, holding Yoshitsune tightly to her breast while two frightened little boys clutched at her skirts. They were captured by Taira warriors a few days later, and once again Kiyomori showed mercy and let the boys live.

When Yoshitsune was six he began studying at a Buddhist temple in the mountains north of Kyoto. At eleven he discovered his family history and, some say, immediately vowed to avenge his father. He spent long hours fencing and became a fine swordsman. According to legend, a spirit trained the boy each night.

When Yoshitsune grew up, one of his retainers was a man named Musashibo Benkei. Nothing is known about Benkei in real life, but in legend he is as famous as his master. According to myth, Benkei was a huge warrior-monk who robbed 999 people of their swords before meeting Yoshitsune on a bridge in Kyoto. As they began to fight, Yoshitsune made the contest more interesting by throwing away his sword; he defeated the powerful monk using only his fan as a weapon. Awed by Yoshitsune's prowess, Benkei gave up being a sword thief and became the young man's loyal retainer.

Yoshitsune was a short, handsome youth of slight build. When he was fifteen he left his mountain temple and wandered about Japan, working as a laborer. Eventually he accompanied a gold merchant on his way to the mines of Mutsu, a province far to the northeast. There Yoshitsune met Fujiwara Hidehara, a nobleman who liked him immediately and brought him into his home. For five years Hidehara was like a father to Yoshitsune.

By contrast, no legends surround the older brother's exile. Kiyomori sent Yoritomo to the castle of a minor Taira chief named Hojo Tokimasa, and there he impressed Tokimasa with his intelligence, ambition, and self-control. He spent time fencing and became an unusually good bowman. He also enjoyed spectacular views of Mt. Fuji when he went riding.

Yoritomo kept up with politics. He followed news from Kyoto closely and held long conversations with local warriors, many of whom were worried that their land was not sufficiently well protected from rival warriors. Like his brother, Yoritomo was short and handsome. He moved with dignity and spoke in a clear, articulate voice. He was skillful at writing verses, and once seduced a young noblewoman, who became pregnant.

Around 1175 the lord of the castle, Tokimasa, moved to Kyoto for three years to fulfill a duty to guard the emperor. While he was away, his daughter, Hojo Masako, and Yoritomo became close friends. Masako was attractive, though not beautiful, and highly intelligent. Because her mother had died young, Masako had spent her teens bringing up a younger brother. Now she was twenty and still single, which was unusual in the twelfth century.

Yoritomo was thirty years old and still in exile, not much of a catch. The only reason Masako had to marry him was love, and this was not good enough to suit her father, who forbade the marriage.

On a dark night in 1177 or 1178, Masako eloped with Yoritomo. After marrying, the lovers hid in a mountain temple until Tokimasa's anger cooled. When it did, he consented; he had always liked Yoritomo anyhow. The couple had two sons and two daughters.

In 1179 Taira no Kiyomori became a dictator when he placed the "retired" emperor under house arrest. Between the eleventh and the fourteenth centuries an older, retired emperor always held the real power at court while a younger emperor was a mere figurehead. Kiyomori replaced court officials with relatives, and even had his two-year-old grandson, Antoku, crowned emperor in 1180.

The aristocracy hated Kiyomori for dominating their court so openly. Warriors disliked him because his many relatives had become governors of provinces and diverted money from the countryside to the capital. The Taira family became especially unpopular in the eastern plain that surrounds Tokyo Bay.

In 1180 an Imperial prince authorized the Minamoto family to "pursue and destroy" Kiyomori in order to end the retired emperor's house arrest. Yoritomo spent several months recruiting warriors, including his own father-in-law, Hojo Tokimasa, who broke with Kiyomori and became Yoritomo's ally.

By November Yoritomo established a headquarters at the seaside village of Kamakura, near modern Yokohama. For 148 years, from 1185 to 1333, it became the military capital of Japan.

Yoritomo bypassed the government in Kyoto and duplicated many of its administrative functions. Using the prince's warrant against Kiyomori as his legal authority, he boldly claimed jurisdiction over the entire eastern plain and offered every warrior—even his enemies—a chance to become his vassal. He confirmed each vassal's title to land with a written deed, and backed up the document with the might of his army.

In essence, what Yoritomo started was a secession movement of eastern landowners against Kiyomori's government in Kyoto. But unlike previous rebels, Yoritomo was in no hurry to march to the capital. Instead, he recruited scholars as administrators and solidified his rule in the East. One branch of the new government was the *samurai dokoro*, which literally means "servant's room," because a samurai is "one who serves." It was actually an office for military affairs, and it oversaw the reward, promotion, and punishment of samurai warriors.

In 1180 a large Taira army advanced to the Fuji River, but when the soldiers saw they were outnumbered they turned around and rode home. Never again would a Taira army march east. Kiyomori died the next year, leaving not one son who was a good general. More significant, Japan suffered one of the worst famines in its history in 1181 and 1182. Hundreds of thousands of people starved to death in western Japan, and for two years fighting stopped because lords did not have enough rice to feed their troops.

Yoritomo's wife, Masako, gave birth to their first son, Yoriie, in 1181, but she did not raise him. By custom, the honor of bringing up a lord's son was given to a trusted vassal who supervised everything from breast-feeding to military training. Unfortunately, Yoriie's new family rarely disciplined him, so the boy became spoiled.

While Masako was pregnant, Yoritomo openly began an affair with a young woman named Lady Kame. When Masako heard about it, she was furious. She ordered an army to destroy Lady Kame's house, and this is the deed for which she is primarily remembered today.

In fact, destroying a mistress's house was then acceptable conduct. The purpose was to give warning. Masako did not want Lady Kame or any other woman to bear Yoritomo a son. The affair could continue, but in the future Yoritomo and Lady Kame would have to be discreet.

In July 1183, when soldiers had rice again, troops led by Yoritomo's cousin Yoshinaka advanced to the outskirts of Kyoto. Taking advantage of the confusion, the retired emperor, Go-Shirakawa, escaped from his house arrest and joined the Minamotos. This gave Yoritomo the legitimacy he needed to attack the Taira clan directly, and to win over neutral warriors. The Taira family abandoned Kyoto and fled west along the Inland Sea, taking Antoku, the boy emperor, with them. A thirteenth-century book about their retreat, *The Tale of the Heike*, is a classic of Japanese literature.

With Kyoto in his grasp, Yoshinaka was no longer content to be his cousin Yoritomo's vassal. He asked Taira generals if they wanted to combine forces against Yoritomo, and entered Kyoto with his rowdy troops in December. When Yoritomo learned of his cousin's treachery, he sent two of his half brothers, Yoshitsune and Noriyori, to attack Yoshinaka's army.

In February 1184 the horsemen forded a swollen river in Kyoto and surprised Yoshinaka, routing his forces. The brothers spent just one week in the capital city, then rode west to Ichinotani, near the modern city of Kobe, where the Taira forces had camped on a narrow beach protected by a high, steep cliff.

Before dawn on March 20, 1184, Noriyori placed his troops at one end of the beach, while Yoshitsune and a few dozen others rode to the top of the cliff and drove a herd of deer over the edge. As the animals safely descended the precipice, Yoshitsune watched them closely. Then at dawn he led his horsemen down the cliff the same way and started a fire on the other side of the army camp. The Taira warriors were trapped by Noriyori's army, the fire, and the sea. Panic-stricken, they ran for their boats and sailed west to the island of Shikoku. It was a brilliant victory.

A year later, in March 1185, Yoshitsune led a surpise attack on Shikoku. Sailing through gale-force winds, he and about one hundred men landed at Yashima and set fire to peasants' homes to make their army appear bigger than it was. The ruse worked. The frightened Taira warriors had prepared only for an attack from the sea. Once again they ran for their boats and sailed west, this time to the northern tip of Kyushu.

Yoshitsune's victory convinced many lords along the Inland Sea to break with the Taira family. Some of them lent ships and seamen to Yoshitsune, and in a month he had assembled a navy of about five hundred boats, about equal in size to the fleet of the Taira clan. Yoshitsune also persuaded several Taira sea captains to change sides.

The climactic battle between the Taira and Minamoto families began on the morning of April 25, 1185, in the narrow strait between the islands of Honshu and Kyushu. As thousands of arrows flew from one boat to another, Yoshitsune reminded his archers to aim for the enemy steersmen. He also bribed an enemy sailor to tell him which Taira boats held warriors and which ones did not. When it was clear to everyone that the Taira clan had lost, many Taira warriors jumped in the sea with their armor and drowned. Kiyomori's widow jumped overboard with her eight-year-old grandson, Emperor Antoku, and they drowned together.

According to *The Tale of Heike*, Yoshitsune outran an especially fierce Taira warrior by leaping from one boat to another. This same fighter, when all was lost, challenged three Minamoto samurai to a duel. In an instant he kicked one warrior overboard, grabbed the other two, and jumped into the sea, drowning three of Yoshitsune's soldiers in the last seconds of his life.

Yoritomo now ruled western as well as eastern Japan. Unlike Kiyomori, he showed no mercy toward his younger captives. Ruthlessly he ordered all Taira boys put to death. He also refused to reward or even thank his victorious brother. Yoshitsune was Japan's greatest general in centuries, but for three weeks he waited in vain at the outskirts of Kamakura. The suspicious Yoritomo would not even let Yoshitsune inside the city.

Yoshitsune had made a terrible mistake in the spring of 1184, after his first victory at the cliffs of Ichinotani, when he let the retired emperor honor him with the titles of deputy commander of the Imperial police and lieutenant of the palace guards. Yoritomo had specifically ordered his vassals not to accept any titles from the Imperial court without his prior approval, and Yoshitsune— whether out of naivete or arrogance—had violated this command.

Yoritomo demanded that his vassals be loyal only to him. Yoritomo knew that if he allowed his soldiers to accept Imperial honors and salaries, there would be no end to intrigue, and no limit to the court's influence over his new government. The wily retired emperor, Go-Shirakawa, knew this, and that is precisely why he gave Yoshitsune the titles. Yoritomo was also angry when Yoshitsune married the daughter of a Taira chief without his prior approval.

Yoshitsune wrote a letter to his older brother pledging him his loyalty, but he also argued that the Imperial titles were an honor to the Minamoto family. Yoritomo responded by dispossessing his brother of twenty-four estates. Yoritomo also received slanderous reports that Yoshitsune was plotting against him, and on the basis of these reports sent an assassin to kill him. The assassin was caught, but Yoshitsune knew that another attempt on his life was inevitable, and went into hiding.

Yoritomo began a nationwide manhunt, and imposed a tax of two percent of the rice crop to pay for a door-to-door and field-to-field search for his brother. To enforce the tax, the retired emperor gave Yoritomo the authority to install a police commissioner in every province, and a revenue collector on nearly every estate. From then on Japan's law enforcement and taxation would be in the hands of the shogun rather than of the court. The court, without an army of its own, was in no position to refuse Yoritomo's requests.

Yoshitsune moved from one hiding place to the next, sheltered by admirers. He stayed at several temples and probably also at the Imperial Palace. But Yoritomo's spies caught Yoshitsune's retainers one by one, and in 1186 they also captured his pregnant mistress, Shizuka, a dancer of extraordinary beauty. According to legend, Shizuka gave a performance for Yoritomo and enraged him by defiantly singing of her love for Yoshitsune. Masako, however, admired her courage. When Shizuka gave birth to a boy, Yoritomo ordered him killed immediately.

In 1187 Yoshitsune fled to Mutsu, the northeastern province where he had lived as a teenager. Sometimes he disguised himself as a laborer. In the most famous legend of all about Yoshitsune, he dressed like a porter as they approached a check-point, while Benkei, the warrior-monk, pretended to be his master.

Despite the disguise, a guard recognized Yoshitsune. Desperate, Benkei reacted quickly. "So he looks like Yoshitsune, does he?" Benkei yelled as he grabbed a walking stick. "It's been one thing after another with you lately. Here, how do you like this!" Benkei asked as he beat Yoshitsune mercilessly.

The guard decided that he was mistaken and let the two men pass; he knew that no servant would dare to beat a master so cruelly. Later, when all was safe, Benkei fell to his knees and tearfully begged Yoshitsune for forgiveness, while Yoshitsune, also in tears, thanked Benkei for saving his life.

When Yoritomo heard that his brother was in Mutsu, he was pleased. He had wanted to attack the province, which was still independent. Now that Mutsu's lord was hiding Yoshitsune, Yoritomo had an excuse. Buddhist priests, however, considered 1188 an unlucky year for war, so Yoritomo waited.

By this time Yoshitsune's old friend, Fujiwara Hidehara, had died at ninety, and his sons were cool to the idea of harboring a fugitive. On June 15, 1189, Yasuhira, Mutsu's new lord, attacked Yoshitsune's home with hundreds of horsemen. The legendary Benkei is said to have killed dozens of men and incurred many arrow wounds to buy his master the time to die with honor. Yoshitsune killed his wife, his three-year-old daughter, and himself. He was just thirty.

Yasuhira's men put Yoshitsune's head in a black lacquer box and filled it with sake, which served as a preservative. For a month they carried the box to Kamakura, where the head was inspected by one of Yoritomo's top generals.

Yasuhira's gift did him no good. In the summer Yoritomo attacked him any-way, cynically using the death of his brother as an excuse to conquer Mutsu and its gold mines.

Yoshitsune managed to be the subject of one last legend. In the late nine-teenth century, as Japanese investment in Manchuria increased, a story spread that Yasuhira had delivered someone else's head to Kamakura. Yoshitsune had escaped to Mongolia, where he began a new life as Genghis Khan.

In 1190 Yoritomo returned to Kyoto for the first time in thirty years. The retired emperor, Go-Shirakawa, gave him several prestigious titles, but after politely accepting each title Yoritomo resigned all of them just days later to show his complete independence from the court.

When Go-Shirakawa died in 1192 his successor gave Yoritomo the supreme rank of *sei-i tai-shogun*, literally "barbarian-subduing great general," but perhaps closer in meaning to "commander in chief." Yoritomo kept this title because it solidified his status as the leading warrior in Japan. Japan continued to be ruled by shoguns for the next 675 years.

In 1192 Yoritomo and Masako had a second son, Sanetomo. This time Masako chose her sister to bring up the boy, which meant that she would have a hand in raising him too.

With his power secure, Yoritomo worked to keep his government honest. His law courts won everyone's admiration because of the impartiality of their judgments. Yoritomo also spent more time hunting. The expeditions were a discreet way for him to be with his mistress, Lady Kame.

Early in 1199 Yoritomo fell off his horse and died, probably of a cerebral hemorrhage. He was fifty-one. Masako took vows as a Buddhist nun, and at seventeen her eldest son, Yoriie, assumed control of the government.

Yoriie quickly became unpopular. He openly favored the Hiki family, who had raised him, and spent too much time playing *kemari*, a kind of kick ball. Once he even planned to kill a vassal because he desired the man's concubine, but Masako put an end to the plot with a letter that said, "Aim your first arrow at me."

In 1202 the retired emperor appointed Yoriie shogun, making the office hereditary for the first time. The following year Yoriie became ill, and a power struggle began between the Hiki and Hojo families. Hojo warriors ambushed and killed most of the Hikis, and Yoriie, who had sided with the Hikis, had to resign as shogun in favor of his younger brother, Sanetomo. A year later Yoriie was murdered.

Masako's father, Hojo Tokimasa, became the regent of his grandson Sanetomo in 1203, and the most powerful man in Japan. But two years later Tokimasa plotted to kill his grandson and shift power to his family by his second wife, Lady Maki. When Masako discovered the plot, she and her brother, Hojo Yoshitoki, forced their father to resign as regent and exiled him to Izu.

Finally, things stablized. Yoshitoki served as regent for nineteen years, from 1205 to 1224. But Masako was equally powerful, and became known as "the nun shogun."

The indirectness of Masako's power was uniquely Japanese. The emperor was a puppet of the retired emperor's, whose powerless court was dominated by the shogun, who was a mere boy led by the Hojo regent, who in turn was influenced by his sister Masako. The complex system worked because the Hojos were talented administrators, and because they did not alienate other families by assuming grand titles. The Hojos were always careful to rule in the name of the Minamoto clan, and did so for 130 years.

Sanetomo was a disappointment to his mother, Masako. Even as a grown man he was content to be a puppet shogun and spent most of his time playing kick ball and writing poetry. In 1219 he was stabbed to death by his nephew Kogyo, who avenged his father Yoriie's death and declared himself the new shogun. Sanetomo's guards killed him immediately, but Masako, whose daughters had died of illnesses, had no more descendants.

She chose a one-year-old boy from the ancient Fujiwara family to be the next shogun, and took care of the baby herself. This was how the Hojo family held power for the next century. They would install a young boy as shogun, rule in his name, then dismiss him when he reached his mid- or late twenties.

In June 1221 Retired Emperor Go-Toba, tired of being powerless, declared the Hojos to be outlaws and called on warriors everywhere to rise up in rebellion. Masako promptly summoned all the shogun's vassals to Kamakura and gave a stirring speech urging an immediate attack on the retired emperor. She called his proclamation a slur on the good name of the Minamoto family and reminded everyone how much they owed her deceased husband, Yoritomo. She added that if any warriors were thinking of joining the retired emperor, he should kill her first.

With almost 100,000 soldiers, the Hojo forces heavily outnumbered Go-Toba's army. The retired emperor was exiled to an island near Okinawa, and his top generals were executed. The government confiscated over three thousand Imperial estates and transferred them to the next retired emperor, but reserved the right to confiscate the estates again at any time. The Hojos also appointed revenue collectors to manage these estates, and Masako personally supervised the appointments. Finally, the Hojos kept two permanent armies north and south of Kyoto.

In 1224 Masako's brother Yoshitoki died. Masako chose his son to be the new regent, and he served with distinction for eighteen years. Before he was formally appointed, however, Masako thwarted one last plot by courageously going to the castle of a key conspirator and asking him in person whose side he was on. The wavering lord, face-to-face with this indomitable woman, abandoned his conspiracy and pledged Masako his loyalty.

With her family's power finally safe from all challenges, Hojo Masako died in August 1225 at the age of sixty-eight. A woman so strong that some say she never shed a tear, Masako prevented other families from destroying her husband's government. She strengthened the shogunate and made it last. The Hojo family ran Japan for a century after Masako's death, and even after they were overthrown in 1333, the military, feudal, and judicial institutions that Yoritomo and Masako created endured.

Few figures in history are more important and less loved than cold, ruthless Yoritomo. But most historians agree that his government of warriors was more honest and better organized than the Imperial government that preceded it. Titles to land were more secure; administrators were more just. This is one reason shoguns ruled Japan until the late nineteenth century.

If Yoritomo had allowed his appealing brother Yoshitsune to keep his Imperial titles, other warriors would also have succumbed to the court's corrupting influence, and the independence and integrity of the new military government might have suffered.

Japan's storytellers would have suffered too. Yoshitsune is the supreme example of a fallen hero, the subject of seventy kabuki plays, twelve *no* plays, ten puppet plays by Chikamatsu, Japan's greatest playwright, and dozens of movies, television shows, and even comic books. And his brother Yoritomo, in spite of his enormous contribution to Japanese history, is nearly always portrayed as a villain.

17
Oda Nobunaga
The Warrior Who United Half of Japan

EVERY JAPANESE schoolchild learns this simple verse that sums up the lives of the men who unified Japan:

Oda Nobunaga pounded the rice,
Hideyoshi baked the cake,
And Tokugawa Ieyasu ate it.

The first leader, Oda Nobunaga, began unifying Japan in the 1560s. A ruthless warrior, he massacred over fifty thousand people and dominated half of Japan before he was killed by a disloyal commander.

The second great unifier, Hideyoshi, was a brilliant peasant who became Nobunaga's top general. With a little force and a lot of diplomacy, he completed Japan's unification in 1590.

The third man, Tokugawa Ieyasu, outlived his two contemporaries. He became shogun in 1603, and his descendants ruled Japan for almost three centuries—until 1868. (See chapters eighteen and nineteen.)

When Oda Nobunaga (1534–1582) was born, Japan had lost the unity it had enjoyed in previous centuries. Following a terrible civil war in the 1460s and 1470s, Japan had split into sixty-six separate provinces, each governed by a regional lord called a *daimyo*. These *daimyo*s were still at war, and during their battles countless farms and villages went up in flames.

Nobunaga grew up in a castle in Nagoya, now Japan's fourth largest city. His father was lord of the castle and one of the three chiefs of the Oda family, rulers of Owari province.

By all accounts Nobunaga was unusually handsome and graceful. He had personal tutors in the arts of war and in the Chinese classics, and exasperated them because he was arrogant and irreverent. One tutor even committed suicide in an attempt to shock Nobunaga into taking a more respectful attitude toward his duties.

Nobunaga also dressed strangely. He wore short sleeves in odd colors and had knickknacks hanging from his belt. His moods shifted so quickly that some people thought he was crazy. It is possible that Nobunaga merely acted the part of the fool to prevent older cousins from seeing him as a rival for power.

At fourteen Nobunaga married the daughter of the lord of Mino province. It was a political marriage lacking in love. Three years later, in 1551, when his father died, Nobunaga wore casual clothes to the funeral, and flippantly tossed incense at his father's corpse when he should have burned it slowly. Nobunaga cared little for the opinion of others.

Gradually, with the help of several of his father's samurai, Nobunaga built a force of about a thousand men. They spent many days in training, jousting and fording rivers, and the drills paid off. Nobunaga's army repulsed two attacks by relatives and another by a bordering province.

When he was twenty-one Nobunaga attacked his chief rival within his family by storming his castle. Two years later a younger brother challenged his leadership. Pretending to be deathly ill, Nobunaga invited the brother to come to his bedside to receive his blessing as the new leader of the Oda family. When the brother naively left his castle to make the visit, Nobunaga had him killed.

Nobunaga's power was not truly secure until 1560. In that year the Imagawa family of Totomi province amassed a huge army of 25,000 men and began to march to Kyoto in a bid for supreme power. The army took some of Nobunaga's minor forts along the way, and relaxed in a narrow valley to celebrate their victories. With only 3,000 men, Nobunaga mounted a surprise attack during a driving rainstorm. They trapped the army in the muddy ravine and cut off heads right and left—including that of the Imagawa family chief.

Nobunaga was suddenly a national figure. He had defeated the largest army in Japan, and neighboring *daimyo*s clamored to make alliances. Tokugawa Ieyasu, lord of Mikawa province, married his son to Nobunaga's daughter, sealing an alliance that lasted twenty years. Nobunaga also gave his sister, O-ichi, said to be the most beautiful woman in Japan, in marriage to Asai, lord of Omi province.

Nobunaga was now the leader of a powerful coalition, but this was only the beginning of his ambitions. He adopted a motto, "The realm, ruled by might," and increased his army to ten times its former size. Nobunaga recruited peasants as foot soldiers to carry spears and lances, and promoted them quickly if they showed talent. One peasant, Toyotomi Hideyoshi, began work as a servant in 1558 but became Nobunaga's top general in little more than a decade.

In 1565 a local Kyoto warlord killed the shogun and put a three-year-old boy in his place. Three years later, at the invitation of the emperor, Nobunaga marched to Kyoto with thirty thousand well-disciplined troops, drove that warlord and his little shogun out of the city, and installed the dead shogun's younger brother, Yoshiaki, as the new shogun. Nobunaga also repaired the palace of the impoverished emperor and gave him land and money.

Ever since 1192, when Minamoto no Yoritomo had become Japan's first permanent shogun, the emperor had been just a figurehead. But after a civil war in the 1330s the shoguns had become nearly as weak as the emperor. Still, a shogun had the power to appoint judges and administrators, and the prestige to mediate disputes between *daimyos*.

For a while, Shogun Yoshiaki was Nobunaga's puppet. He even signed a document giving Nobunaga the power to issue orders in the shogun's name without consulting him. At age thirty-five, Nobunaga was the most powerful man in Japan.

A Jesuit missionary from Portugal named Luis Frois met Nobunaga several times and gave this eyewitness account in 1569:

> A tall man, lean, scantly bearded, with a clear voice, greatly addicted to military exercises . . . contemptuous of all the nobles of Japan whom he addresses brusquely over his shoulder as if they were inferiors. . . .
>
> He scorns the Kami and Buddhas . . . stating unequivocally that there is no Creator, no immortality of the soul, and no life after death.

Nobunaga, however, liked the Jesuits. They shared his contempt for Buddhism, and they gave him interesting gifts: maps, tiger skins, magnifying glasses, and, best of all, new and improved guns.

The first matchlocks in Japan came in 1543 when three Portuguese traders landed on the island of Tanega, just south of Kyushu. Of the many items the Portuguese offered for trade, it was the "iron pipes" that fascinated the Japanese the most. The lord of Tanega bought two matchlocks and immediately gave them to his blacksmiths. They copied the guns, but had trouble getting the gunpowder to explode in the proper part of the barrel. A few months later, when a second and much larger Portuguese ship arrived, a beautiful Japanese girl was given in marriage to a Portuguese gunsmith. He stayed behind and taught the Japanese the finer points of making guns, and before long they were making several matchlocks a week.

The port of Sakai, on Osaka Bay, soon became the gun-manufacturing center of Japan. It was a free city run by its merchants until 1569, but in that year Nobunaga marched south from Kyoto and put the city under his direct rule.

Nobunaga was a skillful administrator as well as a warrior. He made life easier for merchants by standardizing coins and measurements, and by exempting merchants from the "moratoriums" that lords and officials often declared to cancel their own debts. Nobunaga also abolished toll barriers in all his domains, and eliminated guild monopolies in several of his cities. As Nobunaga acquired more territory, Japanese merchants enjoyed an increasingly large area of free trade.

Nobunaga bought thousands of muskets from the merchants of Sakai, and was the first *daimyo* to have his men fire in rotation. Soldiers at that time had to load powder down the gun barrel, which took fifteen seconds, more than enough time to get killed. Nobunaga trained his troops to form alternating rows. As one row of men bent down to reload, a second row fired guns, and a third row took aim. The barrage was devastating. In some battles Nobunaga's armed peasants massacred waves of samurai swordsmen.

In 1570 Nobunaga was attacked by his brother-in-law, Asai, who broke with Nobunaga to help his neighboring lord, Asakura. With the peasant Hideyoshi commanding one of his armies, Nobunaga defeated Asai and Asakura but could not annihilate them. They had retreated to Mt. Hiei, home of Enryakuji, the oldest, largest, and most sacred Tendai Buddhist monastery in Japan.

In the 1500s Buddhist monks were not the saintly men leading simple lives of prayer that we think of today. Many were armed, wealthy, and deeply involved in political affairs. Nobunaga hated Buddhist monks with the same intensity with which his contemporary Henry VIII in England hated Catholic priests. Like Henry VIII, Nobunaga also coveted the priests' extensive landholdings, and resented their use of religion to disguise a pursuit of power.

Nobunaga warned the monks at Enryakuji that he would burn their mountain if they did not stay neutral, but the priests were defiant. They hated Nobunaga because he had confiscated some of their land and threatened to tax what they still had. They also did not believe that anyone, even the "demon king," would dare to burn an eight-hundred-year-old temple city. The gun-toting monks skirmished with Nobunaga, enabling Asai and Asakura to escape to their home castles. Nobunaga's revenge was terrible.

In the middle of a windy night in October 1571, Nobunaga's soldiers surrounded Mt. Hiei and set fire to its dry fields. Within minutes enormous flames engulfed the entire mountain, burning to death over eight thousand warrior-monks and several thousand women, servants, and children. The inferno also destroyed over two thousand homes, schools, temples, and libraries.

All Japan shuddered at Nobunaga's destruction. No one else would have been so ruthless. Even today the burning of the Enryakuji monastery is the first thing Japanese call to mind when they think of Nobunaga. Yet the flames had the effect he desired. The majority of Japan's terrified monks stopped maintaining armies, stayed out of politics, and accepted a loss of land.

One Buddhist sect that continued to defy Nobunaga also went up in flames in 1574. Another was mowed down in a wave of gunfire the following year. But the Honganji monastery on Osaka Bay, the last one to resist, enjoyed naval support from western *daimyo*s. Nobunaga could not take the fortress until 1580, when he destroyed six hundred enemy boats with seven iron-plated ships that preceded by three centuries the iron-plated *Monitor* and *Merrimac* of the American Civil War.

In most of Japan the Buddhists lost their power in 1573, when Nobunaga routed the armies of Asai and Asakura. The two *daimyo*s killed themselves to avoid capture, but their heads were recovered and Nobunaga had their skulls lacquered with gold and silver to use as drinking cups.

Asai's widow, O-ichi, returned to her brother Nobunaga's castle with her three daughters. Her infant son was executed. Still strikingly beautiful, O-ichi was married to Shibata Katsuie, one of Nobunaga's top generals.

For several years Shogun Yoshiaki had been in secret communication with Asai, Asakura, the monks at Enryakuji, the *daimyo* of Kai province, and many other opponents of Nobunaga's throughout Japan. Yoshiaki hated being Nobunaga's puppet, and dreamed of uniting his enemies.

Nobunaga's excellent spies *(ninja)* kept him fully informed of Yoshiaki's activities, and by 1573 he had had enough. Nobunaga and his army reentered Kyoto, expelled Yoshiaki from his palace, and levied taxes on the city to pay for the expedition. Many of Kyoto's richest citizens were friends of the shogun's and refused to pay the tax, but when Nobunaga started burning wealthy neighborhoods one by one, they hurriedly complied.

Nobunaga let Yoshiaki wander around Japan, and for the next thirty years Kyoto had no shogun. The emperor offered to appoint Nobunaga shogun, but the warrior declined. He had no interest in titles.

Nobunaga did have an interest in obedience. He once sent regulations to General Shibata Katsuie that concluded:

> You must resolve to do everything as I say. For all that, do not flatter me when you feel that I am unreasonable. . . . And bear me no evil thought behind my back. Your feelings toward me must be such that you do not even point your feet in the direction where I am.

Central Japan was now at peace, and Nobunaga decided to build himself a magnificent seven-story castle on a high hill in the town of Azuchi, forty miles northeast of Kyoto. Completed in 1579, many of the interior rooms were painted by the finest artist of his time, Kano Eitoku. Each room had a different theme, among them falcons—Nobunaga loved the sport of falconry—horses, wild geese, pine trees, dragons and tigers in combat, Chinese scholars, and, ironically, Buddha and his disciples.

There was also a room painted in gold leaf for tea ceremonies. Nobunaga was an expert in the tea ceremony, trained by the great tea master Sen no Rikyu (see chapter ten). He also collected rare tea utensils, and sometimes gave his generals famous bowls or kettles in gratitude for military victories.

Perhaps the height of Nobunaga's glory came on a bright spring day in Kyoto in 1581. More than half the city came to see twenty-thousand horsemen, gaily dressed in brilliant colors, fly in full gallop past the emperor's reviewing stand.

One general who was not at this parade was Hideyoshi. In 1577 Nobunaga had ordered him to attack Harima province in western Japan, but the western *daimyo*s, united under the leadership of the Mori family, had as many soldiers and guns as Nobunaga. For several years there was a wary, cautious stalemate.

Finally, late in the spring of 1582, the Mori armies approached a castle in Bitchu province. Hideyoshi was outnumbered and sent his fastest rider to ask Nobunaga for more troops.

Nobunaga decided to head west himself, and commanded his best generals to join him. Along the way he spent two nights at a temple in Kyoto to make arrangements for the climactic battle, which never took place.

At dawn on June 21, 1582, one of his generals, Akechi Mitsuhide, did not lead his ten thousand soldiers west, as Nobunaga had ordered, but attacked Nobunaga instead. It was a complete surprise. Nobunaga had less than a hundred men to defend him. Escape was impossible.

For a while the great warrior joined in the battle, but after he was wounded by an arrow or spear he retreated to a locked room and probably commited seppuku, ritual suicide. He was forty-eight. The temple caught fire and burned completely. No part of Nobunaga's body was ever found.

Mitsuhide's army also killed the eldest of Nobunaga's four sons, and a few days later looted his castle at Azuchi, which a mob subsequently burned.

Although Mitsuhide was the most intellectual of Nobunaga's generals, he never explained why he attacked his lord. He did not have time. Within eleven days Hideyoshi's army rushed back to Kyoto, hunted him down, and took his head.

Some people say Mitsuhide was angry because Nobunaga had once sent his mother as a hostage to another province to cement an alliance, and she was executed when the alliance came to an end. Others say Mitsuhide wanted to rule Japan himself. Many Japanese believe that Mitsuhide simply decided that one man had acquired too much power. Like Brutus in ancient Rome, Mitsuhide may have felt that the national interest required him to kill a tyrant.

By conquest or alliance, Oda Nobunaga ruled thirty-one of Japan's sixty-six provinces when he died, and was poised to conquer many more. For a feudal lord, Nobunaga had a surprisingly modern outlook. He revolutionized warfare, broke the power of the Buddhist monks, expanded free trade, ignored titles, and gave peasants opportunities.

Ironically, this fierce warrior who had no qualms about burning thousands of women and children brought peace to a nation racked by two centuries of war. It was a fearful peace, however, based on one man's rule, and when Nobunaga died, even his allies were relieved.

18

Toyotomi Hideyoshi

The Peasant Who United All of Japan

HIDEYOSHI'S LIFE is Japan's greatest rags-to-riches story. Born a peasant, he became the ruler of Japan. His rise is even more astonishing than Abraham Lincoln's ascent from log cabin to the White House, because Lincoln was born in a democracy, while Hideyoshi grew up in a feudal society where ancestry was all-important. A brilliant general, wise statesman, and enthusiastic patron of the arts, Hideyoshi completed Japan's unification in 1590, then began a terrible war against Korea. He also made changes in Japanese government and society that lasted for centuries.

Hideyoshi (1536–1598) was born in a village just outside modern Nagoya, the son of a farmer and part-time soldier who had fought for Oda Nobunaga's family. He did not acquire his family name, Toyotomi, until he was almost fifty. As a child, he was so short and so ugly that his friends called him "Monkey." When he was seven, his father died, possibly of a war injury. For years he and his sister lived only on what their mother could grow. Their meals were rice, bean paste, dried vegetables, and an occasional frog, if he could catch one.

After his mother remarried, Hideyoshi learned to read and write at a nearby Buddhist temple. He worked for a blacksmith, a potter and other craftsmen, but lost interest in each job after just a few months. Eventually he left home because he did not get along with his stepfather. He wandered from one province to another, working at odd jobs and learning about human nature.

At fifteen Hideyoshi became a servant in a castle of the Imagawa family. He worked hard at menial tasks and took the opportunity to learn kendo (fencing with a bamboo sword) and to read Chinese classics such as Sun Tzu's *The Art of War*.

After seven years Hideyoshi decided his prospects for advancement would be best in his home province of Owari. There the young lord Oda Nobunaga, who despised rank and titles, promoted even peasants on the basis of merit. In 1558 Hideyoshi left the Imagawas to begin work as a servant at Nobunaga's castle.

Twenty-two years old and ambitious, Hideyoshi worked unusually hard at all his tasks, whether he was grooming horses, carrying armor, or cooking food. He woke up earlier than his colleagues, worked later, and kept things cleaner. In the winter he even kept the sandals of his superior warm by putting them inside his kimono and holding them tightly against his chest.

Nobunaga took a liking to his witty and cheerful young "monkey." He gave him more responsibility and was not disappointed. Hideyoshi saved Nobunaga money by making the burning of firewood at his castle more efficient, and saved his lord time by speeding up the repair of castle walls. Nobunaga rewarded Hideyoshi with a higher salary, a house of his own, and the chance to command some troops.

At twenty-five Hideyoshi had enough status to marry the girl he loved, Nene, the sixteen-year-old daughter of one of Nobunaga's archers. Pretty and intelligent, Nene could easily have married someone more handsome or of higher rank than Hideyoshi. Probably she chose him because he was more dynamic and amusing than her other, more conventional suitors.

Hideyoshi loved Nene all his life, and even wrote her letters from the battle-field. But after he became a famous general he was often unfaithful. Nene accepted this, partly because her friendship with Hideyoshi continued to be warm, and partly because of her inability to have a child. When Hideyoshi's favorite concubine gave birth to a son, Nene raised him as if he were her own.

Hideyoshi's talent was not fully appreciated by Nobunaga until 1567, when during a battle Hideyoshi and his men built a fortress just a few miles from an important enemy castle. Samurai warriors would have refused to haul the lumber necessary to make this fortress, but the lower-class fighters Hideyoshi brought to the battle were accustomed to heavy lifting. They worked day and night and completed the fort in a week. By the time the enemy attacked it, it was too late, the fortress was secure. The fort gave Nobunaga the protection he needed to storm his rival's castle, and with the castle in his possession he conquered the entire province.

After the battle Nobunaga gave the castle to Hideyoshi. With great pride Hideyoshi ordered his servants to carry his wife and mother (a wrinkled, widowed peasant with callused hands and missing teeth) by litter to join him in his new home.

Slowly Hideyoshi trained his rough brawlers to become skilled and disciplined soldiers. By 1570, when Nobunaga began fighting his brother-in-law, Asai, Hideyoshi was a general commanding 3,000 troops. Three years later, when Nobunaga defeated Asai, he gave most of Asai's land to Hideyoshi. The peasant's son was now a *daimyo:* lord of the northern half of Omi province.

Hideyoshi set up his headquarters in Nagahama, a town with a view of Lake Biwa. To attract merchants and craftsmen, he exempted them from taxes. He also began a detailed survey of his land, and tried to increase the local manufacture of guns.

In 1577 Nobunaga ordered Hideyoshi to attack Harima province in the West. With 7,500 men, Hideyoshi conquered the province easily, but the following year Lord Mori, the most powerful *daimyo* in western Japan, sent tens of thousands of men to take the province back. Nobunaga sent more troops to Harima, and the two armies began a frustrating stalemate that lasted over three years.

Finally, in the spring of 1582, Hideyoshi led 30,000 men farther west into Bitchu province, where they immediately began flooding a key enemy castle. They built a dike three miles long to divert the course of seven rivers at the peak of the rainy season. In two weeks the castle was an island in the middle of a lake, and Hideyoshi's men fired at it from floating barges with stone towers.

Mori hurriedly sent a force of 40,000 men to assist the castle, but the soldiers paused when they saw the lake because they didn't know what to do. The situation was an opportunity because Mori's main armies were all in one place, but it was also dangerous, as Hideyoshi was outnumbered. Hideyoshi needed more troops, and sent an urgent message to Nobunaga asking for reinforcements.

Nobunaga decided to lead his men west himself, but on June 21, 1582, he was ambushed in Kyoto and killed by an army of one of his own generals, Akechi Mitsuhide. The rebel army also killed Nobunaga's eldest son.

A messenger loyal to Hideyoshi rode night and day and delivered the shocking news to him the next evening. The great warrior who had steadily promoted Hideyoshi from peasant to *daimyo* was dead, and Japan, so close to unity and peace, was in danger of reverting back to fragmentation and war.

Hideyoshi could not simply turn east to avenge his lord's death. If he left Bitchu province immediately, all his gains from almost five years of fighting in the West would be lost. He had to make peace with Mori first, and time was of the essence. If Mori learned that Nobunaga was dead, he would never agree to peace. He would simply wait for Hideyoshi to leave western Japan.

To prevent news of Nobunaga's death from spreading, Hideyoshi sealed all roads going west and ordered his guards to arrest anyone who looked suspicious. The next day Hideyoshi proposed a generous peace with Mori, promising not to advance any farther west. Mori agreed, relieved not to have to fight a great battle.

The following day and night Hideyoshi galloped seventy miles east to Harima province, where in just two days he formed an army of several thousand fresh troops, a force that swelled to 20,000 by the time he reached Kyoto.

On June 30 Hideyoshi attacked and routed the treasonous Mitsuhide's army. Mitsuhide fled for his life with a few dozen men, but two days later was killed by peasants, or possibly committed suicide.

During the eleven days it took Hideyoshi to defeat Mitsuhide, other slow-moving generals had not even reached Kyoto. The glory of avenging Oda Nobunaga's death belonged solely to Hideyoshi, and it gave him a commanding position at a conference of Nobunaga's sons and top generals in mid-July.

They met to choose a successor. Nobunaga's eldest son was dead, and no one thought highly of his second or fourth sons. General Shibata Katsuie supported Nobunaga's third son, Oda Nobutaka. But Hideyoshi surprised everyone by walking into the meeting carrying a three-year-old boy in his arms. He argued that under the Oda family's laws the proper successor to Nobunaga should be his grandson Samboshi, son of Nobunaga's firstborn. Everyone agreed, because pledging loyalty to a baby was preferable to losing out to a rival faction.

Hideyoshi was in fact first among equals, but third son Oda Nobutaka and General Shibata Katsuie had trouble accepting this. The two aristocrats still regarded Hideyoshi as an upstart peasant, and invaded his land in Omi province in 1583.

General Shibata sought help from Mori in the West but did not get it. Like many other *daimyo*s, Mori was content to defer to Hideyoshi as long as he could rule his own provinces. The daimyos had been frightened by Nobunaga's drive for personal domination, and were relieved when Hideyoshi seemed willing to share power.

Traveling thirty miles in one night, Hideyoshi crushed Shibata's army before it was prepared for battle. At the same time, Nobunaga's second son surrounded the castle of the third son, Nobutaka. In defeat, the allies Shibata and Nobutaka both committed seppuku, ritual suicide.

Once again Oda Nobunaga's beautiful younger sister, O-ichi, had married a man who lost everything in war. Ten years before, Nobunaga had defeated her first husband, Asai, and turned his skull into a drinking cup. Now Hideyoshi had defeated her second husband, Shibata. This time the war-weary woman chose to die with her husband, but her three daughters, Nobunaga's nieces, became part of Hideyoshi's household. Yodo, the eldest, was as beautiful as her mother. She became Hideyoshi's favorite concubine, and later, the mother of his two sons.

Hideyoshi was now the most powerful man in Japan, stronger even than his predecessor Nobunaga at the peak of his career. Emperor Go-Yozei appointed Hideyoshi *kampaku* (regent) in 1585, the first time a general had ever held this civilian post. Lord Nobunaga had despised titles, but Hideyoshi, born a peasant, felt the need to rule in the emperor's name. The emperor also gave Hideyoshi a family name, Toyotomi, which means "bountiful minister."

The *kampaku* began a nationwide land survey, and sent inspectors to register every farm, paddy, and vegetable plot in Japan. The inspectors measured a field's size and evaluated its fertility, and gave each farmer a document with a red seal that guaranteed his right to the land. They also specified the portion of the village tax that the farmer would have to pay. Taxes were high, usually almost half of a harvest, and anyone caught falsifying figures had his land confiscated.

Taxes went to the *daimyos*, the regional lords, who in turn sent soldiers and laborers to Hideyoshi. But from then on the system of land ownership was national. No one could farm land without the red seal of the central government, and no *daimyo* or local samurai could harass a farmer into paying extra taxes.

In 1587 Hideyoshi sailed to Kyushu and conquered the island with a massive army of 250,000 men. He left the defeated *daimyo*s with several provinces, and turned defiant enemies into grateful allies.

While Hideyoshi was in Kyushu he saw firsthand the growing influence of Christianity. Portuguese Jesuit priests had converted more than 100,000 people to Catholicism, including several *daimyo*s and a majority of the city of Nagasaki, which was virtually governed by the Jesuits.

Hideyoshi encouraged trade with Portuguese merchants and had no objection to an individual's conversion to Christianity. Sometimes he even wore a cross himself as a fashion ornament. But Hideyoshi was concerned that the Jesuits might become as powerful as the Buddhist priests whom Nobunaga had defeated only a decade before. He was also wary of Spain's conquest of the Philippines.

In July 1587, two months after he conquered Kyushu, Hideyoshi ordered the expulsion of all missionaries from Japan. The priests did not obey the order, but instead went into hiding. This seems to have satisfied Hideyoshi. He made no effort to enforce the decree, and apparently meant it as a warning to Christians to stay out of politics. He also assured Portuguese merchants that they were still welcome in Japan.

When Hideyoshi returned from Kyushu that autumn, he celebrated his conquest by giving the greatest tea party of all time. He invited all lovers of the tea ceremony, whether they be "soldiers, townsmen or farmers" to bring "one kettle, one ladle and one cup" to an orchard in Kyoto to serve and be served tea. More than eight hundred people set up tea huts, including Hideyoshi.

The *kampaku* had two portable tea rooms. One was a plain hut papered with old calendars. Hideyoshi used it for the simple *wabi* tea ceremony perfected by Sen no Rikyu. (See chapter ten.) The other tea room was built for the occasion in 1586 when Hideyoshi served tea to the emperor. The entire room was gold plated—cups, kettles, tongs, even the walls and ceiling—everything except the carpet and some linen.

Hideyoshi displayed his golden room to the public, but used his simpler hut to personally serve tea to two hundred people chosen by lottery. Later he visited the rooms of other tea lovers, admiring their utensils and sampling their tea.

In 1588 Hideyoshi began his "sword hunt," a nationwide seizure of swords, spears, matchlocks, and bows and arrows from Japan's farmers, tradesmen, and priests. Hideyoshi disarmed the countryside to prevent armed resistance to tax collectors, but the policy also had the effect of dividing farmers and samurai. Rural samurai had to choose whether to keep their swords or their land; they could not have both. Most samurai stayed armed and moved to castle towns, where they earned salaries as soldiers of their local *daimyo*.

The separation of classes was confirmed in 1591, when Hideyoshi issued laws prohibiting farmers from moving to another village or becoming tradesmen, and forbidding samurai from owning land. The repressive laws restricted the farmers' freedom of movement, making social mobility or even a short trip impossible. But because samurai were no longer in the countryside, the law also gave farmers greater control over their lives. The removal of weapons from rural areas also reduced banditry, making Japan a safer place to travel and do business.

The steady stream of samurai from farm to town increased the power of the *daimyo*s who paid their salaries, and made rural rebellion impossible. The rigid new order Hideyoshi created proved remarkably stable, and continued without much change until 1868.

Early in 1590 Hideyoshi led an army of over 150,000 men to subdue the last powerful family that still defied him, the Hojo, lords of what today would be called the Tokyo metropolitan area. When the Hojo concentrated their forces at Odawara castle, Hideyoshi surrounded the castle and began a long, luxurious siege.

While the Hojo family nearly starved to death, Hideyoshi's soldiers consumed jugs of sake and baskets of fresh fish, and enjoyed the company of wives, mistresses, courtesans, and local girls as well as singers, dancers, jugglers, and other entertainers. Hideyoshi himself summoned his concubine Lady Yodo, daughter of O-ichi, to join him during the siege.

On August 12, 1590, the Hojo family surrendered, and Japan was united at last. Within months even the most remote *daimyo*s in northernmost Honshu pledged their loyalty to Hideyoshi.

Hideyoshi awarded the Hojos' land to a powerful ally, Tokugawa Ieyasu. In a huge land-swap, Ieyasu gave up his five provinces in central Japan in return for eight provinces farther east. Hideyoshi's purpose was to keep Ieyasu as far from Kyoto as possible, but the trade made Ieyasu the biggest landowner in Japan, with an income even larger than Hideyoshi's. Ieyasu moved to the small castle town of Edo (Tokyo), and after he became the ruler of Japan in 1600, it quickly grew to be the largest city in the world.

During Hideyoshi's last years his vanity often clouded his judgment. Perhaps he had enjoyed supreme power for too long. He had a map of Asia painted on his fan, and dreamed of conquering China.

As a preliminary step toward fighting China, Hideyoshi ordered the invasion of Korea. All the *daimyo*s in Japan contributed men and boats, and in May 1592, 150,000 Japanese soldiers landed in Pusan. They marched up the Korean peninsula, took Seoul in twenty days, and continued north to the Yalu River, on the Chinese border. Along the way the Japanese burned and looted cities and sent home grisly trophies—in 1983 a "nose tomb" was discovered near Okayama, west of Osaka, that contained the pickled noses of roughly 20,000 dead Koreans. (The noses were returned to Korea and cremated in 1992.) There is also a tomb in Kyoto known as the "ear mound."

Back in Japan, a triumphant Hideyoshi wrote his nephew a detailed letter on how he planned to divide China's land, but the letter was grossly premature. In 1593 the Japanese suffered the same kind of defeat in Korea that the Americans suffered in 1951. On both occasions Chinese soldiers crossed the Yalu River in great numbers and forced their way down the Korean peninsula.

While the Japanese armies retreated, the surprisingly strong Korean navy cut off supplies from Japan, and Korean farmers burned their crops rather than let the Japanese eat them. Both sides suffered from famine. The weary Japanese finally agreed to discuss peace, and by late summer most of the Chinese and Japanese armies had gone home. Only the southeast corner of Korea remained in Japanese hands. Four years later Hideyoshi launched a second invasion of Korea, but it was even less successful than the first.

Within Japan, Hideyoshi was more constructive. He continued Oda Nobunaga's policy of encouraging free trade through the abolition of toll barriers and guild monopolies. He also enlarged Kyoto and other cities by laying out new streets and city walls, and built several palaces and dozens of temples.

Not content with city building, Hideyoshi took acting and dance lessons early in 1593 and played the lead in eleven classical *no* plays for the emperor later that autumn. The following year he commissioned ten *no* plays about his own life, and played himself in five of them. One critic noted tactfully that Hideyoshi's performances "convey the impression of enormous development."

Hideyoshi loved attention but reacted violently if he felt disrespect. When he learned in 1591 that he had walked under a temple gate that included a statue of the great tea master Sen no Rikyu, and thus had walked under Rikyu's feet, he commanded Rikyu to commit seppuku, ritual suicide. Hideyoshi later regretted his action.

In 1597, when Spanish Franciscan priests ignored Hideyoshi's expulsion order and openly preached on the street, Hideyoshi ordered seven priests and nineteen Japanese converts mutilated, dragged from city to city as a warning, and finally crucified Japanese style (upside down) in Nagasaki.

The crucifixions are occasionally cited as evidence of growing madness on Hideyoshi's part, though Hideyoshi did not punish the Franciscans nearly as harshly as his predecessor had punished Buddhists. Oda Nobunaga and Hideyoshi both wanted priests of all faiths to be subservient to the state. Christians who understood this and kept a low profile, as the Jesuits did, remained unharmed.

Hideyoshi once said that he might have converted to Christianity were it not for its insistence on monogamy. He had a wife, four concubines, and many lovers, yet in spite of this he had only two children, both by Lady Yodo. Their first son died at age two in 1591; a second son, Hideyori, was born in 1593.

Hideyoshi asked five of the most powerful *daimyo*s in Japan, including Ieyasu and Mori, to swear allegiance to his son. He also arranged for the emperor to appoint Hideyori *kampaku* in 1596. Hideyoshi then became *taiko*, retired regent.

In the summer of 1598, as his armies straggled home from Korea for the second time, Hideyoshi became ill. Once again he summoned the five leading *daimyo*s to swear allegiance to his five-year-old son, this time in writing. Hideyoshi chose Ieyasu as Hideyori's guardian, and on his deathbed repeatedly pleaded for his loyalty. "Again and again, I beg you to take care of Hideyori."

Hideyoshi died September 18, 1598. He was sixty-two. Within two years Ieyasu was the undisputed ruler of Japan, and Hideyori was just one of many *daimyo*s. In 1615 Ieyasu, concerned about the succession of his own son, started a war with Hideyori and surrounded his castle. At twenty-two Hideyori committed suicide, along with his mother, Lady Yodo. Ieyasu also executed Hideyori's seven-year-old son and sent his six-year-old daughter to a Buddhist convent; when she died years later, Hideyoshi had no descendants.

Hideyoshi has been an inspiration to generations of lower-class Japanese. Not only did he rise to the top of a society based on family lineage, he also shaped that society for three centuries to come. A genius who learned from life rather than from books, Hideyoshi was a flawed man, but did more good than evil, at least in Japan. He restricted the movement of farmers, but also made the countryside a safer place to live. He started two brutal and useless wars in Korea, but in Japan he frequently made peace with rival *daimyo*s when war would have been fully justified.

By modern standards Hideyoshi was a despot who strengthened a feudal system that took half of a peasant's harvest and gave nothing in return. Nevertheless, Hideyoshi left Japan a better place than he found it. When Oda Nobunaga died in 1582, Japan could easily have returned to being a land of petty states in endless war, with checkpoints and toll barriers making large-scale commerce impossible. But unlike Nobunaga, Hideyoshi had the wisdom to share power with other *daimyo*s. He turned enemies into allies, and forged a lasting national unity based on common interest rather than on one man's domination.

The unity Hideyoshi achieved brought nationwide trade, allowing farmers to grow a greater variety of crops and to make much more money than they could have earned growing only rice. Prosperity led to the rise of merchants and the growth of cities, and with city living came widespread literacy. Literacy enabled the Japanese to enjoy a rich popular culture in the seventeenth century, and a speedy industrialization in the nineteenth century. Hideyoshi could not have foreseen these developments, but he knew that Japan's unification was worth fighting for, and hoped it would lead to great achievements.

19
Tokugawa Ieyasu
The Shogun Who Began
a Three-Century Dynasty

For fifteen generations Tokugawa Ieyasu and his descendants ruled Japan without challenge and controlled nearly every aspect of Japanese life. The dynasty that Ieyasu began in 1603 lasted almost three centuries. Not until 1868 did it come to an end.

Ieyasu (1543–1616) is best known in the West as the character called Toranaga in James Clavell's novel *Shōgun*. But to the Japanese people, he is remembered as the most patient of the three warriors who unified Japan. A poem taught to Japanese schoolchildren recalls the personalities of the three great men:

> *What if the bird will not sing?*
> *Oda Nobunaga says, "Kill it!"*
> *Hideyoshi says, "Make it want to sing."*
> *Tokugawa Ieyasu says, "Wait."*

Nine years younger than Oda Nobunaga and seven years younger than Hideyoshi, Ieyasu (pronounced ee-ay-yasu) allied himself with his two predecessors and sent troops to hasten their unification of Japan. Unlike many lords, he was wise enough not to challenge their superior military strength. Ieyasu slowly built up his forces, and when Hideyoshi died, Ieyasu was by far the strongest lord in Japan. Patiently, he had waited until it was his turn to rule.

Ieyasu was not content merely to hold personal power. He wanted to create a family dynasty that would preserve Japan's hard-won unity. He studied history, hired scholars, wrote laws, and made policy with the future in mind. His influence in Japan was unequaled until the rise of the Meiji leaders in the 1860s.

Tokugawa Ieyasu was born on January 31, 1543, in a small castle in Okazaki, about twenty miles (32 km) southeast of modern Nagoya. His father was a sixteen-year-old chief whose own father had died in battle seven years before. The clan held a thin strip of land between the territories of two more powerful families, the Odas and the Imagawas.

Ieyasu's mother was the fourteen-year-old daughter of a minor warlord.

When Ieyasu was just one year old, the alliance between the families of his mother and father ended and his mother returned home to her family. He was then cared for by an aunt, although his mother continued to send him clothes and sweets.

When Ieyasu turned four, the Oda family kidnapped him and held him hostage. Using children as hostages to insure the peaceful conduct of their parents was a common practice in medieval Japan, and the boys and girls were almost always well treated.

Two years later his father was murdered by a rebellious vassal, and at six Ieyasu became the new leader of his troubled family. Because his father was dead, Ieyasu was no longer of any use to the Odas, so they sent him to a rival clan in a hostage swap. Ieyasu spent the next eleven years at the Imagawa family's castle, but he had plenty of company. Seven vassals sent their sons to accompany him as fellow hostages; five were playmates his own age and two were guardians in their twenties.

The city of Sumpu, where the Imagawas lived, was a pretty and sophisticated town within sight of Mt. Fuji on beautiful Suruga Bay. Ieyasu and his friends swam, rode horses, practiced archery, and spent many hours fencing. His favorite sport was hawking, the use of falcons to hunt cranes, geese, and small game.

Ieyasu's grandmother lived at a Buddhist temple in Sumpu. She taught Ieyasu calligraphy and arranged his early education. Later, one of the finest teachers in Japan, a Zen monk named Sessai, gave him lessons in military tactics and strategy.

Ieyasu would never have received as a good an education at home as he did at Sumpu. But because he spent his entire youth as a hostage, he learned to trust very few people. The short and stocky teenager developed a cool reserve, and also an unshakable poise.

When Ieyasu was fourteen, the Imagawa chief married him to his niece, Lady Tsukiyama, but the newlyweds did not get along. He was uninterested in family life and she was uninterested in military matters. She also had a violent temper, and the handling of her outbursts gave him early lessons in patience.

In 1560 Oda Nobunaga trapped the Imagawas' main army in a narrow valley and killed 3,000 men. Ieyasu, whose duties that day were far from the battlefield, slipped away by night and returned to his ancestral home of Okazaki. Quickly he gathered all his vassals and recaptured his family's castle. At seventeen he was finally free.

Ieyasu took some border fortresses from Nobunaga to show that he could be a nuisance, then began negotiating with him. In 1561 the two young warriors agreed not to attack each other, but instead to expand their territory in opposite directions. It was the beginning of a twenty-one-year alliance, one of the longest pacts in Japanese history. It gave Ieyasu the time he needed to build up his army, and it protected Nobunaga from an attack from the east. The two lords confirmed their pact with the marriage of Ieyasu's son to Nobunaga's daughter.

During the next few years Ieyasu took castles from the Imagawa family. In one battle two bullets lodged in his armor. By 1565 his well-trained army of 5,000 men had conquered all of Mikawa, his home province. At twenty-two Ieyasu was a *daimyo*, a regional lord.

Ieyasu gave land to his most loyal vassals, and sent surveyors into the fields to determine how much tax the peasants should pay. Mikawa was a rich rice-growing area; farmers typically gave over 40 percent of their crop to their lord.

In 1569 Ieyasu and Takeda Shingen, a nearby lord, destroyed the Imagawas completely and divided up their land. Ieyasu took a region called Totomi, his second province.

A bit cocky from his success, he formed an alliance *against* Takeda the following year. When Takeda learned of this pact he was furious, and led an army of 27,000 men to Ieyasu's main castle in 1572. Ieyasu knew his troops could never withstand an attack by so large a force, so he tried deception. He ordered bonfires lit inside and outside the castle and threw the castle gates wide open. Shingen's generals did not know what to make of such a sight, and fearing a trap, decided to turn back home. It was the narrowest escape of Ieyasu's life.

Three years later Ieyasu and Nobunaga combined forces against the Takedas and killed over 10,000 of their soldiers with Portuguese-designed, Japanese-made guns. After this the Takedas were less of a military threat, and turned instead to intrigue.

Lady Tsukiyama, Ieyasu's wife, had never forgiven her husband for the destruction of her family, the Imagawas. She tried to sabotage her husband's alliance with Nobunaga by using a pretty, young noblewoman to lure their son Nobuyasu away from his wife, who was Nobunaga's daughter. She also wrote letters to the Takeda family, urging them to attack Nobunaga.

The letters were intercepted by a friend of Nobunaga's daughter, and were clear evidence of Lady Tsukiyama's treachery. When Nobunaga saw them, he demanded her death and also the death of their son, who he felt was no longer trustworthy.

Ieyasu faced a difficult decision. He could save his alliance with Nobunaga and kill his wife and eldest son, or he could save the lives of his wife and son and fight a disastrous war against the strongest army in Japan. He had no problem deciding to kill his wife, whom he looked upon as a traitor, and quietly sent a vassal to do the bloody deed. But he spent two months trying to decide what to do about his son.

Nobuyasu was a brave warrior twenty years old. Ieyasu's next oldest son was just a toddler. If Nobuyasu died, it would be many years before Ieyasu would have an adult heir again. On the other hand, few of Nobuyasu's vassals spoke up for their lord. In fits of anger Nobuyasu had murdered two women and a priest.

Most of Nobuyasu's vassals argued that the Tokugawa family was better off with another heir, and Ieyasu finally agreed. In October 1579 he ordered his son to commit seppuku, ritual suicide.

Their alliance intact, Ieyasu and Nobunaga attacked the Takedas again in the spring of 1582 and defeated them completely. Ieyasu was an excellent horseman and a fearless general, often shouting, "At them, at them!" in the middle of a battlefield. After the attack Ieyasu acquired the region of Suruga, his boyhood home when he was a hostage. It was his third province.

By contrast, Nobunaga ruled twenty provinces and parts of ten more. So when General Akechi Mitsuhide ambushed and killed Nobunaga and his eldest son in June 1582, it left a huge vacuum of power. Ieyasu marched unopposed into the nearby provinces of Shinano and Kai, and now held five regions and commanded 40,000 men. Only the domains of Hideyoshi, Nobunaga's top general, surpassed his own.

Ieyasu and Hideyoshi skirmished over border forts in 1584, but both men were too cautious to launch a truly risky attack. In December the two warriors agreed to peace, and Ieyasu accepted Hideyoshi's status as the ruler of Japan.

Ieyasu married Hideyoshi's sister, a homely, middle-aged woman named Asahihime, in 1586. It was a political arrangement without the slightest pretence of affection between the partners. When Asahihime died four years later, Ieyasu never married again, although he fathered sixteen children by ten different women. Many of his mistresses were pretty widows from less prominent families.

In the fall of 1586 Ieyasu visited Hideyoshi at his castle in Osaka, and publicly bowed low to him. At the same time, Hideyoshi's mother visited her daughter Asahihime at Ieyasu's castle, in effect acting as a temporary hostage during the conference between Ieyasu and her son. The visit by his mother was Hideyoshi's idea, and it was a gesture of respect almost as great as Ieyasu's bow.

During the late 1580s Ieyasu lived in Sumpu, where as a boy he had spent many days hawking. Not only did he love the sport, it was a useful way for him to exercise, to judge the physical fitness of his vassals, and to see firsthand the condition of the peasants. Often he stopped at a farmer's house in the middle of a hunt and ate a simple lunch of baked sweet potatoes.

After Japan was united in 1590, Hideyoshi confiscated the Hojo family's land and gave it to Ieyasu in a giant land-swap. Ieyasu gave Hideyoshi his five provinces in central Japan, and in return Hideyoshi gave Ieyasu eight provinces farther east. He was farther away from the capital, but he now controlled 12 percent of Japan's tax revenue, a share even higher than Hideyoshi's 11 percent. The swap also kept him busy for years. He had to survey his provinces, install new systems of land ownership and tax collection, improve roads and fortresses, and build a new city to be his headquarters.

In 1590 the town of Edo was just a collection of farming and fishing villages near an old castle that had a leaky roof and mildewed floor mats. But Ieyasu put

10,000 men to work draining swamps, digging canals, laying out streets, building barracks, aqueducts, and warehouses, and repairing and fortifying his castle. To build the castle walls, 3,000 ships carried stones so big that it took over 100 men to move each one.

Ieyasu also invited merchants and craftsmen to the town, enticing them with ample business and moderate taxes. By 1610 Edo was a thriving town of 150,000 people. By 1700 it was the largest city in the world, with over one million people. In 1869 the government gave the city a new name: Tokyo, "eastern capital."

In the summer of 1598 Hideyoshi became gravely ill. He appointed five elders to govern Japan until his five-year-old son Hideyori reached maturity. All five men were *daimyo*s: Ieyasu, Mori, Uesugi, Maeda, and Ukita. Together they controlled 30 percent of Japan's land, although Ieyasu was by far the most powerful of the group. Hideyoshi asked each elder to swear loyalty to young Hideyori, and also promise not to build up personal power through political marriages. Then he died on September 18, 1598.

Despite his oath to Hideyoshi, Ieyasu continued to arrange the marriages of his children and grandchildren into prominent families. It was impossible for him to obey his oath to Hideyoshi because any marriage between his descendants and other families automatically had political consequences. To comply with the oath, Ieyasu's children would have had to stay single.

Nevertheless Ieyasu's rivals objected to the new marriages. His chief critic was a *daimyo* named Ishida Mitsunari. Ishida ordered two assassins to kill Ieyasu in 1599, but they did not get past his guards. A few weeks later a young samurai captured Ishida, but Ieyasu shrewdly let him go. He preferred Ishida to lead the opposition rather than some other lord with closer ties to the deceased Hideyoshi.

By the summer of 1600 Ishida and three of the five elders were amassing large armies to challenge Ieyasu. Ieyasu wrote letters to 108 *daimyo*s asking for support, and received favorable replies from 99 of them. They backed Ieyasu because they had known him for twenty years, and had learned to trust him. Ieyasu's eastern allies blocked the army of Uesugi, one of the elders, and prevented him from marching west to join Ishida.

In July Ieyasu visited a devoted general named Torii at Fushimi castle outside Kyoto. The two friends spent the night reminiscing about old times, and the next morning Ieyasu left the castle in tears. It was the only time anyone ever saw him cry in public. He cried because he knew that Torii and his 1,800 men would soon defend their castle to the death, without reinforcements, in order to give Ieyasu's armies time to rendezvous. In September the loyal men accomplished their mission, killing 3,000 of Ishida's men over the course of ten days before the castle fell.

The climactic battle between Ieyasu and Ishida took place on October 21, 1600, along a mountain road in the village of Sekigahara, about twenty-five miles (40 km) northwest of modern Nagoya. At dawn each side had roughly 80,000 soldiers, but by prearrangement with another *daimyo*, 8,000 men switched sides and joined Ieyasu as soon as the battle began. The result was a rout; Ieyasu's men killed over 4,000 of the enemy. Ishida fled but was captured a week later, and publicly beheaded in Kyoto.

Ieyasu's heir, Hidetada, was twenty-one and in command of 38,000 troops, but arrived at the battle five days late. He had spent too much time taking an insignificant castle, and his father was furious. Ieyasu asked his son whether any of his vassals had told him that the castle was unimportant, and Hidetada replied that yes, Toda Issai had done so. He summoned Toda immediately and said, "It was because your position was not high that your advice was not followed. I will make it high so that it will be in the future." He made Toda a *daimyo*, and increased his land tenfold.

Ieyasu could afford to give away land, because after the battle of Sekigahara he was the master of Japan. He confiscated the land of ninety-one families that had fought against him, and also took seventy-five percent of the vast estates of Mori and Uesugi. He gave large tracts of land to his allies and relatives, and smaller plots and powerful government posts to his vassals. By 1601 twenty-six percent of Japan's tax revenue belonged to the Tokugawa family and its vassals.

Unlike Hideyoshi, who was born a peasant, Ieyasu was a descendant of Japan's first shogun, Minamoto no Yoritomo, and therefore eligible to become shogun himself. The office had been vacant since Oda Nobunaga had expelled the previous shogun from Kyoto in 1573. Thirty years later, in March 1603, Emperor Go-Yozei formally appointed Tokugawa Ieyasu as Japan's new shogun. The emperor owned little land and was largely dependent on Ieyasu for income. Even so, Ieyasu and his family ruled in the emperor's name.

One of the Ieyasu's first actions as shogun was to set up a legal procedure to hear the complaints of peasants against their lords and tax collectors. Usually these involved a request to lower taxes when the harvest was poor, and the government sided with the peasants about half the time. On rare occasions peasants became violent. The shogun's army invariably crushed the uprisings, but often the government met the demands of the peasants even while the leaders of the revolt were crucified or boiled in oil.

On the whole, peasants were more prosperous than before. Unity and peace meant that it was possible for farmers to work on long-term projects such as irrigation and drainage. They also benefited from cheaper hoes and sickles, the use of dried sardines as fertilizer, whale oil as insect repellent, and early-maturing varieties of rice that made it possible to grow two crops a year.

In 1605, after only two years in office, Ieyasu resigned as shogun in favor of his twenty-six-year-old son, Hidetada. By stepping down, Ieyasu made it clear to everyone that his family's claim to the office of shogun was hereditary, and that this was the start of a dynasty. The resignation was particularly designed to thwart the ambition of Hideyoshi's son Hideyori, who lived at Osaka castle and at age twelve was already beginning to dream of recapturing his father's power.

While Hidetada stayed in Edo to do the tedious work of daily administration, Ieyasu retired to Sumpu, his boyhood home, where he continued to make the most important decisions. He was still the leader of the Tokugawa family and the commander of its vassals. But he always treated Hidetada with great respect, and father and son got along very well.

In Sumpu, Ieyasu spent his days hawking and his evenings listening to lectures on Chinese and Japanese history, and Buddhist and Confucian thought. Ieyasu saw himself as a paternal Confucian ruler and closely studied the laws and careers of past leaders, including Ieyasu's own ancestor, Shogun Yoritomo.

Ieyasu learned about the Western world as well. One of his closest advisers was an Englishman, Will Adams (John Blackthorne in Clavell's novel *Shōgun*). Adams was the chief navigator of the Dutch ship *Liefde*, the first vessel to reach Japan from across the Pacific. When the ship landed in Kyushu in 1600, local authorities confiscated it, detained the crew, and sent Adams to Edo, where Ieyasu questioned him for weeks.

Because Adams spoke some Portuguese, Ieyasu was able to talk to him through a Japanese interpreter. Ieyasu learned for the first time of the existence of northern Europe, the Protestant Reformation, and the war between Protestant and Catholic nations. He was immensely pleased that Adams was not a missionary. Ieyasu disliked Christian missionaries and tolerated them only because trade with Spain and Portugal was so profitable. In return for silver, copper, lacquerware, and other handicrafts, all of which Ieyasu had in abundance, he received cotton, spices, and Chinese silk. But if Japan could start trading with the Netherlands instead of with Spain and Portugal, it might be possible to expel the missionaries without suffering any economic loss.

Ieyasu let the crew of the *Liefde* sail home, but kept Adams in Japan as an adviser on shipping and foreign affairs. He made Adams an admiral and a samurai, and provided him with a Japanese wife and an estate with eighty farmers.

A second Dutch ship, the *Brach*, arrived in Japan in 1609. The captain was summoned to Ieyasu's castle at Sumpu, and while Adams interpreted, Ieyasu gave him four copies of a letter that stated: "When Dutch ships come to Japan they are hereby authorized to enter any harbor they like."

That same year a Spanish traveler described Ieyasu as a "heavily built old man," sitting on a raised platform covered with green velvet, wearing "loose robes of green satin decorated with gold brocade." When *daimyo*s approached him, they did so "kissing the ground in humility."

As a student of history, Ieyasu worried about family disputes over succession, and nipped one such conflict in the bud in 1611. Hidetada's second son, Tadanaga, was stronger, brighter, and handsomer than his older brother, Iemitsu, and his mother favored him. When Ieyasu learned of the situation, he visited the boys, placed Iemitsu on a higher platform than Tadanaga, and explained to the younger son that he was a vassal of his older brother. This made it clear that Iemitsu would succeed Hidetada as shogun, and it began a three-century pattern of stability during which older sons succeeded their fathers.

Another potential threat to the dynasty was Christianity. Ieyasu had not enforced Hideyoshi's expulsion of missionaries, and by 1610 there were over 300,000 Christians in Japan, including roughly seven percent of the people of Kyushu. Their priests taught them that the words of Jesus were more important than the laws of the shogun. This became alarmingly clear when 30,000 Christians sang hymns at an execution in 1613. The following year Ieyasu and Hidetada issued a new order expelling Christian priests. They also ordered the destruction of churches and required Christian samurai to renounce their faith. Farmers and craftsmen, however, were free to remain Christian if they wished.

Several Christian warriors went into the service of Hideyoshi's son Hideyori, who was now twenty-one and a threat to Tokugawa legitimacy. Ieyasu decided it was time to pick a quarrel. His scholars charged that an inscription on a giant temple bell built by Hideyori contained a hidden insult to the Tokugawa family. Hideyori sent denials and apologies, but Ieyasu coolly advised Hideyori to leave Osaka castle for a less fortified stronghold. What Ieyasu was really asking Hideyori to do was to forget his father's legacy and accept his status as a *daimyo*. This Hideyori refused to do.

Hideyori asked *daimyo*s throughout Japan for military assistance, but almost all of his father's old friends had died and not one *daimyo* offered any aid. Instead, help came one soldier at a time. When Ieyasu had confiscated the land of ninety-one families in 1600, thousands of warriors lost their jobs. These *ronin*, or masterless samurai, were spoiling for a fight, and more than 60,000 of them streamed into Osaka castle.

Ieyasu could not tolerate such a direct threat to his rule, and ordered 150,000 soldiers to surround the castle in December 1614. The castle was fortified with miles of moats and high stone walls, and hundreds of guns, cannon, and flame-throwing catapults. An assault would have been bloody, so Ieyasu dammed the river that flowed into the outer moat, and on the eleventh day of the siege the water in the moat began to empty. At this point the two sides began talks, and in January 1615 they agreed that if the outer moat were permanently filled in, Hideyori could stay at the castle.

During the truce Ieyasu's soldiers quickly filled in the outer moat, then with lightning speed tore down the castle's outer wall and filled in the middle moat too. Before Hideyori had time to protest, it was too late. Osaka castle was no longer impregnable.

In April, Hideyori began building new walls and accepting more *ronin*. Ieyasu now demanded that Hideyori either leave Osaka and be a *daimyo* somewhere else, or, alternatively, dismiss his *ronin*. It was a reasonable choice, but the *ronin* had nowhere to go, and Hideyori no longer had the power to oust them.

In June, Ieyasu sent 200,000 men to surround the castle once more. This time they bribed a cook to set fire to the kitchen, and as flames spread to the rest of the castle, Ieyasu's troops slaughtered thousands of fleeing *ronin*. Hideyori committed suicide, but his seven-year-old son fled with a nurse to a castle near Kyoto. There one of Ieyasu's vassals captured the boy and beheaded him. It was ruthless of Ieyasu to order the murder of the boy, but the Japanese public understood that his death was necessary to prevent a civil war in the future.

Two months later Ieyasu's son Hidetada summoned all the *daimyo*s in Japan and issued the new Laws for the Military Houses. The *daimyo*s had to swear, first, not to build or repair any castles without the shogun's permission, and, second, not to arrange any marriages without first notifying the shogun. Drafted by scholars, the laws prevented a *daimyo* from building up his military or political power in secret. The stern code also warned that "reason may be violated in the name of the law, but law may not be violated in the name of reason." For the next 250 years Japan's *daimyo*s reaffirmed these oaths whenever there was a new shogun.

In February 1616 Ieyasu became ill. Some say he grew sick from hawking in the middle of winter. Others say it was because he ate rotten tempura. Whatever the cause of his illness, he recovered for a few months and gave Hidetada detailed advice about every major *daimyo* and vassal before he died on June 1, 1616.

Hidetada was harder on Christianity than his father had been. He banned the religion altogether and executed hundreds of people who refused to repudiate their faith. Sometimes even children were burned at the stake. When Hidetada died in 1632 it was grandson Iemitsu's time to govern. Of the fifteen Tokugawa shoguns, Iemitsu (1604–1651) stands second only to Ieyasu in long-term influence.

In 1635 Iemitsu ordered *daimyo*s to spend several months in Edo every other year, and to leave their wives and children in Edo as hostages when they returned home. The effect of this was to make rebellion almost impossible. To enforce the law, Iemitsu placed guards at seventy checkpoints around Edo. No high-ranking woman or child could leave the city, and no weapon could enter it, without written permission from the government. The shogun also maintained a network of spies capable of watching everyone from the most powerful *daimyo* to the humblest peasant.

Iemitsu also issued the famous Exclusion Decrees that isolated Japan from the world for two centuries. For many years Japanese merchants had traded in the Philippines, Thailand, and Vietnam, but in 1633 Iemitsu announced that any Japanese who lived abroad for over five years would be executed if he or she returned to Japan. Two years later the shogun also prohibited all Japanese people and ships from leaving the country.

Foreigners in Japan were forced to move to Dejima, a small island in Nagasaki Bay. This reduced contact between foreigners and Japanese to a minimum, and confined all overseas trade to Nagasaki, a city run directly by the shogun. Iemitsu did not trust the *daimyo*s in western Japan because they had opposed his grandfather in battle, and he wanted to make it impossible for them to buy foreign weapons. This was a reasonable concern. When the Tokugawa dynasty finally fell in 1868, it was precisely because the *daimyo*s in western Japan were able to buy European weapons.

The final exclusionary decree came after a peasant uprising in Kyushu in 1637. When Christians on the island joined the revolt, Iemitsu sent 100,000 soldiers to crush the rebellion, killing over 10,000 people in the process. After this Iemitsu permanently banned all Portuguese ships from Japan, on pain of death, in 1639.

The following year seventy brave Portuguese sailed from Macao to Nagasaki to try to convince the shogun to change his mind. When they arrived, government officials dismantled their ship and beheaded fifty-seven of the crew. They sent the other thirteen back to Macao, and told them: "Let [the Portuguese] think no more of us; just as if we were no longer in the world."

The government had banned Spaniards as early as 1625. Now only the Dutch and the Chinese were permitted to trade with Japan. Unlike the Spaniards and Portuguese, the Dutch were interested solely in trade and had no desire to win religious converts. But even the Dutch were confined to the island of Deshima, which became their permanent home in 1641. For 212 years, until 1853, the Dutch ships that arrived there once a year were Japan's only contact with the Western world.

What would the world be like today if Iemitsu had not issued his Exclusion Decrees? The Japanese might have colonized parts of Asia, or even settled Australia. But it is also possible that the Europeans might have intervened in Japan's domestic affairs, and that the Japanese would have lost not only their unity, but perhaps even their identity.

Tokugawa Ieyasu could not have forseen that his dynasty would bring Japan two centuries of isolation. He was a brilliant and fearless general who fought more than eighty battles and won almost all of them. He was also a talented administrator who wrote laws, distributed land, arranged marriages, and spent money with the single-minded aim of stengthening his family's power.

Ieyasu completed Japan's unification, and made it permanent. By resigning as shogun in favor of his son after just two years in office, he strengthened his family's hereditary claim to the title. By choosing his eldest grandson, Iemitsu, over the boy's stronger younger brother, Ieyasu made sure that his family would be united in times of succession. When Ieyasu finally died, he did not just leave his son an empire, as Nobunaga and Hideyoshi had, he left him a dynasty. The Tokugawa family's reign became an institution, and Japan's unity no longer required a strong warrior. Indeed, Iemitsu never fought a battle in his life, yet he commanded an army of 300,000 men and was the unquestioned ruler of all Japan.

Some Japanese criticize Ieyasu for starting a hereditary military dictatorship based on spies, hostages, and isolation. But in the early seventeenth century, democracy was unknown, and Europe's rulers were as despotic as Asia's. In Ieyasu's day the best way to bring peace and prosperity to a country was to form a strong and stable dynasty, and in this he succeeded. The lasting peace Ieyasu achieved caused farm productivity to rise fifty percent in the seventeenth century, and this new wealth paid for a remarkable growth in literacy and culture. By the nineteenth century, forty percent of Japanese men and ten percent of Japanese women could read and write. When the Tokugawa dynasty finally ended in 1868, millions of Japanese were capable of learning about the modern world immediately.

20

Oishi Kuranosuke

*Leader of the Forty-Seven Ronin
Who Avenged Their Master's Death*

OISHI KURANOSUKE was the leader of forty-seven *ronin* (masterless samurai) whose story is the national epic of Japan. It is known to every schoolchild and is constantly told in movies, plays, and on television. The tale of the forty-seven ronin is as central to Japanese culture as *Hamlet* and "Cinderella" are to the arts in the West—more so, probably, because the story is true.

Oishi (c.1658–1703) was chief vassal to Lord Asano of Ako castle, west of Osaka. He was the son of a samurai, which means "one who serves" in Japanese. Like samurai everywhere, Oishi trained to be a warrior. He learned to fight with swords, daggers, arrows, and sticks. He also read Chinese books on military tactics and Confucian ethics.

Through sheer luck, Oishi's teacher was one of the greatest scholars in Japanese history, Yamaga Soko (1622–1685). Yamaga had been banished to Ako for nine years in 1666 because he had written a book that praised the original teachings of Confucius but criticized the commentaries of many scholars. Some of the shogun's advisers saw the book as an attack on the moral authority of the government.

Yamaga was already famous for his essays on bushido, "the way of the warrior." He taught that a samurai had to be in "physical readiness for any call to service," and be willing even to sacrifice his life, if necessary, to serve his master. Yamaga noted that although a samurai drew a comfortable salary, he did not grow, make, or sell anything, so unless a samurai placed "duty above all," he was simply an idler, no better than a robber.

The famous teacher made an enormous impression on Oishi, who was still in his teens. In the 1600s many samurai had become soft and lazy because it was a time of peace. Oishi, however, continued his physical training, and never forgot that a samurai who shirked his duty was just a parasite.

Tall and handsome, Oishi married when he was about twenty-five. He and his wife had three children and lived happily. Gradually, Oishi rose in rank until he became Lord Asano's chief vassal.

In the spring of 1701, when the story of the forty-seven *ronin* begins, Oishi was in his early forties. Shogun Tsunayoshi had asked Lord Asano and another nobleman, Lord Date, to prepare ceremonies for the annual visit of the emperor's representatives to the shogun's palace in Edo (Tokyo). While Oishi stayed behind to look after the castle, Asano traveled to the great city.

Lord Asano and Lord Date were country warriors who knew nothing about court ceremonies. The shogun asked Lord Kira, the palace's master of protocol, to teach them the required etiquette, but Kira was a corrupt official who expected a bribe. Without telling their master, Lord Date's vassals gave Lord Kira a roll of silk and a purse full of gold, but Lord Asano's servants did nothing. Oishi would have known what to do, but he was back at Ako castle, and Asano's other servants were not bold enough to give gold away without their lord's permission.

Because the wicked Kira did not receive anything from Lord Asano, he insulted him continuously. For two days Asano held his anger, but on the third and final day of the ceremonies Kira said something particularly vicious, perhaps a remark about Asano's wife. Asano drew his sword and lunged at Kira, wounding Kira in the forehead before several men restrained him.

It was a great crime to draw a sword inside the shogun's palace, and the shogun was furious that his ceremonies had been disrupted. He sentenced Lord Asano to death by beheading, but allowed Asano the opportunity to keep his honor by committing seppuku (ritual suicide) instead. The shogun also confiscated Asano's castle and all his land, a total disaster for the Asano family. With this judgment the shogun also turned Asano's upper-class samurai into *ronin* (masterless samurai).

When the terrible news reached Ako, Oishi called a meeting of the district's 300 warriors. They all agreed to appeal the shogun's decision and try to have the land transferred to Asano's younger brother. Oishi also suggested that if the appeal failed, they should fight to the death at the castle when the shogun's troops arrived to take possession. He scheduled a second meeting for the *ronin* to confirm their willingness to fight and die.

As Oishi had anticipated, more than 200 *ronin* suddenly left town or became sick. Only 62 warriors attended the second meeting, but Oishi knew that these were men he could trust. He told them that if the appeal for the transfer of land to Asano's brother failed, they would not fight at the castle as he had announced at the first meeting. Instead, they would avenge Lord Asano and complete his final act—they would kill Lord Kira.

The vendetta had to be secret. By law a samurai was required to register a feud with the police, but without the element of surprise a vendetta was militarily impossible. Even in secret there was nothing Oishi or his men could do as long as Lord Kira lived in the shogun's palace. They simply had to be patient and wait for an opportunity to strike.

In the meantime the *ronin* cleaned and scrubbed the castle and peacefully handed it over to the shogun's representatives. They also took some of Lord

Asano's gold and silver to pay for a monument at his grave, but in reality this money helped finance the vendetta. Finally, the warriors left Ako and went their separate ways, moving to different cities and adopting new professions.

Lord Asano's young wife returned to the home of her parents, but without her daughter. Oishi arranged for a nearby lord to temporarily and secretly adopt the little girl to prevent Kira's men from kidnapping her and holding her hostage to insure Kira's safety.

With his family, Oishi moved into a large house in a small town a few miles east of Kyoto. They lived comfortably but enjoyed little privacy. Lord Kira's spies were everywhere: a cook, a workman, a priest in the street. Each of them reported Oishi's every move.

Because of the incident with Lord Asano, Lord Kira's corruption became common knowledge, and in the autumn of 1701 the shogun's ministers asked him to retire from government service. Kira moved out of the shogun's palace, but his wife's powerful family, the Uesugi, furnished him with over a hundred guards to give him round-the-clock protection in his new home.

When Kira left the palace, many of Oishi's *ronin* wanted to attack him immediately. Oishi had to travel to Edo to calm them down. He reminded them that their first duty was to Lord Asano's brother. They had to wait until the shogun ruled on their appeal for the restoration of Asano's land.

When Oishi returned home from Edo, he divorced his wife to keep her from being connected with the illegal vendetta. He asked her to return to her parents' home and take their two youngest children with her. Their eldest son, Chikara, remained with Oishi. He was only sixteen, but he was one of the sixty-two *ronin* who had pledged to die, if necessary, to avenge Lord Asano. A good student, well-trained in the arts of a warrior, Chikara was already quite muscular.

Once his wife left, Oishi began a spectacular plan to induce the Uesugi family to reduce the number of soldiers guarding Lord Kira: He played the drunk for an entire year to put them off their guard. He moved from one sake house to the next, buying rounds for friends, starting fights in public, and even passing out in the street.

Oishi also spent a lot of money on courtesans. By tradition, his favorite courtesan was a strikingly beautiful geisha named Okaru, who saw through Oishi's drunken ruse and fell in love with him.

Not content with one woman, Oishi also slept with farm girls whose fathers had sold them into prostitution. Many farmers' daughters worked in brothels at this time, because the farmers had no other way to feed their families when their crops failed. Crops were ruined because Shogun Tsunayoshi, who ruled from 1680 to 1709, had outlawed the killing of animals, even insects.

Tokugawa Tsunayoshi is known to history as the "dog shogun." When his four-year-old son died, a Buddhist priest convinced the shogun that it happened because he had killed some living thing in a former life. As a result, in 1687 the shogun issued the Law of Compassion Toward Fellow Creatures. Ironically, the law was not enforced with any compassion toward human beings.

Zealous officials arrested hunters for hunting and fishermen for fishing, and sent thousands of unfortunate peasants to prison camps. Reluctantly, the nation adopted a vegetarian diet. In the capital city the shogun built large, luxurious kennels for hundreds of stray dogs, but in the countryside farmers were forbidden to kill the pests that ate their crops. Many harvests failed, and to feed their families, fathers sold their prettiest daughters into prostitution.

While the nation suffered, Oishi continued his life of decadence. Some of Oishi's own men lost faith in him. What shocked them most was that he allowed his swords to grow rusty. Yet all the while, Kira's spies took detailed notes, and finally, in the summer of 1702, the Uesugi family decided they could trim their expenses by ending the spying and by reducing the number of Kira's guards to about sixty.

On July 18, 1702, the shogun denied Oishi's petition to transfer the land at Ako castle to Asano's brother, and sentenced the brother to permanent exile in Hiroshima. The government also removed the Asano name from the official list of noble families. The legal appeal had failed. The time to strike was near. Oishi stayed drunk awhile longer, but informed his men that he would begin the journey to Edo in November.

Oishi said good-bye to the beautiful geisha Okaru, and disguised himself as a merchant as he smuggled armor into the capital city. He told his *ronin* that they were free to drop out of the vendetta if they wished, and seven men with elderly parents or young children did so. There were now fifty-five *ronin*, and they arrived in Edo a few at a time so as not to arouse suspicion.

For a month Oishi and his men familiarized themselves with Lord Kira's routine and plotted their attack. They carefully studied a floor plan of Kira's house, which one of the *ronin* had obtained by marrying the daughter of the architect who drew it.

Eight more men backed out of the vendetta, but in the middle of January 1703, forty-seven *ronin* met in a restaurant, pretending to be merchants. They ranged in age from seventeen to over eighty, and at Oishi's request they pricked their fingers and signed an oath of vengeance in blood.

A few days later the warriors learned that Lord Kira was giving a tea party late in the afternoon on January 30. He would definitely be home that night.

When the long-awaited evening arrived, snow fell as the ronin put on their battle dress. Above their coats of armor plating were stitchings of black silk and gold cloth that made them look like members of the local fire brigade. This allowed them to walk through the streets unnoticed.

A day or two before the attack, an old samurai who was in his eighties became sick. Only forty-six men actually attacked Kira's compound, but the signers of the blood oath are still known to history as the forty-seven *ronin*.

With rope ladders, several warriors climbed over the front wall, and several more climbed over the back. They overpowered the guards nearby and unlocked the gates to the villa. The younger *ronin* charged into Kira's house before the rest of his guards even knew there was an attack. Nine older *ronin*, in their fifties and sixties, stood guard outside to prevent any of Kira's men from leaving the compound to seek help. They also put a sign out in the street:

WE, THE RONIN SERVING ASANO, THIS NIGHT WILL BREAK INTO THE MANSION OF KIRA TO AVENGE OUR MASTER. PLEASE BE ASSURED THAT WE ARE NEITHER ROB-BERS NOR RUFFIANS AND NO HARM WILL BEFALL THE NEIGHBORING PROPERTY.

The sign worked. The neighbors had never cared for the corrupt Kira, and did nothing to help him.

Inside the house, women and children screamed as Oishi and his men dashed for Kira's bedroom. Kira's bed was still warm, so they knew he was close by. Frantically they searched from room to room, opening every door and closet. They worried that if they did not find Kira in time, the forces of the Uesugi family would come to his rescue, and they would fail to avenge their lord.

Few of Kira's guards put up much of a fight, but one brave man engaged Oishi's son Chikara in a swordfight in the garden. Chikara fought well and wounded his opponent in the leg. Rather than kill him, he took the man's sword, rushed back into the house, and continued the search for Kira.

At last, several warriors ran to the entrance of the kitchen, where one of them thrust his sword into a bin used to store charcoal. There was a muffled cry of pain. Lord Kira staggered out, clutching a dagger. The *ronin* recognized him instantly because of the scar on his forehead from the wound that Asano had inflicted two years before. Kira was bleeding, injured in the thigh. It took just one spear thrust to knock him down.

Accounts differ as to who cut off Lord Kira's head. Some say it was Oishi himself. After the blow, the *ronin* assembled for a roll call. Six men were slightly injured, but not one *ronin* had died.

The warriors wrapped Kira's head in his kimono, and as the first light of dawn appeared on January 31, 1703, the *ronin* began a five-mile walk to the Buddhist temple where Asano was buried. There they washed Kira's head in a well, burned incense, and kneeled in prayer as they placed his head before Lord Asano's tomb. Oishi set down the dagger that Asano had used to kill himself, pointed it in the direction of Kira's head, and left this message:

We could not have dared to present ourselves before you in paradise unless we had carried out the vengeance which you began. Every day that we waited seemed as three autumns to us. . . . Please take this dagger, strike the head of your enemy a second time, and dispel your hatred forever.

Afterward, Oishi sent a messenger to report the vendetta to the police, and later in the day they arrested the *ronin* and divided them into four groups. Each group stayed in the mansion of a *daimyo* (regional lord) until the shogun decided what to do.

Almost everyone in Japan approved of the vendetta and the *daimyos* went out of their way to honor Oishi's men. The *ronin* were carried to the lord's mansions on litters and lavishly entertained with the best food and sake. In a soft and decadent era the *ronin* had thrilled their countrymen by sacrificing everything to fulfill their duty.

Because public opinion was overwhelmingly in favor of the warriors, the shogun took six weeks to decide the case, and asked every major scholar for his opinion. The problem was not just that the vendetta was unregistered and illegal, it also involved an incident that the shogun had already passed judgment on. The vendetta was an implicit rebuke to his justice, and the men who took part in it had to be punished.

The shogun finally sentenced the *ronin* to death, but because of their exemplary loyalty to Lord Asano he allowed them to die honorably by committing seppuku. On March 20, 1703, in the gardens of four separate mansions, the warriors died, one by one.

Oishi was the first in his group. He kneeled on a white cloth covering three mats and thanked the gods for his life and for the opportunity to fulfill his duty as a samurai. Then he thrust his dagger into the left side of his abdomen, and in great pain, slowly moved the dagger to the right. As he did this, one of the *daimyo*'s samurai cut off Oishi's head with one stroke of his sword, and presented the severed head to a government official who served as a witness. Then servants carried Oishi's head and corpse away in a coffin, covered the blood on the ground with sand, put down a new set of mats and cloth, and called the next man in to die.

The *ronin* were buried next to their master, Lord Asano, and today the graveyard of the forty-seven men is one of the most popular tourist attractions in Japan.

The shogun's death sentence angered the Japanese public. Graffiti appeared attacking the shogun, and on a bridge in Edo an old sign that extolled the virtue of loyalty was torn down in disgust again and again until the government finally replaced it with a sign that simply praised the family.

A play about the vendetta was performed just twelve days after the *ronin* died, but the government closed it immediately. Over 150 dramas have followed since then. The most famous by far is *Chushingura* (The Treasury of Loyal Retainers), written in 1748 by Takeda Izumo II with the help of two other playwrights.

Chushingura is set in the 1350s, and Oishi Kuranosuke's name is changed to Oboshi Yuranosuke. This prevented the play from being closed. Originally a puppet play, *Chushingura* has two suicides (not counting the forty-seven at the end of the play), three attempted suicides, a murder, an accidental killing, two other killings, and three deaths in combat. The show was a huge success, and almost immediately the drama became a kabuki play as well. Ever since, Japanese actors have coveted the many-sided role of Oboshi as much as British actors have prized the part of Hamlet.

For dramatic effect, the authors of *Chushingura* took many liberties with the truth. At the beginning of the play, for example, Oboshi rushes to his master's side and opens a sliding door at the moment his lord commits seppuku. "Avenge me!" his master commands, and at the end of the play it is Oboshi who cuts off the villain's head.

The geisha in *Chushingura*, Okaru, is the wife of one of Oboshi's own men. Her husband has sold her into prostitution to raise money for the vendetta, though of course Oboshi does not know this. In addition, late in the play, Oboshi's son marries and enjoys one night of love with his bride before he leaves her to avenge his lord. During the climactic battle, each of the forty-seven *ronin* have letters on their kimonos that correspond to the forty-seven letters of the Japanese alphabet. Finally, in the play's last scene, the men do not wait for anyone's judgment, but immediately prepare to commit seppuku at their lord's grave.

Chushingura and the many other dramas about the forty-seven *ronin* are often shown during the week of December 14, because under the old Japanese calendar the killing of Lord Kira took place on the fourteenth night of the twelfth month. The performances and broadcasts of this story are an annual part of Japanese cultural life, and December would not be the same without them.

Today, after three centuries, we can only look back in awe at Oishi's ability to inspire forty-six other men to divorce their wives, orphan their children, and give up their lives for the sake of their duty to a hot-tempered lord who was already dead. By modern standards such conduct would be insane. But if we substitute the word "freedom" for "honor," we might better understand how men like Oishi could believe that a life without honor was worse than no life at all.

There is no honor in not working for a living, and a samurai's work was to serve his master. The essence of the tale of the forty-seven *ronin* is that these Japanese sacrificed everything to do their job well.

21

Okubo Toshimichi

*The Bureaucrat Who Led Japan
into the Modern World*

I N 1867 Japan was still a backward country isolated from the rest of the world. Within forty years the Japanese had learned to build battleships powerful enough to sink the Russian navy. The three dozen samurai who started Japan's modernization are known today as "the Meiji leaders," because they ordered sweeping changes in the name of Emperor Meiji, who was only fifteen when they took power in 1868. They rank with America's Founding Fathers as among the most successful statesmen in history.

The most capable and influential of the Meiji leaders was Okubo Toshimichi (1830–1878). For ten years Okubo was literally the power behind the throne, and instrumental in transforming Japan from a feudal society into an industrial nation. Although this cool and calculating administrator was assassinated in 1878, his protégés ran Japan for the next forty years.

Okubo was born on September 26, 1830, in the castle city of Kagoshima, on the island of Kyushu. He had four sisters and was the only son of a minor local official. His easygoing father made friends from every social class and seldom scolded his son, not even when Okubo mischievously diverted hot water from a spa and caused bathers to leap out of a suddenly ice-cold pool.

In the morning Okubo went to school and studied the Chinese classics. He also learned Japanese history from teachers who argued that the shogun had taken too much of the emperor's authority. The distant shoguns were never popular in Kyushu. In the afternoon Okubo and his neighbors went to an exercise hall, where they learned judo, fencing, archery, and basic military strategy. They also read about military heroes and discussed fine points of duty and honor.

Okubo was not an athlete, but he was an excellent debater, and won the friendship of Saigo Takamori, a huge, warmhearted warrior three years older than he. Like Okubo, Saigo also became one of Japan's most powerful leaders.

Kagoshima, Okubo's home, was the capital of Satsuma, one of the most powerful of Japan's 261 feudal domains. Because Satsuma was only a short sea voyage from China, its people were especially aware of the spread of European colonialism and the danger it posed to Japan. Many Satsuma officials, including

Okubo's father, wanted to use government funds to buy Western rifles and artillery.

Others in Satsuma were hesitant to spend so much money on the military. When a political conspiracy was exposed in 1849, these citizens gained the upper hand. They exiled Okubo's father to an island three hundred miles to the south, and because young Okubo had served his father as a messenger, dismissed him from a job he held as a librarian and put him under house arrest for six months.

During the five years his father was in exile, Okubo had no income. He borrowed money from relatives to support his mother and sisters, and probably also earned money tutoring students. Despite his efforts, his mother became sick and died, and afterward people said that Okubo became a colder and more reserved individual.

Okubo and his father might never have been pardoned if United States Navy Commodore Matthew Perry had not led steamships into Edo (soon renamed Tokyo) Bay in 1853. Perry delivered a letter from President Millard Fillmore demanding that Japan end its isolation and open up ports to trade with the United States. Perry promised to return the following year for an answer, and implied that he would use force if the government's reply was not favorable.

The Japanese opened two cities to trade in 1854, and six more ports during the next decade. To keep the West from colonizing Japan, the shogun also reluctantly signed "unequal treaties" with Britain, France, Holland, the United States, and Russia in 1858. These treaties violated Japan's sovereignty by setting Japan's import duties at permanently low rates, and by declaring that Americans and Europeans who lived in Japan would be subject to the laws of their own country, not the laws of Japan.

It was humiliating for the shogun's ministers to sign these treaties because the very name "shogun" is a shortened version of *sei-i tai-shogun*, which means "barbarian-subduing great general." Clearly the shogun was not subduing any foreigners. Worse, the shogun agreed to the "unequal treaties" without consulting the emperor, who was against them. In the eyes of many Japanese, therefore, both the treaties and the government that signed them lacked legitimacy. Opponents of the shogun rallied behind the slogan "Revere the emperor, expel the barbarian."

In Satsuma a progressive new *daimyo* (regional lord) began building an iron foundry, a gun factory, and a shipyard. He also pardoned the Okubos and hired the younger Okubo to be an inspector of supplies. By 1858 Okubo was in charge of receiving and distributing the rice sent to the capital by Satsuma's peasants.

This was Okubo's first well-paying job, and at about this time Okubo married a young woman named Masuko. During the next twenty years they had seven sons and one daughter. Although Okubo was unemotional in public, in private he was a warm father who played with his children each morning before he went to work. Compared to most Japanese men of his rank, Okubo was an unusually faithful husband, but in the last years of his life he took a concubine who gave birth to a son five months after his death.

Late in 1858 Okubo lost his job at the rice warehouse because the *daimyo* of Satsuma died and conservatives again took control of the region's government. At the national level too, reactionary ministers purged anyone dissatisfied with the shogun's rule.

Out of work and with no prospects, Okubo helped form a band of forty radical samurai who were determined to kill the shogun's most tyrannical ministers or die trying. But Satsuma's new *daimyo*, Shimazu Hisamitsu, learned of the plot and asked the samurai to wait for a more favorable time to act.

Many young samurai were impatient to become heroes and wanted to march to the capital anyway. But in a calm, quiet voice Okubo pointed out that an action with their *daimyo*'s support would do much more damage to the shogun than an action without it, no matter how heroic. He clinched his argument by telling his cohorts, "If you insist on leaving, kill me first and then go."

Having cooled down his hotheaded friends, Okubo met with Lord Hisamitsu in the spring of 1860. They made an unwritten bargain. If Okubo would restrain his radical friends at home, Hisamitsu would work nationally to persuade other *daimyo*s to oppose the shogun. He also appointed Okubo assistant director of Satsuma's treasury, and within a year the hardworking administrator had become one of Hisamitsu's top advisers.

In the summer of 1862, Hisamitsu led 1,000 troops to Edo (Tokyo) and demanded that the shogun dismiss several unpopular ministers and grant amnesty to political prisoners. The shogun agreed, but Okubo and his followers were bitterly disappointed. Hisamitsu's demands had been too moderate; there was no insistence that the government also expel the Western barbarians. In disgust, Okubo and his angry samurai talked of possibly assassinating the shogun, but their thinking changed completely after a chain of events that began with their march home to Satsuma.

On September 14, just outside Edo, an Englishman named C. L. Richardson defied Japanese custom by neglecting to get off his horse when a *daimyo* went by. Hisamitsu's swordsmen killed Richardson immediately, and Okubo and his friends eagerly anticipated a fight with the British that they knew was inevitable.

Hisamatsu refused to arrest Richardson's killers, and in response a British naval squadron sailed for Satsuma in August 1863. When Satsuma fired cannon at the ships, the British bombarded Kagoshima, burning half the city.

Okubo had worked all year to strengthen Satsuma's coastal defenses, but when he watched the shelling from a rooftop, he understood for the first time how powerful the Westerners were, and the impossibility of expelling them from Japan.

On the western tip of the island of Honshu, 150 miles to the north, another feudal domain, Choshu, also fired cannon at Western ships. A year later, in 1864, a combined force of British, Dutch, American, and French ships bombarded Choshu's coast and captured its guns.

After this even the most radical samurai realized that instead of expelling the foreigners, it would be better to learn the secrets of their industrial strength. The old desire for isolation was replaced by a burning desire to catch up to the West. A new slogan became popular: "Enrich the country, strengthen the army."

During the mid-1860s Satsuma and Choshu imported thousands of breech-loading rifles from Western arms merchants. The new rifles loaded at the back of the barrel rather than at the front, and fired faster, farther, and more accurately. They were vastly superior to the muzzle-loading rifles used by the shogun's army.

The new (and last) shogun, Tokugawa Keiki, turned to France for weapons, in hope of making his army as modern as those of Satsuma and Choshu. But France's military aid to the shogun filled Japan's *daimyos* with fear. Before this they would have been content with a council of lords where the shogun was first among equals. Now they felt that the shogun had to be overthrown completely.

In 1867 the emperor died of smallpox and his fourteen-year-old son succeeded him. The new emperor would later be given the name Meiji, which means "enlightened rule." Because Emperor Meiji was so young when he ascended the throne, the real power at the Imperial court was held by Iwakura Tomomi, the most intelligent and energetic of Kyoto's noblemen. He became one of Okubo's closest allies, and his high rank would lend prestige to Okubo's policies.

Late in 1867 Okubo and Kido Koin, a cultured and forward-looking administrator from Choshu, signed a military alliance between Satsuma and Choshu (the two great western domains) against the shogun. Okubo also requested and received a formal order from Emperor Meiji calling for the shogun's overthrow.

To prevent the desperate shogun from kidnapping the emperor, Saigo (Okubo's childhood friend) led 3,000 troops from Satsuma to Kyoto in December 1867, and Kido sent 2,500 troops from Choshu to Osaka. Okubo coordinated the deployment of the two forces. Finally, on January 3, 1868, Emperor Meiji issued a proclamation, written in part by Okubo, that formally abolished the shogun's government.

Japan's new government was led by the emperor, a Senior Council of lords (including Iwakura), and a Junior Council of deputy ministers, mostly samurai from the more powerful domains. The hardworking deputies held the real power, and included Okubo and Saigo from Satsuma, and Kido and Ito Hirobumi (1841–1909) from Choshu.

Ito was only twenty-eight when he became a junior councilor. The son of a low-ranking samurai, Ito illegally boarded a British ship at twenty-two and sailed to London, where he studied English, science, and naval affairs. His hard work and broad outlook impressed Okubo immediately, and he soon became Okubo's top aide.

Only three weeks after the new government took power, Shogun Keiki attacked Kyoto with 10,000 troops, but was soundly defeated by 5,500 much better-armed troops from Satsuma and Choshu. The shogun fled to Edo, but Saigo drove him out of the city in May 1868. The new government renamed the city Tokyo (eastern capital), and moved the emperor there a year later.

Japan's new leaders quickly discovered that they could not create a modern central government so long as the nation's revenues were divided among 261 *daimyo*s. Okubo and Kido therefore approached their own *daimyo*s and asked them to give up their land for the good of the country. Incredibly, they agreed. In March 1869 the *daimyo*s of Satsuma, Choshu, Tosa, and Hizen voluntarily offered their land and revenues to the emperor, "so that state affairs, both great and small, may be in the hands of a single authority . . . and our country put on a footing of equality with countries overseas."

The four most powerful lords in Japan had set an example of loyalty to the emperor that was impossible for the other *daimyo*s to ignore. By the time the emperor actually ordered the *daimyo*s to return their land to him in July, 247 had already done so.

The *daimyo*s gave up their land for several reasons. They continued to be the nonhereditary governors of their domains, and to draw ten percent of their former revenues, which was still an enormous salary. Also, many of the weaker lords were in debt and happy to have the government take over their obligations.

In 1871 Okubo and Kido created a new army with 10,000 men from Satsuma, Choshu, and Tosa. Led by Saigo, it was Japan's first Imperial Army, and totally loyal to the national government. Four months later, backed by this new army, the government abolished Japan's 261 feudal domains altogether. This time no one consulted the *daimyo*s in advance. Okubo and his allies simply issued a decree in the name of the emperor on August 29, and Saigo announced that he would attack any domain that resisted its dissolution.

The government disbanded the feudal armies and ordered the *daimyo*s to retire and move to Tokyo. For several years, however, they were allowed to keep their high incomes, which many used to start banks and build factories. The Meiji leaders replaced the domains with "prefectures," drew entirely new boundaries, and appointed the new provincial governors themselves.

In September 1871 Okubo became minister of finance, the first low-ranking samurai to be a chief rather than a deputy minister. Okubo not only controlled the budget of every branch of the national government, his ministry also supervised agriculture, commerce, communications, and local government. In reality, if not by title, Okubo was the most powerful man in Japan.

Okubo devoted himself to his work completely; he had no intellectual interests beyond policy formation. He and his staff merged over 1,600 varieties of bank notes into a single, decimal-denominated currency, the yen. They also demanded that Japan's peasants pay their taxes in money rather than crops, and set the tax at three percent (later 2.5 percent) of a plot's value per year, in practice about thirty percent of the crop. They began a national survey to determine the value of each parcel of land, and issued certificates of land ownership which peasants were free to sell.

Okubo's protégé, Ito Hirobumi, helped start a national bank that issued government bonds, and also helped build telegraph lines across Japan. The first two cities connected were Tokyo and Yokohama in 1870, but by 1876 the telegraph linked dozens of cities, and underwater cables extended to Shanghai and Vladivostok.

Ito also organized the building of Japan's first railroad. The nineteen-mile track connected Tokyo and Yokohama in 1872, and reduced freight costs by a whopping ninety-eight percent. It was built by British engineers with British capital, but afterward railroads were financed domestically, and by 1895 Japan had two thousand miles of tracks.

The Meiji leaders also instituted many social reforms in the early 1870s. They declared all classes equal, even the outcast *burakumin*. They also gave farmers the right to leave their villages and work at new occupations, and samurai the freedom to leave their swords home and dress however they liked.

Okubo put his kimonos away and started wearing suits, which in the 1870s were considered a mark of civilization. He cut off his topknot, and grew a mustache that stretched to his sideburns. He also began to smoke cigars. During political meetings he typically puffed silently for an hour before ending a conference with a few short and sharp remarks.

The Meiji government also imposed a military draft. Young men had to serve three years in the army, although there were many exemptions. The draft was unpopular not only with peasants, who didn't want to leave their land, but also with samurai, who didn't want to associate with peasants. Nevertheless both groups obeyed the law, and the enlarged army made the new government much more powerful than before.

The man who installed the draft and modernized Japan's army along Western lines was another protégé of Okubo's, General Yamagata Aritomo (1838–1922). As a young soldier in Choshu, Yamagata had fought bravely for his *daimyo* against foreigners and against the shogun. In 1870, on behalf of the new government, the young army officer traveled to Europe to study modern military organization. He was particularly impressed by the efficiency of Prussia's army, and by the fact that it answered to the kaiser rather than to the parliament. For the rest of his long life, Yamagata fought and succeeded in keeping Japan's army and navy free from the control of political parties.

Of all the Meiji-era reforms, the most important was an 1872 law requiring compulsory elementary education for all Japanese children, including girls and those from peasant families. Local governments began building over 50,000 elementary schools, and many unemployed samurai became teachers. By 1900 more than ninety-five percent of Japan's children were attending school for at least six years.

Most of the government's reforms had already began by the end of 1871, and in December, Okubo, Kido, Iwakura, and Ito did a remarkable thing. They left the government in the hands of their assistants and traveled to America and Europe for a year and a half. The purpose of their trip was to talk to Western leaders about revising the "unequal treaties." Fifty-nine students also accompanied the Meiji leaders, including two of Okubo's sons, whom he enrolled in Western schools. Before leaving, Okubo asked the senior councilors to sign a twelve-point pledge not to change government policy or make any major appointments while he was away.

The Japanese leaders sailed to San Francisco in January 1872, and traveled by train to Washington, where they met President Ulysees S. Grant. In the autumn the Japanese spent four months in Britain, and there Okubo was deeply impressed by the sheer quantity of factories and railroads. "There is no place that the trains do not go," he wrote a friend.

In Europe the Japanese visited Paris, Brussels, and the Hague, but failed to change anyone's mind about the "unequal treaties." They also met German Chancellor Otto von Bismarck in Berlin in March 1873, and Okubo was encouraged by Germany's example of rapid unification and industrialization.

Before the trip Okubo had not realized how far behind Japan was in so many fields. He came home with a much greater appreciation of the importance of economic growth. It was not just a means of financing the military, it was an end in itself.

Upon returning to Japan, Okubo became home minister. He set up an industrial promotion bureau and built model factories where foreigners taught the Japanese how to use machinery to spin cotton, reel silk, and make paper and glass. He also started model farms where peasants could take short courses, and helped finance projects for seed selection, fertilization, irrigation, and drainage. Yields per acre doubled by 1900.

Okubo had a talented and dedicated staff. He always picked men of ability rather than noble birth, and asked them to do their best over and over again. In one letter he used thirty different expressions for the need to make a special effort.

In 1873 Okubo had returned from Europe earlier than expected because the impulsive Saigo was about to attack Korea. The isolationist Koreans had refused to accept Japan's ambassador because they regarded the Meiji leaders as pro-Western rebels, and an outraged Saigo wanted to avenge this insult to Japan's honor.

Okubo was not a member of the Senior Council at this time, and had no standing to oppose the war. But secretly he met with Emperor Meiji and convinced him to postpone a declaration of war until Kido and Iwakura returned home from Europe in September.

Kido and Iwakura joined Okubo in opposing the war, and by autumn Okubo had gained a seat on the Senior Council. There, with a cold logic and a self-assured dignity that Ito once described as "a natural phenomenon," Okubo argued that "a meaningless war" would end Japan's advances in the military and in industry. He concluded:

Should we cross arms with Korea and become like two water-birds fighting over a fish, Russia will be the fisherman standing by to snare the fish.

The peace party in the Senior Council prevailed by a single vote; there would be no war to interrupt Japan's modernization.

Saigo resigned from the government in disgust and returned to Kagoshima, where he started a college and dozens of schools to teach the military arts. Hundreds of army officers from Satsuma followed Saigo home, denouncing Okubo as a traitor.

During the winter of 1874–1875 Okubo proposed several democratic reforms, including a senate that would be the basis for a future national parliament. The senate had no power to initiate legislation or appropriations, however, and could not even stop Okubo from censoring several newspapers in 1875.

In 1876, Okubo's government stopped paying salaries to samurai. It was simply too great an expense for the government to pay wages to warriors when the local armies they served no longer existed. Instead of salaries, the government issued bonds that on average paid only sixty percent of a samurai's previous salary.

For Saigo and his followers in Satsuma, the government's forty-percent cut in samurai pay was the last straw. The new government had eliminated their feudal domain, their local army, and now almost half their income.

By autumn the city of Kagoshima was home to thousands of samurai openly defiant of the government. As a precaution, Okubo ordered the removal of weapons from the city's arsenal in January 1877. But thousands of students occupied the storehouse, carted away its weapons, and convinced Saigo to lead an army north to Tokyo.

Okubo's first instinct was to rush to Kagoshima and have a personal talk with his childhood friend. But Kido, just before he died of tuberculosis, warned Okubo that if he showed any favoritism toward his home province, the people of Choshu might become rebellious themselves. Kido demanded that Okubo send the Imperial Army south to Satsuma to crush Saigo's rebellion, and reluctantly Okubo agreed. Okubo and Saigo, friends since their teens, were now opposing leaders in a bloody civil war.

During the spring and summer of 1877 the island of Kyushu was a huge battlefield, with 60,000 government soldiers fighting 42,000 samurai, sometimes in hand-to-hand combat. The samurai were outgunned as well as outnumbered, and by autumn, half were dead or wounded. One of the wounded men was Saigo. Rather than face capture, he ordered an aide to behead him on September 24.

The civil war in Satsuma marked the end of samurai power and local autonomy. Had Saigo been victorious and restored feudalism, he would have postponed Japan's modernization for decades. Despite this, Saigo is loved by many Japanese today as a romantic hero, while Okubo is only grudgingly admired as an able bureaucrat.

On the morning of May 14, 1878, Okubo rode in a horse-drawn carriage to a meeting at the emperor's palace. Suddenly six samurai surrounded the carriage, cut off the horses' legs, and killed the coachman. One of them thrust a dagger into the middle of Okubo's forehead, and slowly pulled the blade down below his eyes.

The six assassins who avenged the death of Saigo gave themselves up and were tried and executed. Many people hailed them as heroes because they regarded Okubo as a despot unsympathetic to democracy. There was some truth to this, and the government responded by creating prefectural assemblies, the equivalent of state legislatures, during the next several months. It was a course of action that Okubo himself had suggested shortly before he died.

Okubo did not oppose democracy, but he wanted it to evolve slowly. Most Japanese were still illiterate in the nineteenth century, and Okubo was contemptuous of the narrow interests of popularly based political parties. Okubo's beliefs were shared by his top aide, Ito Hirobumi, who succeeded Okubo as home minister and became Japan's first prime minister in 1885. Like Okubo, Ito regarded political parties as a necessary evil, but also as nuisances that interfered with the experts in government who were trying to do their job.

During the 1880s Ito wrote much of the "Meiji constitution" that governed Japan until 1945. He modeled the charter along German lines, with a cabinet that reported to the emperor rather than the legislature, and with the powers of the legislature sharply limited. Neither Ito nor Okubo foresaw that there would come a time, in the 1930s and 1940s, when a government insufficiently accountable to the people would make tragic mistakes.

Still, it would be unfair to blame Okubo for blunders made more than a half a century after his death, especially when he was so instrumental to Japan's rapid progress in the 1870s. No one but Okubo could have kept Saigo and his unruly samurai under control for so long, or avoided war with Korea in 1873. Okubo took on more responsiblity, worked harder, had more courage during a crisis, and thought more coolly and more nationally than any other Meiji leader.

By the time Okubo was assassinated in 1878, he had set the course for Japan's modernization. The Meiji government he dominated had united 261 feudal domains into a single powerful nation. It abolished class distinctions and began the construction of schools, railroads, and factories throughout the country.

Okubo had very little money when he died; even his enemies had to admit that Okubo had been an honest official.

Two of Okubo's protégés, Ito Hirobumi and the even more conservative General Yamagata Aritomo, supervised Japan's economic development for another generation. As boys in Choshu, they had been classmates at school. Now the two rivals took turns as prime minister between 1885 and 1901, extending Japan's power to Taiwan and Korea, and remained the powers behind the throne until their deaths in 1909 and 1922.

Okubo Toshimichi and the Meiji leaders did not abolish class privilege and send peasants to school because they were revolutionaries interested in social justice. On the contrary, they were deeply conservative men who wanted as little change as possible. But they wanted Japan to catch up with the West, and once in power they realized that the social reforms necessary to accomplish this task were huge. Many leaders such as Saigo shrank from making the sweeping changes that Japan needed, but Okubo never hesitated when Japan's national interest required decisive action.

22

Tojo Hideki

Japan's Wartime Prime Minister

D URING World War II the three most hated men in the world were Hitler, Mussolini, and General Tojo Hideki. Tojo ordered Japan's attack on Pearl Harbor, then led his nation in war for three years.

Unlike Hitler and Mussolini, Tojo (1884–1948) was not a dictator. He shared power with other military and cabinet leaders, and with a group of ex–prime ministers known as the "senior statesmen." Most important, he was answerable to the emperor, Hirohito.

Because the emperor by tradition almost never exercised his authority, Tojo was by far the most powerful man in Japan from 1941 to 1944. While he was prime minister, the Japanese invaded Burma, the Philippines, the East Indies, and many islands in the Pacific. Japanese soldiers ruthlessly exploited millions of Asian laborers and caused hundreds of thousands more to die from brutality and untreated disease.

Ultimately, Tojo's policies led to the death of over 2.5 million Japanese, the fire-bombing of Tokyo and Osaka, the atomic bombing of Hiroshima and Nagasaki, and the occupation of Japan by American troops. Yet to the end Tojo never wavered in his belief that in 1941 Japan had no choice but to attack the United States.

He was born in Tokyo on December 30, 1884, the oldest surviving son in an upper-middle-class family of ten children. His mother was the daughter of a Buddhist priest. His father was an army officer who wrote a book on the art of war and eventually became a major general in Japan's war against Russia in 1904–1905.

Like many Japanese children, Tojo was indulged by his mother but disciplined at school. His friends called him "fighting Tojo" because he never backed away from a fight no matter what the odds. Tojo entered a military prep school at fifteen, and later enrolled in the Imperial Military Academy in Tokyo, where in 1905 the hardworking young cadet graduated tenth in a class of 363 students.

At this time Russia and Japan were at war in Manchuria, a Chinese province north of Korea. Tojo was eager for combat, but he was sent to a post far from the front lines, and the war ended just two months after he graduated. His chance for rapid promotion was gone, and he remained a lieutenant for ten years.

In 1908 a young woman from the island of Kyushu named Ito Katsu paid frequent visits to the home of Tojo's parents, who were friends of her family. She was a student at Tokyo Women's College, which made her far more educated than most Japanese women of her time. She was also cheerful and pretty, and she and Tojo married in April 1909. She was nineteen; he was twenty-four. They had three sons and four daughters.

As a young husband, Tojo studied at the Army Staff College, then spent several years as a company commander, a supply officer, and a staffer at the War Ministry. In 1919 Tojo was assigned to Germany as a military attaché. For two and a half years Tojo, now a major, studied the German Army and the Prussian military tradition, which he greatly admired.

When he returned home in 1922 to be an instructor at the Army Staff College, Japan was enjoying a time of peace and prosperity. But the 1920s was a rough decade for the army. To cut the budget, Japan's civilian leaders eliminated four army divisions. Many young officers, the sons of poverty-stricken farmers, resented the cuts and became contemptuous of a democracy that was often led by wealthy retired Mitsui and Mitsubishi executives.

In Manchuria some of these officers took action into their own hands. On September 18, 1931, a bomb exploded on the South Manchurian Railway, which had been Japanese-owned since 1905. Without permission from anyone in Tokyo, the Japanese army that guarded the railroad used the bomb as an excuse to conquer the whole of Manchuria during the next several months, and set up a puppet state called Manchukuo. The army also stationed several thousand troops on the outskirts of Beijing, 150 miles (240 km) away.

Japan's civilian cabinet should have taken measures at this time to control the army. Instead, they accepted the addition of Manchuria to the Japanese Empire, which since 1905 had also included Korea and Taiwan.

Tojo had nothing to do with the "Manchurian Incident," but it is likely that he approved of the outcome. From 1928 to 1931 he commanded the First Infantry Regiment in Tokyo, where his quick mind, his decisiveness as an administrator, and his blunt, rapid speech caused his colleagues to nickname him "the razor." In 1931, at age forty-six, Tojo became a general, and soon served as deputy chief of the Imperial Military Academy.

Tojo became commander of Manchuria's military police four years later, and put discipline into a police force that had been out of control for several years. He did so just in time. On February 26, 1936, over a thousand fiery young soldiers tried to institute a military coup in Tokyo. They murdered several politicians and occupied most of Tokyo's government buildings before Emperor Hirohito ordered the army to crush the rebellion.

Tojo declared an emergency in Manchuria and arrested everyone connected to the uprising, preventing it from spreading. His loyalty was rewarded; in 1937 Tojo became the Manchurian army's chief of staff.

While Tojo moved up the army ranks, the army itself also became more powerful. To keep the unruly army loyal in the aftermath of the 1936 uprising, the civilian government granted the military's request that only generals and admirals on active duty be appointed to lead the War and Navy Ministries. This meant that the army and navy could choose their own leaders, and also, as they soon discovered, that they could bring down an entire government by resigning from the cabinet and refusing to appoint replacements.

Civilian weakness in effect gave the army and navy a veto power over the makeup of the government. Military action soon followed. On July 7, 1937, the Japanese army used some gunfire at the Marco Polo Bridge outside Beijing as an excuse to take over the entire city and fan out over eastern China, once again without any authorization from Tokyo. In Nanjing, China's capital at that time, Japanese soldiers raped a conservative estimate of 20,000 women in December 1937, and killed over 250,000 people.

Rather than reassert civilian control over a renegade army, Japan's new prime minister, Prince Konoe Fumimaro, sent additional troops to China and advocated a "new order" for East Asia. The Chinese continued to resist, and in the end it took one million Japanese troops just to hold China's cities and coastline.

As in Manchuria in 1931, Tojo had nothing to do with the outbreak of these hostilities, but because he regarded China's army as a threat to Manchuria, he approved of the new war. To protect Japanese troops from an attack from the north, Tojo swiftly led his soldiers into Inner Mongolia and conquered the province. It was the only combat Tojo would ever see, and it was against a badly equipped Chinese army, but it was sufficient to advance his career. In 1939 Tojo became inspector-general of the army air force.

The patriotic feeling the war in China aroused in Japan was so strong that in 1938 the Diet, Japan's parliament, passed the National General Mobilization Law, giving the government the power to control prices, wages, hours, trade, and even newspapers and the radio. By June 1940, Japan's political parties dissolved themselves with almost no debate and merged to form a single new party called the Imperial Rule Assistance Association.

The next month Prince Konoe appointed Tojo as minister of war in a one-party cabinet. The short, bald, fifty-five-year-old general was chosen for his administrative ability and for his desire to press the war in China vigorously.

Beginning in 1938, the United States sent a small supply of weapons to the Chinese to help them fight Japan. To secure an ally of its own, Japan signed an alliance with Nazi Germany in September 1940. The Nazis in turn pressured their puppet government in France to let Japan send troops to the northern part of Vietnam, which was then a French colony. Japan wanted to cut the land route by which the United States sent weapons to China.

But Japan was no longer content just to rule China. When the Netherlands fell to the Nazis, their oil-rich colony, the Dutch East Indies (known today as Indonesia), seemed ripe for the taking.

As a first step toward an advance to the south, Japan made peace in the north, signing a neutrality pact with the Soviet Union in April 1941. Then in July, Japanese troops in northern Vietnam moved south to Saigon. This put Japan's air force within striking distance of British Malaya and the Dutch East Indies.

But the Japanese badly underestimated the anger their alliance with the Nazis and their advance to Saigon had created. On July 26, 1941, the United States, Britain, Australia, and the Dutch East Indies froze Japanese assets in their countries and banned all trade with Japan, including the export of oil from the United States and from the East Indies.

The Western nations had hoped to shock Japan into realizing that its aggression had to stop, but the Japanese saw the action as a conspiracy of hostile powers. Japan was completely dependent on foreign oil: Its stockpiles could last only two years. On September 6, Japan's cabinet decided that if by October 15 it could not negotiate an agreement with the West to resume oil imports, Japan would go to war.

Japan offered to withdraw its troops from southern Vietnam, because this is what had brought on the Western trade embargo. But the United States and Britain had no confidence that Japan would not put troops back there again, and demanded that Japan withdraw troops from China as well.

Tojo was adamant. Japan could not withdraw troops from China. More than 165,000 Japanese soldiers had died there, and it would break the army's morale to just pick up and go home. Besides, troops in China were needed to protect Japan's control of Manchuria and Korea.

In October, Prince Konoe met with Tojo privately and expressed his doubt that Japan could win a war against the West. Tojo said, "America has her weaknesses too." In the samurai tradition of defying the odds, he added, "There are times when we must have the courage to do extraordinary things—like jumping, eyes closed, off the veranda of the Kiyomizu Temple." Konoe replied that people in responsible positions should not think that way, but Tojo insisted that if Konoe lacked the courage to follow through on the September 6 decision for war, he should resign as prime minister. Konoe did so a few days later on October 15, 1941.

Two days later, Japan's former leaders, the "senior statesmen," recommended that the emperor pick Tojo as the next prime minister of Japan. They chose him for two reasons. First, they asked the emperor to command the new premier to reconsider the September 6 decision for war, and they thought that since Tojo was loyal to the emperor he would work for peace if commanded to do so. Second, the senior statesmen knew it would not be enough for a new prime minister simply to negotiate an agreement with the United States and Britain. He would also have to make the army accept the troop withdrawals necessary for peace. Tojo, they felt, could not only lead the army in war, he could also restrain it in peace.

In the autumn of 1941 Tojo's new government both prepared for war and made initiatives for peace. The army and navy drew up attack plans and trained troops for combat in the tropics, and the foreign office sent two proposals to the United States secretary of state, Cordell Hull. One proposal was for a neutral zone in Southeast Asia in return for an end to United States aid to China. The other was for a slow withdrawal from China over a twenty-five-year period. Tojo and his generals do not seem to have considered that since Japan had been the aggressor in China, perhaps Japan should make a major concession.

Secretary Hull replied to the Japanese proposals on November 26, 1941. He offered to renew oil shipments and remove American trade barriers to Japanese goods, but he also insisted that Japan withdraw all of its troops from China and Vietnam.

Hull's hard line was fully supported by Britain, Australia, and the Netherlands. They refused to accept the Japanese conquest of China, especially since Japan was an ally of the Nazis. By late 1941 the Nazis had conquered nearly all of Europe, and with the fate of the world at stake, the era of appeasement was over.

For the Japanese, Hull's note of November 26 came as a thunderbolt. The United States was demanding that Japan give up everything it had gained since 1931. Even those who had been advocating peace with America recognized the impossibility of Japan's withdrawing *all* its troops from China. As the Japanese saw it, they faced three choices: to commit political suicide by giving in to the American demands, to commit economic suicide by doing nothing and gradually running out of oil, or to go to war.

On December 1, 1941, Emperor Hirohito ratified the unanimous decision by General Tojo and his cabinet to begin war against the United States, Britain, and the Netherlands. In a speech several weeks earlier, Tojo had predicted: "If one hundred million people merge into one iron solidarity and go forward, nothing can stop us."

The plan of the Japanese military was to knock out the United States Navy in a decisive blow, take the oil and metals of the East Indies, and set up a defense perimeter in the South Pacific.

On December 7, 1941, Japanese planes bombed Pearl Harbor, the United States Navy base near Honolulu, Hawaii. They sank twelve ships, destroyed 188 planes, damaged 159 more, and killed 2,403 Americans. Within forty-eight hours the Japanese also attacked Hong Kong, which fell in eighteen days, the Philippines, most of which fell in twenty-six days, and Malaya, where the Japanese took seventy days to advance down the long peninsula to Singapore.

The Dutch East Indies were now defenseless, and the Japanese took the islands in March 1942, with little damage to the oil fields. The Japanese also occupied Burma, most of New Guinea, and the Solomon, Gilbert, and Marshall islands in the Pacific.

Scholars estimate that the Japanese caused over one million civilians and prisoners of war to die from brutality, overwork, starvation, or disease. In the Pacific, twenty-seven percent of the American and British POWs died in captivity, compared with four percent in Europe. The Japanese did not respect prisoners because they themselves preferred to die in battle. On the island of Iwo Jima in 1945, for example, American marines killed 15,000 Japanese; only nine surrendered. Yet in previous wars the Japanese had treated POWs well in spite of their contempt for prisoners. Only during World War II did the Japanese military have so little regard for a foreigner's humanity.

In China, Tojo's repeated command that prisoners who did not work should not eat caused many Japanese officers in the field to work tens of thousands of sick and wounded POWs to death. In Thailand, where Tojo suggested using civilians and POWs to build the Burma-Thailand railroad—featured in the 1957 film *The Bridge over the River Kwai*—no one took precautions to protect anyone from disease or from the tropical sun. Over 12,000 Allied POWs and 60,000 Asians died during the building of this railroad.

The worst abuse by far was in Japanese army Unit 731 in Manchuria. Army doctors tortured Chinese, Koreans, and Russians in gruesome experiments, including freezing limbs, injection with germs, drilling into skulls, and dehydrating people to twenty percent of their weight. At least 10,000 victims died; one was a baby three days old. Tojo walked out of the room when a film of Unit 731's experiments was shown to him, but he did nothing to stop the torture.

The Japanese tried to win the goodwill of their fellow Asians by forming the Greater East Asia Co-Prosperity Sphere. To promote this idea, Tojo hosted a conference of Japan's Asian supporters in November 1943. But the brutality of the Japanese army and the arrogance of many Japanese businessmen gave the lie to Japan's promise of Asian brotherhood. The vast majority of the people of East Asia thoroughly hated Japanese rule.

In Japan the public knew nothing of the army's atrocities because censorship was tight. Tojo reviewed troops, toured factories, and gave speeches urging people on to greater effort. Dressed in a khaki uniform with a red collar and several medals, Tojo liked to ride a white horse in the morning and chat with people in the street. Once, when some fishermen complained that a shortage of gasoline made it difficult to get their fish to market, Tojo gruffly replied, "Never mind gasoline, get up earlier!"

But willpower and self-discipline could not make up for the hundreds of ships sunk by American airplanes and submarines. On June 4, 1942, off the island of Midway, United States Navy dive-bombers destroyed four Japanese aircraft carriers and 332 planes—half of Japan's naval air force. Some of the pilots were in the air when their ships were sunk, and having nowhere to land, ran out of gas and crashed into the sea.

With fewer airplanes to protect their ships, Japanese losses began to mount. The oil, rubber, and metals in the East Indies that the Japanese had gone to so much trouble to take in 1942 became hard to ship back to Japan in 1943. By 1944 aircraft and weapons production fell despite the fact that women and teenagers worked in factories for sixty hours a week and more. Tojo's government rationed rice and other food to save resources, and closed ten thousand places of amusement.

Tojo became unpopular. Navy officers criticized him for wasting men and weapons in China. Civilian leaders criticized him for surrounding himself with yes-men and transferring opponents to distant posts. The public resented that his two grown sons were not in the army. (One was nearsighted; the other was an engineer in the weapons industry.)

Discontent with Tojo climaxed in July 1944, when the United States took Saipan, an island just 1,500 miles (2,400 km) south of Tokyo. Twenty-five thousand Japanese soldiers died defending the island, but now American bombers were within range of Japan's largest cities.

On July 17, 1944, Japan's "senior statesmen" sent a resolution to the emperor calling for Tojo's resignation. Tojo resigned as prime minister the next day, and moved back to his modest home in suburban Tokyo. While he spent his time gardening and writing, his successor, Koiso Kuniaki, continued the war.

American B-29s began bombing Tokyo, Osaka, and other large cities in October 1944. By May 1945, when a bomb destroyed a small cottage in Tojo's backyard, millions of Japanese were already homeless.

Tojo continued to believe in the war and was confident that the army and navy could keep Japan's home islands secure. Even after the atomic bombing of Hiroshima and Nagasaki on August 6 and 9, 1945, an unyielding Tojo told his wife, "Our ancestors must have lived in caves at one time and so can we. . . . If we don't take baths for seven months we aren't going to die and if we can stand it that long, we will win." But on August 15, when Emperor Hirohito went on the radio and asked his subjects to "endure the unendurable" and surrender, Tojo finally accepted defeat.

Four weeks later, on September 11, United States military policemen came to Tojo's house to arrest him for war crimes. Tojo looked out his window, sat down in an armchair, and shot himself in the heart. Military policemen rushed into his house, and as news photographers popped flashbulbs, a Japanese doctor bandaged Tojo's wounds. Later an American doctor gave Tojo six blood transfusions.

The previous day, Tojo had written a last testament stating his hope that his dying would atone for having brought death to so many of "His Majesty's faithful subjects." But Tojo did not die. He had missed his heart by millimeters.

When Tojo recovered, he was sent to a Tokyo prison, where he washed dishes, scrubbed floors, and prepared for his trial. Allied prosecutors charged Tojo with conspiracy to commit aggressive war and with willfully permitting atrocities. Twenty-eight of Japan's top wartime leaders (but not the emperor) were brought before the International Military Tribunal for the Far East, which began in May 1946, and was presided over by judges from eleven countries. The trial lasted two and a half years. Not until December 1947 did Tojo finally take the stand. He assumed full responsibility for Japan's decision to go to war in 1941, but said it was necessary because of the Allied trade embargo. He stressed that the emperor had no choice but to ratify his cabinet's decisions. He apologized for atrocities to POWs, and lamely said he had forwarded reports of their ill treatment to the proper departments. On November 4, 1948, the court found Tojo guilty of the majority of the crimes he was charged with, and a week later, sentenced him to death.

During Tojo's last months in prison he read Buddhist scriptures. He said he regretted that he had only discovered them in prison. Tojo also told a priest, "I fully realize my responsibility for not making His Majesty's benevolence generally known to the world."

Tojo, five other generals, and an ex–foreign minister were hanged by the United States military police on December 23, 1948. Prisoners not only of the United States Army but of the beliefs formed in their youth, the seven condemned men shouted three "Banzai!" for the emperor just before they entered the gallows. Several hours later American soldiers cremated their bodies, and to prevent a memorial to them in the future, mixed their ashes together and scattered them to the winds.

Japanese workers secretly saved some of the ashes and divided them into seven urns. They buried the urns under a boulder at the Yasukuni Shrine in Tokyo, a Shinto structure that honors the spirits of Japan's war dead. The boulder is a simple monument, but to many foreigners its very existence is provocative.

23
Yamamoto Isoroku
The Admiral Who Planned Pearl Harbor

ONE OF THE greatest ironies in history is that the man who planned Japan's attack on Pearl Harbor in 1941, Admiral Yamamoto Isoroku, strongly opposed going to war with the United States.

Yamamoto (1884–1943) knew how strong America's economy was. He had lived in the United States for four years during the 1920s, studying the oil industry at Harvard and serving as the naval attaché at Japan's embassy in Washington. As a student, Yamamoto hitchhiked across America and saw the steel mills of Pittsburgh, the automobile factories of Detroit, and the oil wells of Texas. As a diplomat, he played poker at night with United States Navy officers, and knew that Americans were not the soft, luxury-loving people most Japanese military men thought them to be.

Yamamoto opposed Japan's conquest of Manchuria in 1931 and the invasion of China in 1937. He wanted to avoid a war with the West. In September 1940, just before Japan signed an alliance with Hitler, Yamamoto warned Prime Minister Konoe Fumimaro,

> In the first six to twelve months of a war with the United States and Britain I will run wild and win victory after victory. But if the war continues after that, I have no expectation of success.

The militarists who led Japan's government tolerated Yamamoto because he was the most dynamic and capable admiral in the navy. From 1930 to 1933, and again in 1935, Yamamoto had served as technical director of Japan's naval air force. During this time he was instrumental in developing the highly maneuverable Zero fighter plane, the Nakajima torpedo bomber, and the long-range, twin-engine bomber that Americans later called the Betty. Yamamoto trained his pilots relentlessly until they mastered the art of taking off and landing at night and in fog.

Most important, Yamamoto convinced his colleagues that aircraft carriers were the wave of the future. At a time when the world's navies, including Japan's, were still relying on battleships, Yamamoto created an aircraft carrier strike force with hundreds of combat-ready planes. By the late 1930s Japan had the most powerful naval air force in the world.

Yamamoto Isoroku was born on April 4, 1884, outside Nagaoka, a small city 150 miles (240 km) north of Tokyo, just inland from the Sea of Japan. He was the youngest of seven children. His father had fought for the shogun against the Meiji government, and later became principal of an elementary school. Fifty-six years old when his new son was born, the father named him Isoroku, "fifty-six."

Nagaoka is in one of the snowiest regions of Japan; as a child Isoroku grew strong shoveling footpaths in the winter. He ran to school each morning, and excelled in gymnastics. One of his teachers was an American missionary; sometimes Isoroku went to his house after school and practiced English.

Isoroku entered the Imperial Naval Academy in 1901. He was only five feet three inches tall, but stocky and very strong. Sometimes he amused his fellow cadets by standing on his head and twirling two plates on the palms of his hands, finishing with a somersault, plates still twirling. Even as an adult, Isoroku sometimes enlivened a party with his plate dance. He was a serious student, however, and graduated seventh in his class in 1904. He was then assigned to the cruiser *Nisshin* as a gunnery specialist.

When the Japanese sank the Russian navy in 1905 during the battle at Tsushima Strait, a shell hit Isoroku and ripped the index and middle fingers from his left hand. Ignoring the pain, he wrapped his hand in a handkerchief and remained at his post until the battle was won. Afterward, the head of the navy, Admiral Togo Heihachiro, wrote Isoroku a personal letter of commendation. Years later, because Isoroku had only eight fingers, geishas refused to charge him the usual price of one hundred sen for a manicure, and gave him the nickname "Eighty Sen."

After finishing postgraduate studies at Japan's naval staff college in 1916, Isoroku agreed to be adopted by (and take the name of) the Yamamotos, a prominent military family from his hometown having no male heir. Two years later, on August 31, 1918, he married Mihashi Reiko, the plump, homely twenty-two-year-old daughter of a dairy farmer. They had two sons and two daughters.

As a staff officer with a promising future, Yamamoto had passed up several opportunities to marry an admiral's daughter. He may have felt that a woman from a humble background would be more likely to put up with long absences at sea, and infidelity, than would a wife from an upper-class family. In the same year he married, he also made the first of many visits to a young geisha who lived near a naval base in Kyushu. Later, when he was fifty, Yamamoto fell in love with Kawai Chiyoko, a thirty-year-old Tokyo geisha who delighted in his playful, easygoing nature. Her professional name was Umeryu (Plum Dragon), and she was the mistress of a well-known real estate tycoon. Both Yamamoto and the tycoon accepted her two-sided love life.

Yamamoto lived in America for four of the first ten years of his marriage, but even when he was back in Japan he was rarely at home. In the early 1920s he commanded a cruiser, taught gunnery at the staff college, and studied aviation late at night. Although airplanes at that time were still made of wood and canvas, Yamamoto was convinced that they represented the future of war. He learned to fly in 1924, though he was already forty years old.

Assigned to the Japanese embassy in Washington in the mid-1920s, Yamamoto learned everything he could about the United States Navy and the American aviation industry. He also perfected his English by reading several biographies of Lincoln. When he returned home in 1928 he was given command of Japan's first aircraft carrier, the *Akagi*. Two years later he became a rear admiral, and was sent as a delegate to the London Naval Disarmament Conference of 1930.

The purpose of this conference was to monitor the Washington Naval Treaty of 1922, in which Britain, the United States, and Japan had agreed to limit battleship and aircraft carrier tonnage to a 5-5-3 ratio, with Japan's navy as the smallest. Many Japanese officers felt humiliated by this treaty and called for its cancellation so that Japan's fleet could be equal in size to that of the United States and Britain. This group became known as the "fleet faction." By contrast, the "treaty faction," which included Yamamoto, supported the arms limitation. They knew that Japan could not afford to build a navy as big as America's, and that in the Pacific, where Japan kept all its ships, it actually enjoyed a superiority over Britain and the United States.

Although Yamamoto was unpopular with the fleet faction, he was appointed technical director of the navy's air force in the autumn of 1930 because he knew more about airplanes and aircraft carriers than any other admiral. To get the airplanes he wanted, he made daily phone calls to the Mitsubishi Heavy Industries aircraft factory in Nagoya. If the company was short of men or materials, Yamamoto made sure they quickly received whatever they needed. One result of his effort was the twin-engine Betty bomber, which had a range of 1,200 miles (1,930 km) and was instrumental in destroying China's air force in 1937.

Before war with China began, however, another naval disarmament conference took place in London in 1934. The purpose of this meeting was to renew the 1922 5-5-3 treaty, which was due to expire in 1936. This time Yamamoto was one of Japan's two chief negotiators. He dined with Prime Minister Ramsay MacDonald and played bridge in the evening with British admirals.

The fleet faction, which had grown in power, demanded that Yamamoto ask for an end to the unequal 5-5-3 ratio, but after Japan's conquest of Manchuria in 1931, the British and Americans were too suspicious of Japan to agree to any change. A renewal of the treaty was impossible.

When Yamamoto returned to Japan in 1935, his militarist enemies gave him nothing to do. For a while he thought about resigning from the navy and going to Monte Carlo to gamble professionally, but after several months he was finally able to resume his work for the naval air force. He helped develop a carrier-based fighter plane that was eventually known as the Zero because it made its debut in the Shinto centennial year 2600 (1940). He also persuaded the navy to convert a battleship under construction into an aircraft carrier. By the end of the 1930s Japan had ten carriers, while the United States Pacific Fleet had just three.

In 1936 the moderates regained power briefly after a coup by right-wing army officers failed. Yamamoto became vice minister of the navy, a post that enabled him to stop young navy officers from starting an incident that could lead to war. He was powerless, however, to restrain the hotheads in the army. When gunshots at a bridge near Beijing led to full-scale war with China in July 1937, Yamamoto told friends, "Those damn fools in the army are at it again!" He particularly detested General Tojo Hideki, the future prime minister, whom he regarded as a pompous windbag.

By 1939 Yamamoto had so many enemies in the military that he received threatening letters every few days. A reappointment as vice minister might easily have led to his assassination. For Yamamoto's protection, the outgoing navy minister appointed him commander in chief of the Combined Fleet, a supreme but nonpolitical command that he held for the next three and a half years.

Within six weeks Yamamoto intensified the training of his men. Ships followed one another at night in radio silence, pilots made emergency takeoffs and landings from carrier flight decks, and bombers dropped torpedoes that sailed safely underneath their "target" ships.

In September 1940 Japan signed a military alliance with Nazi Germany. In a meeting with Japan's top generals Yamamoto argued that Germany had nothing to offer the Japanese, and that in response to the pact the West would soon stop selling them oil. His plea fell on deaf ears because the army was already planning to conquer the oil-rich territories of Burma, British Malaya, and the Dutch East Indies (now Indonesia), among other nations.

Yamamoto thought it was "risky and illogical" for Japan to go to war with the United States and Britain when it was still fighting China. He warned that unless the navy destroyed the United States Pacific Fleet at the start of such a war, American aircraft carriers would head west and launch bombing raids against Tokyo.

To prevent this, Yamamoto proposed sending aircraft carriers to bomb Pearl Harbor, the United States Pacific Fleet's headquarters near Honolulu. He hoped a devastating attack would bring Americans to the peace table and induce them to accept Japan's conquests in Asia. In January 1941 he wrote the navy minister a nine-page memorandum outlining his plan, then asked Commander Genda Minoru, a brilliant young officer, to work out the technical details.

Genda concluded that there were two impediments to a successful raid on

Hawaii. First, the navy had to preserve the element of surprise. Second, they had to find a way to prevent their torpedoes from sinking in the shallow mud of Pearl Harbor. To maintain surprise, Yamamoto decided that his fleet should sail in radio silence through the choppy waters of the less-traveled North Pacific. To prepare for the trip, Yamamoto ordered his ships to practice refueling in rough weather.

As for the torpedoes, dive-bombers made training runs at Kagoshima, a port geographically similar to Pearl Harbor, and at first the torpedoes simply sank to the bottom. By autumn, however, engineers had added wooden stabilizers to the fins, and this kept the torpedoes from sinking.

On September 16 and 17, Yamamoto presented his detailed plan for an attack on Pearl Harbor to his colleagues during war games at the naval staff college. Many high-ranking officers said the plan was too risky. They argued that it would be safer to wait for American ships to sail to the western Pacific, where they would be numerically inferior and far from their supply lines.

The officers stated their objections again at a meeting on October 3. Yamamoto listened to them in silence, then asked,

> What would you do if . . . the U.S. fleet launched air raids on Japan from the east? Are you suggesting that it's all right for Tokyo and Osaka to be burned to the ground so long as we get hold of oil?

Yamamoto threatened to resign unless the attack on Pearl Harbor was carried out, and this clinched the decision to make the raid. No one wanted the brilliant commander to retire at the beginning of the war, especially since there were enough airplanes for simultaneous attacks on Malaya and the Philippines. By the first week of November, the navy's leaders agreed that six of Japan's ten aircraft carriers could be spared for a raid on Hawaii.

After ten months of planning, a huge strike force left the Kurile Islands in the far north of Japan on November 26, 1941. Only then were the flight crews told of their mission. Many aviators were given postcards showing an aerial view of Pearl Harbor.

The six carriers held 423 planes, and were accompanied by two battleships, eleven destroyers, three cruisers, eight refueling tankers, and three submarines. The carriers were ordered to turn back if detected before December 6, but although they sailed eleven days and 3,500 miles (5,600 km), they remained unobserved.

The air force included 143 torpedo bombers, 131 dive-bombers, 79 fighters, 30 reconnaisance planes, and 40 planes held in reserve. Yamamoto had hoped to command the carriers personally, but the navy minister felt that he would be more useful at his headquarters on the battleship *Nagato* in Hiroshima Bay. The ministry chose Admiral Nagumo Chuichi to command the mission instead.

By December 6 the strike force was just 250 miles (400 km) north of Pearl Harbor. Shortly before dawn the next morning, on Sunday, December 7, 1941, under a three-quarter moon, 353 pilots on six ships finished their breakfast, drank a tiny cup of sake, said a brief Shinto prayer, shouted three Banzai! ("Ten thousand years!") for the emperor, climbed into their cockpits, and started their engines. At dawn, within fifteen minutes 183 planes took off, flying south for another one hour and fifty minutes before beginning the attack.

At 7:02 A.M. two American radar operators on a mountain near Pearl Harbor detected dozens of airplanes 137 miles (220 km) to the north. They made two telephone calls to report their discovery, but a lieutenant assured them that it was just a squadron of American planes. At 7:53 the lead Japanese pilot radioed *Tora! Tora! Tora!* ("Tiger! Tiger! Tiger!"), code for the fact that they had achieved complete surprise. Five minutes later an American admiral broadcast a message heard around the world: "Air Raid on Pearl Harbor! This Is No Drill!"

In two attacks of 183 and 170 planes, Japanese pilots sank four American battleships, damaged four more, wrecked dozens of other ships of all kinds, destroyed 188 planes, and damaged 159 more. The surprise raid killed 2,403 Americans. More than 1,100 died on the battleship *Arizona* when a bomb struck a room storing explosives. The Japanese lost only 29 planes, eight percent of their force, but they made a costly mistake in not targeting the navy's repair facilities during the first two attacks. Admiral Nagumo did not want to lose any more pilots and planes. His aviation experience was limited, and he failed to press his victory. By not ordering a third attack he left Pearl Harbor's repair docks intact, and in roughly a year the Americans had rebuilt all but five ships in the harbor.

The Japanese destroyed or damaged all eight of the American battleships, but not one of the Pacific Fleet's three aircraft carriers was in Pearl Harbor that day, and Nagumo made almost no effort to search for them. He probably could have found and sunk the *Enterprise*, because it was only 200 miles (320 km) to the west.

Back in Japan, Yamamoto's aides begged him to order Nagumo to launch a third attack immediately. But Yamamoto was reluctant to overrule a commander in the field. "Even a burglar," he said, "hesitates to go back for more."

At a victory party afterward, Yamamoto was quiet. He later wrote a friend: "This war will give us much trouble in the future. The fact that we have had a small success at Pearl Harbor is nothing."

As Yamamoto had predicted, for several months the Japanese "ran wild" and conquered Hong Kong, Malaya, Singapore, the Philippines, Burma, and the Dutch East Indies. But even Yamamoto failed to predict the fury Americans felt following the sneak attack on Pearl Harbor. Within hours of the raid, 135 million Americans were at work to defeat the Japanese Empire.

If Japan had carefully avoided United States territory and left Hawaii, Guam, and the Philippines alone, it is likely that an isolationist America might never have fought Japan with anything more than protests and boycotts. For this reason Samuel Eliot Morison, the great naval historian, has called the attack on Pearl Harbor "a strategic imbecility," although in the short run it was a tactical success.

Once war began, Yamamoto knew that time was short. Japan had to sink the Pacific Fleet while it was still small, before American industry had time to build new ships. He proposed sending over 160 ships to invade the Midway atoll, home to a small United States Navy base 1,500 miles (2,400 km) northwest of Hawaii. From Midway, Japan's navy could threaten aircraft factories in California and Washington. Yamamoto knew America would never give up Midway without a fight. What he was trying to do was use Midway as bait, to lure American aircraft carriers to the islands and sink them.

Many senior Japanese officers told Yamamoto that it was too risky to concentrate so many ships in one area. They wanted to conquer the South Pacific and cut America and Australia off from each other. Once again Yamamoto threatened to resign, but what decided the issue was Lieutenant Colonel James Doolittle's raid on Tokyo on April 18, 1942. The humiliation of having sixteen American B-25's drop bombs near the Imperial Palace convinced almost every military leader of the need to take Midway and extend Japan's defense perimeter eastward.

The strike force that left Japan at the end of May was even bigger than the one that attacked Pearl Harbor. It included four large aircraft carriers, two very small carriers, eleven battleships, sixteen cruisers, fifty-three destroyers, twenty submarines, eighteen transports carrying five thousand men, and several dozen more fuel tankers, minesweepers, and patrol craft. The surface area of the ships was greater than that of the Midway atoll.

This time Yamamoto accompanied his force. His new battleship, the *Yamato*, was the largest warship in the world, the length of three football fields. At dawn Yamamoto put on his snow-white uniform and read almost one hundred reports from ships in the fleet before breakfast. In the evening, after dinner, he played *shogi*, Japanese chess, before reading himself to sleep. Characteristically he liked to begin even a game with an attack.

As much as Yamamoto enjoyed going into battle himself, it was a mistake. To keep their locations secret, the ships sailed to Midway in radio silence. This not only made it difficult for Yamamoto to get timely information, it also meant he could not give an order without breaking the silence. By contrast, the United States fleet commander, Admiral Chester Nimitz, stayed in constant communication with his ships from his office at Pearl Harbor.

Yamamoto expected the invasion of Midway to be a surprise. He had no idea that United States Navy mathematicians had cracked the Japanese navy's radio code and learned almost everything about the planned attack. In response to the threat, Admiral Nimitz ordered the Pacific Fleet's three aircraft carriers, the *Enterprise*, the *Hornet*, and the *Yorktown*, to rendezvous 300 miles (480 km) east-northeast of Midway, just out of range of Japanese reconnaissance.

It was a miracle the United States still had a third carrier. In the battle of the Coral Sea in May, two Japanese and one American aircraft carrier had been badly damaged. But while the Japanese took several months to fix their carriers, 1,400 men at Pearl Harbor worked around the clock and repaired the *Yorktown* in only two days. It made it to Midway just in time.

Because the Japanese did not expect to encounter any American carriers so soon, the overconfident strike force commander, Admiral Nagumo Chuichi, did not launch any search planes until the moment he began his attack.

Seven minutes before dawn, on June 4, 1942, under a full moon, 108 Japanese planes took off from their carriers and flew 240 miles (390 km) southwest to bomb Midway in preparation for an invasion by five thousand Japanese troops scheduled two days later. The planes destroyed more than half of Midway's small air force, but the runway remained undamaged. Admiral Nagumo decided to make another attack, and ordered that the ninety-three planes on the flight decks that were then carrying torpedoes be reloaded with bombs.

Admiral Raymond Spruance, the American strike force commander, felt that the best moment to attack the Japanese would be when they were refueling, so he launched his raid earlier than first planned. It was at about this moment that Admiral Nagumo learned there was an United States carrier off to the east. He now faced an excruciating decision: send a few bombers out right away without torpedoes and without the cover of the fighter planes returning from Midway, or wait an hour and launch a massive attack with torpedo bombers and plenty of fighter cover.

Still thinking there was just one American carrier, Nagumo decided to wait, and ordered the sailors who were putting bombs on the ninety-three planes to remove them and reload the planes with torpedoes. Amid the confusion, stacks of bombs and torpedoes filled the decks of the Japanese carriers.

At this point Yamamoto's failure to concentrate his forces proved fatal. He had not expected any American carriers for several days, and therefore kept his battleships 550 miles (880 km) to the rear, to increase the subsequent surprise. Now, when they were desperately needed in battle, they were too far away.

Yamamoto disagreed with Nagumo's decision to wait an hour to attack and considered ordering him to strike immediately. He did not do so because he did not want to break radio silence and reveal the existence of his ships to the Americans. But for all the good they were doing, the eleven battleships might just as well have stayed in Japan.

While the Japanese were reloading their planes, forty-one American torpedo bombers flew in just above the water and fired their deadly projectiles at the Japanese carriers. The American planes were no match for the maneuverable

Zero fighters, however, and rarely had a decent shot. All the torpedoes missed their targets, and the Japanese shot down all but six of the planes.

The thirty-five American pilots who died then did not do so in vain. They kept the Japanese Zeroes down at low altitudes, so that at 10:22 A.M.—when sixty-seven dive-bombers from the *Enterprise* and *Yorktown* entered the battle at a height of 15,000 feet (4,600 m)—there were no fighters high enough to challenge them.

Suddenly three of the Japanese carriers were sitting ducks as the direction of the entire Pacific war turned around in just five minutes. Swooping almost straight down at a speed of three hundred miles per hour (480 km per hour), Lieutenant Earl Gallagher dropped a bomb on the Japanese carrier *Kaga* that hit a group of refueled airplanes and turned the entire flight deck into an inferno. Lieutenant Richard Best dropped two bombs on Yamamoto's old carrier, the *Akagi*, that started a chain reaction of exploding bombs and torpedoes. Lieutenant Paul "Lefty" Holmberg scored three hits on the carrier *Soryu*, and began another chain reaction of exploding fuel tanks and torpedoes.

The only large Japanese carrier left was the *Hiryu*, and in the afternoon two of its planes fired torpedoes that destroyed the *Yorktown*. Two hours later, dive-bombers from the *Enterprise* destroyed the *Hiryu*.

The Japanese lost four aircraft carriers, 332 planes, and over 2,500 men—half their naval air force—in just one day. The Americans lost one carrier, 147 planes, and 307 men. Many sailors on both sides burned to death, and some were eaten by sharks.

When Yamamoto heard that three of his aircraft carriers were burning, he immediately ordered his battleships to Midway. But that night, when Admiral Spruance refused to risk a further engagement and wisely retreated to the east, Yamamoto knew the battle was over. At 2:55 A.M. the following morning he canceled the invasion.

Ashen and exhausted, Yamamoto kept to his room during the long trip back to Japan. He ordered cakes, money, and fresh underwear for the survivors, and warned one of his aides not to criticize Admiral Nagumo. "The failure at Midway was mine," he said firmly.

Yamamoto's biggest mistake, shared by many Japanese in 1942, was overconfidence. "Victory disease," the Japanese later called it. His Midway attack had no contingency plans as to what to do if surprise was lost, or if a battleship's guns were suddenly needed.

If Japan had won the Battle of Midway, America might have had to abandon its "Germany first" policy and concentrate on defending California. Because they lost, the Japanese had to cancel their plans to take Fiji and New Caledonia and cut off Australia. Instead, they were mired in hard-fought retreat for the rest of the war.

Some of the most grueling fighting took place in the steamy, smelly, mosquito-infested jungle of Guadalcanal, one of the Solomon Islands. In the summer of 1942 the Japanese tried to build an airstrip there to prepare for an attack on nearby New Guinea. To prevent this, 17,000 United States marines landed on the island on August 7, forcing the Japanese troops to retreat to dugouts and caves. Using bulldozers, the marines completed the airstrip within a week, but on August 9 the Japanese navy sank four Allied cruisers and six destroyers, and took control of the sea. The marines had received only half of their food and supplies, and had to live on half-rations for the next four months.

Yamamoto immediately sailed south and established new headquarters at Truk, in the Caroline Islands, 1,400 miles (2,250 km) north of Guadalcanal. By night his ships sent food and men to the island, but in the day United States air power ruled the sky. Neither side could prevent the other from sending minimal supplies, nor could they send enough food to feed their own troops adequately. Soldiers on both sides began to eat roots and weeds, but the Japanese had far less food, and died of malaria, beriberi, and dysentery.

The Allies and Japanese fought thirty-four naval engagements near Guadalcanal that autumn, and sank sixty-five ships all told. Yamamoto's hair turned gray as the water around the island was nicknamed the Ironbottom Sound, for the many ships sunk there.

By January 1943, United States air power had become so strong that the Japanese situation was hopeless. The only thing left to do was withdraw. Yamamoto organized an evacuation of 13,000 troops on the nights of February 1 through 6 that was so gradual, the Americans did not realize what was happening until the last man was gone and the Japanese guns were silent.

Some 24,000 Japanese and 1,592 Americans died on Guadalcanal, mostly from disease. The Americans had at least gained something from their sacrifice: a "stepping-stone" on the way to Tokyo.

Two months later, on April 18, 1943, Yamamoto flew to the island of Bougainville to visit pilots on the front lines. His itinerary had been carelessly broadcast over the radio and was decoded by the Americans. President Franklin Roosevelt ordered the navy to seize this opportunity and shoot down Yamamoto's plane. At 9:40 A.M., sixteen P-38 fighter planes arrived from Guadalcanal and ambushed Yamamoto's bomber and his seven escorts. A machine-gun bullet entered Yamamoto's left jaw and exited his right temple, killing him instantly. Other bullets started a fire in the plane's left engine, causing it to crash in the jungle.

Japanese soldiers recovered and cremated Yamamoto's body. Six weeks later, on June 5, 1943, over one million people lined the streets of Tokyo to mourn their boldest admiral. At the funeral altar were roses sent by Mussolini. The admiral's ashes were put into two urns. One was buried at his family's plot in his hometown, Nagaoka. The other was buried in Tokyo, next to the grave of Admiral Togo Heihachiro, whose fleet sank the Russian navy in 1905.

Two other military men who can be compared to Yamamoto are Erwin Rommel and Robert E. Lee. Each of them was a remarkable wartime leader. Rommel despised Hitler, yet fought brilliantly for Germany. Lee hated slavery, but battled valiantly for the Confederacy. Yamamoto loathed militarism, yet fought with fierce audacity for the Japanese Empire. All three commanders were noble men who fought for their homeland on the wrong side of history.

24

Emperor Hirohito

*His Role in the Final Week
of World War II*

H IROHITO (1901–1989) IS THE ONE Japanese leader almost everyone in the West has heard of. He was emperor of Japan for sixty-three years, from 1926 to 1989, but has only a short chapter in this book because, as biographer Stephen Large has observed, Hirohito "was less important for what he did than for what elites did in his name."

Hirohito exercised real power only twice in his life. Once was in February 1936, when he demanded that the army suppress a military coup by radical young officers. The second time was in August 1945, when he brought World War II to an end. Even critics of the emperor call this period his finest hour.

When Crown Prince Hirohito became emperor in 1926, the Japanese stopped calling him by his first name. Instead, they called him *Tenno*, "Emperor," and since his death he has been known as *Showa Tenno*, "Emperor during the Showa period." *Showa*, which means "enlightened peace," is the name of the era of Hirohito's rule. For a Japanese to call the Showa Emperor "Hirohito" is a bit like calling the Queen of England "Liz." Nevertheless it is the custom in the West to call monarchs by their first names, so Showa Tenno continues to be known around the world as Hirohito.

As a teenager he was more interested in marine biology than court ceremony, and later in life he wrote over a dozen scientific articles, half of them on hydrozoans, the class of sea life that includes jellyfish. As a grown man Hirohito was short, nearsighted, shy, and walked with a stoop. He married for love at twenty-two, and was a faithful husband even when his wife gave birth to four daughters in a row. His aides hoped he might take a concubine to have a son, and introduced him to one beautiful girl after another. Hirohito refused them all, and finally in 1933 the empress gave birth to a boy, Akihito, the current emperor of Japan.

In the 1930s Hirohito failed to prevent the army's gradual takeover of the government. Some historians think this was because the emperor craved military conquest, but the overwhelming majority of Western and Japanese scholars believe that as a constitutional monarch Hirohito had much prestige but little power. In 1931, for example, the army ignored his instruction to keep the dispute in Manchuria "within bounds," and conquered the entire province without any authorization.

Six years later, when the army began fighting in China, Hirohito made the mistake of trusting his boyhood friend, Prime Minister Konoe Fumimaro, to manage the situation. Instead of firing disobedient army officers and negotiating a peace, Konoe ratified the decision of his generals to "annihilate" the Chinese army. Once war had begun, it was too late for Emperor Hirohito to stop it.

Hirohito is also criticized for endorsing the attacks on Pearl Harbor and Southeast Asia in December 1941, but at that moment there was too strong a consensus for expanding the war for the emperor to have bucked the tide. America, Britain, and the Netherlands had grown tired of fueling Japan's brutal conquest of China, and stopped the sale of oil to Japan after it invaded southern Vietnam in July 1941. Because Japan was now an ally of Nazi Germany, they refused to resume the sale of oil unless Japan withdrew all its troops from China and Indochina.

This condition was a shock to the Japanese. After four years of war, even Hirohito thought that a total withdrawal from China was unthinkable. Faced with a complete cutoff of oil, he reluctantly endorsed the unanimous decision of the cabinet to declare war on the three Western nations.

During the war Hirohito often appeared in public in uniform on a white horse. His duties were ceremonial, and he never attended a cabinet meeting. Yet at the end of the war Hirohito was momentarily the most powerful man in Japan. To understand how this happened, it is necessary to look briefly at the events of the summer of 1945.

The United States had just taken the islands of Iwo Jima and Okinawa, both within 1,000 miles (1,600 km) of Tokyo. Their posession made it possible for the United States to bomb nearly every city in Japan, but the battles for the two islands had been extraordinarily bloody. On Iwo Jima, an island one third the size of Manhattan, 6,812 Americans died and 19,089 were wounded.

At Okinawa the carnage was worse because of attacks by over 3,300 kamikazes: 12,513 Americans died and over 36,000 were wounded as the Japanese fought almost to the last man. Almost 150,000 Japanese died on the island, many of them civilians. Americans feared that the battle was just a taste of the bloodbath to come when the United States invaded Japan's home islands.

On July 26, 1945, at Potsdam, a suburb of Berlin, United States President Harry Truman called for "the unconditional surrender of all Japanese forces." The alternative was "utter destruction." Some historians have criticized Truman for insisting on unconditional surrender, arguing that if he had let the Japanese know that they could keep their emperor, the war might have ended several weeks sooner and the atomic bombs would not have had to be dropped.

But if the Japanese were truly ready to end the war on this basis, all they had to do was ask. They never did. Instead, they sought a last-minute alliance with the Soviet Union, thinking that this would bring them better terms.

The Potsdam Proclamation included an assurance that "we do not intend that the Japanese shall be enslaved as a race or destroyed as a nation." This phrase was censored from Japanese newspapers, and Japan's prime minister, Admiral Suzuki Kantaro, said publicly that the proclamation was unworthy of comment.

Suzuki's dismissal of the Potsdam ultimatum solidified President Truman's decision to drop atomic bombs on Hiroshima on August 6 and Nagasaki on August 9. Truman hoped the use of nuclear weapons would shock the Japanese into surrendering quickly. He believed the bombs would save Japanese as well as American lives if the conventional bombing of Japan's cities by B-29s each night came to an end and if an invasion could be avoided. The bombs were dropped without warning because the Americans feared that if the Japanese were forewarned, they would move POWs to the target as hostages, or shoot down the plane carrying the bomb.

The suffering caused by the atomic bomb is vividly described in the novel *Black Rain*, discussed in chapter thirty on writer Ibuse Masuji. Recoiling from the bomb's horror, some historians have criticized Truman's decision to drop it.

First, they argue that the bombs were unnecessary because the Soviet Union had pledged to declare war on Japan and invade Manchuria, which it did on August 8, and that this alone would have compelled Japan to surrender. But if true, Japan would surely have been split into Communist and non-Communist zones, particularly because the Soviets had planned to invade the island of Hokkaido on August 22. Whether it is worse for 300,000 people to die in Hiroshima and Nagasaki, or for five million people in Hokkaido to live under communism for fifty years and the nation to be divided is a difficult question. Critics of the decision to drop the bomb understandably avoid the issue.

Second, Truman's detractors often cite a United States Strategic Bombing Survey made after the war, which concluded that the conventional bombing of Japan was so intense that the war would have ended by December 1945 even without an American invasion. Nuclear bombs, they argue, were not necessary to force Japan to surrender. But even four more months of war would have spelled death for hundreds of thousands of Japanese civilians and tens of thousands of Allied sailors and POWs. These historians also ignore the inherent bias of the 1946 Strategic Bombing Survey, which naturally sought to maximize the role of the United States Air Force in winning the war.

In presuming a Japanese willingness to surrender by December, these scholars also overestimate the rationality of the top Japanese generals. Having amassed two million soldiers on the home islands, they were actually looking forward to a United States invasion as an opportunity to inflict massive casualties and win a decisive victory. In preparation for the great battle, women and children near the coastline were given bamboo spears, and over 8,000 kamikazes trained for their final, violent moment. There were also plans for civilians to strap explosives to themselves and dive under American tanks. Admiral Onishi Takijiro, who was in charge of the kamikazes, said that if Japan could recruit twenty million men and women for suicide missions, it could win the war.

In 1945, of course, the Bombing Survey had not yet been made, and nearly all of America's top military leaders thought an invasion of the island of Kyushu would be necessary to end the war. The attack, scheduled for November 1, would have involved 770,000 Americans, more than were needed at Normandy. Estimates of probable American dead and wounded ranged from 100,000 to 500,000. Japanese casualties, including civilians, would have been much higher.

For those who question whether dropping the atomic bombs was necessary, and those who ask, "Maybe Hiroshima, but why Nagasaki?" the August 9 meeting of Japan's Supreme Council for the Conduct of the War is revealing. Held below the Imperial Palace in a sweltering underground bunker, the council of six was divided into two factions.

Prime Minister Suzuki, Foreign Minister Togo Shigenori, and Navy Minister Yonai Mitsumasa agreed that Japan's situation was hopeless and favored surrender if Japan could keep its emperor. Army Chief of Staff Umezu Yoshijiro, Navy Chief of Staff Toyoda Soemu, and the minister of war, General Anami Korechika, opposed surrender unless the United States also agreed not to occupy Japan, not to try war criminals, and to trust the Japanese to disarm themselves.

Inexplicably, the council waited three days after the bombing of Hiroshima before convening at eleven A.M. on August 9. War Minister Anami began the meeting by questioning whether America had a second atomic bomb, and said that even if it did, it would not use it for fear of offending world opinion. Japan, he said, should wait for the United States invasion and kill as many Americans as possible in order to negotiate peace from a stronger position.

Thirty minutes later an aide stepped into the room and informed the men that Nagasaki was in ruins. Even then, the three militants, Anami, Umezu, and Toyoda, refused to end the war. When the meeting resumed in the evening, it was presided over by Emperor Hirohito. As the six men on the council continued to argue, General Umezu said that better antiaircraft fire could prevent further atomic attacks, and General Anami announced that "100 million people are ready to die for honor!"

After two hours Prime Minister Suzuki, fearing a third nuclear blast, decided to break the three-three deadlock by taking the unprecedented step of asking Emperor Hirohito for his opinion. Everyone gasped in astonishment, then listened attentively to their emperor. "I cannot bear to see my innocent people suffer any longer . . ." he said, his voice choked with emotion, ". . . the time has come when we must bear the unbearable . . . [and] accept the Allied proclamation." As he finished, every man in the room shed tears.

On the morning of August 10, Foreign Minister Togo cabled Switzerland that Japan accepted the Potsdam Proclamation, provided "that the said declaration does not comprise any demand which prejudices the perogatives of His Majesty as a Sovereign Ruler."

Now it was the Americans' turn to have meetings. Japan's cable was almost an unconditional surrender, but not quite. Most of President Truman's advisers favored letting Japan keep its emperor. As a practical matter his cooperation would make the occupation and disarmament of Japan infinitely easier. But the Americans also knew that the Russians, Australians, and Dutch wanted to try Hirohito as a war criminal. So did a majority of Congress. On August 11, after consulting with the allies, United States Secretary of State James Byrnes sent the Swiss his careful reply to Japan's surrender offer:

> From the moment of surrender the authority of the Emperor and the Japanese Government to rule the state shall be subject to the Supreme Commander of the Allied Powers. . . .
>
> The ultimate form of government of Japan shall, in accordance with the Potsdam Declaration, be established by the freely expressed will of the Japanese people.

Because the American reply implied but did not guarantee that Japan could keep its emperor, the Supreme Council was once again evenly divided over whether or not to surrender. On the morning of August 14, however, the emperor practically ordered the council to end the war. Looking straight at General Anami, he said, "It is my desire that all of you, my ministers of state, obey my wishes and accept the Allied reply immediately."

That night Hirohito recorded a speech to be broadcast on the radio the next day. He knew that many of Japan's soldiers would lay down their arms only if they heard the news of the surrender in his own voice. To hide the vinyl recording of the emperor's speech from armed fanatics who were out to destroy it and continue the war, Hirohito's chief servant stored the disk in a lady-in-waiting's safe overnight, then in the morning dressed shabbily and took it to the radio station in an ordinary lunch bag.

At noon on August 15, over sixty million Japanese both at home and abroad gathered around radios and, standing at attention, heard the emperor's high-pitched voice for the first time in their lives. They did not know whether he was going to announce a surrender or ask them to die fighting, and they had trouble understanding him because he spoke in formal, old-fashioned Japanese. Still, the gist of his message was clear.

The war situation has developed not necessarily to Japan's advantage. . . .
Moreover the enemy has begun to employ a new and most cruel bomb. . . .
We have resolved to pave the way for a grand peace for all generations to
come by enduring the unendurable.

The emperor never used the word "surrender," nor did he refer to the acts of
aggression in China and Southeast Asia that had united the world against Japan.
Instead, the Japanese were victims of "a new and most cruel bomb," a position
that even today keeps many Japanese from properly examining their nation's
warlike past.

The humiliation of surrender was coupled with relief that the war was finally
over. Within hours, police confiscated thousands of airplane propellers to prevent
any stray kamikazes from continuing the war. Hirohito also sent his relatives to
visit troops overseas and assure them that the surrender really was his will.

Four months later, on January 1, 1946, Emperor Hirohito renounced his
divinity in a historic message to the people.

The ties between us . . . do not depend upon mere legends and myths. They
are not predicated on the false conception that the Emperor is divine. . . .

The next year, in May 1947, Japan adopted a new constitution that redefined
the status of the emperor. Instead of being "sacred," he was now "the symbol of
the state . . . deriving his position from the will of the people." Some Japanese
were upset by this new charter, but Hirohito said, "I rejoice that the foundation
for . . . a new Japan has been laid according to the will of the Japanese people."

Hirohito had always seen himself as a constitutional monarch. Now it was
the law of the land. In 1945 he stepped out of his constitutional role briefly
when Japan's very existence was at stake. After the war he was content to be a
figurehead again. In Japan's long history, this has been the emperor's usual role.

25
Yoshida Shigeru
*Prime Minister of Japan
During the American Occupation*

A T THE END OF World War II, Japan was in ruins. Almost three million Japanese had died and over eight million were homeless. Seventy percent of Tokyo, 80 percent of Osaka, and 90 percent of Nagoya were destroyed. Food was scarce and money was worthless. Trains were jammed with passengers headed for the country, hoping to trade family posessions for sweet potatoes and cabbages. Soap was rationed to two bars per person per year.

The two men who led Japan back to prosperity were General Douglas MacArthur, Supreme Commander of the Allied Powers, and Yoshida Shigeru (1878–1967), Prime Minister of Japan. MacArthur ordered sweeping economic and political reforms, most of which the conservative Yoshida opposed. Yoshida implemented them dutifully, however, serving as prime minister for almost seven years, from 1946 to 1947, and again from 1948 to 1954.

During this time Yoshida cemented an alliance of big businessmen and government bureaucrats that even today is still powerful. His three-point policy of emphasizing exports, avoiding a big defense budget, and maintaining an alliance with the United States has continued for half a century, and most Japanese agree that this policy has been remarkably successful.

Starting in 1946, Yoshida's Liberal Party, and its direct descendant, the Liberal-Democratic Party, governed Japan for all but three of the next fifty years. During this span five men from Yoshida's bright young staff were elected prime minister: Ikeda, 1960–1964; Sato, 1964–1972; Tanaka, 1972–1974; Ohira, 1978–1980; and Miyazawa, 1991–1993.

Yoshida was probably the most influential prime minister of the twentieth century. Yet only one year before he took office in 1946, the elderly diplomat was not only retired, but in jail.

Yoshida Shigeru was born on September 22, 1878, a few miles south of Tokyo. His father was a politician from the island of Shikoku, his mother an unknown geisha. Because the father already had four sons, he had promised that his next son could be adopted by his friends, Yoshida Kenzo and his wife, Kotoko, who were childless. He gave them his baby when it was nine days old, and from then on Yoshida had almost no contact with his natural family.

Yoshida's adoptive father had studied in England and worked for a British shipping firm before starting his own shipping business, exporting silk and importing weapons. He made a fortune and bought a large estate in Oiso, a seaside town southwest of Tokyo with a view of Mt. Fuji. It remained Yoshida's home all his life.

When Yoshida was nine, his adoptive father died, leaving Yoshida a huge inheritance, perhaps $30 to 40 million in today's money. Despite his wealth, Yoshida once described his childhood as "a lonely life in a lonely house." He was an only child, and his adoptive mother was a strict, haughty woman lacking in warmth.

Like his mother, Yoshida became proud and self-confident, but he also developed a cheeky wit and sense of humor. In school he studied the Chinese classics, calligraphy, English, English literature, and some economics. In the 1890s schoolteachers encouraged an especially great reverence for the emperor, and as an adult Yoshida built a shrine in his garden to Emperor Meiji and his ministers, whom he honored as the modernizers of Japan.

Yoshida studied at a college for diplomats for two years, then transferred to Tokyo Imperial University, where he earned a law degree in 1906. After graduation Yoshida began working for Japanese consulates in Manchuria, London, and Rome.

In June 1909 Yoshida married Makino Yukiko, daughter of Count Makino Nobuaki. Count Makino was the second son of Okubo Toshimichi (leader of Japan in the 1870s, and the subject of chapter twenty-one) and one of Japan's highest government officials. It was an arranged marriage in the purest sense. Yoshida brought great wealth and a promising career; in return, Count Makino introduced Yoshida to Japan's aristocracy.

Yoshida was thirty, handsome, but short—just five feet tall. Yukiko was twenty, plain, refined, and somewhat prudish. Together they raised two sons and two daughters. Yoshida was unfaithful from the start, seeing geishas discreetly. It didn't seem to bother Count Makino. Father- and son-in-law remained good friends for forty years, sharing a strong interest in diplomacy.

From 1912 to 1916 Yoshida was consul at Antung (Dandong), China, near the Korean border. He helped Japanese companies develop Manchurian timberland, and also judged civil disputes between Koreans. Japan had annexed Korea in 1910.

In 1919 Yoshida accompanied his father-in-law to the Paris Peace Conference that followed World War I. He remained in Europe for two years as an official at the Japanese embassy in London.

Yoshida was fascinated by Britain, but admired its power more than its liberalism. He rode in a Rolls-Royce, wore Savile Row suits at work (but a kimono at home), and smoked Cuban cigars after meals. Yoshida's English was fluent though heavily accented, but his eldest daughter learned to speak English flawlessly, and would later serve as a hostess for Yoshida when he became prime minister.

In 1922 Yoshida returned to China to be consul general, first in Tianjin, and then in Mukden (Shenyang), both cities with many Japanese-owned sweatshops. Yoshida worked to protect Japanese firms from any new taxes, tariffs, strikes, or boycotts, and regarded Japanese expansion as an economic blessing for the Chinese.

In 1928 Yoshida was appointed vice foreign minister. Three years later he became ambassador to Italy, although he talked to the British more than to the Italians. He defended Japan's annexation of Manchuria in 1931, but also sent cables to Tokyo warning his government of the deep British and American anger at the action.

Yoshida felt useless in Italy, and resigned in the fall of 1932. During the next three years he made a number of high-level trips for Foreign Minister Hirota Koki. He visited the United States several times, and had two frosty meetings with Secretary of State Cordell Hull. In 1936 Prime Minister Hirota wanted Yoshida to be his foreign minister, but the military vetoed Yoshida as being too pro-Western. In consolation, Hirota appointed Yoshida ambassador to Great Britain.

It was a difficult job. British irritation with Japan turned into outright hostility after Japan signed the Anti-Comintern Pact with Italy and Nazi Germany in November 1936. Yoshida himself was deeply opposed to the pact.

Yoshida had great contempt for the peasants' sons who were running the Japanese army. He thought they had no understanding of the immense economic power of the United States and the British Commonwealth. Even when the Nazis conquered France, Yoshida still thought that Germany was too small a country to win a world war.

During 1936 and early 1937 Yoshida tried to interest the British in a plan that, had it been adopted, might have avoided war in Asia and preserved the Japanese Empire. If Britain would recognize Japan's annexation of Manchuria, Yoshida proposed, Japan would uphold British trading interests in the rest of China. Because Britain had its hands full with the threat from Germany, many British officials were tempted by Yoshida's offer.

Unfortunately Yoshida never had the backing of his own government, and in July 1937 the Japanese army invaded China. Japanese and Western interests in China were now totally at odds. Yoshida returned to Tokyo in 1938, having accomplished nothing. Sixty-one years old, he retired from the Foreign Service in 1939, but as a member of the elite he continued to be well informed.

In 1941 Yoshida's wife, Yukiko, died of throat cancer. She was fifty-three. A year or two later, a retired geisha named Korin moved in with Yoshida, and in effect became his second wife.

The year 1941 was also when General Tojo Hideki became prime minister of

Japan. Yoshida hated him, calling him in private "the son of the devil." In November 1941 the Tojo cabinet decided to go to war with the United States, Britain, and the Netherlands because they refused to sell any more oil to Japan unless it first withdrew from China, which it refused to do. Yoshida begged Foreign Minister Togo Shigenori to resign rather than declare war on the United States, but the foreign minister declined to do so.

When Yoshida heard the news of the bombing of Pearl Harbor, he felt "rage" at the recklessness of Japan's military leaders. Despite the success of the raid, Yoshida predicted privately that Japan would lose the war. For over three years there was nothing he could do but listen to foreign news broadcasts on shortwave radio.

In February 1945 Yoshida helped write a paper that Prince Konoe, a former prime minister, submitted to Emperor Hirohito. It said defeat was inevitable, warned that further chaos could lead to communist revolution, and recommended surrendering to the United States as soon as possible.

The military police, which had spies in Yoshida's home working as domestic servants, obtained a copy of the paper and arrested Yoshida on April 15, 1945, on charges of spreading "groundless rumors" about the war effort. Korin, Yoshida's geisha, hurriedly smuggled other papers out of the house in the sash of her kimono, and later burned them.

The police questioned Yoshida in detail about his antiwar activities, but treated him well. Because he had powerful friends, his cell was clean and he received food from home, which made him popular with the guards and other prisoners. Yoshida spent just seventy days in prison, but it was enough. After the war, when the United States army purged 200,000 Japanese from public office, Yoshida was one of the few men of stature unaffected by the sweep.

In September 1945, one month after Japan's surrender, Yoshida became the foreign minister in Japan's first postwar cabinet. His real job was to help implement the orders of General Douglas MacArthur, Supreme Commander of the Allied Powers in the Pacific, who, like Yoshida, was in his mid-sixties, arrogant, and politically conservative.

The first priority was for seven million Japanese soldiers to put down their arms. They did, and during the entire American occupation not a single American soldier was killed.

Disarmament went smoothly because the United States decided to let Emperor Hirohito remain on his throne. MacArthur wrote Washington that if the Allies put the emperor on trial, it would be comparable to the crucifixion of Christ. One million troops would be necessary to keep order. With the emperor secure, however, MacArthur needed only 200,000.

America's second priority was democratization. Even before the war ended, United States State Department officials had drawn up detailed plans for radical change in Japan. Now, during his first six months as supreme commander,

MacArthur ordered the Japanese to dissolve the secret police, end censorship, give women the vote, release all political prisoners, including Communists, give unions the right to organize and strike, break up large companies, distribute land to tenant farmers, and disestablish Shinto as the state religion.

The reforms delighted many Japanese, but dismayed conservatives. Yoshida could not believe that Communists were out of jail and free to form unions and start strikes. To Yoshida, radical change by the United States was unnecessary and dangerous. All the United States needed to do, he thought, was remove the military fanatics who had caused Japan to "stumble" in the 1930s.

Americans thought Japanese militarism had deeper roots, and demanded as a start that the role of the emperor be redefined in a new constitution. Hirohito helped on New Year's Day, 1946, by announcing that he was not divine. But a parliamentary committee assigned to revise Japan's 1889 constitution recommended only that the emperor be "supreme" instead of "sacred."

At this point General MacArthur and his staff decided to write the new constitution themselves. Twenty-seven people wrote different parts of the document and produced a draft in just one week in February 1946. Remarkably it has been Japan's constitution for a half a century and has never been amended.

MacArthur had kept the Russians and Australians, who wanted to abolish the monarchy, from getting involved. The Japanese understood that if they did not ratify the American document, other nations might write the next draft and turn Japan into a republic.

The postwar constitution defines the emperor as "the symbol of the state and of the unity" of the people, deriving his position from the will of the people. It also directs Japan's cabinet to report to the Diet (parliament) and not to the emperor, as it had in the past. In addition, the constitution enumerates many human rights, including the right of equality between men and women.

Most important is Article 9, originated by MacArthur himself:

> The Japanese people forever renounce war as a sovereign right of the nation and the threat or use of force as a means of settling international disputes . . . land, sea and air forces, as well as other war potential, will never be maintained.

Yoshida had misgivings, but realized that adopting this constitution was the only way to save the monarchy. He felt better about the document when Emperor Hirohito told him that he approved of every word, including the phrases limiting his power. The press was favorable too, and in April 1946, with women voting for the first time, the Japanese chose candidates in favor of the "no-war" constitution by large majorities. (The Diet later ratified the charter by a vote of 342 to 5.)

The voters gave the Liberal Party the most seats in the Diet, but just when its founder, Hatoyama Ichiro, was on the verge of becoming prime minister, General MacArthur purged him from public life. He had written a book in 1938 praising Hitler and Mussolini for their handling of labor unions. Hatoyama asked Yoshida if he could lead the Liberal Party instead, and on May 22, 1946, the sixty-eight-year-old diplomat became prime minister of Japan.

Surprisingly Yoshida appointed a left-wing minister of agriculture. Yoshida agreed with MacArthur that the best way to prevent revolution in Japan was to give land to the tenant farmers. Yoshida sympathized with the landlords, who were paid for their land in bonds made almost worthless by inflation. (Payment for one acre had about the same value as a carton of cigarettes on the black market.) On the other hand, four million Japanese became landowners as one third of Japan's land changed hands. The new farmers worked harder and harvested more than ever before, and people everywhere soon had more food to eat. Farmers became prosperous, and delighted Yoshida by voting conservatively.

In the cities the Yoshida government tried to boost the economy by giving loans to six "priority" industries: coal, steel, fertilizer, shipbuilding, textiles, and electric power.

Over half of Japan's industrial workers had joined unions by 1946, mainly because inflation was cutting the value of their paychecks. Strikes were rare, but slowdowns became a nuisance everywhere. (For a while, even can-can dancers kicked only half as high as usual.) To Yoshida it seemed as if "a sea of red flags" were engulfing Japan, but MacArthur refused to intervene.

Finally, in 1947, radical labor leaders planned a general strike on February 1 unless wages tripled and unless Yoshida resigned. More than half of Japan's workers were set to strike, shutting down railroads, telephones, electricity, mines, factories, and even schools. Nine hours before the walkout was set to begin, General MacArthur ordered the strike canceled. He said Japan was still too poor to withstand such a shock to its economy.

Most Japanese blamed communist union leaders for taking the nation to the brink of chaos, but they were also disatisfied with Yoshida, who was against even the eight-hour day. (At American insistence, it became law anyway.) The moderate Socialist Party won elections in April 1947, and Yoshida resigned as prime minister.

The Socialists made no headway in fighting inflation, and were replaced by a socialist-centrist coalition a year later. But this new government was scandal-ridden, with sixty-four of its members charged with taking bribes, including the prime minister. After mass resignations, Yoshida became prime minister a second time on October, 15, 1948. He strengthened his power in elections three months later when his Liberal Party won a majority in the Diet.

Also in 1948 the American occupation began to "reverse course." In July, MacArthur announced that government employees, including teachers, railway, and telephone workers, would no longer have the right to strike. Equally important, President Harry Truman decided that Japan was costing the American taxpayer too much money.

Truman sent banker Joseph Dodge to Tokyo in February 1949 on a mission to end Japan's inflation and begin its economic recovery. Day after day Dodge met with Finance Ministry officials, pored over the government's budget, and questioned every subsidy. He slashed 260,000 workers from government and railroad payrolls, and balanced Japan's budget for the first time since the 1930s. Inflation stopped cold, but many small businesses went bankrupt.

Yoshida put his brightest young officials in the Finance Ministry, and they fought with Dodge over the severity of his cuts. In general, however, Yoshida firmly supported the "Dodge line," and did not flinch in the face of the heavy criticism he received during the 1949–1950 recession.

The payoff came much sooner than anyone expected. In June 1950 the Korean War began and the United States Army began ordering grenades, bullets, trucks, radios, barbed wire, cotton fabric, and prefabricated buildings. Exports tripled, and by October 1950 industrial production exceeded prewar levels for the first time. The Korean War, said Yoshida, was "a gift of the gods."

The Japanese deeply admired Dodge's firmness in cutting their expenditures, and balanced their budgets for the next twenty years. They also hardened their attitude toward Communists. Yoshida fired over 10,000 Communists from the government in 1949, and private companies fired another 10,000 in 1950. Most of those dismissed were labor activists. Not surprisingly, Japan's unions became docile from then on.

By late 1950 Yoshida was happier than he had been in a long time. Japan's economy was booming, its radicals were in retreat, a new Ministry of International Trade and Industry was helping business increase exports, and, best of all, the Americans were no longer interested in reform.

One task remained: to end the American occupation itself. Yoshida decided that independence would come faster if the United States were assured that Japan would remain an ally after the occupation. So he let American officials know that Japan would be willing to permit United States military bases on its soil long after the occupation. A communist leader opposed to the bases compared Yoshida to "a dog wagging its tail to its master," but Yoshida predicted that

> Just as the United States was once a colony of Great Britain but now is the stronger of the two, if Japan becomes a colony of the United States, it will also eventually become the stronger.

President Truman sent John Foster Dulles to Japan to negotiate a peace treaty. A staunch foe of communism in Asia, Dulles wanted Japan to rebuild its military, but Yoshida resisted. Yoshida had become one of Article 9's biggest defenders, because the constitutional prohibition against maintaining an army was a perfect excuse not to have one.

Yoshida thought a large army would be a waste of money, and also worried that it would end up fighting in Korea. His main fear, however, was that a revived Japanese military would frighten other nations in Asia and hurt Japanese trade.

Yoshida understood, perhaps more than any other leader of his time, that lasting power is not military but economic. A large army would have been an expensive distraction. What Japan truly needed was industrial growth at home and access to foreign markets and technology abroad.

MacArthur started a National Police Reserve of 75,000 men in 1950, and Dulles wanted to turn this into a full-fledged army of 350,000. Yoshida stalled and demurred and made excuses, but he never let the "self-defense" force grow beyond 152,000 men. Of all the many things that Yoshida discussed with American officials, this was the issue on which he was the most firm.

MacArthur sided with Yoshida against Dulles, but in 1951 his career came to an abrupt end. After trying to widen the Korean War with military action against Communist China, MacArthur was fired by President Truman on April 11. The dismissal was a powerful example to the Japanese of civilian control of the military.

Under the security pact between the United States and Japan that accompanied the peace treaty, American troops had to leave the cities within ninety days and move to rural military bases, and American soldiers arrested while off duty were to be tried in Japanese courts. Even so, the security pact was highly unpopular with the Japanese public. The United States was keeping 1,400 army bases, airfields, naval installations, training areas, and barracks. Polls showed that while 90 percent of the Japanese felt they had benefited from the American occupation, only 18 percent wanted United States bases to remain.

Yoshida mocked intellectuals and rival politicians who failed to understand that Japan's choice was continued United States bases or prolonged occupation. He also criticized those who were neutral in the cold war for taking "a cowardly attitude," and reminded them that friendship with the United States had been "the main road of Japanese diplomacy" since the nineteenth century.

On September 8, 1951, in San Francisco, forty-nine nations signed a peace treaty with Japan. The signing was televised, but later in the day, away from the cameras, Yoshida signed the less popular security treaty with the United States.

Among the few nations that did not sign the peace treaty were the Soviet Union and Communist China. Yoshida had intended to begin diplomatic relations with Communist China, but fifty-six United States senators threatened to vote against the treaty's ratification, and thus continue the American occupation, unless Yoshida recognized the Nationalist Chinese government in Taiwan instead. Yoshida did so, and as a result Japan did not trade with China until the 1970s.

The peace and security treaties took effect on April 28, 1952. Japan was independent at last, and Yoshida finally enjoyed the full powers of a prime minister. The government reversed several American policies during the next few years. It halted the breakup of large companies and re-centralized education, law enforcement, and the financing of local government. But the most important reforms of the occupation were left intact.

In November 1954 Hatoyama Ichiro, the man who had asked Yoshida to be prime minister in 1946, formed an anti-Yoshida "Democratic" Party. Yoshida's popularity had declined for several years, partly because of his imperious manner (he called a socialist leader a "stupid fool" on the floor of the Diet), his support for United States military bases, and his party's involvement in a scandal over shipbuilding contracts. The Democrats joined forces with the Socialists and passed a motion of no confidence on December 6, 1954. Yoshida resigned the next day, and Hatoyama became prime minister.

Yoshida felt betrayed and angry, but once the cherry trees on his estate began to bloom, he started to enjoy retirement. He remained in the Diet eight more years, and his advice carried great weight. In 1958 he published his memoirs. By then Japan was the world's leading shipbuilder, a source of great pride to him.

Yoshida Shigeru was eighty-nine when he died from an inflammation of the gallbladder on October 20, 1967. His funeral was televised, Japan's first state funeral since World War II.

During his lifetime Yoshida was widely criticized for being a flunky of the United States, but Yoshida thought the way to wealth and power was for Japan to ally itself with the richest and most powerful country. While other nations maintained large armies and independent foreign policies, Japan quietly acquired patent licenses and market shares—and spent only one percent of its national income on the military.

Yoshida was an old-fashioned gentleman more interested in power for his own class than he was in a better life for working people. Yet because he had a true understanding of the source of power, and pursued national wealth rather than military pride, the ordinary citizens of Japan today are among the most prosperous and powerful people on earth.

26

Kato Shidzue

Birth Control Pioneer

IN 1920 a young Japanese baroness met Margaret Sanger in New York and learned about her efforts to make birth control available in America. Eight decades later, Kato Shidzue still remembers the day vividly. "The minute I met her," she has said, "I was inspired to take up this great work in Japan."

Shidzue (as she is always referred to because she has had three last names) opened Japan's first nonprofit birth control clinic in 1934. Four years later the police closed the clinic and jailed her briefly for having "dangerous thoughts." After World War II Shidzue was elected to the national Diet, where she served twenty-seven years. She was crucial in winning public approval for the legalization of birth control and abortion in the late 1940s.

Because of her role in helping to lower Japan's birth rate, Kato Shidzue, who turned 102 in 1999, has contributed as much to Japan's prosperity as the founders of Sony and Toyota. Between 1950 and 1985 the world's population doubled, but in Japan it rose just 45 percent. One hundred twenty-five million Japanese live in a country smaller than California. If the birth rate had been only slightly higher, tens of millions more would have competed for land and resources.

Shidzue was born in Tokyo on March 2, 1897, the second of six children. Her father was a mechanical engineer who often traveled to Europe to buy machines, and became rich helping companies build factories. Shidzue's mother was also well educated. She learned to read Shakespeare in English, but taught her daughter that "a man comes first, a woman follows," and that romantic love was a "wild feeling" appropriate only among vulgar people.

At the Peeresses' School, Shidzue's classmates included four princesses, three marchionesses, and fourteen countesses. When they were twelve, Shidzue and her classmates began high school. They studied geometry, physics, and world history, but spent more time learning calligraphy, Japanese literature, painting, and sewing.

Three weeks after she graduated, Shidzue received a proposal of marriage from Baron Ishimoto Keikichi, a young mining engineer who spoke English and whose father had recently been minister of war. The broad-minded Ishimoto had studied mining not because he loved machines, but because he wanted to help Japan's poorest laborers.

Shidzue accepted the proposal and married Ishimoto on December 23, 1914. She was seventeen. Shortly before the wedding Shidzue's servants drove four trucks full of her possessions to the baron's house, including forty-five pieces of furniture and 147 kimonos, "which were expected to last me for the rest of my life."

One month after the wedding the Ishimotos moved to a smoky and muddy mining town near the Miike coal mines on the island of Kyushu. Ishimoto was an engineer for the Mitsui Mining Company, and worked underground twelve hours a day, with only two days off a month. The newlyweds lived in a small, dimly lit thatched hut, but they were happy and had two sons, Arata and Tamio, in 1917 and 1918.

Shidzue was shocked by the lives of the miners' wives. Half-naked women worked in coal pits with babies on their backs, and sometimes even gave birth underground. At home, exhausted, the women fetched water, started fires, cooked, washed, and nursed, but still could not prevent some of their babies from coughing up dust and dying. On payday the wives quarreled with their husbands because many of the demoralized men spent their earnings drinking. Often the drunken husbands beat their wives.

Seeking answers, the idealistic baron and his wife read widely, studying both the Bible and Karl Marx. They were excited by the Russian Revolution in 1917, but by then Ishimoto's health suffered, and the following year he moved his family back to Tokyo, where he took a new and less demanding job in a laboratory.

Bored with lab work, Ishimoto decided to travel to America to meet radical leaders. He left his wife and two sons early in 1919, but soon invited Shidzue to join him, writing: "Don't come abroad if you seek pleasure and new fashions in clothes . . . come to me if you will educate yourself."

It was unheard of for a Japanese woman to leave her babies in order to travel, but Shidzue felt her first duty was to her husband. She left her sons with her mother and arrived in New York in September.

To Shidzue's surprise, Ishimoto told her that she needed to be self-supporting, and enrolled her in an eight-month course to learn typing, shorthand, and bookkeeping. Then he left for Washington to attend a labor conference before sailing to Europe.

For three months Shidzue spoke only English and avoided the temptation to meet Japanese people. Finally she had tea with a Japanese banker, and it was this man who introduced her to Margaret Sanger, the woman who first coined the phrase "birth control."

While talking to Sanger, Shidzue realized that nothing would help the miners' wives back in Japan more than access to contraception. She was determined to help these wretched women win some control over their lives.

But at the moment Shidzue found her purpose in life, her husband seemed to lose his. He tried again and again to enter the Soviet Union to meet Lenin and Trotsky, but Soviet officials had no interest in meeting a titled aristocrat and never gave him a visa. Disillusioned, the baron realized that his travels had accomplished nothing, and he and Shidzue returned to Japan in the fall of 1920.

Ishimoto opened a bookstore in Tokyo and sold foreign works cheaply. In the same building, Shidzue began selling imported yarn. A baroness working as a merchant was news, so the store had plenty of publicity and customers. By contrast, her husband's bookstore did poorly, and soon after the great 1923 earthquake Shidzue tactfully decided she would close her store permanently.

Her real passion was birth control. In 1921 Shidzue, Baron Ishimoto, a labor leader named Kato Kanju, and several others formed the Birth Control League of Japan to study fertility issues and contribute articles to newspapers and journals. The group later started a research institute and a publication, *Small Family*.

A few months later a magazine asked Margaret Sanger to speak in Japan. Sanger agreed, but when her ship arrived in March 1922, the government refused to give her a visa. The denial was front-page news, and embarrassed officials finally granted a visa on the condition that Sanger not speak about birth control in public. What might have been an ordinary lecture tour was now a sensation. Sanger spoke at private homes overflowing with people, and usually Shidzue served as her translator.

Many Japanese were deeply opposed to birth control. Some said that using contraception was "like leaving a restaurant without paying the bill." Others hissed at Shidzue when she walked by.

In the spring of 1923, union leader Kato Kanju invited Shidzue to speak about birth control to miners and their wives at the Ashio copper pits in northern Japan. It was Shidzue's first experience in public speaking, and the short, demure young woman spoke both gently and forcefully.

The following year Ishimoto decided to travel again, and once more Shidzue left her children, six and five, with her mother. In Britain, the Ishimotos had lunch with the great economist John Maynard Keynes, and in America they noticed that even servants ate better food than most Japanese. Despite Marx's predictions, capitalism seemed strong in 1924, and the six-month trip marked the end of Baron Ishimoto's radicalism.

The baron lost interest in unions, birth control, and all other progressive causes. His new enthusiasm was for national expansion and empire. "My husband was always ahead of his time," Shidzue said later. Ishimoto spent evenings in geisha houses with businessmen who flattered him, then financed their schemes for Manchurian railroads and Korean canals, almost all of which lost money.

To rescue their faltering marriage, Shidzue did little political work in the late 1920s, but nothing changed. Ishimoto became even more conservative, and told a friend, in Shidzue's presence, "Never shall I be weak enough to have to consult a woman." He also told Shidzue her looks were "losing charm" for him.

Reluctantly Shidzue realized that their marriage was over. Ishimoto was willing to give her a divorce, but it required the additional permission of two male relatives, and none would grant it. For a while the unhappy Shidzue took solace in comic books.

In 1931 the Japanese army started occupying Manchuria. Ishimoto was joyous, and later moved to Manchuria, but Shidzue was appalled. She shared her dismay with her friend Kato Kanju, and in October they began a secret affair.

Five years older than Shidzue, Kato was born poor and studied law before leading miners, printers, and ironworkers in various strikes. After the occupation of Manchuria, he broke with most Japanese labor leaders and led a small group of antimilitarist unions. Kato's wife, who was unintellectual and often sick, never knew of his affair with Shidzue, but Shidzue's sons knew and liked Kato because he was warm, calm, and reliable.

As Ishimoto slowly squandered his entire fortune, Shidzue decided to accept an invitation arranged by her uncle to earn money lecturing in America. For four months, during the winter of 1932–1933 she put on a kimono and talked to audiences across the United States about Japanese feminism, birth control, and art.

After she finished the lecture tour, Shidzue spent three months studying Margaret Sanger's birth control clinic in New York. She learned how to make a variety of foams and jellies, and was especially impressed by the systematic way the clinic recorded the case histories of its patients. The information enabled the clinic to give women individual advice and options.

Using money she made from her lectures, Shidzue opened Japan's first nonprofit birth control clinic on March 1, 1934, operating from a doctor's office in Tokyo. She did not merely sell women contraceptives, as some doctors had already done. She explained how they worked, then sent each woman to a gynecologist to determine which method of birth control would best meet the woman's needs.

Shidzue kept file cards on thousands of women. The most common reason women wanted a small family was to be able to save enough money to give their existing children a good education. Shidzue also received thousands of letters from rural women, and later opened a clinic in a small town in northern Japan.

In addition to working long hours at her clinics, Shidzue wrote her autobiography in English, at the suggestion of Mary Beard, an American historian, and in 1935 Farrar & Rinehart published *Facing Two Ways: The Story of My Life*. The book was well reviewed and earned a substantial amount of money, but Shidzue invested all of it in a small factory run by a young friend of Kato Kanju's, and the business failed completely.

Shidzue soon had to close her clinics because a new government regulation made it difficult for physicians to discuss contraception. Shidzue made plans with a courageous woman doctor to open a new clinic, but first went to America during the winter of 1937 to raise money lecturing.

Shidzue came home in May and celebrated Kato Kanju's election to the national Diet. Kato was the only member of the legislature who was both anti-militarist and pro–women's rights.

Shidzue opened her new birth control clinic on July 31, 1937, but war with China had begun July 7, and within five months the government arrested 473 left-wing leaders for having "dangerous thoughts." Policemen came to Shidzue's house at six in the morning on December 15. As agents searched in vain for illegal publications, Shidzue calmly packed a wool sweater and long underwear for the unheated jails of Tokyo.

Because Shidzue was a baroness, the police interrogated her gently. They asked her many times whether she knew any Communists, and also asked her why she was trying to limit the population at a time when Japan needed more soldiers. The absurdity of encouraging large families at home so that bigger armies could conquer more living space abroad was not apparent to the detectives. Shidzue told them that she was simply trying to help "poor Japanese mothers who could not afford to have more children."

The police released Shidzue after two weeks, and warned her not to engage in any political activity. They also ordered Shidzue to close her birth control clinic, and confiscated the confidential records of her clients. Shidzue continued to answer letters from rural women, however, and often sent them contraceptives that her diplomat friends smuggled in from abroad.

Kato Kanju was not as lucky as Shidzue. Though still a member of the Diet, he remained in prison for over two years.

Through her foreign friends, Shidzue had access to overseas newspapers and knew the full horror of the rape of Nanjing and other Japanese atrocities. But there was nothing she could do but read, write letters, and wait. "I will live in this insane Japan . . . while I await the return of law and order," she wrote Mary Beard.

Shidzue's two sons shared her political beliefs. Tamio, her youngest, was intelligent, athletic, and popular, but died of tuberculosis in 1943. Arata, the oldest son, graduated in physics from Kyoto University in 1942 and was immediately drafted. Although two of his father's brothers were generals, Arata opposed the war and deliberately failed his officer's examination. He became a truck driver and spent the rest of World War II on the island of Sumatra, a safe place to be as it turned out. After the war he became a professor of mathematics and symbolic logic.

In 1944, at the age of forty-seven, Shidzue became pregnant again. This prompted a brother and a brother-in-law to finally sign the forms that allowed Shidzue to get a divorce. Shidzue and Kanju married in November; Kanju's wife had died three years earlier.

When the United States Air Force firebombed Tokyo in March 1945, Shidzue was eight and a half months pregnant, but she welcomed the B-29s as liberators. She recalled later that "the planes flew so low that often I could see the pilots, and wondered whether any of them might be a son of one of my American friends."

Miraculously Shidzue's house was undamaged by the bombing, and a healthy daughter, Taki, was born on March 30. Milk was scarce, so Shidzue pawned kimonos and other valuables.

One day in September, a month after Japan's surrender, Shidzue returned home from the countryside carrying a sack of potatoes. She was astonished to see an American soldier in a jeep waiting to take her to Allied headquarters. Several American officers had read her autobiography, and they knew that an expert on women's issues who spoke English and liked Americans was a great asset. They consulted Shidzue regularly on a wide range of issues.

General Douglas MacArthur, Supreme Commander of the Allied Powers in the Pacific, ordered Japan's wartime Diet, still in session, to pass a law giving women the right to vote, which they did on December 15, 1945. The occupation authorities scheduled new elections, and barred eighty-three percent of the members of the wartime Diet from running again. Japan's postwar legislature would be filled almost entirely with new people. Both Shidzue and her husband announced their candidacies for the Diet, and Shidzue joined her husband's new political party, the Japan Socialist Party, which demanded a minimum wage, unemployment insurance, and a forty-eight-hour work week.

Shidzue campaigned on an even more practical agenda: more food, more clothing, more contraceptives, and more soldiers coming home from China and the Pacific. She talked to voters in school auditoriums, on crowded streetcars, and on radio programs such as *Women's Hour* and *Round Table of the Air*. Shidzue also received a large campaign contribution from the young factory owner who had lost all of her investment of her book royalties ten years before. Finally, on April 10, 1946, thirteen million Japanese women voted for the first time in history. Shidzue was one of thirty-nine women elected to the Diet that day, and her husband Kato Kanju also won a seat. Newspapers called them "the love bird representatives."

On June 20, the first day the new Diet was in session, the thirty-nine women legislators met with General MacArthur, much to the envy of their male colleagues. Shidzue spoke for the group in English. She thanked the general for giving women the vote, but asked him to import "more wheat and soya beans for our people and milk for the babies," telling him, "we are all hungry in Japan now." She also promised that "we Japanese women will never vote for the militarists . . . we shall never have war again."

Shidzue was assigned to one of the Diet's most important committees, Constitutional Revision. She helped strengthen Article 24 of the new constitution, which says that

Laws shall be enacted considering choice of spouse, property rights, inheritance . . . and other matters pertaining to marriage and the family from the
standpoint of . . . equality of the sexes.

The Diet had been too busy in 1946 to think about birth control, but
Shidzue continued to write pamphlets and give speeches on the need for contraceptives. She also moderated a radio program, "Should Birth Control Be
Legalized?" Contraceptives were still illegal under Japan's wartime laws, but
after this broadcast a poll of listeners found that sixty-three percent approved of
their legalization.

In 1947 Shidzue and her husband were reelected and the Socialists took
power in a coalition government. She and others introduced a bill in August that
would have legalized abortion and provided for the distribution of contraceptives,
but the bill died in committee because the government was more concerned with
nationalizing coal mines. In addition, General MacArthur ordered allied officers
to maintain a strict neutrality on abortion and birth control. He felt these were
deeply personal issues that the Japanese should decide for themselves.

Shidzue personally opposed abortion, but felt that legal abortions in a doctor's
office were preferable to illegal ones elsewhere. Birth control was, of course, a
much better alternative. Throughout 1947 Shidzue continued to promote the use
of contraceptives in articles, pamphlets, lectures, and radio broadcasts.

By 1948 even conservatives saw the need for some kind of population control. Millions of soldiers and civilians from the many territories that Japan had
lost had come home, and food and medical supplies were so limited that thousands of Japanese women were having abortions without anesthesia.

Shidzue and other Socialist women worked for a more moderate law in 1948,
and had the bill cosponsored by several conservative doctors. The Eugenic Protection Law was passed by the Diet on June 28, but fell far short of what
Shidzue wanted. It legalized abortion and contraception only when a pregnancy
endangered the life or health of the mother, and said that only licensed obste-
trician-gynecologists could prescribe contraceptives. The bill also made no
provision for birth control education or clinics.

The Diet was far behind public opinion on this issue, and by the following
year most of its members knew it. In May 1949 the legislature amended the
Eugenic Protection Law to permit abortions for "economic reasons." The
amendment also permitted the manufacture and sale of contraceptives, and
authorized hospitals and clinics to distribute them. There was still no effort to
finance birth control programs, however, and doctors proved reluctant to give
patients contraceptives because abortions were much more lucrative. By 1953
Japanese women were having over one million abortions a year. Even today the
reported number is about 500,000; abortions in Japan have become a common
substitute for birth control.

In 1949 a Conservative Party landslide caused both Katos to lose their seats. The public was disillusioned by the Socialist Party's unfulfilled promises. Kato Kanju returned to the Diet in the next election and kept his seat for a decade and a half, but in 1950 Shidzue decided instead to run for a seat in the much less powerful "upper" house, the House of Councilors. The Councilors can amend legislation passed by the lower house of the Diet, but the lower house is free to reject the amendment if it wishes.

For Shidzue the chief advantage of being in the House of Councilors was that its term of office was six years, which meant she could campaign much less often than if she were in the lower house of the Diet. This was an important consideration because her daughter Taki was just five.

Shidzue campaigned in 1950 for public financing of birth control education and contraceptives as the best way to reduce the high number of abortions, and received the sixth highest vote in Japan. Two years later the governnment finally agreed with her. It authorized over seven hundred health clinics to provide counseling on family planning, though it did not give them enough money or manpower to make them effective, and few doctors participated.

By 1954 the government's birth control program had come to a standstill, so health officials helped Dr. Kunii Chojiro set up a private organization, the Japan Family Planning Association, to distribute educational materials and contraceptives. Once again the government failed to provide any funding. Shidzue also started an organization, the Family Planning Federation of Japan, to coordinate the activities of birth control organizations across the country. It was short of money too.

In October, Shidzue and Dr. Kunii came up with a novel way to raise funds. They approached the Okamoto Rubber Company and began buying millions of condoms at half the wholesale price. They resold the condoms to their clients at the wholesale price, making enough money to finance their organizations. By 1957 condoms were so widespread that Japan's birth rate was half what it was in 1947.

Today most Japanese couples use condoms as their chief method of birth control. This is partly because the Japanese government has never fully authorized the use of the birth control pill. Doctors can prescribe a high-dosage pill, though they rarely do, but the pill cannot be advertised and family planning workers are not allowed to furnish information about its use. Japanese officials claim to be worried about the pill's side effects, but their deeper fear may be that the use of the pill will increase premarital sex among young people. Recently, women's groups have pressured the government to allow the general sale of birth control pills, and early in 1999 the Ministry of Health gave the idea its preliminary approval. Meanwhile, to Shidzue's deep dismay, her dream of modern clinics that offer women a full range of contraceptive choices based on the best medical advice is still well in the future.

In 1960 Shidzue became the only Socialist in either house of the Diet to support the renewal of the Japan's security treaty with the United States. The treaty was extremely unpopular, and on June 15 twelve thousand students stormed into the Diet building, injuring almost six hundred people. The next day Shidzue denounced the demonstration as a "dangerous attempt to throw out the government by violence," and apologized for the fact that the Socialists had failed to criticize the increasingly violent marches. Many Socialists were furious with Shidzue, and her influence within the party shrank considerably.

During Shidzue's fourth term, which began in 1968, she became chairman of the Industrial Pollution Committee, and helped strengthen five antipollution laws in the early 1970s. She also co-wrote a book, *Protecting Japan's Environment*, in 1972.

Two years later Shidzue lost her reelection bid because she and a leading feminist split the women's vote. At seventy-seven Shidzue retired from politics but not from public life, becoming president of the Family Planning Association of Japan. After her husband died in 1978, Shidzue left the Socialist Party because it seemed to her to be out of date and incapable of changing Japan.

In her old age, once every six or weeks or so, if someone did "the right thing at the right moment," Shidzue wrote a letter of praise. She used shocking pink stationery because, she said, "busy men are more likely to open a pink envelope, in hopes that it comes from an admirer."

To commemorate her one-hundredth birthday, Shidzue wrote a short book called *Living*, in which she said that she stayed positive "by appreciating ten things a day." She also encouraged young women to enter politics, but hoped that they would join the newer political parties.

Despite Shidzue's work, many Japanese men continue to have a feudal attitude toward women. Of Japan's top 8,500 officials, only 0.8 percent are women, and the average Japanese man spends just twenty-four minutes a day in home activities.

In addition, birth control in Japan remains cumbersome, a matter primarily of condoms and abortion. But if Japan's methods of contraception are onerous, their results are solid. When Shidzue founded the Birth Control League of Japan in 1921, the average Japanese mother had five children. Today she has two. Modern women not only have more time to develop personal interests, or a career, they also have more money to spend on their children's education. Japan's literacy rate today is over ninety-nine percent, the highest in the world.

Shidzue never held much political power, and she did not lower Japan's birth rate by herself. But for eight decades she led more fights for women's reproductive freedom than anyone else in Japan. At the end of her life, she was still looking to the future.

27

Tanaka Kakuei

Modern Japan's Most Powerful but Corrupt Prime Minister

THE MOST POWERFUL man in Japan from 1972 to 1985 was Tanaka Kakuei. A construction contractor who never went to college, he built a national political patronage machine that still exists today, dwarfing such American parallels as Richard Daley's dominance of Chicago or Huey Long's control of Louisiana.

Tanaka was Japan's prime minister for only two years. Like Richard Nixon, his contemporary, Tanaka opened diplomacy with China in 1972 and resigned because of a scandal in 1974. Unlike Nixon, Tanaka (1918–1993) remained a legislator and pulled so many strings behind the scenes that he became known as "the shadow shogun." He was also the chief architect of Japan's "money politics."

Tanaka was born on May 4, 1918, in Nishiyama, a small town 150 miles (240 km) north of Tokyo, in poor and mountainous Niigata prefecture, a Japanese counterpart to West Virginia. He was the only son in a family of seven children. His father was a horse dealer who drank too much and lost most of his money gambling at racetracks. His mother was an intelligent woman who worked long hours growing rice, and sewing.

As a child, Tanaka stuttered. He got into fights with schoolmates who teased him, but overcame his defect by learning to talk in a rapid, machine-gun style. He worked so hard that classmates called him "the mole."

Although Tanaka finished first in his class in junior high school, his parents did not have enough money to continue his education. At fifteen, Tanaka worked as a laborer, pushing hand cars full of rocks and dirt at a construction site. The following year he moved to Tokyo and took night classes in architectural drafting and civil engineering, supporting himself by working as an apprentice to a building contractor and as a reporter for an insurance industry newspaper. In night school he was so tired that to keep himself awake he often held a small knife in the palm of his hand to gently prick his forehead if he nodded off.

When Tanaka was nineteen he started a one-man company, drawing blueprints for factories and supervising the subcontractors he hired to build them. In 1939 the business came to an end when Tanaka was drafted and sent to Manchuria, where he spent two years but was discharged when he contracted pleurisy and pneumonia.

Five months after returning home, on March 3, 1942, the cheerful and stocky Tanaka married Sakamoto Hana, the homely daughter of the owner of a large construction company. In 1943 Tanaka took over his father-in-law's company, renamed it Tanaka Civil Construction, and secured several government contracts. The following year Tanaka won a multimillion-dollar contract from the army to move a piston ring factory to Korea to keep it out of range of American bombers. Shortly after the government paid him a large advance to start work in 1945, the war ended. Tanaka no longer had to build a thing. He returned some of the money, hid much more, and because of the chaos following Japan's surrender, never had to make a full accounting. At twenty-seven he was rich.

Tanaka's wife was a divorcee seven years older than he. They had two children, a son who died when he was four, and a daughter, Makiko. Before they married, Tanaka's bride asked him to promise three things: that he would never threaten to throw her out, that he would never kick her as her previous husband had, and, finally, that when he became famous he would escort her to the Imperial Palace to meet the emperor.

Tanaka kept all three promises, although he was not a faithful husband. He had at least two mistresses. One, Tsugi Kazuko, was a geisha who bore him two sons in the 1950s. Tanaka lived with her for many years, and their older son, Kyo, did not know that he was illegitimate until Tanaka told him when he was fourteen. The other mistress, Sato Akiko, became his most trusted aide, and handled millions of dollars worth of campaign contributions.

In 1946, in return for a donation equal to about one million dollars in today's money, Tanaka was invited by the Progressive Party to run as a candidate for the Diet (parliament) in the third district of Niigata prefecture, his childhood home. In spite of the large contribution, Tanaka lost the election. Some local officials had brazenly spent the money on the campaigns of rival candidates.

The following year Tanaka opened a branch of his construction company in Niigata, then used his employees and relatives as campaign workers. Visiting eight or nine villages a day, Tanaka gained three thousand additional votes and won a seat in the Diet. At twenty-nine he was the youngest man there.

In 1948 Tanaka switched to Prime Minister Yoshida Shigeru's Liberal Party, which was actually conservative and the forerunner of the Liberal Democratic Party (LDP) that has dominated Japan since 1955. At that time it was unusual for a rural representative to join a party of urban bureaucrats, but Tanaka signed up because it was the best way to bring government money into his prefecture. He worked long hours raising funds for Prime Minister Yoshida, and lobbied for roads, bridges, tunnels, railroads, harbors, and snow-removal equipment for his district.

The people of Niigata approved. In 1949 they reelected Tanaka even though he spent the last weeks of his campaign in jail after he was convicted of taking a bribe from a coal mine owner who opposed the nationalization of the industry. Tanaka claimed that the campaign contribution and his vote against nationalization were unrelated, and in 1951 an appeals court agreed and overturned his conviction. The following year Tanaka was reelected again, by a landslide, the first of many.

Accusations of bribery are common in Japan because members of the Diet need so much campaign money—twice as much as hard-pressed American legislators do. Like other members of the Diet, Tanaka gave money at births and weddings, left wreaths and candles at funerals, and helped voters to find jobs, arrange marriages, and organize trips to Tokyo. By 1962 Niigata was the nation's fifth-highest prefecture in government spending per person, and Tanaka's campaign organization had tens of thousands of loyal members.

In 1957 Tanaka became minister of posts and telecommunications, the youngest cabinet member since the 1890s. At a time when Japan had few television stations, he issued forty-three broadcasting licenses in a single weekend. One night he also sang Japanese folk songs on the radio. His voice was raspy, like that of Don Corleone in the film *The Godfather.*

As Tanaka acquired seniority in the Diet, he grew increasingly involved in the politics of party factions. In Japan it is usually not an election but a caucus of the Liberal Democratic Party that determines who will be prime minister. The election itself has often been a foregone conclusion because most Japanese have never regarded the Socialists and other opposition parties as credible alternatives to the LDP. But one-party rule has not had the disastrous consequences in Japan that it has had in so many other countries, because the LDP is divided into fiercely competing factions, with each group of Diet members loyal to the man who raises the most campaign money for his followers.

Until single-member districts were introduced in 1994, almost every district in Japan elected between three and five people to the Diet. Candidates from different LDP factions ran against each other, and this vastly increased the amount of money that a Diet member needed to raise to win an election.

Factions multiply their power by forming coalitions. Often an alliance of two large factions is all that is necessary to form a majority within the LDP, which in turn commands a majority in the Diet. Whoever the Liberal Democrats choose as their party president almost always becomes prime minister, because even losing factions within the LDP will vote for a conservative from their own party rather than a more left-wing candidate from another party. By constituting a majority within a majority, the largest factions of the LDP run the government year after year, although an LDP prime minister always sets aside several cabinet posts for the leaders of his rival factions, to preserve party unity.

By 1960 Tanaka's contacts in the construction and telecommunications industries had made him the second largest fund-raiser in a faction led by Sato

Eisaku. Tanaka persuaded Sato to postpone running for prime minister that year and form a coalition with another faction led by Ikeda Hayato. In return, Ikeda promised to support Sato as prime minister four years later. In 1962 Prime Minister Ikeda rewarded Tanaka for negotiating this deal by appointing him minister of finance.

The power of Japan's Finance Ministry is enormous. An American equivalent would combine the powers of the Office of Management and Budget, the Federal Reserve Board, the Internal Revenue Service, and the Commerce Department in a single agency. Many finance ministers, overwhelmed by the administrative task involved, are content simply to make speeches and let subordinates run the ministry.

By contrast, Tanaka possessed a detailed grasp of the laws, departments, and budgets involved in each government contract. His motto was "decide quickly and act," and admiring officials called him "the computerized bulldozer." But Tanaka was not content merely to win the respect of his subordinates. He also worked to put as many in his debt as he could. He gave promotions to some deputies, and bonuses of thousands of dollars to over two hundred others. He also let the most promising men in the ministry know that he could help them run for the Diet or become a director of a corporation in later years. As a result, no one could get bureaucrats to grant a permit or approve funds as quickly as Tanaka could. And he developed a reputation among businessmen as a politician who kept his promises.

With the Finance Ministry bent to his will, Tanaka steered large government contracts to companies that donated campaign funds to his faction. In later years Tanaka demanded contributions equal to three percent of the value of a government contract.

Tanaka also enriched his friends and himself by buying private land or selling public land shortly before a nearby highway, railroad, or other improvement made the land more valuable. Tanaka set up "ghost corporations" with no telephone numbers to buy and sell land, and to deduct imaginary business expenses that sheltered huge profits from taxation. He also sold government land in central Tokyo to the city's three major daily newspapers, and predictably, all three papers treated Tanaka gently for the next ten years.

Tanaka once said that since parents and dogs do not live forever, the only thing you can depend on is money. He was eventually worth hundreds of millions of dollars, and built himself a twenty-five-room mansion in Tokyo and a summer compound in the Japanese Alps.

Tanaka's faction leader, Sato Eisaku, tolerated corruption because he needed campaign money. In 1964, when Sato was elected prime minister, a single one of Tanaka's ghost corporations may have funneled over $1.7 million to Sato's campaign.

Sato was so pleased with Tanaka's fund-raising that in 1965 he asked Tanaka to leave the Finance Ministry and raise money for the party directly. Tanaka became the LDP's secretary-general, a post he held for four of the next six years.

During Sato's final year as prime minister, Tanaka was minister of trade and international industry. With the help of assistants at the ministry, Tanaka wrote a best-selling book called *Building a New Japan: A Plan for Remodeling the Japanese Archipelago*. It called for the construction of over sixty medium-sized, park-filled cities as a way to ease the overcrowding and pollution in Japan's largest metropolitan areas. It also recommended building 11,800 miles of high-speed railroads and highways, and hundreds of bridges and tunnels. To pay the $1.5 *trillion* price tag for this construction industry dream, Tanaka recommended deficit financing:

> We should free ourselves from the idea of annually balanced budgets . . . debts are not in themselves inherently evil. . . . A fair distribution of the costs among the generations is necessary if we are to build a beautiful and pleasant nation to live in.

Although in hindsight Tanaka's book seems like a plea for wild pork-barrel spending, many Japanese were troubled by the increasing ugliness of their cities, and at the time, the book seemed bold and thoughtful. Few of the book's plans were carried out, but some of the projects that were completed include Tokyo's Narita Airport, Tsukuba Science City, a fifteen-mile (24 km) tunnel to the island of Hokkaido, and two long bridges between Honshu and Shikoku.

In June 1972 Prime Minister Sato retired after eight years in office. By then Tanaka was one of the two men most likely to succeed him. The other was Fukuda Takeo, who led his own faction, and was Tanaka's opposite in many ways. Fukuda had graduated first in his class at Tokyo University Law School and become a top official at the Ministry of Finance before entering the Diet. And while Tanaka was decisive and warm, Fukuda was cautious and aloof.

In public Sato was neutral. In private he favored Fukuda, a fellow graduate of Tokyo University Law School, over the uneducated Tanaka. But Sato no longer controlled his own faction. Tanaka had become both the chief administrator and chief fund-raiser of the group, and he was especially popular among younger Diet members who were in greater need of campaign money. Raising $20 million, Tanaka won the loyalty of eighty percent of Sato's faction, and also formed a coalition with three other factions that had grown tired of being led by graduates of Tokyo University Law School.

At the Liberal Democratic Party convention on July 5, 1972, the LDP members in the Diet (and forty-seven additional delegates) voted for party president. On the second ballot they gave Tanaka 282 votes and Fukuda 190. The party used its majority in the Diet the next day to vote for Tanaka as prime minister.

At fifty-four, Tanaka was the first prime minister of the century who had never attended a university or a military academy.

On most days Tanaka woke up at four, took a hot Japanese bath, read several newspapers while eating a breakfast of rice and vegetables, and admired his fish pond with its rare carp worth thousands of dollars each. At seven he began a fifteen-hour day of meetings. Usually he carried a white fan and wore a dark suit. In the morning Tanaka saw anywhere from thirty to three hundred people—groups of businessmen, contractors, and ordinary citizens from Niigata. Often he served them tea and cakes and posed for snapshots, but what they really wanted was Tanaka's *"yossha yossha"* (okay okay) to their requests. Lunches were typically with top politicians and senior bureaucrats, and in the evening Tanaka read documents and drank scotch or sake with his closest advisers.

As prime minister Tanaka funneled more money than ever to his home province. He allocated $5 billion to build a bullet train line from Tokyo to Niigata City, and also provided his district with super highways, a university, a nuclear power plant, and, most important, continued farm subsidies. One tunnel cost the government $4.5 million to build, but served a village of only sixty families.

The peak of Tanaka's career was probably his trip to Beijing in September 1972, when he and Chinese Foreign Minister Zhou Enlai signed a joint statement formally opening diplomatic relations between their countries. Returning home, Tanaka called a general election in December to capitalize on his popularity, but in a surprising result the LDP lost seventeen seats in the Diet. Although the LDP still had a comfortable majority, the Socialists gained thirty-one seats and even the Communists won ten percent of the vote. Many Japanese were tired of pro-business policies that promoted economic growth at all costs. They wanted environmental regulation, and some of the government safety nets that people enjoyed in Western Europe.

Tanaka gave them what they wanted. He sponsored some of the toughest antipollution laws in the world, doubled pensions to over forty percent of final earnings, increased health insurance to cover seventy percent of costs, and provided free medical care for the elderly. The cost was huge. Social welfare spending jumped almost thirty percent in 1973, and public works spending rose thirty percent. Because there were no tax increases to pay for these benefits, inflation also climbed twenty-three percent the same year.

Tanaka's book, *Building a New Japan*, made the inflation even worse. Giant corporations bought land in areas where the book had recommended construction, and also speculated in building materials such as lumber and concrete. Prices soared.

The public's approval of Tanaka declined from sixty-two to twenty-seven percent during 1973, but the deathblow to his dream of rebuilding Japan came from the Arab oil boycott that began in October. Japan was completely dependent on oil from the Middle East, but had only four days worth of reserves. Frightened consumers began hoarding soap, detergent, toilet paper, salt, sugar, and soy sauce. The price of oil quadrupled, and Tanaka realized that he needed a new finance minister.

He turned to his rival, Fukuda Takeo, the former bureaucrat who had years of experience cutting budgets. Fukuda was unable to cut medical and social welfare entitlements, but he did cancel over thirty percent of the government's construction projects. Within a year inflation was under control, and by the early 1980s Japan had almost five months worth of oil reserves.

On October 9, 1974, a prestigious magazine, *Spring/Fall Literary Monthly*, published an article by a young freelance journalist named Tachibana Takashi, who would soon become famous. Entitled "A Study of Tanaka Kakuei: His Money Network and His People Network," the article described in detail Tanaka's ghost corporations, his buying and selling of land, his awarding of government contracts to contributors, and his tax evasion. In 1973, Takashi wrote, Tanaka had bought stock and land worth $425 million, yet declared an income of only $260,000.

For two weeks not a word about the piece appeared in the rest of the Japanese press. Although the article was well documented, it did not tell journalists in Tokyo anything they did not already know, and therefore did not seem newsworthy.

In America, however, the story was picked up by *Newsweek* and *The Washington Post*. Then on October 22 Tanaka gave a speech at the Foreign Correspondents Club of Japan. During the question period that followed, reporters ignored the speech and asked about the article. Tanaka said that his business and political dealings were separate, but when the questions got tougher he abruptly left the room. The next morning Japanese newspapers finally ran front-page stories about the magazine article and the disastrous press conference. Tanaka's popularity fell to just twelve percent.

Younger Diet members in the other factions of the LDP were on the verge of open revolt, so for the good of the party Tanaka had to leave office. He waited until United States President Gerald Ford completed a trip to Japan, then resigned as prime minister on November 26, 1974. He'd had trouble sleeping for weeks and was exhausted; he watched the news that morning in tears.

The public was content with a resignation. The LDP-controlled Ministry of Justice did not investigate Tanaka's financial dealings, and Tanaka continued to lead his party's biggest faction.

The new prime minister, Miki Takeo, was "clean" because as the leader of a small faction he had done relatively little fund-raising. Quietly Tanaka made his own faction even larger, but in 1976 news from America made it impossible for him to ever be prime minister again.

In hearings before the United States Senate Subcommittee on Multinational Corporations, a vice president of the Lockheed Corporation testified that his company had paid $1.6 million in bribes to Tanaka's personal secretary while Tanaka was prime minister.

In return for the bribe, Tanaka persuaded All Nippon Airways to buy a fleet of Lockheed's double-aisle TriStar jets at $17 million each, rather than McDonnell Douglas's single-aisle but quieter DC-10s. Through middlemen, Lockheed made the payments in four installments during 1973 and 1974, in cardboard boxes filled with high-denomination yen notes that were quickly put in Tanaka's safe. On one occasion Lockheed was given a typed receipt for cash that said "I received 100 peanuts," a peanut being one million yen.

To the dismay of the rest of the LDP's leaders, Prime Minister Miki ordered a full investigation, and asked the United States Senate and the Securities Exchange Commission for the relevant documents. Five months later, on July 27, 1976, prosecutors arrested Tanaka and took him to jail for questioning.

The arrest was big news. A Japanese bribe to a party politician was one thing; a foreign bribe to a prime minister was another. Across Japan, almost everyone watched television coverage of his imprisonment. Sensational news came only days later when Tanaka's chauffeur committed suicide by asphyxiating himself in his car, just hours before he was to be questioned by prosecutors.

Prosecutors indicted Tanaka for bribery and for not reporting foreign income. Tanaka denied the charges. He did not feel he had done anything unusual, only that his enemies were changing the rules in the middle of the game. After three weeks in jail, Tanaka was freed on $700,000 bail. But justice in Japan is even slower than it is in America; the trial, which took place on Wednesdays, lasted seven years.

Tanaka resigned from the Liberal Democratic Party but remained in the Diet as an independent. In Niigata, which now received three times as much government money as it paid out in taxes, voters reelected him by a landslide in 1976, 1979, 1980, 1983, and 1986.

Tanaka continued to lead his faction even though he was no longer a member of the party. As one young Diet member explained, "Mr. Tanaka has helped me and there is no legal judgment against him. I cannot cut my ties with him. It would be too disloyal."

Tanaka's strategy was to prevent anyone from his own faction from becoming prime minister, a post that could allow someone to challenge his leadership of the faction. He also prevented anyone from a rival faction from serving more than two years as prime minister. In exchange for giving up his faction's turn at the prime minister's post, Tanaka could appoint men he trusted as minister of construction, which helped him to raise money from construction companies; as LDP secretary-general, which allowed him to distribute party money; and as minister of justice, which insured that there would be no more investigations of his finances.

The LDP waited as long as it could before calling an election, but the Diet's maximum term of four years ended in December 1976, and a vote could no longer be avoided. As party leaders had feared, the LDP lost twenty-two seats in the Diet, and clung to a majority of just one seat.

Prime Minister Miki's willingness to arrest and prosecute Tanaka had saved the LDP from a greater defeat, but the leaders of the LDP were furious with Miki for allowing an investigation in the first place. They quickly used the poor election results as an excuse to force Miki's resignation. To get rid of him, Tanaka even swung his faction behind the candidacy of his rival, Fukuda Takeo. In return Fukuda agreed to a mere two-year term as prime minister.

When Fukuda's term expired at the end of 1978, Tanaka's years in the political wilderness were over. His indictment for bribery was no longer news, and the trial moved so slowly that he could once again exercise power proportionate to the size of his faction.

For the next seven years no one became prime minister without Tanaka's approval, and it was during this period that he became known as "the shadow shogun." One prime minister, Suzuki Zenko, was a complete nonentity. His moment in the sun began when his faction leader, who had succeeded Fukuda as prime minister in 1978, died ten days before an election, in June 1980. Tanaka knew that Suzuki had difficulty making decisions, and saw this as an opportunity. With his huge faction behind him, he supported Suzuki as the party's president and the nation's prime minister.

During the two years of Suzuki's weak leadership, party and cabinet officials grew increasingly independent. This heightened Tanaka's power, although budgets were tight because the government was still paying off construction bonds Tanaka had issued a decade earlier. Unfortunately, foreigners began to notice how little respect Japanese politicians and bureaucrats paid to Suzuki, and soon most of the world's leaders were too busy to see him.

By 1982 even Tanaka realized that Japan needed a smarter and more forceful prime minister. He chose Nakasone Yasuhiro, the leader of a small faction that had supported him when he ran for prime minister in 1972. Nakasone brought stability to Japanese politics, remaining in office five years, between 1982 and 1987.

Tall, handsome, and an excellent speaker, Nakasone is conservative even for a member of the LDP. His brother died as a kamikaze pilot, and as a young Diet member Nakasone wore a black tie in mourning throughout the American occupation. In later years he often tried to increase Japan's defense budget. Nakasone changed political allegiances so smoothly that critics called him "Mr. Weathervane," but by 1982 he had been a Tanaka ally for some time and had served in several cabinets before becoming prime minister.

It was rare for a faction to hold more than four cabinet posts at a time, but Nakasone appointed six members of Tanaka's faction to his cabinet, as well as two independents closely allied to Tanaka. Newspapers called the new government "the Tanakasone cabinet," and Tanaka himself said, "Nakasone may be a first-class geisha capable of dancing on the international stage, but I am the one who molds the clay of his administration."

With Tanaka's approval, Nakasone privatized the telephone company and the national railway. He also let Japan's defense spending reach one percent of its gross national product for the first time.

Nakasone's hawkish views on defense made him popular with United States President Ronald Reagan. During a summit conference in 1983, Nakasone told Reagan to think of Japan as "a big aircraft carrier" in the struggle against the Soviet Union. From then on "Ron" and "Yasu" were on a first-name basis.

Meanwhile Tanaka's bribery trial finally reached a verdict: guilty on all counts. On October 12, 1983, the Tokyo District Court sentenced Tanaka to four years in prison, pending a 3,024-page appeal that took another court four years to decide. Opposition parties immediately demanded that Tanaka resign from the Diet, and polls showed that over eighty percent of the public agreed with them. But Tanaka refused, and Nakasone would not permit the matter to come to a vote. In disgust, the opposition parties boycotted the Diet for five weeks, until finally Nakasone resolved the deadlock by allowing the opposition to pass a motion of no confidence, which forced a new election.

Tanaka still denied that he had done anything wrong, which angered the Japanese people, because they expect remorse from a wrongdoer. But public condemnation did not hurt Tanaka's political machine. Although the LDP lost thirty-six seats in the "Tanaka verdict election" of December 1983, the Tanaka faction lost just two of those seats. Nakasone's new cabinet once again included six members of Tanaka's faction, but many voters were deeply frustrated that they had been unable to hold the LDP accountable for the crimes of its most powerful leader.

By 1985 even members of Tanaka's faction were grumbling about being led by a convicted criminal. This was partly because Tanaka was no longer the biggest fund-raiser in his faction. The new champion was his top aide, Takeshita Noboru, a "god of elections" who held giant parties at hotels that raised millions of dollars in a single night. Companies bought $200 tickets in blocks of fifty and a hundred, but rarely used more than a few of them. Businesses also gave money to "policy research institutes" that did little research.

Short, very polite, and with a black belt in judo, Takeshita had been training to be a kamikaze pilot when World War II ended. In the Diet he became a Tanaka favorite and an expert in deal making, but in January 1985 he finally challenged his mentor. Takeshita started a "policy study group" that was in fact a new faction inside Tanaka's faction. Eighty-four Diet members expressed an interest in joining, and when Tanaka found out, he was furious. Through persuasion and intimidation he managed to reduce the study group's size by half, but could not stop forty people from meeting.

Three weeks later, on February 27, 1985, Tanaka suffered two massive strokes that paralyzed his right side and left him unable to walk or speak clearly.

He spent two months in a hospital, then returned home under the care of his wife and daughter. The two women would not let Tanaka's illegitimate sons visit him, and even returned their letters unopened.

Despite Tanaka's stroke, Takeshita could not take over the faction until he won more followers. To gain time, he supported Nakasone's bid to be prime minister for a fifth year, then waited until July 1987 before creating a new faction that drew 113 of the 140 Diet members who had once been loyal to Tanaka.

That same month the Tokyo High Court upheld the lower court's verdict that Tanaka was guilty of bribery. Tanaka filed an appeal to the Supreme Court of Japan, and continued to be free on bail.

When Nakasone retired in November 1987, he paid his debt to the men who had backed him by supporting Takeshita as Japan's new prime minister. But it was soon clear that another protégé of Tanaka's was operating behind the scenes. Takeshita's shadowy alter ego was Kanemaru Shin, nicknamed "the don," a big, gruff bear of a man who taught judo and ran his family's sake brewery before running for the Diet and later becoming Tanaka's minister of construction. Like Tanaka, whom he served for years, Kanemaru raised millions of dollars from construction and telecommunications firms, often making a secret deal in return for a contribution.

Learning from Tanaka's experience, Kanemaru declined to run for prime minister and let Takeshita administer Japan's day-to-day affairs. Kanemaru trusted Takeshita—his son was married to Takeshita's daughter, and the two leaders shared grandchildren.

Kanemaru avoided the prime minister's office because the publicity was too dangerous. It might lead to an investigation. As one faction leader put it, "The powerful man has to collect political funds not only for himself, but also for dozens of other people. . . . We have to raise money any way we can. Clean people are not powerful."

In 1989 the incapacitated Tanaka finally resigned his seat in the Diet and retired from politics. Takeshita also resigned as prime minister when an investigation revealed that he had lied to a Diet committee about taking a $400,000 loan from a communications company, the Recruit Group.

Kanemaru took over Takeshita's faction and led it for three years. He propped up three weak prime ministers, but had to resign from the Diet in 1992 when the public learned that he had taken $4 million in bribes from a parcel delivery company with ties to organized crime. Kanemaru was also charged with tax evasion in 1993 after the police searched his home and found $2 million in cash and gold bars and $30 million in bank and corporate bonds.

In spite of this spectacular corruption, the leaders of the LDP refused to pass any campaign or electoral reforms. When Kanemaru was fined less than $2,000, younger Diet members, keenly aware of the public's disgust, feared for their careers.

On June 18, 1993, thirty-four Diet members, led by Ozawa Ichiro, a former aide to both Tanaka and Kanemaru, deserted the LDP and joined the opposition in a vote to bring down the government. For the first time in thirty-eight years, the LDP lost its power. A coalition of eight parties chose a new prime minister and created single-member districts, but their shaky alliance lasted just eleven months. Since 1994 a weaker LDP has returned to power, but only by forming coalitions with other parties or attracting independent Diet members. The Tanaka-Takeshita faction, recently led by Prime Minister Obuchi Keizo, is still powerful.

Tanaka never served a day of his prison sentence because he died before the Supreme Court upheld the conviction he had appealed. On December 16, 1993, six months after the LDP fell from power, Tanaka died of pneumonia and a failure of the thyroid gland. Several days before the public funeral, Tanaka's family held a private service. The daughter, Makiko, refused to let her half brothers attend.

Shortly before her father died, Makiko campaigned for her father's Diet seat in Niigata and won. This is common in Japan. It takes an average of $4 million to win a seat in the Diet, and children of politicians have an easier time raising that kind of money than most other people do. According to a 1990 survey by the *Tokyo Shimbun* newspaper, forty-seven percent of all Diet representatives are second-, third-, or fourth-generation politicians.

In 1995 a Japanese magazine, *New Tide Weekly*, reported that accountants valued Tanaka's estate at $110 million, from which the family paid about $70 million in inheritance taxes. Tanaka's two illegitimate sons, a management consultant and a concert promoter, have filed a lawsuit that claims the family has hidden tens of millions of dollars in unreported assets, an allegation many Japanese think is quite likely.

Many people had high hopes that Tanaka Kakuei, a former construcution worker, would shake up Japan's bureaucracy and make the government more accountable to the people. Instead, he corrupted the government even more and made it resemble Japan's tainted construction industry. Just as in America a developer may make campaign contributions to influence a local zoning board, so Tanaka used construction company money to win power over an entire nation.

Money has always been significant in Japanese politics, but Tanaka "changed the digit" so that ten times as much money circulated as before. Yet for all the money that Tanaka spent on public works, Japan's cities are still unsightly and congested. And despite all the time and energy Tanaka's faction spent campaigning, ordinary Japanese continue to have little say in the choice of who leads their government. The decision is still usually made in secret by a few extremely powerful old men.

PART FOUR
Modern Writers

28

Fukuzawa Yukichi

The Writer Who Helped Japan to Understand the West

FUKUZAWA YUKICHI was the most popular and important Japanese writer of the nineteenth century. His many books about the West were huge best sellers, and widely read even in Japan's smallest villages.

Before Fukuzawa (1835–1901) began writing, most Japanese thought the only things they needed to learn from the Western "barbarians" were their techniques of cannon making and shipbuilding. In matters of spirit the Japanese felt completely superior. Fukuzawa changed this attitude. In plain, simple language he explained that an army and navy are merely the external forms of a civilization. Britain had hundreds of warships because it had thousands of factories and tens of thousands of engineers. Japan could not build warships until it had those things too.

Fukuzawa charged that Confucian ethics had stifled "the spirit of science" and "the spirit of independence" in the Japanese people. He said for the moment the West had superior spirit, as shown outwardly by its continual stream of new inventions. If Japan wanted to catch up to the West and be "strong in the arts of both war and peace," it would have to acquire Western science and Western enterprise as well as Western weapons.

Fukuzawa founded Keio University, Japan's most prestigious private college, and started the nation's first daily newspaper. He was also a strong champion of women's rights throughout his career, and a vigorous critic of polygamy.

Fukuzawa was born in Osaka on January 10, 1835, the youngest of five children. His father was a Confucian scholar who had been ordered by his lord to work as an accountant, a job he hated. He died when Fukuzawa was an infant, and the family moved back to its ancestral home in the town of Nakatsu, on the island of Kyushu.

Nakatsu was a rigid town. Fukuzawa was the best student in his class, yet he had to speak to higher-ranking children in respectful language, while they nearly always spoke arrogantly back to him. Fukuzawa's mother cared little about rank, however, and made friends from all classes. Sometimes she even picked lice out of a local beggar woman's hair.

In his teens Fukuzawa spent long hours studying Chinese and Japanese literature, but he had no belief in Buddhist or Shinto gods. As a test, he once stomped on a paper charm that had a god's name written on it. When nothing happened, he used another charm as toilet paper.

One day a letter that Fukuzawa's older brother had written to a local official was returned unopened because the address had not been written in a humble enough style. Fukuzawa fumed, "How foolish it is to stay here and submit to this arrogance!" He vowed at that moment to leave Nakatsu at all cost.

His opportunity came soon after United States Navy gunboats arrived in Japan in 1853. The Japanese desperately wanted to learn Western methods of making guns and cannon, but had only a few books on the subject, in Dutch. For two hundred years the Dutch—because they did not send missionaries— had been the only Westerners permitted by the shoguns to trade with Japan. Once a year a Dutch ship sailed to a small island off Nagasaki, the only place in Japan where foreigners were allowed.

An open-minded old scholar in Nagasaki taught Dutch and gunnery, and since the city was only ninety-five miles (155 km) from Nakatsu, Fukuzawa decided to become his pupil. Because Fukuzawa had been an excellent student, the chancellor of Nakatsu gave him permission to go, and also sent along his own son. When Fukuzawa jubilantly began his journey and walked past the last street in Nakatsu, he spat on the ground and swore never to return.

Fukuzawa mastered the basics of Dutch and gunnery within a year, but the chancellor's son was lazy and learned very little. The son's envy made it difficult for Fukuzawa to stay in Nagasaki, so in 1855 he joined his brother in Osaka, where, like his father before him, he was unhappily working as his lord's accountant.

Fukuzawa was fortunate that Osaka had Japan's best school of "Dutch studies," as the Japanese called the sciences. Under the direction of a doctor named Ogata, students slowly penned their own copies of Dutch books in medicine, chemistry, physics, and astronomy. The young men worked hard and late into the night, but they also drank heavily and played practical jokes. One of their favorite pranks was to fake a fistfight and empty a busy street in seconds. Another was to steal the sealed envelopes that people left at a local shrine, open them, and laugh at the prayers inside.

In 1858 the lord of Nakatsu asked Fukuzawa to start a school in Edo (soon to be called Tokyo) and teach Dutch to his agents in the capital. This tiny school eventually became Keio University. Fukuzawa also earned money translating Dutch books into Japanese.

The next year the shogun opened the port of Yokohama to foreigners. Fukuzawa eagerly went to the port to talk to Americans and Europeans, but was crushed when none of them spoke Dutch. He had naively thought Dutch was a universal Western language, and now quickly realized that he would have to learn English.

After many weeks Fukuzawa got hold of an English conversation book and a Dutch-English dictionary. To help with pronunciation, he also found some Japanese fisherman who had once been rescued by a British ship. Slowly, Fukuzawa became one of the first half-dozen Japanese to learn English.

With his new knowledge, Fukuzawa served as an interpreter aboard the *Kanrin-Maru*, the first Japanese ship to sail to America. Despite five weeks of stormy weather, the vessel reached San Francisco safely in March 1860.

The people of San Francisco proudly showed Fukuzawa a telegraph office, a sugar refinery, and other technical wonders, but Fukuzawa was more interested in their daily life. He was fascinated by matches, ice cubes, horse-drawn carriages, and, especially, dancing.

We could not make out what they were doing. The ladies and gentlemen seemed to be hopping about the room together. As funny as it was, we knew it would be rude to laugh, and we controlled our expressions with difficulty.

Fukuzawa bought a Webster's dictionary before returning home. Within months he wrote and published the first English-Japanese dictionary, with 2,200 words and 500 phrases and short sentences.

Tall and handsome, Fukuzawa married Toki Kin in 1861. She was the sixteen-year-old daughter of a high-ranking samurai who served the lord of Nakatsu. Their marriage was happy. Fukuzawa was a faithful husband, and the couple had four sons and five daughters.

The following year Fukuzawa joined a diplomatic mission to France, Britain, the Netherlands, Germany, Russia, and Portugal. He saw factories, army and navy bases, banks, clubs, zoos, churches, and the homes of many important people. He was particularly fascinated by political parties. They permanently opposed each other, he observed, yet never fought a battle.

Fukuzawa took notes everywhere he went, and they became the basis for his first popular book, *Things Western*, published in 1866. The book is simply a neutral description of ordinary Western institutions such as public schools, libraries, and hospitals, and makes no comparison to conditions in Japan. In the 1860s the slightest written criticism of Japanese society could have led to Fukuzawa's execution by the government, or his assassination by an antiforeign fanatic.

Not only was *Things Western* the first Japanese book about Western society, it was also concise and easy to read. Fukuzawa had asked his maid to read the manuscript, and simplified anything she did not understand. As a result, the book was an enormous success. Sales exceeded 250,000 copies, making Fukuzawa a wealthy man at age thirty-one.

During the next several years Fukuzawa wrote a flood of books, including *Western Ways of Living* (about food, clothes, houses, and furniture), *All the*

Countries of the World (written for children, in rhyme), *The Illustrated Book of the Physical Sciences* (the manuscript was first read to illiterate women), *The English Parliament, Bookkeeping, How to Hold a Conference* (similar to Robert's Rules of Order), *The Rifle Instruction Book*, and *An Outline of the Western Art of War.*

With money from his books, and with modest tuition fees, Fukuzawa built a dormitory for his school in 1868 and soon had over two hundred students. Even adults attended his school, because after his second trip to America in 1867 Fukuzawa returned with the finest collection of English-language books in Japan.

At first almost all the teachers were Americans and Europeans. They taught the Western alphabet, English grammar, elementary science, and, one year later, geography, history, and physics.

During the battles between the armies of the shogun and the Emperor Meiji in 1867 and 1868, Fukuzawa stayed neutral. He despised the repressive bureaucracy of the shogun, but also feared the supporters of the emperor who wanted to "expel the [foreign] barbarians," a policy he knew would be disastrous.

Fukuzawa was surprised when Emperor Meiji's new government abandoned the idea of expelling foreigners, and delighted when they began to modernize Japan as fast they could. Suddenly reforms Fukuzawa had only dreamed about, such as universal elementary education, became real.

Perhaps the most important reform of the 1870s was free speech. At last Fukuzawa could express his opinions. He renounced his samurai status and stopped wearing the customary two swords, saying, "Only a fool in this enlightened age would carry the instruments of murder at his side."

Fukuzawa also began writing his most important work, *An Encouragement of Learning.* The book is a series of seventeen essays published between 1872 and 1876. Each one sold hundreds of thousands of copies, which in turn were passed along and read by many more, including millions of students.

Fukuzawa caused a sensation with his very first sentence: "Heaven does not create one man above or below another man." In a nation as hierarchical as Japan, this was a revolutionary thought. Fukuzawa explained that although men "differ like the clouds above and the mud below, still from the point of view of inherent human rights all men are equal." And no matter how powerful a government official seems, "the people are the real masters and bosses." The official "is just their representative and manager." Therefore people should have "the spirit of independence" to challenge an official when they think he is wrong.

In the same vein, Fukuzawa wrote that "all nations are equal," and that national power "can be changed by the diligent efforts of men. . . . If we Japanese will begin to pursue learning with spirit and energy . . . why shall we fear the Powers of the West?"

Fukuzawa made fun of the fanatics who wanted to "expel the barbarians" as being as "narrow-minded as the proverbial frog in the bottom of the well. . . ."

We should mutually teach and learn from each other . . . acknowledging errors even before the black natives of Africa . . . and not being afraid of even the warships of England and America.

Fukuzawa offended conservatives by criticizing the study of the Chinese classics as impractical. Most children, he argued, would be better off learning letter writing and the use of the abacus, or, if they have talent, Western languages and the physical sciences. Fukuzawa compared Confucian scholars who ignored modern science to merchants "who stock mosquito nets with the coming of winter, still mindful of the good business they enjoyed in the summer."

Fukuzawa's strongest attacks were against polygamy, a common practice in Japan in the nineteenth century. "From ancient times forward we have never heard of a harmonious home with a plurality of wives," he wrote. Polygamy causes quarrels and "leaves poison to future generations." Anyone who supports polygamy, "even if he be Mencius or Confucius, should unhesitatingly be called a criminal."

Fukuzawa savagely criticized Confucian ethics, but did not blindly advocate everything Western. He was not a Christian, and had no desire to overthrow the emperor and make Japan a republic. He also disapproved of the West's unequal distribution of wealth.

Most important, Fukuzawa hated Western colonialism. He feared that Japan, like India, might lose its independence. To prevent this, he urged the Japanese to adopt Western science and freedoms wholeheartedly, because they were the key to national strength.

In his next important book, *An Outline of a Theory of Civilization*, Fukuzawa wrote; "The only means of preserving our independence is to adopt Western civilization." He added, "There is no use talking about Japanese civilization if there is no country."

In this work, published in 1875, Fukuzawa traced the growth of European freedom following events such as the Protestant Reformation and the beheading of England's King Charles I. His account of Europe's "progress" was a new idea in Japan. Confucian scholars believed that after a golden age of wisdom, men had degenerated, not progressed.

Fukuzawa argued that Japan fell behind the West not because of moral degeneration, but because for 250 years

Publications were official publications . . . no newspapers existed . . . nor assemblies for the discussion of public opinion. . . . In short, there was not one private attempt at intellectual development.

Educated Japanese still had "the spirit of subservience," Fukuzawa complained. "If a young student reads only a few volumes, he immediately aspires for a government post," and thinks he "cannot accomplish anything except through the government."

Fukuzawa was frequently offered but never accepted a government position. He disliked the arrogance of government officials, and said it was "a foolish game" to be in a position to bully those below you while being bullied by those above.

He also wrote that a government can only command, but it is better to persuade than command, and still better to offer a personal example. Fukuzawa thought he could be a better example of "the spirit of independence" if he remained in the private sector, writing and teaching.

Even so, Fukuzawa had a huge impact on Japan's government. In 1879 he wrote a long newspaper article advocating the immediate establishment of a national parliament. Other newspapers in Tokyo took up the call, and within three months petitions demanding a parliament were circulating all over Japan. By 1881 public opinion on the subject had grown so strong that the government agreed to establish a written constitution and a national legislature by 1889. It was the beginning of Japanese democracy.

In 1882 Fukuzawa started a newspaper, *Jiji-shimpo* (The News of the Times). It remained one of Tokyo's leading dailies until shortly after World War II. Fukuzawa felt the need for an unbiased newspaper, and because he was wealthy but unconnected to the government, decided that he should be the one to launch it.

"I encouraged the reporters to write bravely and freely," Fukuzawa wrote, "but I warned them that they must limit their statements to what they would be willing to say to the victim face-to-face."

Fukuzawa also helped start a newspaper in Korea. In 1883 he sent printers to Korea to cast metal typeface in the Korean phonetic alphabet. Until then Koreans had done nearly all their reading and writing in Chinese. Fukuzawa helped revive the Korean alphabet because he wanted ordinary Koreans who were too poor to learn Chinese to have a chance to read about the modern world.

When young reformers took over Korea's government in 1884, Fukuzawa was delighted. But the coup failed when China's Manchu dynasty sent troops to Korea to restore the old order. After this defeat Fukuzawa took a more imperialistic attitude in matters of foreign policy. If China or Korea were going to be carved up by colonial powers, Fukuzawa wrote in 1885, Japan should be "a guest at the table," and not just an onlooker.

Fukuzawa did not think only of young men when he looked to the future. The father of five daughters, Fukuzawa wrote dozens of articles in his newspaper advocating equality for women.

For two centuries the classic Japanese book on female etiquette had been *The Greater Learning for Women*, a summary of four much older Chinese books. According to its teachings,

A wife must look to her husband as her lord, and must serve him with all worship and reverence. . . . The great life-long duty of a woman is obedience . . . and the style of her address should be courteous, humble and conciliatory. . . . A woman should look on her husband as if he were Heaven itself.

The Greater Learning for Women also stated that a woman should never leave home without her husband's permission, never disobey her in-laws, and never be jealous if her husband is unfaithful.

Fukuzawa called these teachings "outrageous," "against human nature," and as obsolete as a spear in modern war. By contrast, Fukuzawa advised,

In a woman's schooling and other education, never discriminate because of her sex . . . have her learn a profession of her own by which she will some day be able to make a living . . . without depending on a man.

Fukuzawa expanded these ideas in a long essay called *The New Greater Learning for Women* in 1898.

Fukuzawa continued to attack polygamy, which he described as a shameful "stain on our new Japan." He also criticized the conservative morality that kept young men and women apart, arguing that it led only to an increase in prostitution. Instead, men and women should attend

parties to enjoy blossoms, birds and the moon, or even just tea . . . big or small, intellectually uplifting or only for fun . . . any excuse should be used to bring people together.

Fukuzawa looked forward to a "new world of decency" where "the association of the sexes will be lifted to nobler planes so that . . . illicit affairs under cover will become a thing of the past."

Perhaps Fukuzawa hoped his students would enjoy such noble friendships. In 1890 Fukuzawa's school officially became Keio University when three American professors began teaching graduate-level English-language courses in law, economics, and literature. Several years before, the Keio school had moved to a high hill with a spectacular view of Tokyo Bay, where it remains today. Later, after Fukuzawa's death, graduate schools were also established in medicine and engineering.

As proud as Fukuzawa was when his school become a university, he was even more pleased when Japan defeated China in the war of 1894-1895. He described the triumph as a "victory for Japanese civilization," because it meant Japan was now too strong to lose its independence to the West. His only regret was that many of his friends had not lived to see the victory.

By the mid-1890s Fukuzawa's older children had grown up. His two eldest sons earned degrees at Cornell and M.I.T., and after their father's death one son became Chancellor of Keio University while the other became president of the *Jiji-shimpo* newspaper. Fukuzawa's second eldest daughter married into the Iwasaki family, the fabulously rich owners of the Mitsubishi enterprises.

Fukuzawa loved family life,

> I find my greatest pleasure in seeing my children and grandchildren assembled around me, playing with them, or watching them play . . . the sounds of their happy voices and laughter . . . are the sweetest music I can think of.

Fukuzawa remained healthy nearly all his life, walking four miles before breakfast every morning with any students who cared to join him. But in 1898, just two months after finishing a lively autobiography, he suffered a stroke. He recovered, but stopped writing. Two years later Fukuzawa suffered a second stroke and died on February 3, 1901. Before he slipped into his final coma, his last words were mumbled ramblings about women's rights.

Over fifteen thousand people attended Fukuzawa's funeral. Emperor Meiji sent a special messenger, and the national Diet passed an unprecedented measure of condolence.

When Fukuzawa published the first English-Japanese dictionary in 1862, Japan was a feudal society isolated from the outside world. By 1905, only four years after Fukuzawa's death, Japanese battleships had sunk the Russian navy. In just four decades Japan became one of the most powerful nations on earth.

No one did more to lead the Japanese people into the modern world than Fukuzawa Yukichi. For over three decades he wrote dozens of books on subjects as mundane as bookkeeping and as lofty as a theory of civilization. In an easy style any peasant could understand, Fukuzawa explained what was good about Western civilization without becoming blind to the West's faults. He attacked the evils of Japanese society with such homespun logic that he never seemed too radical or threatening to the general public.

The range of Fukuzawa's interests, along with his scientific mind, common sense, and clear writing, make Fukuzawa Yukichi a figure comparable to Benjamin Franklin. Both men were public-spirited citizens famous for their wisdom and their activities outside, not inside, the government. Both men left their hometowns in their teens, learned four languages, published an almanac, printed a newspaper, started a school that became a great university, and wrote a vivid autobiography. Both men were also great patriots, helping the people of their country at the dawn of a new era.

Today the two men have something else in common. Fukuzawa is on Japan's 10,000-yen note. Franklin is on America's 100-dollar bill. The two notes are roughly equal in value.

29

Natsume Soseki

The Early Twentieth Century's
Most Highly Regarded Writer

A N AUTHOR'S JOB, Natsume Soseki once wrote, is to "perform an autopsy on his soul and report to the world any malaise he may discover." The malaise Soseki describes is alienation. Most of the main characters in his novels are intellectuals who retreat from the modern world, and Soseki (1867–1916) examined their neuroses with subtlety and precision.

The theme of alienation was fresher when Japan was newly industrialized than it is now. Soseki has relatively few readers abroad, but he is still highly regarded in Japan. In 1984 the government put his picture on the 1,000-yen (roughly $10) note.

A poll of Japanese university graduates in 1968 revealed that Soseki's novel, *Kokoro* (*The Heart*), was second only to Dostoyevsky's *Crime and Punishment* as the work of fiction that had most influenced their thinking. Like Dostoyevsky, Soseki had a profound understanding of human psychology.

Soseki was born with the name Natsume Kinnosuke in Tokyo on February 9, 1867, the year before the Meiji government overthrew the shogun. The Natsume family had been city government officials since 1702, but lost their income when the shogun fell. His father was fifty-three, his mother forty-one, and they put the child, the youngest of eight, up for adoption. The new father was Shiobara Masanosuke, a city official in the new government. For years Soseki believed that Shiobara and his wife, Yasu, were his real parents.

In an autobiographical novel, *Grass on the Wayside*, Soseki recalled the possessiveness of his new parents. "Who are your real father and mother?" they asked. When he pointed to each of them they asked him again, "Whose child are you really? Come on, tell me the truth." Sometimes Soseki remembered, he "felt more anger than pain, and would stand stiff as a board, refusing to answer."

He was never allowed to eat a cake or wear a new kimono without being told that it had come from "your father" or "your mother." They seemed not to know that such desperate attempts to win his gratitude would only make him resentful.

When Soseki was seven, Shiobara began an affair with a young widow. He quarreled with his wife, and often Soseki awoke to the sounds of beating, kicking, and screaming. When they divorced two years later, Soseki was returned home to his biological parents. He thought they were his grandparents and continued to call them "grandma" and "grandpa," until one night a maid told him the truth.

"To his father he was a nuisance," Soseki recalled in *Grass on the Wayside*, "an unwanted piece of furniture." His mother was kinder. Often she took him to see *rakugo*, performers who told funny stories in a snappy style. She died when Soseki was just fourteen.

As a child Soseki had gone to public schools. As a teenager Soseki entered a private school and memorized thousands of lines of Chinese poetry. He also took English, a compulsory subject, and trigonometry, because for a while Soseki wanted to be an architect.

Soseki had never been a good student and failed an examination when he was nineteen. The humiliation of flunking made him resolve to work harder in the future, and from then on he was always at the top of his class. He adopted the name Soseki, Chinese for "refusing to admit defeat," when he was twenty-two. One of his classmates was Masaoka Shiki (1867–1902), who would soon become the greatest haiku poet of modern Japan. The two men became lifelong friends.

In 1890 Soseki entered the department of English literature at Tokyo Imperial University. He wrote a magazine article introducing the poems of Walt Whitman to Japan. To Soseki, Whitman's *Leaves of Grass* had a "strange tone free from the traditional rules of poetry . . . showing a spirit of independence worthy of an American."

After Soseki graduated in 1893 he taught English for a year at Tokyo Normal School, but wrote a friend that he "felt not the slightest interest in my work as a teacher."

Soseki left Tokyo in 1895 to teach at a middle school on the island of Shikoku. Despite the decline in status, he may have felt that he could get more reading and writing done away from the capital city. He did not worry about what friends thought. "What varies according to the praise and censure of others," he wrote, "is a man's market price and not his real value."

With the encouragement of Masaoka Shiki, who lived in Shikoku, Soseki began writing Chinese poetry. Most of his work has yet to be translated into English, but it is widely thought to be the finest collection of Chinese poems written by a Japanese in modern times. Soseki's best poems were written in the last year of his life, and are admired by many Chinese.

In the autumn of 1895 Soseki exchanged photographs with Nakane Kyoko, the nineteen-year-old daughter of the chief clerk of the House of Peers, then the upper house of Japan's parliament. Years later Kyoko recalled that the writer's "photograph pleased me very much. There was a gentlemanly and quietly settled air about him . . . a calm and trustworthy expression." In December, Soseki went to Tokyo to meet Kyoko and her family, and they married on June 10, 1896. By then Soseki was teaching at a more prestigious high school in Kumamoto, on the island of Kyushu.

The Sosekis did not have a happy marriage. "Even the simplest remarks could not be exchanged without misunderstanding," Soseki once wrote. Perhaps because he was insufficiently loved as a child, Soseki was poor at giving and receiving love as an adult. After their wedding, one of the the first things he said to his bride was "I am a scholar and therefore must study. I have no time to fuss over you. Please understand this."

Kyoko, in turn, suffered bouts of depression and hysteria. In 1898 she tried to drown herself in a river, but was rescued by fishermen. Afterward Soseki tied their kimono sashes together at night to prevent her from attempting suicide again.

"When the tension reached a certain point," Soseki wrote in *Grass on the Wayside*, "the two from necessity would unwind themselves and treat each other with more gentleness." Physically attracted to each other despite their quarrels, they had five daughters and two sons.

In 1900 the Ministry of Education asked Soseki to study in England for two years. The government gave him little money, no instructions, and no letters of introduction. It was enough if he simply lived in England and improved his English.

Disappointed in marriage and bored with teaching, Soseki felt free when he left Japan in September and sailed to Singapore, Suez, and Genoa before boarding a train for London. In London, Soseki lived in a succession of dingy boardinghouses and spent what little money he had on books. He decided that lectures at the University of London were a waste of time and spent most days alone in his room reading. He lived in almost complete isolation, "like a frightened mouse in a cell-like room."

Soseki began to doubt whether any foreigner could ever really master another nation's literature. On the edge of madness, he formed a ten-year plan to create a grand theory of literature. The book he had in mind, he wrote his father-in-law, "starts with the question, how to view the world; moves on to the next, how to look at life . . . then goes on to define civilization . . . and discusses its impact on the evolution of literature. . . ."

Soseki read feverishly. He devoured dozens of great novels, read Shakespeare's plays and many works of philosophy and psychology. He filled thick notebooks "with letters as tiny as flies' heads." He also concluded that the Japanese needed to distance themselves from Western trends and form their own literary judgments.

During the two years Soseki lived in London, his wife wrote only half a dozen letters. When Soseki returned to Japan in 1903, he brought home crates full of books, but not one gift for his wife.

After so much time alone, the strain of family life caused Soseki to suffer a nervous breakdown. He grew angry and smashed things at the slightest provocation, and was convinced that he was being followed by detectives. In July his wife and two daughters left him for two months.

Soseki had promised the government to teach English for four years after he came home. Now he became the first Japanese to teach English literature at Tokyo Imperial University, replacing Lafcadio Hearn, an Irish writer whose classes had been enormously popular. By contrast, Soseki disappointed his students because his lectures were so theoretical.

The theory of literature that Soseki dreamed of writing in London became the basis of his lectures back home. The subtitles of the theory make one feel sorry for his students: "Classification of Literary Content," "Quantitative Change in Literary Content," "Characteristics of Literary Content."

Fortunately Soseki stopped giving these lectures after 1905, and turned instead to criticism. He gave a series of talks on eighteenth-century English writers that were later published under the title *A Criticism of Literature*. Daniel Defoe's novels, he said, were too long and detailed to leave anything to the reader's imagination. Soseki admired Alexander Pope's skill as a poet, but felt that too much of his talent had gone into the excessively contrived verse that was then fashionable. The writer he liked most was Jonathan Swift, which is not surprising because Soseki's first book of fiction is a satire.

I Am a Cat first appeared as a short story in a literary magazine in January 1905 and won Soseki instant fame. Public enthusiasm was so great that Soseki wrote ten additional chapters during the next year and a half. The narrator is a cat without a name who lives in the house of a schoolteacher named Mr. Sneeze. Mr. Sneeze, the cat notes,

> pretends to be hard-working. But ... when he has read a few pages, he becomes sleepy. He drools onto the book . . . if it's possible to sleep this much and still be a teacher, why, even a cat could teach.

The cat pokes fun at government officials, the newly rich, and half-educated followers of Western fashion. He also visits Miss Tortoiseshell, the beautiful and pampered cat of "the thirteenth shogun's widowed wife's private secretary's younger sister's husband's mother's nephew's daughter."

Still teaching, Soseki somehow managed to write two novels in 1906. The first, *Botchan* (*The Young Master*), continues to be one of the most widely read books in Japan. Botchan is a brash and not very bright young man from Tokyo who teaches math at a middle school in Shikoku. The students torment him with insults on the blackboard and grasshoppers under his blanket. Two teachers, "Redshirt" and "Clown," are petty schemers who succeed in getting him blamed for starting a fight which in fact he had tried to stop. At the end of the novel, however, Botchan and a friend catch Redshirt and Clown outside a brothel and give them a good beating.

The Japanese love Botchan's directness. But in the West, where this character trait is commonplace, Botchan may strike many readers as an unread fellow who is too quick to scorn other people.

Soseki wrote his second novel that year, *The Three-Cornered World*, in two weeks. It has also been translated under the titles *Pillow of Grass* and *Unhuman Tour*. Soseki once described the experimental novel as "haiku-like." The narrator is both a painter and a poet, and there are descriptions on almost every page.

While hiking through the mountains the hero decides to think of people "as moving about in a picture, and . . . avoid any undue emotional current." But at an inn he meets a beautiful young divorcee named Nami, who startles the painter several times with tantalizingly brief appearances. The most dramatic sight was at a hot spring, when "she stood there [nude] surrounded by swirling eddies of mist . . . crowned with billowing clouds of jet-black hair."

The artist gradually becomes friends with Nami, but cannot paint her because he feels something is missing. Only at the end of the book, when her ex-husband boards a train to fight the Russians in Manchuria, does a look of compassion in Nami's eyes provide the artist with the "final touch" he needs to create a great painting. Her compassion, however, reconnects him to the "emotional currents" that he had tried to avoid, and ends his retreat from the world.

By the end of 1906 Soseki had become a magnet for young writers who wanted to discuss literature. To accommodate them he set aside time on Thursday afternoons. Later, one of the members of "the Thursday group" was Akutagawa Ryunosuke (1892–1927), who would write the well-known short story "Rashomon."

In 1907, having fulfilled his promise to teach for four years, Soseki resigned his post at Tokyo Imperial University and signed a contract with the *Asahi Shimbun* (*Morning Sun*), which is still one of Japan's two leading newspapers. Soseki agreed to serialize one long (or two short) novels a year, roughly four installments a week, and not to write fiction for anyone else. In return, *Asahi* paid Soseki a large salary and promised not to interfere with his work. For nine years both sides kept their promises, and Soseki wrote for *Asahi* until he died.

Soseki's first novel for *Asahi* was *The Poppy*, a melodrama about a beautiful and manipulative woman that has been panned by critics because of its predictable characters. The public enjoyed it, however, and newsboys boosted sales by crying, "Read Soseki's *Poppy!*"

The novel was soon followed by a collection of short stories called *Ten Nights of Dream*. The most haunting dream is the third, in which the narrator carries his blind six-year-old boy piggyback into a forest. Finally the boy asks, "Father, it was at the cedar's root, wasn't it . . . exactly one hundred years ago that you murdered me?"

In the autumn of 1908 Soseki began *Sanshiro*, the first novel in what is often called Soseki's first trilogy. In fact, the three books, *Sanshiro*, *And Then*, and *The Gate*, have no characters in common and can be read in any order. Their only continuity is that the man in love is slightly older in each successive book.

Sanshiro is a novel about doomed innocence. The main character, Sanshiro, is twenty-three. A country boy who has come to Tokyo to study, he is unduly impressed by long-winded professors and by students who use European phrases. Soon he falls in love with a beautiful but more sophisticated woman his own age named Mineko, who enjoys leading him on.

One day Mineko whispers something in Sanshiro's ear just to make another man nearby jealous. Sensing Sanshiro's displeasure at her game-playing, she tells him, "You're not the one I was toying with." The admission is only a pin-prick in his awakening, and doubtless the first of countless disillusionments to come.

Soseki's next novel, *And Then*, was serialized in 1909. Its main character, Daisuke, is older, richer, more sophisticated, and more intelligent than San-shiro. Yet at thirty he is still unemployed and living on an allowance from his father. He has no wish to contribute to Japanese society, which he thinks is warped from trying to catch up to the West too quickly.

Daisuke's idleness ends when he realizes that he loves his best friend's wife, Michiyo, and that she also loves him. Michiyo's husband has never loved her and agrees to leave her, but Daisuke's father is furious at his son for breaking up a marriage and disowns him. To earn money, Daisuke looks for a job. But the end of the novel is uncertain because Michiyo is seriously ill, and because Daisuke, under the stress of losing family, friends, and income, suddenly shows signs of madness.

The last book in the trilogy, *The Gate* (1910), is about the consequences of stealing a friend's wife. The hero, Sosuke, is middle-aged and had to leave his university when he eloped with a friend's wife, Oyone. They are still happy together, but they are poor and cut off from society. They live under a cliff that blocks the sun, cannot have children, and are unable to take solace from reli-gion. In the last chapter Oyone tells her husband that spring has come. "Yes," Sosuke says, "but it will soon be winter again."

In the summer of 1910 Soseki began suffering from stomach ulcers. He vom-ited blood, briefly lapsed into a coma, and was hospitalized for six months. When he returned home in February 1911, the Ministry of Education offered him an honorary doctorate in literature, but Soseki refused it. He did not want to lend prestige to the repressive government of Prime Minister Katsura Taro, which often imprisoned and even executed left-wing opponents on false charges. Soseki's refusal won nationwide publicity and approval, and guaranteed him large audiences when the *Asahi Shimbun* sponsored a series of five lectures by Soseki in August. In one talk, Soseki expressed his fear that scientific progress had a psychic cost, and that the continuing race to keep up with the West could one day cause the Japanese people to suffer a national nervous breakdown.

In 1912 Soseki began his second trilogy of books, *To the Spring Equinox and Beyond, The Wayfarer,* and *Kokoro.* As in the first trilogy, none of these works has any characters in common. What links the books is that each one is narrated by a young man who observes the suffering of an elder. *To the Spring Equinox and Beyond* is not a novel at all but a collection of six short stories that have the same listener. The most moving of them, "A Rainy Day," describes the death of a baby girl. It was inspired by the death of Soseki's one-year-old daughter, Hinako, in 1911. At the end of this story a young niece asks the grief-stricken mother to have another child "just like Yokio-san." Sadly, the woman replies, "It's not like making a porcelain plate or a hat. Even if I did have a new baby to take her place, we'd never forget the lost one."

Installments of Soseki's next book, *The Wayfarer,* began in December 1912. The main character, Ichiro, is a brilliant professor in a loveless marriage who is continually ill at ease. He suspects his wife of being unfaithful, but after arranging to tempt her finds that it is not so. He is also uneasy about science:

> Never once has science . . . allowed us to pause . . . from carriage to train, from train to automobile, on to the dirigible, further on to the airplane. . . . How far it will sweep us along, nobody knows for sure. It is really frightening.

When a friend suggests that Ichiro turn to religion, Ichiro asks sarcastically whether there is any god as trustworthy as a ricksha man. Because Ichiro has ruled out both religion and suicide as ways to relieve his anxiety, his final choice is to either find a greater purpose for which to live, or go mad.

The last book in Soseki's second trilogy is his finest novel, *Kokoro (The Heart),* written in 1914. The book is about betrayal, and "the heart" of human nature is this: "Under normal conditions, everybody is more or less good . . . but tempt them, and they may suddenly change. That is what is so frightening about men."

The narrator is an unnamed student who becomes friends with an intelligent older man he calls Sensei (Teacher). Like many of Soseki's heroes, Sensei has no job and no children. He is sophisticated and has a pretty wife, but is also lonely and cut off from the world. Gradually the student realizes that he cares more for Sensei than he does for his own father, and also that Sensei is hiding something from his past.

While the student is home visiting his dying father, he receives a book-length testament from Sensei, accompanied by a note that says, "By the time this letter reaches you . . . I shall in all likelihood be dead." Realizing that the testament is a long suicide note, the student promptly takes a train to Tokyo in the vain hope of seeing Sensei before he dies. In doing this he risks cutting himself off from his family, because they are unlikely to forgive him for leaving his own father, who is dying. The student may therefore have doomed himself to be a lonely outsider, like Sensei.

On the train he reads Sensei's life story. At nineteen Sensei inherits a fortune when both his parents die. But his uncle, who manages his estate while he is away at school, betrays him by embezzling most of the money. This betrayal makes Sensei mistrustful of people.

At his university, Sensei and his best friend, "K," become boarders at the home of a widow and her beautiful daughter, Ojosan. Secretly, both students fall in love with Ojosan, and one day K reveals his true feelings to Sensei.

Instead of dealing with the problem honestly, Sensei betrays his friend by immediately asking Ojosan's mother for her daughter's hand in marriage. The proposal is accepted, and K kills himself several days later. "With a shock, I realized I was no better than my uncle. I became as disgusted with myself as I had been with the rest of the world. Action of any kind became impossible for me."

Sensei buries himself in books and drowns himself in sake, but remains obsessed by guilt. His wife knows something is wrong, but Sensei refuses to "taint" her "pure, spotless" nature by telling her the true reason for K's suicide. Keeping a secret from a wife is another form of betrayal, and Sensei only succeeds in making both of their lives more lonely.

Unable to bear his guilt as he grows older, Sensei kills himself in such a way that his wife thinks it is a natural death. Before the suicide he mails his testament to the young narrator so that his life can "serve as an example to others." He asks the student to keep the document secret as long as Ojosan, his wife, is alive.

The final betrayal then is the existence of the book itself. Although the narrator/student says nothing to Ojosan and she knows nothing of Sensei's testament, he has in fact betrayed Sensei by telling us this story sooner than Sensei wished.

In 1915 Soseki suffered another ulcer attack. The severity of the illness may have prompted him to write his only autobiographical novel, *Grass on the Wayside*, which began serialization in June. The book is a merciless but even-handed portrait of his relationship with his wife during the years when he was so irritable after he returned from London. They lived "with their backs toward each other," Soseki wrote, so that even well-meant gestures went awry. Once, for example, Kenzo (Soseki) worked especially hard so that his wife could have more money.

> He pulled out the envelope containing the bills and threw it down in front of his wife.... Neither of them said a word.... I could have shown pleasure, she thought, if only he had said something kind.

Some critics dislike *Grass on the Wayside* because it is a cheerless book about an unhappy marriage. But for an autobiographical novel it is unusual because Soseki describes his own character flaws with brutal honesty.

By the time Soseki began his last, unfinished novel, *Light and Darkness*, in 1916, he had resumed writing Chinese poems and was more interested in them than he was in his prose. Though some critics admire the finely drawn portraits of the novel's two main characters—a self-centered husband and his calculating wife—the book has almost no plot development. Donald Keene, the respected American critic of Japanese literature, is unusually blunt when he writes that the "ponderous" book "bores me from beginning to end."

During the last months of his life, when Soseki was not writing, he enjoyed painting and the study of Zen Buddhism. In November he wrote a young monk, "Everything I do—walking, standing, sitting, lying—is full of falsehood. . . . I am a fool who, at the age of fifty, has for the first time realized the need to seek the way."

One month later, on December 9, 1916, Soseki died from an ulcer that caused massive internal bleeding. The next day newspapers across Japan published long obituaries mourning his loss.

Natsume Soseki did not have a happy childhood, marriage, or disposition, and was uncomfortable with modern progress. Yet there is little doubt that his anguish made him a keen student of human behavior, and a profound writer.

It took thirty-eight years for Soseki to begin writing full-time, but in his last dozen years he wrote a well-loved satire, a popular humorous novel, two trilogies of fine psychological fiction, and a vivid autobiographical novel. Most of his work was available to anyone who could afford a newspaper, and eagerly read by men and women from all regions and classes.

Because Soseki was a psychological rather than an erotic, social, or a political writer, conservative Japanese could appreciate his work without having to question his beliefs, or their own. Both right- and left-wing intellectuals acknowledged Soseki as the leading voice of his time. Today he is still on any list of modern Japan's most important writers.

30

Ibuse Masuji
The Novelist from Hiroshima

A T SIXTY-SEVEN Ibuse Masuji could have retired after a long and successful career as a writer. Instead, he wrote *Black Rain*, the most powerful and moving novel about the atomic bombing of Hiroshima. Based on the diary of a friend who survived the blast, *Black Rain* shows the city's destruction in human rather than political terms, focusing on the suffering of just one family.

Black Rain sold millions of copies in Japan and has been translated into many languages. The novel overshadows the rest of Ibuse's work, but during his long life Ibuse (1898–1993) wrote dozens of historical novellas and many essays and short stories.

Ibuse almost always portrayed ordinary people coping with disasters or oppression. His spare writing style is so close to common speech that in the 1980s many of his books became popular on audiocassette, read aloud by famous actors.

Ibuse Masuji was born on February 15, 1898, in Kamo, a village fifty miles (80 km) east of Hiroshima. He was the third of four children in a prosperous, landowning family, and grew up in a large house with a hillside view of pine trees and wild azaleas.

Ibuse's father was a lover of literature who died of pleurisy when Ibuse was five. To compensate for the lack of a father, Ibuse's mother became quite strict. Perhaps because she was lonely, she also complained a lot. Ibuse was happier when he was with his grandparents, both of whom were great storytellers. Ibuse's grandmother talked about the famines and peasant revolts that she lived through as a child, while his grandfather told stories of brave warriors from feudal times.

When Ibuse's older brother suffered from pleurisy in 1905, his grandfather took the children to Sensuijima, a terraced island of orchards, cedar trees, and sandy beaches on Japan's warm Inland Sea. It was the first of many happy summer vacations.

At fourteen Ibuse went to a school where scholars had taught the Chinese classics for over a hundred years. He also studied English and painting, and read Japanese literature in the evening. He decided to study literature more deeply at Waseda University in Tokyo, and at nineteen left his village to live in the most populous city in the world.

For years Ibuse lived in dingy boardinghouses just off campus. Sometimes he joined other aspiring writers at coffeehouses and noodle shops, but often he suffered long bouts of loneliness and lethargy. He slept late and skipped many of his classes during his four years as a student, but always attended lectures on Basho, Shakespeare, and Blake, and on the French writers Hugo, Balzac, Flaubert, and Baudelaire.

Ibuse's best friend at Waseda was a classmate named Aoki Nampachi. Aoki encouraged Ibuse to write, and in the summer of 1919 Ibuse responded by sending him seven short stories. One was "The Salamander," Ibuse's first published work. An allegory about a lonely intellectual, the story describes a salamander whose head has grown so big that he is stuck in a cave. The salamander cannot move, but he can see clearly, and with contempt he watches schools of fish that veer now to the left, and now to the right.

Ibuse shied away from left-wing politics at a time when most of his fellow writers were part of the "proletarian literature movement." Perhaps Ibuse knew too many working people back in his village to put his faith in an ideology. He once told a friend that he would read Marx only if his friend underlined the most important passages.

In 1921 Ibuse resisted the sexual advances of a Russian literature professor. The vengeful man forced new course requirements on Ibuse, and in dismay Ibuse left Waseda University altogether. By this time his writing was more important to him than his classes. For seven months Ibuse retreated to an island in the Inland Sea, writing, fishing, drinking sake, and reading translations of Tolstoy and Chekhov. He returned to Tokyo in the spring of 1922, and a few weeks later his friend Aoki died of a respiratory disease.

Ibuse was devastated. He had not known that Aoki was sick. Now he felt guilty. He began to work harder and write more, and over the next few years published stories in five literary magazines.

In 1923 Tokyo suffered a terrible earthquake. Ibuse fled his boardinghouse for the Waseda University baseball field. From third base he could see the flames downtown, the first of three times in his life when he would see a city burn.

Several months later Ibuse met an essayist named Tanaka Kotaro. Tanaka was eighteen years older than Ibuse, but they shared a love for writing, sake, and the sea. Tanaka became Ibuse's mentor, editing his short stories and finding him odd jobs translating, proofreading, and ghost writing.

Tanaka even found Ibuse a wife. In October 1927 Ibuse married Akimoto Setsuyo. She was only sixteen at the time, but a keen student of literature. Ibuse borrowed money from his older brother to buy a house in Ogikubo, a new suburb still surrounded by wheat fields and cedar forests. The Ibuses had one son three years later and lived happily in Ogikubo all their lives. Today the area is fashionable and considered close to the heart of Tokyo.

In the 1930s Ibuse began writing short novels. One book, *Waves, a War Diary*, took eight years to finish. Set in the 1180s, *Waves* purports to be the diary of a teenage soldier in a defeated army as it retreats before the forces of Japan's first shogun. Slowly the entries reveal the boy's transformation from a sensitive aristocrat into a hardened warrior. *Waves* is a difficult book for the Western reader, however, because it assumes a knowledge of this period of history.

Like many of Ibuse's works, *Waves* also lacks a plot. "I simply don't know how to construct a plot," Ibuse once confessed, "perhaps I'm plot-deaf." This may explain why Ibuse became interested in the true stories of Japanese castaways; certainly as a country boy in Tokyo, Ibuse must often have felt like a castaway himself.

Ibuse wrote four books on castaways in the mid-1930s, two about sailors who drifted to Siberia and two about men marooned on a deserted island. In 1937 Ibuse wrote a fifth novel, *John Manjiro: A Castaway's Chronicle*, his most acclaimed book before *Black Rain*.

In this true story, Nakahama Manjiro was fourteen when he and four other fisherman were shipwrecked in 1841 on an uninhabited island five hundred miles south of Japan. For five months the men had nothing to eat but birds that they caught by hand, and nothing to drink except rainwater trapped in the crevices of rocks.

At last they were rescued by an American whaling ship, the *John Howland*. The Japanese were amazed by the size of the ship, and tried to be useful. Young Manjiro learned English faster than the others, and the American sailors called him "John Man."

The ship's captain, William Whitfield, dropped four of the Japanese off in Honolulu, but asked them if he could take John Man home with him to New Bedford, Massachusetts, where he would give him an education. John Man wanted to see the world, and after some discussion the other Japanese consented. In Hawaii three of the men became farmers. The fourth worked as a barrel maker.

By the time the *John Howland* arrived in New Bedford early in 1844, John Man was seventeen years old and an experienced seaman. In New Bedford he stayed with friends of Captain Whitfield's and helped with farm chores. At school he studied reading, writing, mathematics, and surveying, and also made friends with a boy who became Franklin Roosevelt's grandfather. After three years, however, John Man yearned to be back on a whaling ship.

In the fall of 1846 he joined the crew of the *Franklin* and sailed to Africa, Indonesia, and China. When the ship passed the Ryukyu Islands in southernmost Japan, John Man approached some local fishermen and greeted them in Japanese. But the frightened fishermen pretended not to hear him because contact with foreigners was forbidden. Reluctantly John Man went back to his ship.

When the *Franklin* returned to New Bedford in the fall of 1848, the crew had sailed around the world and caught over five hundred whales. The sailors had chosen John Man as the ship's first mate, and at the end of the voyage he received a share of the profits made from the sale of whale oil. The following year John Man traveled to California and prospected for gold, then sailed to Honolulu.

In Hawaii one of the Japanese fishermen had died, and another chose to stay in Honolulu. But two others joined John Man and boarded the *Sarah Boyd*, a steamship on its way to China. The ship surreptitiously dropped them off in Okinawa in 1851, and the three fishermen were back in Japan.

Their troubles continued. For a year and a half they were interrogated by different ranks of officials in Okinawa, Kagoshima, and Nagasaki. John Man told each of them about the "rail-row," the telegraph, and the American king, currently Taylor, who rules for four years. Finally an official ordered the three men to stamp their feet on a picture of Jesus to prove they were not Christians. At last they were free to return to their village. John Manjiro, almost twenty-six, saw his mother again after twelve long years.

The following year, 1853, United States Commodore Matthew Perry sailed his gunboats into Tokyo Bay, and Japan's isolation came to an end. John Manjiro, a lowly fisherman, suddenly became the shogun's adviser on shipbuilding and surveying. Manjiro dreamed of being the captain of a Japanese whaling ship, but political turmoil made the outfitting of a whaler impractical. After the shogun fell in 1868, Manjiro taught English and navigation until he retired.

John Manjiro: A Castaway's Chronicle won the Naoki Prize in 1938. A judge later joked that he gave the award to Ibuse because Ibuse was in debt to half the pubs in Tokyo. A more serious reason for the book's success was that Ibuse had abandoned the poetic style of his early short stories and written instead a straightforward narrative in unusually simple language. Another interesting feature of *John Manjiro* was its timing. In 1937 Japan was at war with China and hostile to the West. Yet here was a book that portrayed Americans as open and friendly, and Japanese officials as rigid men who distrusted new people and ideas.

In 1939 Ibuse wrote *Tajinko Village*, a nostalgic portrait of a rural village as seen through the eyes of a kindly policeman. The book was an escape for readers in the middle of a war, and became a big best seller. Critics regard it as lightweight, however, and the book has never been translated into English.

At forty-three Ibuse was drafted into the army in November 1941. He was on a fishing trip with a friend when his wife sent news that they both had just three days to report to duty. The two men fished for two more days, but hardly said a word.

Ibuse was put on a ship heading south. "Our final destination was unknown to us," he later recalled, "we were in the same position as the slaves of old." The ship's commanding officer shouted, "Your lives are in my hands now. Any complaints and I'll cut you to pieces." A few days later, when the news of the attack on Pearl Harbor reached the ship, the fanatical commander ordered his men to bow low in the direction of the Imperial Palace.

Ibuse sailed to Vietnam and Thailand, then rode in the back of a truck as the Japanese army advanced down the Malay peninsula. He was just a few miles outside Singapore when Japanese planes bombed the city's oil tanks in February 1942. It was the second time he watched a city burn.

Ibuse became editor in chief of Singapore's English-language newspaper. He could see that the people of Singapore resented Japan's conquest, and he was horrified when the Japanese military police executed forty thousand ethnic Chinese. But he was powerless to protest. When Ibuse published a diary, *Sailing South*, the following year, all he could do was leave the diary blank on the days when the executions took place.

Ibuse became sick during his only summer in the tropics, and flew back to Japan in the fall of 1942. The next year he published a story, "A Young Girl's Wartime Diary," written from the point of view of a teenage girl in Singapore. Then, with censorship at its height, Ibuse stopped writing fiction for three years.

As food grew scarce, the Ibuse family left Tokyo in 1944 and eventually moved to Kamo, Ibuse's home village, where they stayed until 1947. On August 6, 1945, Ibuse did not see the mushroom cloud over Hiroshima because hills blocked the view, but many people from his village died in Hiroshima that day, and others straggled back with hideous burns. Ibuse also saw the nearby city of Fukuyama burn on the night of August 7, when it was targeted by conventional American bombers—the third time he saw a city in flames.

During the postwar years Ibuse wrote several antiwar stories. Perhaps the finest is "Lieutenant Lookeast," written in 1950 and inspired by Ibuse's commander on the ship to Saigon. Like the ship's commander, Lieutenant Yuichi orders his men to bow to the east whenever news of a victory comes on the radio, even when the same news is repeated during a later broadcast.

Later, Lieutenant Yuichi falls out of a truck, bangs his head, and is sent home to his village. There he barks commands at his neighbors: "Look sharp!" "Take cover!" "Fetch me the corporal!" During the war no one thinks this is strange. But when the war ends and Yuichi continues giving orders, his neighbors realize that he is mad. Of course, the lieutenant's behavior is not that different from what it was before his injury. He appeared normal then because during wartime the whole nation was insane.

During the 1950s Ibuse wrote essays on fishing that were widely read by Japanese men. He also translated Hugh Lofting's Doctor Dolittle books for children into Japanese, as well as Daniel Defoe's great castaway novel, *Robinson Crusoe*, in 1961. Many bilingual Japanese insist that Ibuse's translations are better than the originals.

Ibuse undertook the greatest challenge of his career in the 1960s. A fishing companion, Shigematsu Shizuma, begged Ibuse to write a novel about his niece, Yasuko, who survived the bombing of Hiroshima only to die later of radiation sickness. Shigematsu, who also survived the blast, provided Ibuse with over three hundred pages of diaries, records, and accounts of the bombing. In addition, Ibuse interviewed more than fifty other survivors.

Black Rain is Ibuse's only long novel. He serialized the book in *Shincho* magazine in 1965 and 1966, finishing a chapter a month for twenty months.

The hero of the book is Shizuma Shigematsu. (Ibuse merely switched the first and last names of his friend.) He is an office worker at a clothing factory just outside Hiroshima. His niece Yasuko lives with him because she works at the same factory. Shigematsu worries that Yasuko will not find a husband because of rumors that she was in the center of Hiroshima at the time of the blast. To counter these rumors, Shigematsu decides to make a copy of Yasuko's diary to prove to a marriage broker that she was over six miles from the center of the city when the bomb was dropped. Later Shigematsu includes his own much longer diary to show that a man could be just one mile from ground zero and still survive intact. Shigematsu also attaches the short diary of his wife, Shigeko, and that of a doctor, Iwatake.

Black Rain is a composite of these four diaries. Shigematsu's diary takes up most of the book, but with four accounts Ibuse can describe the atomic blast several times without being repetitive.

❖

The diary entries for August 6, 1945, all begin normally. At eight-fifteen in the morning Yasuko was having a cup of tea with a friend. Suddenly a flash of bluish-white light rushed from the city "like a shooting star the size of hundreds of suns," followed a few seconds later by a terrifying roar.

At the same moment, Dr. Iwatake was being scolded by a military officer for not looking snappy enough. Iwatake, a little nearer to the city than Yasuko, felt a wave of searing heat before he heard a roar and lost consciousness. His nephew, an eighth-grade student, was burned to death at his desk at school.

Shigematsu was waiting for a train. He saw a ball of intense light, followed instantly by total darkness. He was temporarily blind, but he could hear shouts, curses, and screams of pain. Shigematsu was shoved to and fro until he felt a pillar, and instinctively he clung to it with all his strength. Like many victims in Hiroshima, he thought at first that he had been directly hit by a conventional bomb. Only when he could finally see did he realize that his entire neighborhood had been destroyed.

Yasuko saw smoke rising high above the city as if it were spewing from a volcano. But the cloud bank also moved out horizontally like a giant umbrella. Shigematsu, who was close enough to see the cloud boil and churn, thought it was shaped more like a jellyfish. But this monstrous animal emitted flashes of red, blue, purple, and green light—"an envoy of the devil himself."

Whole neighborhoods were in flames as Shigematsu tried to walk home. Sometimes he dodged a smoldering beam or window frame that fell to earth after having been sucked up into the sky. Because the air was choked with smoke, Shigematsu soon felt a terrible, overpowering thirst. Tap water was too hot even to touch, but Shigematsu was lucky enough to find a bucket of water half full. He stuck his head in like a dog and "just drank."

Shigematsu's house was tilting fifteen degrees, but still standing. He and his wife were writing a note for Yasuko, when by chance she arrived. Yasuko and Shigeko shed tears of joy.

Thousands of others were not so lucky. Mothers shouted for their children, and children for their mothers. One mother, seeing that she had the wrong child by the hand, shook her hand free, but the little boy burst into tears and ran after her.

Yasuko saw a mirror and noticed that her skin looked as if it had been splattered with mud. Then she remembered that earlier that morning, after the blast, a brief shower of black rain had fallen. Ice-cold raindrops the size of jelly beans had fallen for just a few seconds—and in the months to come nothing would get the spots off her skin.

Shigematsu, Shigeko, and Yasuko decided to walk across Hiroshima to the clothing factory where they worked in hope of finding friends and getting food and water. Along the way they saw countless corpses and thousands of hideously injured people. A young man's skin was hanging from his body like shreds of wet newspaper. A boy's face was so swollen that his own brother couldn't recognize him. A horse, burned black, was still breathing.

The Shizuma family reached the factory safely, but in hindsight it was a mistake for them to walk across the city. While crawling at one point to avoid some dangling electric wires, Yasuko scraped herself, and the wind blew radioactive ash into her wound. Months later Yasuko's hair fell out, her teeth became loose, her sight grew blurry, and she suffered fever, violent pain, and a constant ringing in her ears.

Soon Shigematsu realizes that Yasuko will never find a husband. She will not even live. He decides to keep copying the diaries anyway and donate them to a school library. It will be his contribution to history.

The book moves back and forth in time and closes with Shigematsu's diary entry for August 15, 1945. The emperor is on the radio announcing Japan's surrender, but Shigematsu is not interested. He walks to a canal and watches a parade of baby eels swim upstream. "On you go, on up the stream," he tells them. Unharmed by the blast, they are a sign of renewal.

❖

Soon after *Black Rain* was published, Ibuse won the Order of Cultural Merit, Japan's highest honor to a writer. Ibuse lived serenely for another twenty-seven years, continuing to write even into his late eighties. Often he wrote memoirs about people he knew in his youth. A 1974 essay, "Someone I Miss," is about his young protégé, Dazai Osamu, author of the acclaimed novel *The Setting Sun*, whose suicide in 1948 continued to haunt him.

In the mid-1980s Ibuse serialized another novel based on a diary, *The Record of Tea Parties at Tomonotsu*. It is an account of fifteen dinner parties given during the 1590s, when Hideyoshi had just unified Japan. Priests and samurai talk about castles and politics, and nearly everyone criticizes Hideyoshi's two unsuccessful invasions of Korea. The novella is Ibuse's parting shot at the stupidity of war.

Ibuse Masuji died of pneumonia on July 10, 1993. He was ninety-five. He used the voices of ordinary people to bring history to life, and then used the past to illuminate the present. He wrote about injustice and tragedy calmly, and never wasted a word. A modest writer, Ibuse avoided grand passages even when describing one of the worst horrors of all time.

31
Hayashi Fumiko
*Modern Japan's Most Popular
Woman Writer*

HAYASHI FUMIKO IS perhaps the most popular woman writer in twentieth-century Japan, but she is still little known in the West. Only one of her novels and a half dozen short stories have been translated into English, out of a body of work that includes twenty-five books and over 250 stories and essays. Yet even this tiny sample reveals her extraordinary power.

Most of Hayashi's books were best sellers, and the Japanese public still loves her as a working class girl who made good. Hayashi (1903–1951) endured extreme poverty until she became rich at twenty-six, and drew upon her early hardship to write with compassion about the troubles ordinary women have with jobs, money, husbands, and lovers. In a simple and poetic style Hayashi wrote bittersweet stories about poor women who never give up hope.

Hayashi was born on December 31, 1903, in a rented room above a tin shop in Moji City, at the northern tip of the island of Kyushu. Her father was a peddler, and opened a secondhand thrift store in the nearby city of Shimonoseki soon after her birth.

Hayashi's mother worked as a chambermaid at a hot springs inn before she was pregnant. A high-spirited woman, she cared little for social convention and already had three children by two different men. At thirty-five, she was fourteen years older than her new lover. Hayashi's parents never married.

When Hayashi was six, her father brought home a concubine. Within months her mother ran off with a handsome clerk at the thrift shop who was twenty years her junior. Taking Hayashi with them, the couple moved from city to city, peddling secondhand goods. Hayashi's stepfather was kind, but the young girl switched elementary schools thirteen times in six years, and made no friends her own age. She read a great deal, and also spent time with her hall mates at cheap boardinghouses. Among her companions were a coal miner who picked lice out of Hayashi's unwashed hair, a prostitute with a snake tattooed on her belly, and a street singer with a glass eye.

When Hayashi was twelve, her family moved to Onomichi, a small seaport forty miles east of Hiroshima. An elementary-school teacher there admired

Hayashi's writing and encouraged her to enter high school in 1918; Hayashi's mother then insisted that the family not move again until Hayashi graduated.

Hayashi earned her tuition by working nights at a canvas-sail factory. Her grades at high school were average, but still another teacher encouraged her literary ambitions. She discovered the poetry of Basho, Walt Whitman, and Heinrich Heine, and wrote poems of her own for local newspapers.

Okano Gunichi was Hayashi's first love, a friend from Onomichi who shared her interest in literature. When Hayashi graduated from high school in 1922 she followed him to Tokyo, and for a year they lived together while he finished his university studies. Despite the fact that Hayashi was very pretty and highly intelligent, Okano did not marry her when he graduated because his family strongly objected to a match with someone poor and illegitimate. Hayashi was devastated, but decided to stay in Tokyo, and supported herself with a variety of jobs: as a cashier at a public bathhouse, a saleswoman at a pawnshop, a nanny for an author's children, a clerk in a stockbroker's office, an assistant at a maternity hospital, a painter of toys in a basement factory. Usually she worked as a waitress in cheap cafés, but she also helped her parents sell socks and underwear at a night stall they operated when they came to Tokyo.

Once Hayashi had so little money, she stole turnips from a vegetable patch and slept in a public toilet. Another time she attempted suicide because she felt it was the only way she could avoid the financial temptation to become a prostitute. When the sleeping powder she took failed to work, she decided that she would "toil on by daring to live."

Hayashi also had hard times with men. In 1924 she supported a young actor for months until she discovered that he had a bankbook with deposits of over 2,000 yen (several years' income) and love letters from another woman. She dropped him immediately, but her next lover was worse. Nomura Yoshiya was a mediocre anarchist poet who beat Hayashi frequently. The miserable affair ended only after he kicked her to the floor, stuffed her into a burlap bag, and threw the bag under the floorboards of their kitchen.

In 1926 Hayashi finally met a supportive and level-headed man, a European-style painter named Tezuka Ryokubin. They began living together almost immediately, but did not bother to legalize their happy relationship until 1944.

Throughout these difficult years Hayashi was determined to be a writer. She kept a lengthy diary, and also wrote poems. Some of her poems were published in a left-wing journal called *Literary Front*. Hayashi also read translations of Baudelaire, Tolstoy, O'Neill, and the Norwegian writer Knut Hamsun.

In 1927 Hayashi rewrote her diary under the title *A Vagabond's Story*, also translated as *Vagabond's Song*. She sent the manuscript to several publishers, all of whom rejected it. A literary magazine, *Women and the Arts*, began to print installments of the diary in October 1928, and an editor who liked what he read published the diary as a book in 1930.

A Vagabond's Story describes Hayashi's life as she works at a variety of menial jobs. Although the book has a stream-of-consciousness feel, each thought is complete and concise.

Hayashi writes concretely about her lack of money:

> I'd like to eat some pickled scallions and some sweet beans. I'd also like to buy some benzine to clean the stains on my kimono. . . .
>
> The boarding house is noisy at dinnertime. The aroma of food that others are able to buy makes me envious.

A Vagabond's Story is not an exposé of poverty, however; it is a record of Hayashi's moods, her despair—"I want to scream like a crazy person"—and also her ambition:

> We decide to publish five hundred copies of the magazine, which should cost eighteen yen. . . . I consider pawning one of my good kimonos. . . .
>
> To write. Only that. To lose myself in my writing. It's phony to pose as a European poet. I can forget the posing.

The book has many unforgettable images: a hundred women waiting on line to apply for two jobs at a grain store, a group of construction workers who quarrel and vomit after drinking ten bottles of sake, and a knife-throwing ex-boyfriend whom Hayashi both hates and adores.

Sometimes Hayashi puts her poems into the book. Here is a powerful couplet:

> *I wasn't prepared for my youth, it was all guessing*
> *And now it has rotted into ashes.*

A Vagabond's Story was an instant success, selling hundreds of thousands of copies even before critics had a chance to review it. Many Japanese women led lives like Hayashi's, and they hailed her for putting their experiences and feelings into words.

"The only ideal I ever had was to get rich quick," Hayashi once wrote, and at twenty-six she had succeeded. She gave money to her proud and weary mother, then treated herself to a month-long trip to China. When she returned, she published some additional chapters of her diary to meet the public's demand for more material. About this time she also released a book of poetry, *I Saw a Pale Horse*.

In the summer of 1931 *A Vagabond's Story* was staged at a theater in Tokyo. Four years later it became a popular film, the first of three movie adaptations.

Yet more than sixty years later only a few excerpts of this remarkable book have been translated into English.

The year 1931 was also when Hayashi published *Town of Accordions and Fish*, a memoir of her childhood in Onomichi, and *Honest Poverty*, a collection of short stories about the first four years of her relationship with Tezuka. During this time Hayashi and Tezuka were desperately poor, but deeply in love. As Hayashi gradually began to feel secure in her marriage, she also regained the faith she had lost in the basic goodness of people.

Honest Poverty was a success with both the critics and the public, and substantially boosted Hayashi's royalty income. Traveling again, she took the Trans-Siberian Railroad to Moscow, then continued on to Paris, where she spent four months going to operas, plays, and museums. But even the royalties from a best seller could go only so far in this expensive city. Hayashi helped make ends meet by eating lightly and by writing articles for Japanese magazines before returning to Japan by ship in June 1932.

Back home, Hayashi was inundated with offers not only to write magazine articles, but also to give talks to women's groups and literary societies. She rarely refused a request, partly because she was very hardworking, and partly because she enjoyed traveling around Japan. During each of the next ten summers, however, she and Tezuka rented a quiet cottage in Onomichi, where she could write and he could paint undisturbed. By 1933 Tezuka was making a decent living as an artist.

In 1934 Hayashi began for the first time to write stories that were not drawn from her own life. *Cry Baby* is about an unwanted boy who is passed from one relative to another while his mother begins a new marriage. *Oyster*, published in 1935, describes a pouch maker who gradually retreats into madness after his young wife, who married him only for money, deserts him. Both novellas were highly praised by critics, and this gave Hayashi the confidence to continue writing fiction.

In the fall of 1936 Hayashi visited troops in Japanese-occupied Manchuria. She enjoyed being a reporter, but never challenged the militarism of her time. Perhaps it was too dangerous. Only three years earlier the police had thrown her into jail for nine days merely for subscribing to a communist newspaper. Although she had many left-wing friends, Hayashi was basically uninterested in politics. She preferred to write personal stories about ordinary people coping with hardship.

When Japan invaded China in 1937 Hayashi's lover was drafted into the army. In December, Hayashi went to China herself as a war correspondent for the *Mainichi Shimbun*, one of Japan's leading newspapers. She was the first Japanese woman in the city of Nanjing after its conquest, but she wrote articles from the Japanese point of view and ignored the fact that the Japanese soldiers had raped over twenty thousand Chinese women. Censorship was severe, and perhaps Hayashi knew better than even to try to report such horror.

During the next several years Hayashi wrote articles about Japanese troops in China, Manchuria, Vietnam, and Borneo, and often gave speeches to the soldiers. Although she never questioned the harshness of Japanese military rule in public or in print, she did try to live with local civilians so that she could see what their lives were like. Her rather luxurious stay in the highlands of Vietnam in the winter of 1942–1943 proved especially useful because the area became the setting of her final novel, *Floating Cloud*. In that book she wrote that the Japanese "were nothing but sheer outsiders who came to ransack someone else's property."

By the time Hayashi returned to Japan for good in May 1943 it was almost impossible to write. The search for food and necessities was too time-consuming, and censorship grew tighter as even *A Vagabond's Story* was banned for being too self-absorbed and insufficently patriotic.

Fortunately, Tezuka was discharged from the army, and in December 1943 he and Hayashi adopted a baby boy whom they named Tai. Four months later Hayashi and her son left Tokyo for a hot springs inn in the mountains near Nagano. They stayed at spas in the region for the rest of the war, but the care of her baby left Hayashi with little time for writing.

After the war Hayashi made up for lost time. She was free at last from censorship, and in a defeated nation there was a wealth of material to write about because everyone was poor and deserving of compassion. Hayashi published several short stories in Kawabata Yasunari's literary magazine, *Humanity*, in 1946, and began serializing a novel about war widows, *Swirling Currents* (not yet translated), the following year.

One of her best stories from the postwar years is "Borneo Diamond." Manabe, a mining engineer, sends his wife a large diamond that he has dug up himself and dreams of seeing her wear. Instead, to his disgust, his wife donates the diamond to the war effort.

> Manabe felt something in common [between] the ignorant conquerors who despised the native population as an inferior race . . . and the heart of a Japanese woman who did not know the worth of a diamond.

In another story, "Splendid Carrion," a war veteran abandons the tiny apartment of his sister's family for life in the streets, because "the life of a vagabond promised a more comfortable world than that of a bed in the entrance hall."

It is probably no coincidence that Hayashi wrote her best work once her son was old enough to go to elementary school. Between 1948 and 1951 she completed eight novellas, a full-length novel, and her finest short stories.

In one story, "Bones," a widow is the sole support of her family. Her husband had died in Okinawa, her brother suffers from tuberculosis, and her aging father's pension has been cut off. She is too frail to make a living knitting, and turns to prostitution. On her first night with a customer "she felt such remorse that it seemed to set her ears ringing," but before long she learns "to guess the worth of a wallet at a glance."

Another work by Hayashi, "Late Chrysanthemum," written in 1948, is regarded by some critics as not only her finest short story, but also as one of the best accounts of a geisha ever written. It concerns a middle-aged geisha's dashed expectations.

Kin, who is fifty-six and comfortably retired, eagerly awaits a visit from Tabe, a former lover who is twenty-five years younger than she is. Before the war Tabe was a fresh-faced student, but years of fighting in Burma have taken their toll. He arrives with a bottle of whiskey, and drinks it in greedy gulps. His business is failing, his marriage is stale, and his mistress is pregnant. He asks Kin to lend him 400,000 yen. "A cold chill crept over Kin. . . . 'Did you come to talk about money, then, and not to see me?'"

Kin loved Tabe once, and kept his photograph for years. Now, as Tabe falls into a drunken sleep, she burns his picture. Although Kin still has a wealthy patron, she is unlikely to fall in love again. Money will be her chief comfort in her old age.

"Downtown," also written in 1948 and sometimes translated as "Tokyo," is perhaps Hayashi's most vivid story. In only a dozen pages Hayashi conveys the bleakness of postwar Tokyo, the beginning and end of a romance, and the start of a new life.

Ryo makes a meager living trudging from house to house shouting, "Tea for sale." She has a son six years old, the length of time that her husband has been a prisoner in Siberia, if he is alive at all. On a cold, windy day a kindhearted truck driver invites her into his home so that she can warm herself by a fire. She returns the next day and the day after, and they become friends. One night they go to a movie and stay at an inn. The following day the truck driver is killed in an accident, and the friendship has ended almost as soon as it has begun. At the end of the story Ryo sells tea to four women who are sewing a pile of shirts and socks by a warm stove; perhaps Ryo will join them.

During 1949 and 1950 Hayashi wrote several novellas, but her most important work during this period is her last novel, *Floating Cloud*, which she published in installments between 1949 and 1951.

Floating Cloud is a novel of defeat. It is about a man and a woman who cannot adjust to the bleak realities of postwar Japan. Tomioka is a forestry engineer, Yukiko is a typist, and they meet in 1943 in the wooded highlands of Japanese-occupied Vietnam, where they live luxuriously at a French colonial villa. Everywhere there are tropical flowers, white peacocks, and mountain views. For Yukiko especially, life is paradise. She is the only young Japanese woman in the area, and is sought after. She falls in love with Tomioka, a handsome man who is married and also has a Vietnamese mistress. Tomioka desires Yukiko but does not love her nearly as much as she loves him. Nevertheless the two have plenty of time to explore the woods, the gardens, and each other.

By contrast, Japan in 1946 is a nation of shortages and fatigue. Skies are gray, blankets are thin, pillows are soiled, and breakfast is boiled barley. At home Tomioka is demoralized and weak. He cannot bring himself to tell his wife about Yukiko, or to tell Yukiko that he doesn't love her. He sells his house to start a lumber business, but it fails quickly, and eventually he lives with relatives.

Yukiko is also weak. She sees Tomioka's faults clearly enough, but cannot stop "chasing the shadow of a lost love." When Tomioka's wife dies and Tomioka takes a forestry job on the rainy island of Yakushima, Yukiko follows him there even though the damp weather worsens her tuberculosis. Lying sick in bed, Yukiko realized

> that what she imagined was the rustling of trees swaying in the wind in the Indochina paradise was actually the beating of drizzling rain against the window panes. Her spirits dropped like a shot.

Yukiko dies, and Tomioka has no wife, no lover, no home, and no purpose. He is a floating cloud, one of the millions of lost souls in postwar Japan.

Two months after finishing *Floating Cloud*, Hayashi suffered a heart attack and died the following day, June 28, 1951. She was forty-seven. (Her son died in a train wreck in 1959, when he was only sixteen.) Kawabata Yasunari, author of *Snow Country*, led her funeral service, but thousands of ordinary women with aprons and shopping bags also came by to pay their respects.

Hayashi literally wrote herself to death. At the time she died she was writing installments for three novellas simultaneously, and in March she had also begun a new full-length novel, *Meals*.

Why did she work so hard? She once said that "to eat and to write are the two reasons for living." Because of her firsthand experience with poverty, Hayashi had many more tales to share than do most women who write. She could tell the stories of ordinary women better than anyone else in Japan, and perhaps it was because she knew this that she drove herself so hard.

Hayashi Fumiko loved common people, and they love her in return. In Onomichi, her hometown, a statue of Hayashi stands on the main street, and nearby is an exact replica of her office. In Sakurajima, Kyushu, at the hot springs inn where Hayashi's mother once worked as a chambermaid, tourist buses stop daily at a shrine dedicated to Hayashi. Two lines of her poetry are carved in stone:

> *The life of a flower is short,*
> *only bitter things are long.*

32
Mishima Yukio
The Modern Novelist Inspired by the Samurai Tradition

HAD MISHIMA YUKIO not stabbed himself to death at age forty-five, he very likely would have won the Nobel Prize for Literature in later years. During his short, dramatic life Mishima wrote thirteen serious novels, two dozen plays, and more than a hundred essays and short stories. Of all modern Japanese authors, Mishima is the most widely translated.

Mishima (1925–1970) also found time to be a bodybuilder, a kendo swordsman, a world traveler, a film actor, a film director, and toward the end of his life, a right-wing nationalist with his own private army.

Though Mishima had a wife and two children, he is known for his intense and powerful explorations of homosexuality, violence, and death. Because of this, Mishima is somewhat embarrassing to many Japanese, though few deny his enormous talent. The great novelist Kawabata Yasunari once declared that Mishima was the kind of "genius that comes along perhaps once every 300 years."

Mishima Yukio was born with the name Hiraoki Kimitake in Tokyo on January 14, 1925. His mother was a well-educated woman, the daughter of a middle-school principal. His father was deputy director of Japan's Bureau of Fisheries. His grandfather had been governor of Sakhalin island (part of Russia today), but later started several businesses and lost the family fortune.

The dominant person in Mishima's childhood was his paternal grandmother, Natsu. She came from a proud, aristocratic family, but by the time Mishima was born she lived with her son and his family in a rented house. She was a bitter woman, suffering severe pain from sciatic neuralgia, the result of a venereal disease she caught from her philandering husband.

Her son a minor bureaucrat, her husband a complete failure, Natsu decided that she would have to be the one to pass on her family's drive. She insisted on raising her eldest grandson exclusively, and Mishima's father assented. Mishima later wrote:

> My grandmother snatched me from my mother's arms on my forty-ninth day. My bed was placed in my grandmother's sickroom, perpetually closed and sti-

fling with odors of sickness and old age, and I was raised there beside her sickbed.

Natsu refused to let Mishima play outside with other boys, and permitted his mother to take him for walks only to and from elementary school, or sometimes to a nearby park. Even Mishima's younger brother and sister seldom came to Natsu's room. Trapped, Mishima's only diversions were his books, and, later, his fantasies.

When Mishima came home from school he had to dress his grandmother's sores and help her walk to and from the toilet. He also listened to her moan at night. Once her pain was so intense that she pulled out a knife and threatened to kill herself.

We do not know what determines one's sexual orientation; still, it is not hard to understand why as an adult Mishima would fail to be attracted to feminine flesh. Nor is it hard to see where he first developed his preoccupation with blood and death.

For all her many faults, Mishima's grandmother was a well-read woman and a great storyteller. Every day she told Mishima tales from her childhood or from Japanese history, and sometimes he retold these stories excitedly to his brother and sister.

At last, when Mishima was twelve, Natsu became too sick to care for her grandson any longer. Mishima moved back with his parents and began middle school in 1937. His teachers quickly recognized his talent and encouraged him to write poetry and short stories. Mishima also read foreign authors such as Oscar Wilde and Rainer Maria Rilke in translation.

His father, by contrast, looked upon literature as "girlish" and angrily tore up many of Mishima's poems and stories. For a while Mishima had to hide his work, but when he was thirteen his father became director of the Bureau of Fisheries, a position that required him to move to Osaka, 250 miles (400 km) away. During the next four years Mishima saw his father only two or three nights a month. He continued writing, and his mother, who edited her son's work throughout his life, kept it a secret from her husband.

As a boy Mishima was weak and pale, but as a writer he towered over his classmates. His metaphors were fresh, his vocabulary was rich, his touch was subtle. When he was sixteen Mishima's teachers asked him to contribute a long story to an adult magazine.

Despite the honor, he could not use his real name. To conceal his identity from his father, he took a pen name, Mishima Yukio. Mishima is a town near Mt. Fuji, and Yukio is a poetic variation of *yuki*, the Japanese word for "snow."

In 1942 Mishima's father moved back home. He quickly discovered that his seventeen-year-old son was writing every night almost until dawn, a routine Mishima continued for the rest of his life. Enraged, he often barged into his son's room and tore up every manuscript he could find. Mishima wrote a friend that his father is frozen stiff with the bureaucratic spirit. . . . "The practice of literature," he informs me, "befits only the people of a degenerate nation." . . . He harps on one string only: Nazis, Nazis, Nazis.

Ironically, although Mishima tried to revive Japan's martial spirit in 1970, as a teenager he had no interest in World War II. He thought Japan's generals were uneducated and bureaucratic, and in any case, he loved knives and swords, not guns and artillery.

Mishima was not drafted until February 1945. He caught a fever immediately, which an army doctor misdiagnosed, and Mishima was declared unfit for duty. He was free to return to school.

Mishima graduated at the top of his high school class in 1944, and was personally given a silver watch by Emperor Hirohito. Proud as his father was, he still insisted that Mishima stop studying literature.

Instead, Mishima studied German law at Tokyo Imperial University. He graduated in 1947 and passed the exceedingly difficult advanced civil service exam, which virtually guaranteed him a high-powered career in government. Early in 1948 Mishima began working in the Banking Bureau of the prestigious Ministry of Finance.

All the while, Mishima continued to write until three or four in the morning. He published short stories in fourteen different literary magazines in 1948, an astounding output considering that he had a full-time job and averaged only four hours sleep a night. After nine months of this grueling pace, Mishima quit his job at the Finance Ministry in late September.

His father was angry, but there was nothing he could do. Mishima was making money from his writing. Characteristically his father told him, "All right, quit your job, but make sure you become the best writer in the land." Two months later Mishima began writing *Confessions of a Mask*, one of his finest books.

"I will attempt to dissect myself alive," Mishima wrote his editor, and that is exactly what he did. *Confessions of a Mask* is an amazingly honest autobiographical novel. Mishima even recalls his first ejaculation at age twelve. He saw Guido Reni's painting of the young martyr, St. Sebastian, half naked, hanging by a rope, with three arrows in his sides. "My hands, completely unconsciously, began a motion they had never been taught."

Mishima also describes his fantasy of a "murder theater":

Young Roman gladiators offered up their lives for my amusement . . . [with] mournful, pathetic cries . . . [and Mishima's] own shout of exultation, answering the victim cry for cry . . . my imagination slaughtered many . . . princes of savage tribes, hotel elevator-boys, waiters, young toughs, army officers . . . I would kiss the lips of those who had fallen to the ground and were still moving.

Everyone Mishima fantasized about was male, but years would pass before he fully understood what this meant. In his novel Mishima hopes that if he kisses a woman, "surely then I will discover my normality." But when he does kiss a woman, he feels nothing. Later, at a dance hall, he almost ignores his female friend when he sees a shirtless young man and promptly imagines him stabbed to death and drenched in blood. At last, "as though a thunderbolt had fallen," Mishima realizes he is both attracted to men and obsessed with death.

Confessions of a Mask was a best seller for much of 1949, and was praised even by critics who were horrified by Mishima's explicitness. At twenty-four Mishima was recognized as one of Japan's leading writers.

Mishima continued to explore sexuality in his 1951 novel, *Forbidden Colors*, which describes the "sticky meeting of glances" that goes on in Tokyo's gay bars. He also wrote modern versions of several Japanese *no* plays, as well as plays for the kabuki theater. Critics and actors agreed that Mishima had a better mastery of classical Japanese than any other living writer.

In 1952 Mishima traveled to Greece and acquired what he would later call a "will to health." The man who spent his childhood in his grandmother's shuttered sickroom discovered the sun. He maintained a tan for the rest of his life by reading in his garden for an hour every afternoon.

Mishima also began weight lifting and kendo (fencing with bamboo swords). He went to a gym five days a week, even when he traveled abroad. "I had to make my body beautiful," Mishima wrote, and soon he did have a muscular build.

His physical training was more than just a pursuit of beauty. In a 1970 article for *Sports Illustrated* Mishima wrote that the scream of a kendo swordsman "recalls the flow of new-shed blood . . . the cry of our race bursting through the shell of modernization." And in a short book called *Sun and Steel*, Mishima confessed that he wanted "muscles suitable for a dramatic death."

In 1954, when Mishima was just beginning his new life of physical strength, he published his most wholesome book, *The Sound of Waves*. It is the only love story he ever wrote that was both heterosexual and happy. Set in a modern fishing village on a remote and beautiful island, *The Sound of Waves* is the story of Shinji and Hatsue, a handsome boy and a beautiful girl.

Meeting by chance on top of a mountain, Shinji and Hatsue agree it is best not to tell anyone of the encounter, and so

> Their well-founded fear of the village's gossip changed what was but an innocent meeting into a thing of secrecy between the two of them.

Before long they face the temptation of premarital sex, the gossip of neighbors, a severe storm, and the objections of Hatsue's rich father before they finally become engaged. "I'll take the exam and get a first mate's license," Shinji tells Hatsue, "then I guess it'd be all right to have the wedding."

The Sound of Waves sold so well, it broke postwar records. It was also adopted by the Education Ministry for use in high schools.

Mishima's next major book, *The Temple of the Golden Pavillion*, published in 1956, sold even more widely. Based on a true story, this psychological novel is about a young Zen Buddhist monk in Kyoto with a severe stutter who deliberately burns down a 550-year-old temple because he is haunted by its beauty and wants to free himself from his obsession.

"Like some beautiful ship crossing the sea of time" the Golden Temple constantly enters the monk's mind, and even interferes with his sex life. At the moment "I slipped my hand up the girl's skirt," he confesses, "the Golden Temple appeared before me . . ." Impotent again and again, the monk finally decides to "decrease the volume of beauty" and burn the temple which has "separated me from life." "When people concentrate on the subject of beauty," Mishima observed, "they are, without realizing it, confronted with the darkest thoughts that exist in this world."

Some critics think *The Temple of the Golden Pavillion* is Mishima's greatest work, and certainly it sealed Mishima's reputation as perhaps the foremost Japanese writer of his generation. The *Asahi Shimbun* said that at thirty-one, Mishima had become "a mature observer of human nature." In America, *The Temple of the Golden Pavillion* was translated into English and published by Knopf, along with *The Sound of Waves.*

Mishima described his method of writing a novel in an essay entitled "My Art of Writing." After slowly choosing a theme, he would carefully study relevant material such as newspaper articles, police reports, technical terms, dialect, and slang. He would also visit the locale. For *The Sound of Waves*, for example, he used his father's connections at the Bureau of Fisheries and arranged to live briefly in a fishing village. Mishima then outlined the plot in great detail, including the climax. Only after this preparation did Mishima begin writing, and then always with his theme in mind.

Mishima said he "weighed each word carefully on a scale like a pharmacist," and was not afraid to use an archaic Japanese word when it had the right nuance of meaning. Once Mishima justified his lifestyle of Western food, Western clothes, a Western home, and Western friends (he was fluent in English) by claiming that "my true life as a writer is the pure Japan of the Japanese language I use every night in my study."

Most nights Mishima dined out with friends. He enjoyed new and expensive restaurants, and went to the movies often. But he drank only moderately and always left for home by eleven. Mishima worked each night until six in the morning, then slept until one.

Not every night was spent writing literature. Mishima wrote serialized fiction for women's magazines, and purposely reduced his vocabulary for these "potboilers." Mishima regarded these books with contempt, but they sold extremely well.

In 1958 Mishima decided to fulfill his duty to his parents and get married. He wanted an intelligent, pretty woman who was not interested in literature and would not disturb him when he was working. Go-betweens introduced Mishima to several women, and on May 30, 1958, he married Sugiyama Yoko, the twenty-year-old daughter of a famous traditional painter. It appears to have been a marriage of convenience.

The new couple built a large Italian-style house with a marble statue of Apollo in front. Mishima told his architect, "I want to sit on rococo furniture wearing Levis and a Hawaiian shirt."

The Mishimas had two children, a daughter, Noriko, born in 1959, and a son, Iichiro, born in 1962. Unlike many Japanese, Mishima included his wife in his conversations and took her on trips, including two around the world. And though Mishima was rarely home for dinner, he did set aside several days a month for his children, and spent all of August with them by the seashore.

Mishima's first novel after his marriage was *Kyoko's House*, published in 1959, a book he once called "a study in nihilism." Its main characters are a boxer, a painter, a businessman, and an actor. Each represents a part of Mishima's personality, and all are preoccupied with death. The actor commits suicide with his mistress, but not before discovering the excitement of masochism, where "blood and pain completely certified his existence, and . . . seemed to merge with pleasure." Critics agreed that Mishima did not succeed in weaving the four characters together, and *Kyoko's House* has yet to be translated into English. One writer called the book "Mishima's first big failure." Another said, "Balzac would have created a fresco; all Mishima requires is a mirror."

The following year Mishima bounced back and published *After the Banquet*, one of his finest novels. Based on an actual romance between a former foreign minister and the owner of one of Tokyo's most elegant restaurants, the book's elderly hero and heroine, Noguchi and Kazu, are too set in their ways to adapt to each other and make their marriage work.

The real theme of the novel is the ruthlessness and duplicity of big-money politics. Friends betray Kazu in the middle of her husband's election campaign, then after it is over help her reopen her restaurant as if nothing had happened.

Her glimpses of Conservative Party politicians at [her restaurant] had given Kazu a splendid notion of the nature of their work. Politics meant . . . forcing a man's back to the wall while cheerfully gazing at the same fire, making a show of laughter when one is angry or flying into a rage when one is not in the least upset . . . in short, acting very much like a geisha. The exaggerated odor of secrecy clinging to politics confirmed its resemblance to the business of romance; politics and love affairs were in fact as alike as peas in a pod.

Three years later, in 1963, Mishima finished his most gruesome book, *The Sailor Who Fell from Grace with the Sea*. In this novel a sailor marries the owner of a chic clothing store and gives up his life at sea to help her run the shop. But the woman's teenage son cannot forgive him for giving up his masculine way of life. He poisons the sailor's tea, then asks his vicious friends to bring their scalpels and saws.

The Sailor Who Fell from Grace with the Sea won only lukewarm praise and moderate sales. Some critics wondered if Mishima's talent as a novelist had peaked. Mishima's short plays and short stories, however, continued to win acclaim.

One story, "Patriotism," offers special insight into the last years of Mishima's life. Written in 1960 and set during the attempted coup by right-wing army officers in 1936, "Patriotism" is about a lieutenant whose friends had kept him unaware of the revolt because he was newly married. Ordered to attack his comrades as "rebels," the lieutenant decides instead that he will commit seppuku, ritual suicide, and his wife decides that she will join him in death.

Their final moments, Mishima writes, "make the gods themselves weep." They make love for the last time, and the imminence of death "refines their awareness of pleasure." Mishima then gives a 1,500-word description of the lieutenant's seppuku, the most detailed and gory in Japanese literature. The lieutenant's wife watches, then cuts her throat.

Five years later Mishima produced, directed, and wrote a half-hour film based on "Patriotism." He also played the role of the lieutenant. Mishima had acted in films before, playing gangsters, but this was the only movie he ever directed. It won high praise in France, then became a box office smash in Japan in 1966. No one realized that the film was Mishima's dark fantasy, and that he would try to make it real just four years later.

Why did Mishima glorify the failed army coup of 1936? Why was he attracted to emperor-worship and right-wing extremism? In an article for *The Times* (London) in 1969, Mishima wrote:

In the first twenty years of my life national culture was controlled by the unnatural puritanism of the militarists. For the past twenty years pacifism has been sitting heavily on samurai spirit.

"My ideal," Mishima said in a speech that same year, "is to restore the balance. To revive the tradition of the samurai."

Mishima knew that writing alone could not put the sword back into Japanese culture. He felt he needed to take action. In 1968 Mishima and eleven young men formed the Shield Society. With blood they signed an oath to protect the emperor from communists and radicals if Japan's small army should prove inadequate to the task. Mishima called the society "the world's least armed, most spiritual army," and paid for its elegant uniforms and boot camp training himself. Soon there were eighty members, mostly college students from rural areas.

Mishima dreamed of a heroic death, but he did not want to die until he had revived his career and written a new masterpiece. Even before Mishima founded the Shield Society he was working on the most ambitious project of his career: a four-volume set of novels called *The Sea of Fertility*. The title is a reference to the lifeless sea on the moon, Mishima's metaphor for the moral state of modern, commercial Japan.

One character, Kiyoaki, is reincarnated from novel to novel, although he never remembers his previous lives. He is always beautiful, always has three moles on his left breast, and always dies by age twenty. The other principal character, Honda, is aware of these transmigrations, and helps his friend in each novel.

By far the best of the four novels is the first, *Spring Snow*, which Mishima finished in 1966. The title is a symbol of the fleeting love affair between two striking young aristocrats, Kiyoaki and Satoko, set in the years 1912 to 1914. Mishima's feel for the era and for the attitudes of the Japanese nobility is faultless, a result, perhaps, of his grandmother's storytelling. Novelist Kawabata Yasunari considered *Spring Snow* to be Mishima's finest book, and many others agree.

Satoko is the most intelligent and enchanting woman in any of Mishima's novels, but she is engaged to a dull, soldierly prince of the Imperial family. Risking everything, she frequently meets Kiyoaki in secret; "elegance disregards prohibitions, even the most severe." Later, she declares,

> I've known supreme happiness, and I'm not greedy enough to want what I have to go on forever. Every dream ends. Wouldn't it be foolish, knowing that nothing lasts forever, to insist that one has a right to do something that does?

The two lovers face the inevitable consequences of their illicit affair with great courage. Satoko, after getting pregnant and having an abortion, becomes a nun in a Buddhist monastery. Kiyoaki, facing death, assures his classmate Honda, "I'll see you again. I know it."

Unfortunately, the next three novels in *The Sea of Fertility* are widely regarded as flawed. *Runaway Horses* is devoted entirely to the ultranationalism of an extremist who is on trial for the murder of some businessmen. *The Temple of the Dawn* is as much thesis as novel; nearly a third of the book is a discussion of Hindu, Buddhist, and ancient Greek theories of reincarnation and karma.

In Mishima's last novel, *The Decay of the Angel*, Honda visits Satoko, who is now a priestess, and begins to question whether Kiyoaki or any of his reincarnations ever existed. Despite its moments of mysticism, *The Decay of the Angel* is a swamp of shabby characters. The book is interesting chiefly for what it reveals about Mishima during his last year. In it, old Honda ponders,

> With what a shallow awareness men slipped through time that would not return! . . . Time dripped away like blood. Old men dried up and died. In payment for having neglected to stop time . . . Endless physical beauty. That is the special perogative of those who cut time short.

By 1970 Mishima was forty-five years old. If he was truly going to "cut time short" and die young, it was now or never. His wife, Yoko, suspected a suicide was coming, but thought he would wait until he finished *The Decay of the Angel*. She did not know that Mishima was a year ahead of schedule.

A follower of Mishima's who was just as eager as he was to die heroically was Morita Masakatsu, a twenty-five-year-old student and captain in the Shield Society. Mishima was highly attracted to this uncomplicated, unintellectual youth, but no one knows whether the two men were actually lovers. Carefully Mishima and Morita approached three other men in the Shield Society, and each of them agreed to commit himself "to the very end."

Mishima wanted to speak to Japanese troops and denounce Article 9 of the postwar constitution, which gives up "war as a sovereign right of the nation." Mishima hoped the soldiers would then march to the Diet building and force the legislature to repeal Article 9. He must have known that the chances of success were almost nil, but he was determined to make the statement.

Mishima and his men talked about how to force soldiers to hear a speech, and drew up a detailed plan in September 1970. They bought rope, wire, pliers, and cotton cloth, and rehearsed their plan of action eight times. Mishima also made final visits to his parents, his best friends, and other members of the Shield Society.

On the morning of November 25, 1970, Mishima put the final chapters of *The Decay of the Angel* in an envelope and placed it on a table in his hallway. In his entire life Mishima had never missed a deadline. Then he and his four followers drove to the headquarters of the eastern division of the Japanese army.

Mishima had scheduled an appointment to see General Mashita Kanetoshi, commander of the division. He began by showing the general the sixteenth-century sword he had with him. Then the five men gagged the general with a handkerchief, tied him to his chair, and barricaded the office. Several officers burst in through one of the doors, but Mishima stabbed at their arms with his sword, shouting "Out, out!" They left, bleeding.

Mishima demanded that the general command his troops to listen to his half-hour speech. If the general complied, Mishima guaranteed he would be released unharmed in two hours. If he did not, Mishima said he would kill him and commit seppuku, ritual suicide.

On General Mashita's orders, eight hundred soldiers assembled in front of division headquarters. Mishima stepped out on the flat roof at noon and began his speech. Amid the whir of police helicopters he shouted that the army was the soul of Japan, criticized the Japanese constitution, and asked the soldiers to rise in rebellion. But the soldiers were hostile. "Asshole," they shouted, "come down from there." "Stop playing the hero." "Madman." "Asshole."

Mishima intended to speak for thirty minutes, but after seven he had enough. He stepped back into the general's office, shouted three "Banzai!" to the emperor, and thrust a dagger into the left side of his abdomen.

"At the moment the dagger entered, the sun rose glowing red behind his eyelids," Mishima wrote three years before in *Runaway Horses*. Slowly he moved his blade across to his right side, then slumped forward. Once Mishima finished hara-kiri (belly-cutting), it was time for Morita to complete the ritual of seppuku. Morita swung his sword but missed Mishima's neck and cut his back and shoulders instead. Then he missed again. Finally, a third cadet, Koga Hiroyasu, grabbed Morita's sword and cut Mishima's head off with a single chop. Morita also committed seppuku, and Koga sliced his head off too. The three surviving followers quickly picked up the heads of Mishima and Morita, placed them upright on the bloody carpet, and bowed in prayer.

Mishima had given the three students strict orders to stay alive, release General Mashita, and represent the Shield Society in court. In 1972 a Tokyo court sentenced each of them to four years in prison. The Shield Society disbanded about the same time.

On the morning of his suicide Mishima left a note on his desk: "Human life is limited, but I would like to live forever."

A poignant parting line. Mishima's life was limited. He did not grow up in a happy family, he rarely wrote about families, and he abandoned the family he created. He also had an aristocratic contempt for business that kept him from appreciating the modern and useful ways in which Japan's samurai ethic lives on.

But Mishima's fame will endure. Not only was he a superb writer, honest enough to share his most private fantasies, he was also a man of action who lived and died to make them real.

33
Ariyoshi Sawako
The Writer Who Gave Voice
to Silent Women

A RIYOSHI SAWAKO, who died in 1984, wrote dozens of best-sellers about women, yet rarely wrote about romantic love. In a simple style, she focused on other issues in women's lives—tension between mothers- and daughters-in-law, care for the elderly, environmental dangers, and racism.

Ariyoshi (1931–1984) was not interested only in modern problems, she was also a lover of the traditional Japanese arts. She wrote a *no* dance drama, a bunraku puppet play, several historical novels, and dozens of short stories about Japanese artists.

Many of Ariyoshi's works have been made into movies and television shows in Japan; she herself wrote several screenplays. She is still little known outside Japan, partly because to date only half of her many books have been translated into English.

Ariyoshi Sawako was born on January 20, 1931, in Wakayama City, thirty miles (50 km) southwest of Osaka. Her father was an international banker who spent five years working in New York and was well read in English, French, and German. Her mother came from a conservative family of landowners, but nevertheless worked for women's rights.

When Ariyoshi was six her father was stationed in Jakarta, Indonesia. The family lived luxuriously, with many servants, and Ariyoshi and her older brother went to an elementary school for overseas Japanese. She was often sick and spent many days at home reading the books in her father's library. There she began her lifelong enthusiasm for the literature of traditional Japan.

In 1941, only a few months before Japan attacked Pearl Harbor, the Ariyoshis returned to Japan. It was a shock for the young girl. Crowded and dirty, modern Tokyo was nothing like the Japan she had read about in books, and Ariyoshi began seeing Japanese society more objectively than most girls her age. She particularly disliked the subordinate role of women.

As the war grew worse for Japan, Ariyoshi left Tokyo in 1943 to live with her grandmother in Wakayama. Her school days were tedious because she and her classmates spent much of their time sewing army uniforms.

In 1945 Ariyoshi's house in Tokyo was bombed, her father's bank was dissolved, and by order of the United States military, her grandmother's land was sold cheaply to its tenants. Ariyoshi stayed with her grandmother one more year, then rejoined her parents in Tokyo. For three years during the American occupation she completed high school while her parents scrounged for money and food.

The contrast between the bleak postwar years and Ariyoshi's happy childhood in Jakarta temporarily soured the young woman on things Japanese. Sensing this, her father tried to rekindle her interest in Japanese culture by taking her to kabuki plays. It worked. Ariyoshi loved the first performance she saw and remained interested in the theater for the rest of her life.

In 1949 Ariyoshi entered Tokyo Women's Christian College, the school her mother had also attended. Unlike her mother, Ariyoshi decided to join the Catholic Church. Perhaps she was disillusioned with the Shinto religion, which until 1945 had been closely tied to Japanese militarism.

At college Ariyoshi majored in English literature. When her father died in 1950, she supported herself by working part-time. She dreamed of becoming a drama critic, and regularly wrote articles for a magazine called *Theater World*.

In 1954, two years after her graduation, Ariyoshi became the corresponding secretary for a kabuki troupe that was unusual because it was led by a female performer. She also helped produce and direct the company's plays.

In her spare time Ariyoshi wrote short stories for literary magazines. One story, "Jiuta" ("Ballad"), is about a famous and blind ballad-chanter who disowns his daughter when she marries a nisei, a Japanese-American. What particularly saddens him is the knowledge that his daughter, who plays the stringed koto beautifully, will not be carrying on the Japanese musical tradition. The story ends when the father relents and goes to the airport to say good-bye to his daughter as she leaves for America.

Without Ariyoshi's knowledge, her friends entered "Jiuta" in a literary competition in 1956. The story was a finalist for the Akutagawa Prize, the highest award a new writer in Japan can aspire to. Some of the judges thought her story's theme was old-fashioned; the criticism may have spurred Ariyoshi to seek bolder and more original topics in the future.

Another short story, "Prayer," is about the continuing dread a family feels when a woman who survived the Nagasaki atomic bombing has a child. First, the family worries that the child will be born with deformities. Then they worry the child will be retarded and not learn to talk. They worry each time the child has a fever, wondering if it could be leukemia. The ordinary anxiety of parents and relatives is multiplied a hundred times, and out of love for the child each member of the family offers a silent, fervent, and continuing prayer for his well-being.

In 1959, when she was only twenty-eight, Ariyoshi finished her first important novel, *The River Ki*. The book is highly autobiographical and spans the lives of three generations of strong women. Hana, the first, is a traditional wife who works hard to help her politically powerful husband; when she is married in 1899, five festive wedding boats float gently down the Ki River. By contrast, when her rebellious daughter Fumio marries an international banker in 1925, the wedding is at a Tokyo hotel, followed by a Western-style banquet. The third woman, the granddaughter Hanako, is modeled after Ariyoshi herself, who inherits her mother's modern outlook but also shares her grandmother's affection for Japan's past.

After *The River Ki* was published, Ariyoshi won a Rockefeller Foundation grant to spend the 1959–1960 school year at Sarah Lawrence College, just north of New York City. She studied the works of Christopher Fry, a British playwright she admired, and took many trips to Harlem to research her next novel, *Not Because of Color*.

Not Because of Color tells the story of Emiko Jackson, a young Japanese woman who marries a black American soldier during the occupation of Japan in the late 1940s. Their daughter, Mary, is mercilessly teased by her Japanese classmates because she is half black. To give Mary a brighter future, Emiko moves to the United States, but she and her husband can afford only a one-room apartment in Harlem. They have three more children, and Emiko works hard to support them as a waitress and later as a servant for the Japanese wife of a Jewish professor. She also makes friends with a Japanese woman married to an Italian-American, and another married to a Puerto Rican.

Emiko comes to the conclusion that it is "not because of color" that prejudice exists, because

> Even among whites, the Jews, Italians, and Irish are often looked down upon and regarded with disdain. They, in turn, discriminate against the blacks . . . the blacks look down upon the Puerto Ricans . . . the intelligent make fun of the ignorant. . . . No matter who he is, a human being establishes another as his inferior. . . . Unless he does this, he doesn't feel secure.

In 1961 Ariyoshi met Jin Akira, director of the Art Friend Association, an organization that brought foreign performers to Japan. A cosmopolitan man, he enjoyed the fact that Ariyoshi was outspoken about so many artistic and political issues. He may also have been charmed by the fact that she was a good golfer and a knowledgeable fan of the Yomiuri Giants baseball team.

They married in March 1962, and had one daughter, Tamao, in 1963. By then Ariyoshi was making money from her writing. Later she bought a house and hired a live-in housekeeper. She also had her widowed mother move in. This allowed Ariyoshi to work long hours and even travel abroad with the knowledge that her daughter was well cared for.

Ariyoshi's marriage lasted just two years. She and Akira divorced in 1964, when Tamao was just six months old. Akira and his parents may not have understood that Ariyoshi's commitment to her writing was full-time, and that when she was not at her typewriter she felt she needed to be out interviewing, traveling, or doing research in a library. Under different circumstances Ariyoshi might have changed her lifestyle and given more time to her marriage. But at this time the Art Friend Association was in financial difficulty, and this made her own income important and a shortening of her work hours impractical.

In 1965 Ariyoshi wrote *Time of Distrust*, a female-revenge novel that caused a sensation in Japan and quickly became a movie. The work may also reflect Ariyoshi's state of mind after her divorce. In the book, an unfaithful husband has an affair with a bar waitress, and soon both his wife and his mistress become pregnant. When the two women meet by accident, they plot their vengeance. The waitress files a claim for a large share of the husband's pension. But the wife, who makes a good salary teaching, declares that her child is not her husband's, but instead the result of artificial insemination. The book ends with the hapless husband not knowing for certain if he is the father of either child.

The following year Ariyoshi published *The Doctor's Wife*, one of her two finest works. It is a historical novel based on the diary and records of Hanaoka Seishu (1760–1835), the first doctor in the world to perform surgery with a general anesthetic. Using an extract from datura and other poisonous flowers to keep his patient unconscious and numb, Hanoka successfully removed a breast cancer in 1805—thirty-seven years before Dr. Crawford Long began using ether in the United States.

The real story of this novel, however, is the subtle but constant tension between Hanaoka's wife, Kae, and her mother-in-law, Otsugi. The two women even compete to be the first one to test Hanaoka's anesthetic. In the end, both women take the dangerous drug, and Kae goes blind before the anesthetic is perfected. Hanaoka's sister observes,

> Don't you think men are incredible? It seems that an intelligent person like my brother would have noticed the friction between you and Mother. But throughout he shrewdly pretended that he didn't see anything ... tension between females is to the advantage of every male. . . .
>
> The only luck I've had in my entire lifetime is that I didn't get married and didn't have to be somebody's daughter-in-law.

The Doctor's Wife became both a movie and a play in 1967. Ariyoshi wrote the script of the play herself. She also began writing *Kabuki Dancer* the same year. The book is a fictional biography of Izumo no Okuni (the subject of chapter eleven), the graceful dancer and flamboyant actress who created kabuki theater on the streets of Kyoto around the year 1600. Only in 1629 did kabuki, by law, became an art for men only.

Most of the women in Ariyoshi's novels are strong and appealing, but in *Sun-*

set Hill Apartment Complex No. 3, written in 1970, the housewives are petty and neurotic. They spend hours gossiping, but compete fiercely when it comes to their children's grades. The ambitious mothers constantly pressure their sons and daughters to study harder, until finally their children are exhausted.

Ariyoshi not only portrays the banality of middle-class life, a common theme in literature, but also condemns the brutally competitive system of college admission, which creates the "examination hell" endured by millions of Japanese teenagers.

During the winter of 1970–1971 Ariyoshi accepted an invitation to teach at the University of Hawaii, where she led a graduate seminar on kabuki theater. She took her daughter with her and enrolled her in a nearby Catholic school. She also visited many nursing homes in Hawaii, researching the problems of senility for her next book, *The Twilight Years*.

In the summer of 1971 Ariyoshi sent her daughter back to Japan, then spent a month each in New York and London to see dozens of plays and visit more nursing homes. When Ariyoshi returned to Tokyo in August, she began to write her most widely read book, *The Twilight Years*, published in 1972. The novel tells the story of Shigezo, an eighty-four-year-old man so senile he can no longer recognize his son, his daughter, or even a picture of his dead wife. But he does recognize his daughter-in-law, Akiko, and because his daughter Kyoko lives far away, it is Akiko's duty to take care of him at home.

Akiko is a typist for a law firm, but soon she can go to work only three days a week because taking care of Shigezo is so exhausting. She gets up two or three times a night to help him urinate, and finally swaddles him in diapers, changing them several times a day. She bathes him every evening after dinner, and is embarrassed each time. Because he is constantly hungry, she also gives him snacks at odd hours.

Akiko cannot put Shigezo into a nursing home because sometimes he wanders off into the streets of Tokyo, and the nursing homes are too understaffed to take "runaways." Gradually Akiko discovers that many of her friends also take care of senile relatives. There are millions of old people throughout Japan, but surprisingly few facilities to take care of them.

"Men are so helpless," Akiko complains at one point. For over a year Akiko works at her law office, cleans house, cooks dinner, and takes constant care of Shigezo. Her husband and teenage son mean well, but do little to help.

For a long time Akiko wishes Shigezo were dead. But as Shigezo becomes more infantile, he also becomes more likable. The crotchety old man develops a beautiful angelic smile, like some wise priest in a meditative trance. His vocabulary shrinks to a single word, *moshi-moshi* (hello), and he spends entire days happily watching a caged songbird. In the end Akiko feels that Shigezo has somehow transcended the human condition. When he finally dies, she is the only one who mourns.

The Twilight Years sold two million copies in hard cover before it became a paperback. In a nation that reveres its old, the book had obviously touched a nerve.

Ariyoshi tried to donate all the royalties from her book to a number of nursing homes, but the Japanese government insisted on its share of taxes. After a furor in the press, the government finally allowed her to deduct a quarter of her royalties as a charitable contribution. It also began to loosen its tax laws on donations, and eventually built a few more nursing homes.

After writing *The Twilight Years*, Ariyoshi helped translate Father Daniel Berrigan's anti–Vietnam War play, *The Trial of the Catonsville Nine*, from English into Japanese. Then she directed the play, which was performed in Tokyo.

In 1974, Japan's second largest newspaper, *Asahi Shimbun*, invited Ariyoshi to write a serial novel on any subject she chose.

She decided instead to write a nonfiction book on the cumulative effects of agricultural chemicals and food additives. *Compound Pollution* explained difficult scientific issues simply, and many commentators said it had a greater impact than anything else previously written about the environment in Japan.

Ariyoshi reveals, for example, that because pickled vegetables are sold by the pound, modern wholesalers add water to make them weigh more. Water reduces their shelf life, so they also add preservatives, which decrease the flavor. The wholesalers then insert artificial flavoring agents to restore the lost taste, which, of course, would not be necessary if they had not added water in the first place.

Ariyoshi knew that *Compound Pollution* was not literature. But she felt that "someone has to do this kind of work. And because I knew I could do a good job, I felt obligated to do it."

In the spring of 1977 Ariyoshi was hospitalized for exhaustion from overwork. She was researching her last important novel, *Her Highness Princess Kazunomiya*, and told friends that she had been pouring all of her creative energy into the book.

Written in 1978, *Her Highness Princess Kazunomiya* is about the lowborn girl who married the next-to-last shogun in 1862 and her adjustment to Japan's modernization. The novel is full of detailed descriptions of the makeup, hairstyles, and dresses of the court ladies, as well as their music, manners, and style of talking.

An entire chapter of *Her Highness Princess Kazunomiya* is devoted to how the nobility performed the tea ceremony. Ariyoshi was a devoted practitioner of the tea ceremony, and had her own collection of tea utensils.

Her Highness Princess Kazunomiya was adapted as a series for television in 1980. Two years later Ariyoshi wrote a mystery, *The Bell at Curtaintime Rings Merrily*. Although Ariyoshi was a great admirer of Agatha Christie and Rex Stout, she wrote only one mystery. Her astounding output of books slowed down considerably after she finished *Her Highness Princess Kazunomiya.* She started a book about prostitution, for example, but serialized only a few chapters in a newspaper before discontinuing the project.

Still tired, Ariyoshi despaired that she was losing her creativity. Perhaps this depression was compounded either by menopause or by the fact that her only daughter was away at college. By 1984 Ariyoshi had difficulty going to sleep. She took sleeping pills and started drinking heavily, and it is likely that a combination of pills and alcohol caused her to die in her sleep on August 30, 1984. She was fifty-three.

Ariyoshi Sawako widened the scope of Japanese literature by writing about problems that were common to millions of families yet new to Japanese fiction. With restless compassion, she wrote about a radiation victim having a child, an interracial couple, exhausted students with competitive mothers, a young wife living with her mother-in-law, a woman caring for a senile father-in-law, and many other harried people. Considering that Ariyoshi also wrote historical novels that capture in careful detail the exquisite beauty of Japan's past, the range of her work is astonishing.

In an era when many writers, especially Japanese, have looked inward and examined every aspect of their psyches, millions of readers find it refreshing that Ariyoshi almost never wrote about herself. She was too busy describing the suffering of others.

34
Kawabata Yasunari and Oe Kenzaburo
Nobel Prize–Winning Novelists

Though the awards began in 1901, only two writers from East Asia have won the Nobel Prize in Literature: Kawabata Yasunari and Oe Kenzaburo. The prize may be the one thing these two men have in common.

Kawabata Yasunari (1899–1972), author of *Snow Country* and *The Sound of the Mountain*, won the Nobel Prize in 1968. He loved the traditions and crafts of ancient Japan, ignored modern politics, and never seemed comfortable in the twentieth century. In a simple style Kawabata wrote poetic novels about man's yearning for beauty. Using descriptions of the seasons to set a mood, he preferred to paint a portrait rather than tell a story, and most of his novels end ambiguously.

By contrast, Oe Kenzaburo (b. 1935), author of *A Personal Matter* and *The Silent Cry* and winner of the Nobel Prize in 1994, is very much a twentieth-century postwar writer. An outspoken opponent of the Japanese monarchy, he seems indifferent to Japan's national traditions and prefers the literature of Europe and the folklore of his native village. He is a passionate advocate of nuclear disarmament, and has written complex novels about personal responsibility in the modern world. Oe's writing is often dense, with long sentences packed with adjectives and similes; he struggles against the Japanese language's tendency to ambiguity. He also often uses images of ugliness and deformity.

Few critics would suggest that Kawabata and Oe are the two greatest writers of modern Japan. Nobel prizes are given to the living, and many great Japanese authors either died young or did not have their works translated during their lifetimes. Kawabata and Oe are certainly *among* the finest writers of their time, and many of their books will remain influential.

Kawabata

KAWABATA YASUNARI was born in Osaka on June 14, 1899. His father, a doctor, died of tuberculosis when Kawabata was just two. His mother died a year later of the same disease, and the young orphan was raised by his grandparents in a farm village outside the city.

When Kawabata was seven, his grandmother died. For the next eight years he lived alone with his grandfather, a small landowner whose eyesight slowly deteriorated until he was nearly blind. Although Kawabata was an excellent student, he was lax about going to school and missed fifty-six days one year.

On warm days the thin, frail Kawabata liked to climb a tree, perch on a branch, and read. He enjoyed adventure stories, but also read *The Tale of Genji* by Lady Murasaki.

In 1914 Kawabata's grandfather died. The boy had nursed the old man during his last days and kept a journal that he rewrote and published a decade later, called *Diary of My Sixteenth Year.*

Alone once more, Kawabata moved to a boarding school in Osaka. When his English teacher died, Kawabata attended yet another funeral and nicknamed himself "the funeral director."

Kawabata moved to Tokyo in 1917 to attend First High School, a prestigious academy with young men from all over Japan. Three years later he entered Tokyo Imperial University. He changed his major from English to Japanese literature because the English professors took attendance. At twenty-one Kawabata already knew that he liked to spend most of his time outside the classroom, writing.

Kawabata wrote a short story about circus entertainers in 1921 that was praised by prominent critics. He also fell in love with a coffee shop waitress just fifteen years old. The couple made plans to marry, but after a month the girl broke off the engagement.

While still a student Kawabata began to review fiction for monthly magazines, an occupation he continued for sixteen years. He praised stories by many new writers, including those by Ibuse Masuji and Hayashi Fumiko, and eventually became known as Japan's foremost discoverer of new literary talent. He particularly liked the fresh outlook of new writers, and once said, "I hate a professional in whom an amateur has stopped living."

After Kawabata graduated from Tokyo University in 1924, he helped start *Literary Age*, a magazine that emphasized the importance of using the senses in writing. He also wrote short tales (two to five pages long) that he called *Palm-of-the-Hand Stories.* He published 146 of these stories during his life, but wrote over half of them in the 1920s.

In one charming story, "The Grasshopper and the Bell Cricket," written in 1924, children with lanterns hunt insects at night. A boy catches a grasshopper and gives it to a girl, but she sees that it is a bell cricket, a much rarer insect. The narrator observes: "Probably you will find a girl like a grasshopper whom you think is a bell cricket. [To a] clouded, wounded heart, even a true bell cricket will seem like a grasshopper."

One year after this story was published, Kawabata met his future wife, Matsubayashi Hideko, at the home of a friend. She was an eighteen-year-old student, the daughter of a fisherman. The couple began living together in 1926, but did not register their marriage for another five years. In 1927 they had a daughter who died within days of her birth. During the next decade the childless couple kept as many as nine dogs and over a dozen birds.

Kawabata's most famous short story, "The Izu Dancer," was published in 1926. A young student meets a group of traveling entertainers and falls in love with a dancer who has large eyes and "a flower's laugh." When he accidentally sees the girl naked at a public bath, he realizes she is "a child, a mere child," probably no more than thirteen years old. The student feels relief rather than disappointment, because now he can have a pure friendship with the girl, free of sexual tension. The little dancer responds to his genuine affection, and renews his faith in human nature.

Like *The Catcher in the Rye*, "The Izu Dancer" is a mature work about the hopes and insecurites of adolescence. It is also the first of many Kawabata stories about a man's love for a beautiful but unobtainable young girl. The story has been filmed five times, because the little dancer is a perfect role for a young pop star who wants to begin a new career as an actress.

In the late 1920s Kawabata spent many days exploring the streets of Asakusa, a district in Tokyo that was once full of cafés, music halls, and casinos. By 1930 he turned his notes into a best-selling novel, *The Asakusa Crimson Gang*, about a group of young women who work at a variety of odd jobs.

In the early 1930s Kawabata became an editor at *Literary World*, a new magazine that published the work of both Marxists and those who believed in "art for art's sake." Kawabata could bring diverse groups together because everyone knew that the nonpolitical author cared only for good writing.

In 1935 Kawabata began serializing magazine installments of his most famous novel, *Snow Country*. A rich and idle man from Tokyo, Shimamura, is on his way to visit a geisha at a mountain resort.

> The train came out of the long tunnel into the snow country. . . .
>
> A woman's eye floated up before him. He almost called out in astonishment. But . . . it was only the reflection in the window of the girl opposite . . . the eye became a wierdly beautiful bit of phosphorescence on the sea of evening mountains.

The eye belongs to Yoko, who adores a man too sick to return her love. Shimamura is attracted to Yoko, but she takes little notice. Komako, the geisha who is the main character of the novel, loves Shimamura deeply, yet he lets a year go by without writing her.

Snow Country is a novel about wasted effort. Komako knows her love for Shimamura is futile. So is her reason for becoming a geisha in the first place—to pay the doctor bills of a young man who was dying. Kawabata also describes insects that die in the autumn, weavers who never wear what they make, and Shimamura's pretense of being a dance critic. He seems to suggest that life itself is mostly wasted labor, and that the sincere effort that Komako and others make each day is the bravest response to this predicament.

Kawabata felt that modern novels ignored nature, so *Snow Country* describes something beautiful on nearly every page. The public responded with great enthusiasm to his book, filled with haikulike lines. Kawabata earned enough money to buy a summer home in the mountains; most of the year he and his wife lived in Kamakura, a seaside town with many writers an hour south of Tokyo.

Oddly enough, Kawabata never knew how to end *Snow Country*. He wrote two new installments in 1940 and 1941, then deleted them and added two more chapters in 1946 and 1947. Twenty-five years later, just before his death, Kawabata reduced the entire book to a short story that completely ignores the last two thirds of the novel. The 1947 edition, however, is still considered definitive.

During World War II Kawabata sold his summer home and lived off the proceeds to avoid writing wartime propaganda. He edited the works of dead soldiers once a year, and judged a nationwide contest of children's writing. Mostly Kawabata retreated from the world and reread *The Tale of Genji* and other Japanese classics. He and his wife also adopted a cousin from his village in 1943, a baby girl named Masako whom they raised to maturity.

By the end of the war Kawabata was convinced that he was one of the few writers who could preserve Japan's ancient culture. "I felt that there was a beauty that would perish if I died," he once wrote, "I would live for the sake of the traditional beauty of Japan."

Kawabata and several friends started a new literary magazine, *Humanity*, in 1946. One writer whose work they published was Mishima Yukio, then just twenty-one years old. The two great authors became close friends, and Kawabata served as master of ceremonies for both Mishima's wedding and his funeral.

Perhaps because many of Japan's best writers died during the years after the war, the mature Kawabata often seemed to have an air of "slight sadness." He took solace in his art collection. Art was cheap then, and Kawabata bought tea bowls, eighteenth-century paintings, and masks from *no* dramas. He once said that just looking at a work of art could sustain him during a long night of writing.

In 1948 Kawabata's fellow writers elected him president of the Japanese branch of the P.E.N. (poets, playwrights, editors, essayists, and novelists) Club, the international association of writers. Kawabata held this position for seventeen years, and was surprisingly good at fund-raising and administration. As president of P.E.N., Kawabata visited Hiroshima twice, but was unable to write about the city's devastation. He once said that "no work of art is born from observation of sufferings alone."

Instead, in *Thousand Cranes*, a novel he serialized from 1949 to 1952, Kawabata uses a tea bowl to symbolize the degradation of Japan's postwar culture. The four-hundred-year-old bowl is used as a flower vase and, worse, is permanently smeared with lipstick.

The only person in the novel who performs the tea ceremony correctly is a beautiful girl who wears a kerchief with a pattern of a thousand cranes. It is a Japanese tradition that a sick person who folds one thousand paper cranes will get well, so the title of the book may imply that if someone takes pains to perform the tea ceremony properly, he or she will also help to restore the nation's spirit.

Kawabata wrote about beautiful young girls all his life, but the men who admire them grew steadily older as Kawabata advanced in age. In *The Sound of the Mountain*, serialized between 1949 and 1954 and perhaps Kawabata's finest novel, the protagonist is a gentle old man named Shingo. He hears "the sound of the mountain":

> . . . like the wind, far away, but with a depth like a rumbling of the earth. . . . A chill passed over him, as if he had been notified that death was approaching. . . .

The old man knows he is in decline. Sometimes he forgets how to tie his tie, or pours tea into an ashtray. Yet his memory of a girl who died young is quite clear. Compared to her, Shingo admits, his wife is homely. Nor does he care for his ill-tempered daughter or his philandering son.

The son's wife, beautiful Kikuko, is Shingo's "window looking out of a gloomy house." As a daughter-in-law she is unobtainable, like so many of Kawabata's heroines. Though no longer a virgin, she is still inexperienced, for despite her good looks and sweet nature her husband ignores her and starts an affair with a war widow. Both Kikuko and the war widow get pregnant, and the second half of *The Sound of the Mountain* deals sensitively with the question of whether each woman should keep her child or have an abortion.

Kawabata was particularly productive during the 1950s because he suffered from insomnia; by 1954 he was addicted to sleeping pills. This dependency may have affected his writing, because Kawabata's next two works of literature are strangely perverse. *The Lake*, published in 1955, is a portrait of a voyeur who stalks young girls. *The House of the Sleeping Beauties*, completed in 1961, is set in a secret brothel where an almost impotent old man spends five nights sleeping next to naked virgins who are drugged unconscious. Each girl arouses a memory of a different woman from the man's past, making each night quite distinct.

Kawabata finished his last major novel, *The Old Capital*, the following year. It features twin sisters, separated at birth, who rediscover each other at a Shinto festival in Kyoto. One sister lives in the city; the other lives in the mountains.

When an admirer of the girl in Kyoto meets her sister in the mountains, he proposes to her, but the mountain twin refuses, explaining to her sister,

> Hideo wants to marry me as an illusion of you . . . [but] even when I'm an old woman of sixty, won't . . . his illusion still be as young as you are now? . . . The time never comes when a beautiful illusion turns ugly.

When Kawabata completed *The Old Capital* in 1962, he decided to stop taking sleeping pills, but during his withdrawal he lapsed into a coma that lasted ten days. After he recovered, the writer published his last important story, "One Arm," in 1964. It begins with the memorable sentence: "'I can let you have one of my arms for the night,' said the girl."

In October 1968 Kawabata became the first Japanese writer to win the Nobel Prize in Literature. He flew to Sweden to give his acceptance speech, "Japan, the Beautiful, and Myself," and expressed his admiration for *The Tale of Genji* and for Zen's "emptiness," which he described as "a universe of the spirit in which everything communicates freely with everything."

Kawabata was hailed by the press and gave lectures in Hawaii and Taiwan, but now wrote little fiction. *Dandelions*, a novel about a girl who loses both her father and her fiancé, remained unfinished.

During the winter of 1971–1972 Kawabata suffered from appendicitis. Shortly after his recovery, on April 16, 1972, he went to his office, inhaled gas from a bathroom water heater, and died. He left no suicide note.

Many people have asked why Kawabata took his life, but fear of rapidly declining health seems a likely answer. As a boy he had nursed his sick grandfather and perhaps was determined that no one should have to do the same for him. "People should go away while they are still loved," Kawabata wrote in *The Sound of the Mountain;* a dying man "would at least wish to choose his own time."

In his final essay, "The Existence and Discovery of Beauty" (1969), Kawabata describes sunlight dancing brightly off rows of glasses at a resort in Honolulu and asks, "Is not precisely this kind of encounter the very essence of literature and also of human life? . . ." If Kawabata was more interested in the glimmer of the glasses than in the problems of the people who cleaned them, it is still significant that even in his seventies, he never lost his fresh eye for beauty.

Oe

OE (PRONOUNCED *oh-ay*) KENZABURO was born on January 31, 1935, in Uchiko, a mountain town in western Shikoku, the smallest of Japan's four main islands. He was the third son in a family of five children. His father owned a bark-stripping business that furnished the raw materials used to make paper for Japanese currency; he died when Oe was nine.

Because Oe stuttered, he spent more time than most children do just reading and listening. He especially liked to hear his grandmother tell stories of village myths and folklore.

Oe began school at the height of Japanese militarism. His teacher claimed that the emperor was a living god, and asked him every morning, "What would you do if the emperor commanded you to die?" Dutifully Oe would reply, "I would die, sir. I would cut open my belly and die." But in bed at night Oe guiltily admitted to himself that he was not so eager to die for his monarch.

After Japan's defeat Oe realized that he had been taught lies, and the sense of betrayal he felt would later fuel his writing. When he was fourteen and in a local boarding school, he particularly enjoyed reading *Huckleberry Finn* because Huck was willing to defy society and protect Jim from re-enslavement. Years later, when Oe began reading French literature, he admired Huck Finn even more as the perfect example of an existential hero.

Oe was an outstanding student, and in 1954 he left the island of Shikoku for the first time to enter Tokyo University. He majored in French literature because at the time the Japanese considered it more serious than American or British writing. Oe wrote a thesis on the use of imagery in the fiction of Jean-Paul Sartre, but also admired the "grotesque realism" of François Rabelais and the gritty reporting of Norman Mailer. He disdained the works of Kawabata Yasunari as "vague" and "simplistic."

Because of Oe's stutter, owlish appearance, and thick provincial accent, he was shy, and spent most evenings reading and writing well into the night. By the time he graduated in 1959 he had finished twenty short stories, including "The Catch," also known as "Prize Stock," a story of lost innocence that won him the Akutagawa Prize, Japan's top award for relatively unknown writers.

In this story a black American pilot survives a plane crash near a small Japanese village during World War II. At first the villagers keep the pilot in chains, but gradually the boy who brings him food learns to trust him and takes him out for walks. One summer day the children of the village play with the soldier, naked in a spring, and their voices are "hoarse with happiness."

When it is finally time to take the pilot to a nearby town, the soldier who everyone had grown to love takes the boy hostage. In a bloody fight the boy's father kills the soldier with a hatchet but smashes his son's hand in the process. "I was no longer a child," the boy recalls later; "all adults were unbearable to me."

Oe also wrote his first novel in 1958, *Nip the Buds, Shoot the Kids.* In a story reminiscent of *Lord of the Flies*, a group of juvenile delinquents takes over a plague-ridden village that has been abandoned by its citizens.

Oe's next novel, *Our Era*, published in 1959, received uniformly bad reviews, partly because it is so grotesque. One character, Yasuo, describes his relationship with a woman this way:

> What you and I are going to do for the next twenty years is to shake our butts, breathe heavily, and dump five liters of sperm mixed with filth down into the dark drainage pipe.

Oe's characters are *never* romantic. Lovers grope rather than caress, their sweat looks like flies' eggs rather than dew, and ecstasy is climaxed by a grunt instead of a quiver. "I use sex to shock people," Oe admits, "to wake them up." In *Our Era* Yasuo becomes impotent, a condition symbolizing Japan's dependency on the United States after the war.

Like most Japanese of his generation, Oe was against Japan's security treaty with the United States, which authorized American military bases on Japanese soil and was up for renewal in 1960. Oe spoke against the pact at huge student rallies, and also traveled to China to meet Mao Zedong. Four years later Oe cut his ties to China to protest its testing of an atomic bomb.

Oe married in 1960. His wife, Itami Yukari, is the daughter of a scriptwriter who sometimes directed his own films. Her brother, Itami Juzo, a high school friend of Oe's, became a well-known filmmaker, directing the acclaimed comedies *Tampopo* and *A Taxing Woman*. The Oes' marriage is happy, and Oe has publicly described his wife as "the very image of patience."

Early in 1961 two novellas, *Seventeen* and *The Death of a Political Youth*, created a sensation when they were published in *Literary World*. They were inspired by the seventeen-year-old right-wing fanatic, Yamaguchi Otoya, who had killed the chairman of Japan's Socialist Party with a sword on October 12, 1960, and then killed himself in prison three weeks later.

Seventeen describes an awkward teenager who escapes his problems at school by attending and later speaking at right-wing rallies. It ends with the boy fantasizing about the emperor while masturbating. "Ooh! Your Imperial majesty, my radiant sun. Ah, ah." It was *The Death of a Political Youth*, however, that really angered Japan's right wing. The hero of *Seventeen* could have been any troubled teenager, but the hero of the sequel assassinates a left-wing politician and hangs himself in prison, and thus is clearly modeled on Yamaguchi, who by early 1961 had already become a martyr for the extreme right. Oe's story demystifies the assassin, and ends with the sentence: "The officer who dragged down the hanging body said that he smelled of semen."

Oe and his publisher received death threats day and night for weeks, and soon *Literary World* published an apology to everyone offended. Oe nervously chewed antiacid tablets but refused to apologize for his stories. Since then *The Death of a Political Youth* has never been reprinted or translated, and today it is almost completely unavailable.

In 1963 Oe's wife gave birth to a son so deformed that he looked as if he had two heads. Without an operation to remove the swelling he would die. With an operation he would live, but with permanent brain damage. While Oe and his wife struggled to decide whether or not to raise the child, Oe traveled to Hiroshima to do some journalism. "I was escaping my baby," he later recalled.

In Hiroshima, Oe met radiation victims "who had every reason to commit suicide but didn't." When he returned to Tokyo, "I knew that I must face my baby, ask for the operation, and make every effort to care for him . . . with the birth of my son my heart opened."

The Oes named their son Hikari ("light"). He is uncoordinated, epileptic, has crossed eyes, and talks like a young child. When he was eleven he began piano lessons, and today although he is a poor player, he is a successful composer. His first two compact discs, released in 1992 and 1994, have sold over 100,000 copies. Lindsley Cameron of the *The New York Times* described his classical-style piano sonatas as "extremely moving, with haunting melodies and striking elegance." Recently Hikari has composed duos for piano and flute and piano and violin as well. The Oes also have two younger children, a son and a daughter, fully grown and completely normal.

Oe made eight trips to Hiroshima by 1965. The result was *Hiroshima Notes*, a collection of essays that was a huge best seller. In one essay Oe shows his disgust with factionalism among antinuclear groups by describing a loudspeaker that drowns out the speech of a dying A-bomb survivor. In another Oe is impressed by the dignity of Hiroshima's people. He warns that a failure to preserve peace would be a betrayal of the bomb's victims.

While Oe wrote *Hiroshima Notes*, he also wrote *A Personal Matter*, probably his most famous novel. The main character, Bird, dreams of going to Africa, but his wife has given birth to a severely deformed boy. Bird rebels against the prospect of bringing up a "monster," and approves a doctor's suggestion that they try to kill the baby by feeding it sugar water instead of milk.

He also starts an affair with a college friend named Himiko, a woman who gives him much more sexual pleasure than his wife does. As Bird wrestles with the problem of whether or not to bring up his baby, Himiko provides a powerful argument for letting the baby die.

Your son would never be more than a vegetable! . . . You'd be nurturing a life that meant absolutely nothing to this world! Do you suppose that would be for the baby's good?

Bird finally decides to raise his son, but avoids the question Himiko asked. "It's for my own good," he tells her. "It's so I can stop being a man who's always running away."

Near the end of the book, in a plot twist critics resented, the baby turns out to be normal after a successful operation. The brain hernia was just a benign tumor. At the hospital Bird is pleased that he has acted responsibly. He feels more adult, and his wife's parents are smiling. Critics asked whether the parents would still have smiled if the baby had truly been brain damaged.

Oe's second most important novel at this writing is thought to be *The Silent Cry*, published in 1967. The literal translation of the Japanese title is *The Football Match in the First Year of the Man'en Era* (i.e., 1860). Two brothers return to their home village with little in common except an interest in an ancestor who led a violent but unsuccessful peasant rebellion. The romantically wild younger brother wants to recreate the thrill of leading a revolt. He forms a soccer team and goads his players into looting a Korean-owned supermarket. Later, troubled by memories of incest with his sister, he kills himself.

By contrast, his quieter older brother seeks only the truth about the 1860 rebellion. After several false leads, he learns that their ancestor hid in a cellar for eleven years before reemerging to lead a nonviolent but effective uprising in 1871.

The Silent Cry was an experimental novel of simultaneity, but Oe made no effort to get the reader to care about the events of 1860, or, for that matter, the two modern brothers who are deeply flawed. One critic praised Oe for freeing himself from the limitations of a biography or a historical novel. Another complained that the book "is written in a style of deliberate obscurity." A third writer found that "there is a tactile quality about every scene." A fourth warned that "the novel's basic unpleasantness is apparent on every page."

Oe's 1969 novella, *Teach Us to Outgrow Our Madness*, also has piecemeal accounts of an event long past, but they come only at the beginning and end of the story. In between is a fascinating look at Oe's life with his retarded son. In the novella the boy is named Eeyore; in real life Hikari was called Pooh.

Oe describes his daily bicycle trips with his son sitting in a seat attached to the handlebars. At the end of a ride they would eat pork noodles and drink Pepsi-Cola at a Chinese restaurant. He also gives a chilling account of the impossibility of getting Eeyore to sit still during an eye examination, and of the panic the boy feels when a doctor shines a penlight in his eyes.

Oe's next novella, *The Day He Himself Shall Wipe My Tears Away*, published in 1972, is a satire inspired by the 1970 suicide of the great writer Mishima Yukio. The story begins with a man in a hospital bed who wears dark goggles and dictates a rambling "history of the age." It ends when the emperor appears to him as a huge golden chrysanthemum that covers all of Japan. Even Oe's translators have called this work "tortuous" and "difficult to follow." Some Japanese critics simply declined to finish it.

The Pinch-Runner Memorandum, published in 1976, is only marginally easier to read. The novel is a father's fantasy. The main character wakes up one morning with a body twenty years younger, while his retarded son is suddenly twenty years older. The "Cosmic Will" behind this transformation directs the son to kill a villain named Big Shot and stop his evil plan to rule the world through the manipulation of student radicals and nuclear scientists. The retarded boy completes his mission, and like a crowd at a baseball game that cheers a pinch runner who reaches home plate, the father is very proud of his heroic son.

Oe wrote *The Pinch-Runner Memorandum* without using any quotation marks, and because the narrator of the book is only a ghostwriter for the father, it is often difficult for readers to figure out who is talking. As in *The Silent Cry*, opinion about this novel was divided. One critic praised the book as "a treasure-trove of meaning." Another called it "obscure in both style and content."

Oe has continued to write a new book about every three years. These include *A Contemporary Game* (1979), a multilayered novel about a village in Shikoku that separates itself from the rest of Japan and has its own local gods and legends, and *The Trial of 'Nip the Buds, Shoot the Kids'* (1980), a sequel to his first novel told from many conflicting points of view.

By the 1980s, after fifteen years of writing experimental books, Oe decided that the Japanese were not as interested in literature as they used to be. Young people, he said, seem "content to exist within a late adolescent or post-adolescent subculture."

From 1983 onward Oe began writing easier, more straightforward narratives. *Rouse Up, O Young Men of the New Age!* (1983) is about the joys and trials of bringing up his retarded son Hikari, climaxed by the young man's rejection at age twenty of his childhood nickname, Pooh. *The Story of M/T and the Wonder of the Forest* (1986) is a simplification of Oe's 1979 novel *A Contemporary Game*. M/T stands for matriarch-trickster.

A Quiet Life, published in 1990, is a complex autobiographical novel about how well Oe's grown children take care of themselves while their parents are away for a semester at a university in California. In the book the daughter keeps a diary of the distress she suffers when she contemplates taking care of her retarded brother in her old age, and of the joy she feels watching him compose music and learning to swim. Oe adds subplots involving a child molester, a protest at an embassy, and interpretations of the movie *Stalker*—and a sexual assault by a swimming coach upon his daughter that is so crude that in *The New York Times Book Review* novelist John David Morley called it "ludicrous" and "unworthy of Mr. Oe." The sheer number of secondary plots detracts from the otherwise poignant themes of the young woman's diary.

In 1992, after *The Story of M/T* was translated into Swedish (no English translation of this book has yet been published), Oe gave a lecture tour through Scandinavia and expressed his admiration for Scandinavian writers such as Isak Dinesen and Selma Lagerlof.

Two years later, in October 1994, Oe Kenzaburo won the Nobel Prize in Literature. In his acceptance speech Oe said: "As someone living in present-day Japan and sharing bitter memories of the past, I cannot join Kawabata in saying

'Japan, the Beautiful, and Myself.'" Oe criticized the use of ambiguity in Japanese culture, but hoped that the arts would help bring mankind together.

Later in the year the Japanese government sought to give Oe the Imperial Order of Culture, but Oe refused any award given by the emperor. "I do not recognize any authority, any value, higher than democracy," he said. It was an unheard-of affront to the monarchy, and once again Oe was subject to threats.

Ironically, one month before Oe won the Nobel Prize he finished a trilogy of novellas set in Shikoku called *The Burning Green Tree*, then told reporters that he would not write any more novels. He said his mission since 1963 had been to speak for his son Hikari, but since Hikari was now composing music, he had no more need to write novels. Two years later he changed his mind and began writing *Somersault*, which is expected to be his longest novel to date.

As an older writer Oe has tried to revive the legends and mythology of his native Shikoku as a possible alternative to Japan's traditional emperor-centered culture, though it is doubtful that urban Japanese will be drawn to regional folklore.

Oe is most powerful when he writes in a straightforward way about raising his son Hikari. In 1995 he published *A Healing Family*, a moving series of essays. In one, Oe contrasts Hikari's difficulty in speaking (Beethoven and Chopin are "Bebe" and "Unpa") with the ease with which he works with a pianist rehearsing one of his compositions. In another essay, Oe concludes,

Though I dream of finding a way in my writing to express something that transcends this world, it is in Hikari's music that I most often get a premonition of a world beyond our own.

PART FIVE

Two Film Directors,
Two Athletes

35
Ozu Yasujiro
Director of Poignant Films
About Families in Transition

I n the future when people want to see what Japanese life was like before and after World War II, they will watch the movies of director Ozu Yasujiro. His quiet films have no heroes, no villains, no violence, and no rags-to-riches successeses. Usually they are about a family in transition, and the plot is as simple as a daughter's impending marriage or a parent's unwanted visit. The dialogue in an Ozu movie is so natural, the characters so lifelike, the emotions so universal, viewers are deeply moved.

Ozu (1903–1963) used simple camera techniques and kept his movies in the present. He never once used a flashback or a dream. His films unfold slowly, taking whatever time they need to show someone's feelings. In Ozu's later films an average shot lasts a lengthy seven seconds, but this leisurely tempo is what allows viewers to feel the emotions of his characters so deeply.

Because Ozu's films are understated (and the Japanese love understatement, feeling that a flower looks best in a simple vase) Ozu has often been called the most Japanese of all directors. Six of his films were rated number one in *Kinema Jumpo* magazine's annual poll of movie critics, Japan's equivalent of the Academy Award for Best Picture. His films, however, did not begin to be appreciated in America and Europe until the 1970s, and even today his two greatest films, *Late Spring* (1949) and *Tokyo Story* (1953), remain largely unknown to the Western public.

Ozu was born on December 12, 1903, in Tokyo, the second son of four children. His father was a fertilizer wholesaler. His mother was noted for her kindness and humor. As a child, Ozu explored a neighborhood of sprawling markets and busy shipyards, but when he was nine his father moved the family to his hometown of Matsuzaka, a small coastal city southwest of Nagoya.

Ozu's father remained in Tokyo, and rarely came home. An undisciplined child and lazy student, Ozu did not even show up for a college entrance exam. Instead, he spent the afternoon watching the silent film *The Prisoner of Zenda*. Ozu later wrote that "film had a magical hold on me." He saw American movies whenever he could, and studied English in school in order to understand them.

In America, silent films were accompanied by a piano, but in Japan they were narrated by chanters called *benshi*, who also provided commentary. Ozu wrote letters to *benshi*, and collected programs with information about a movie's plot, cast, and credits.

In 1920 Ozu was kicked out of a high school dormitory for writing a love letter to a younger classmate. In Japan this was not so unusual, but a new principal was uncommonly strict and expelled several boys for writing the same young man. Ozu still attended classes, but commuted from home. He had to account for his hours in a passbook signed by his mother and his teachers, but often he forged his mother's seal and went to the movies after school.

At eighteen Ozu had no prospects of attending a university. He taught for a year at an elementary school in a mountain village near home, but drank so much at night that his father had to wire money to pay for his son's debts.

Perhaps as a result of this fiasco, Ozu's father brought his family back to Tokyo in 1923. An uncle who leased land to the Shochiku Motion Picture Company got Ozu a job interview, and Ozu impressed the studio manager with his extensive knowledge of foreign films. He hired Ozu as an assistant cameraman, and the strong, broad-shouldered nineteen-year-old moved cameras, tripods, and other heavy equipment.

Ozu made friends with other youths at the studio, playing catch during lunch hour and drinking with them in the evening. They discussed the techniques of Japanese and American film directors; Ozu was deeply influenced by Ernst Lubitsch and particularly admired his 1924 comedy *The Marriage Circle*, in which the facial expressions of the actors often directly contradict the lines on the screen.

In 1926 Ozu became an assistant director. He chose to work for an especially lazy boss because often this director failed to show up for work, let his assistant finish the shooting, but then generously gave him credit for the film. Ozu shared a house with several other assistant directors, and together they revised one another's scripts and swapped ideas for gags.

One year later Ozu directed *The Sword of Penitence*, the first of his thirty-four silent and twenty sound films. The movie, which no longer exists, was about an ex-convict who tries to reform but eventually returns to crime. The script was written by Noda Kogo, the first of twenty-seven collaborations between Ozu and this best friend. One young actor with a minor part in this film was Ryu Chishu, who eventually became Ozu's leading star. Ryu (1904–1993) had at least a walk-on part in all but three of Ozu's movies.

By 1931 Ozu had made twenty-two films, an average of one every ten weeks. Each of them was a comedy about students, office workers, or young couples. Although he experimented with film techniques such as pans, fades, and dissolves, he gradually rejected them as "attributes of the camera" rather than of the story. For Ozu a stationary camera and a simple cut from one scene to the next were sufficient. Of the seven movies from this period that have been preserved, the best known is his 1931 work *Tokyo Chorus*, a film about an office worker who is fired for sticking up for a fellow employee.

Several roles in *Tokyo Chorus* are played by children, and they were the subject of the low camera angle for which Ozu is famous. In one scene he films parents only from the waist down; when the children come in we see the room from their point of view. Ozu discovered the low angle when he was sitting on the ground in a garden one night, drinking sake. He realized immediately that this angle is also the viewpoint of someone sitting on a tatami mat, the most natural position in a Japanese home. From then on the height of the camera in an Ozu movie ranged from 1.5 to 4 feet (45 to 120 cm), depending on the height of the person being filmed and the nature of the room. The camera is always respectful, looking up at people rather than across or down at them.

Ozu filmed *I Was Born, But . . .*, perhaps his greatest silent movie, in 1932. "I started to make a film about children," Ozu said later, "and ended up with a film about grown-ups." The picture's turning point comes when two little boys who are the leaders of their neighborhood gang see a home movie of their father meekly clowning around in front of his boss, who is the father of Taro, one of their weakest playmates.

"Why do you have to bow to Taro's father?" the boys ask their dad.
"Because Taro's father is a director of my company. He pays me my salary."
"Don't let him."
"If I didn't, you couldn't go to school, you wouldn't eat."
"From tomorrow, let's not eat!"

The boys begin a hunger strike. The next day, however, they cannot resist eating the fresh rice balls their mother has made. By ending their strike, they have begun to adjust to reality. Though Taro is neither strong nor smart, his father is rich. "It's a problem they'll have to live with for the rest of their lives," the boys' father says sadly.

Despite its disillusioning theme, *I Was Born, But . . .* is quite funny. For example, when the father asks "Like your new school?" the older boy answers, "We like to go and we like to come home. It's the part in between that we don't like."

By 1932 most of Ozu's roommates had married, so Ozu moved back home with his parents. His father died soon after, and for the rest of his life Ozu lived with his mother in a suburban house that he bought with his earnings. Ozu may have had one or two brief affairs with actresses, but it seems more likely that he was celibate.

At home Ozu's study was lined with books, though one shelf was usually filled with bottles of sake and whiskey. A gramophone stood in one corner of the room; Ozu particularly enjoyed Robert Schumann's piano work *Traumerei*. He also had a half dozen ink brushes lying about because he was constantly sketching scenes for upcoming movies.

In 1934 Ozu filmed *A Story of Floating Weeds*, a movie which was remade in sound and color in 1959. The title refers to a traveling group of actors. The lead actor takes his third-rate troupe to a small town where twenty years before he fathered a son during a casual affair. The son thinks the actor is his uncle, but learns the truth at the end of the movie. By then the father realizes that he cannot just show up and exert parental authority. Before he leaves town, however, he assures his former mistress that when he returns next time he will be a famous actor that she can be proud of. This is highly unlikely, and in the silent film the ex-mistress is bitter at being deserted again. In the remake, by contrast, she lets him go without protest, understanding that the actor's dream of fame is vital to his sense of self.

By the mid-1930s "talkies" were replacing silent films. The change took a bit longer in Japan because of the resistance of the *benshi*, narrators of silent films, who formed a labor union and sometimes even grew violent. Ozu did not make his first sound feature until 1936.

The Only Son is one of Ozu's darkest movies. A mother gives up her retirement so that she can send her son to a university, and works long hours boiling fabric at a silk-spinning mill. Eventually she visits her son in Tokyo, but finds that he is teaching part-time at a night school, with barely enough money to support his wife and a child.

In the 1930s almost half of Japan's college graduates could not find a job, yet Ozu was the only film director who dealt with this harsh fact of life. The search for work is a theme of many of Ozu's silent films, including *I Graduated, But . . .* (1929), *The Life of an Office Worker* (1929), *I Flunked, But . . .* (1930), *Where Now Are the Dreams of Youth?* (1932), and *College Is a Nice Place* (1936).

In 1937, however, Ozu began making films about the upper middle class. It was during this year that he and his mother moved to the suburbs, and he recalled later; "I realized that very few directors had worked on the lives of people in these residential areas."

The year 1937 was also when Japan invaded China. Ozu was drafted immediately and made a corporal in the infantry. He served in the poison gas unit and was present at Nanjing in December, when Japanese soldiers raped over 20,000 women and killed over 250,000 people. He never said anything about it after the war, nor did he feel a need to recreate the horror on film. But in the film *Early Spring* (1956), two veterans drink and discuss the war.

There are a lot of pretentious guys nowadays who go around saying, "I opposed the war." They're all frauds and fakes.

Yeah, big fakes . . . If we'd said something like that, we would've been shot on the spot.

After two years of combat, Ozu returned to Japan in 1939, and was amazed to find that almost every movie made was propaganda. He ran into censorship difficulties himself with a script about a married couple's last meal before the husband goes off to war; army censors objected to the choice of food and use of Western phrases. Rather than rewrite, Ozu put the script aside and made a new movie in 1941, *The Brothers and Sisters of the Toda Family*, about a soldier home on leave who finds that his rich brothers and sisters have not taken good care of his widowed mother and youngest sister. The film is an attack on the selfishness of the rich, and was Ozu's first big commercial success.

The following year Ozu made one of his greatest films, *There Was a Father*. It is seldom seen today because the quality of the original wartime negative is poor, as is the sound track. The movie is about a father, a son, and the obligations that keep them apart. The father's work compels him to send his son to boarding school, and later the grown son teaches in the far north of Japan. They see each other only during vacations, and in two famous scenes Ozu shows them fishing in unison and casting their lines in an identical manner. Just when it seems that father and son might finally live together, the son is drafted. As he leaves for war his father dies, and their separation is final.

Ryu Chishu plays the father, and many critics consider his performance one of the finest by any actor in the history of Japanese cinema. Ryu has a friendly manner and a deep voice, and even when he is just listening and says "Hmmm," he says it with such resonance that he seems to understand every aspect of his companion's problem.

Ozu was meticulous about sets. Often he moved a cup or a glass three centimeters to the right, then back one centimeter to the left. As a joke he would say "Move this four centimeters toward Hollywood," or "Move that two centimeters toward Tokyo." When the set was finished, he always said, "Call the produce market!" a humorous reference to the fact that in Japan, "radish" is slang for a bad actor.

Sometimes Ozu asked his actors to rehearse a scene twenty and even thirty times. He liked to use real food and liquor on the set, so a mealtime scene often felt like a party. But Ozu was demanding. One poor actress had to spend two full days rehearsing a single shot in which she simultaneously stirs tea and glances to the left as she turns her head. Imamura Shohei, an assistant who later became a famous director himself, quit working for Ozu because he felt that he drained all the spontaneity out of his actors.

Ryu Chishu, on the other hand, once wrote that Ozu taught him to be "an empty page." Ozu, he said, already "had the complete film in his head before we went on the set, so all we actors had to do was to follow his directions, from the way we lifted and dropped our arms to the way we blinked our eyes."

In one film, for example, Ryu plays an impoverished student who sells his new suit to a pawnshop, then feels sorry about what he has done. "I had no idea how to do it," Ryu recalled. "Ozu told me that when I got the money I should look first at one of the bills, then at the other, and then look up. And there it is, up on the screen—sorrow."

"He told me what to do," Ryu once wrote, "and let me discover the feeling."

Ozu was drafted again and sent to Singapore in 1943. For over a year Ozu did little but lounge by a pool and watch American movies that the army had confiscated. Ozu saw more than a hundred films, including *Gone With the Wind*, *Citizen Kane*, and director John Ford's *My Darling Clementine* and *The Grapes of Wrath*. In these last two films he especially admired the rapport between Ford and actor Henry Fonda, who could convey deep emotions with barely a facial movement.

Finally, the army assigned Ozu to do an anti-British documentary about India's independence movement, but the war ended before he could finish it. Ozu carefully burned every foot of the film before the British arrived to retake Singapore in August 1945.

Ozu was a prisoner of war for six months. As ships became available, the POWs drew lots to determine who would get on board, but Ozu gave his right to go home early to a homesick friend who missed his children. He finally returned to Japan in February 1946, but was unable to make a movie for another year.

His first postwar film, *Record of a Tenement Gentleman* (1947), features a hard old woman who softens as she takes care of a war orphan. His second, *A Hen in the Wind* (1948), is about a wife who becomes a prostitute for a night to pay for her son's medical bills. The two movies, most critics agree, are not as distinguished as the rest of Ozu's later films.

In 1949, after fourteen years, Ozu resumed his collaboration with scriptwriter Noda Kogo and filmed *Late Spring*, the first of their thirteen "home dramas." When they wrote a script together, Ozu and Noda, who was married, stayed at an inn for as long as four months until the job was done. They had guests and ate hamburgers in the evening and drank over a gallon of sake a day. Ozu numbered the bottles and laughed as the pile grew bigger.

Ozu once said that writing a script was the hardest part of making a film, and that "you cannot write a script unless you know who is going to play the part. . . . It is not a matter of how good an actor is," he added, "it is a matter of . . . what he really is."

Before Ozu and Noda began a script, they had specific actors and actresses in mind. Indeed, they used practically the same cast in film after film. Ryu Chishu usually played the father, and Hara Setsuko played the daughter. Hara is known to the Japanese public as "the eternal virgin" because she is so bright and cheerful that even when she says "excuse me" her voice ripples with laughter.

The two scriptwriters began their work by talking about character rather than plot. "Pictures with obvious plots bore me," Ozu said, "I want to make people feel what life is like without resorting to dramatic ups and downs."

Once the characters were clear, Ozu and Noda outlined scenes on note cards, one scene to a card. Only then did they begin to write dialogue. The routine, Ozu said, was to "write and correct, write and correct, day and night." If they disagreed, Noda recalled, "we said scarcely a word . . . but after a few days, mysteriously enough, one of us would come up with a new idea."

The emotion of a character is always clear from the dialogue. As critic Donald Richie has observed, in Ozu's scripts "the character delineation achieved is so great, yet the economy so extreme," that many writers regard the scripts themselves as literature.

With rare exceptions, Ozu's post-1949 films have just five settings: home, office, restaurant, tea salon, and bar. Introductory shots establish the location: a quiet suburban street, a hallway in an office building, a small but colorful neon sign. Ozu spent hours walking through country lanes and downtown alleys to find just the right spot for a shot.

At the end of a scene, after the characters have left, Ozu lingers and shows us an empty room for a second. The sudden absence of activity reminds us that everything in life is temporary. This feeling of transience, known in Japanese as *mono no aware*, is particularly strong in Ozu's 1949 masterpiece *Late Spring*, but is present in all of his later films.

In *Late Spring* Ryu Chishu plays Professor Sumiya, a widowed father, and Hara Setsuko plays his daughter, Noriko. The title refers to the fact that at twenty-seven Noriko is a little past the typical age of marriage. She stays single because she likes taking care of her father.

Professor Sumiya wants Noriko to meet a prospective husband, but when she seems reluctant to do so, he tells her that he will soon marry himself. Shocked, Noriko quizzes him.

> You'd remarry? (He nods)
> You'd marry again? (He grunts)
> Was she the one? (He nods)
> Is it definite? (He grunts)
> You're being honest?

The professor nods again, but because his honesty is directly questioned, his cheek twitches for perhaps a quarter of a second. It is enough. In the most subtle way possible, Ozu lets us know that the professor is lying. "If I'd said otherwise," he tells a friend later in the movie, "she'd never have married . . . it was the biggest lie of my life."

Fortunately Noriko likes her suitor and agrees to marry him. But her father, who has a modern outlook, wants to make sure that he is not forcing this marriage on her.

You've no objections?	No.
Not just resigned are you?	No.
Or still undecided?	No I'm not.

As Noriko's marriage approaches, the feeling of transience increases. When she and her father go to Kyoto for a weekend, he points out that "this is our last trip together." Later, she too has the feeling of *mono no aware*, and asks, "Please, Father, why can't we remain as we are?"

Noriko's unease about marrying is momentary, but her feeling of transience remains strong. Moments before the wedding, in full bridal dress, she bows before her father and says, "I want to thank you for everything during these long years." "Be happy," her father replies, "and be a good wife."

The final scene of the film is perhaps the most powerful. The wedding is over and the professor has just returned home. He is alone in the house for the first time. As he sits down he starts to peel a Japanese pear. A closeup shows his hands at work. Suddenly the peeling stops—the hands are still. The emotion is clear. The professor feels old and alone. No shot of his face is necessary. We simply see his head droop.

Four years passed before Ozu made another film of this caliber, but many people consider *Tokyo Story*, released in 1953, to be his greatest film. It is a movie about the thoughtlessness of children. When an elderly couple decides to visit their two children in Tokyo, they discover that the children are too busy and too selfish to spend much time with them.

Shige, the daughter, owns a beauty parlor, and pinches her pennies. She serves her parents sukiyaki instead of sashimi, and tells her husband, "Don't buy expensive cakes for them, they don't need it." She can't be bothered to take a day off and show her parents the city, and her brother Koichi, a doctor, is also busy.

The one person who is kind to the parents is the young widow of their son who died in the war. The widow is played by Hara Setsuko, and once again her character is named Noriko. Noriko cheerfully shows her in-laws the sights of Tokyo, and her kindness contrasts with the selfishness of Shige and Koichi.

Shige decides to send her parents to Atami, a seaside resort, as a way to get rid of them for a few days. "Atami is less expensive, really" than showing them around Tokyo, she tells her husband. But because she has chosen a cheap resort, it is noisy at night. In a long and agonizing scene Ozu shows the old couple in bed, wide awake, unable to sleep because of mah-jongg players in the next room and musicians on the street below.

The next morning the parents decide to go home, a tacit admission that they no longer have a warm relationship with their children. On the way home the father, played by Ryu Chishu, confides to his wife;

FATHER: Shige used to be nicer when she was younger . . .
MOTHER: Koichi's changed too. He used to be such a nice boy.
FATHER: No, children don't live up to their expectations.

This is the Tokyo story. The daily struggle to make money in a city where there are "too many people" has made the children hard and insensitive. Even when the mother dies later in the film, Shige and her brother go back to Tokyo just one day after the funeral, greedily taking their mother's best clothes with them.

Kyoko, a younger sister who still lives at home with her father, is appalled by her older sister's selfishness. But Noriko, who is sensitive enough to spend a few extra days with her father-in-law, takes a more charitable point of view toward Shige:

NORIKO: A woman has her own life at Shige's age . . . everyone has to look after himself.
KYOKO: Isn't life disappointing?
NORIKO: I'm afraid it is.

The richness of *Tokyo Story* cannot be captured in a page, but the movie was a huge success with both critics and the public. Oddly enough, it was not shown in foreign theaters until 1972, when it won praise everywhere. Critic Stanley Kauffmann called it one of the ten best films of all time.

Ozu's last movies do not approach the greatness of *Tokyo Story* or *Late Spring*. By 1956 younger Japanese preferred films about sex, science fiction, and rock and roll, and many of them disdained Ozu as old-fashioned. He tried to be more up-to-date in *Early Spring* (1956), which examines a marriage after a husband has had an affair, and *Tokyo Twilight* (1957), about a daughter who has an abortion and later commits suicide. Neither film is among Ozu's best, and Ozu himself admitted that "whenever I try to handle that high a volume [of emotion], somehow vibrations always appear."

Ozu made the first of his six color films, *Equinox Flower*, in 1958. He described it in an interview with *Kinema Jumpo* magazine:

[The father's] daughter has gotten engaged without consulting him. He realizes that her fiancé is a good man, but because he was neglected, he feels . . . injured. . . . This intricate tension of the father is what I wanted to present.

At the beginning of his career, Ozu made films about college students and recent graduates. Now, in his fifties, most of his characters were middle-aged men. "A director's observations must be made from the viewpoint of his own age," Ozu said in the same interview. He added that he was "sympathetic" to old people who are "displeased by the aimless rebellion of the young."

In 1960 Ozu released *Late Autumn*, a film patterned after *Late Spring*, but less moving. During the filming, one million students protested the renewal of Japan's alliance with the United States, sometimes violently. But just as Jane Austen's families ignored the Napoleonic Wars, so Ozu's families are oblivious to current events.

Ozu's final movie, *An Autumn Afternoon* (1962), is one of his best. Like *Late Spring*, the movie is about a widowed father (played by Ryu Chishu), who decides that it is time for his daughter to marry. Unlike *Late Spring*, *An Autumn Afternoon* is shot from the father's point of view. It has many scenes of men eating and drinking together in restaurants and bars, and their banter makes the movie much lighter in tone than *Late Spring*.

In one scene, the father and a sailor who served under his command during World War II are having drinks in a bar. The old sailor wonders what things would be like if Japan had won the war.

It's because we lost that the kids are all shaking their behinds dancing to this rockabilly thing. But if we'd won, then all the blue-eyed foreigners would be wearing geisha wigs while plunking out tunes on the samisen.

The father laughs and says, "Then it's lucky we lost."

As in *Late Spring*, *An Autumn Afternoon* ends when the father returns home from his daughter's wedding. Softly he sings the "Battleship March" to himself: "In defense or attack . . . floating castles guard the nation." By instinct he is singing a song that gives him courage. The enemy he faces now is not the United States Navy, but a lonely old age. In the hallway he fights tears as he looks upstairs toward his daughter's bedroom. To compose himself, he walks into the kitchen, sits down, and drinks some water. In the last shot of Ozu's career, the camera remains in the hallway. The father's grief is seen only from a distance.

In February 1962 Ozu's mother died of pneumonia. One year later a cancerous swelling appeared on Ozu's neck. Cobalt treatments were ineffective, and Ozu died, painfully, on December 11, 1963, one day short of his sixtieth birthday. Shortly before his death, the president of Shochiku Studios paid a visit. From his hospital bed Ozu looked around the room with the eye of a film director and joked, "Well, sir, it's a home drama after all."

"In every Ozu film," critic Donald Richie has written, "the whole world exists in one family." In the 1930s Ozu's families mirrored the Great Depression, as husbands were demoralized by the difficulty they had supporting their wives and children. After the war, by contrast, Ozu's more prosperous families reflected the liberal influence of the American occupation, as fathers tried to balance traditional family arrangements with the modern idea of marrying for love.

More than twenty years before the phrase "empty nest" was coined, Ozu had already shown how lonely a parent in a nuclear family can be once his children leave home. The passage of time breaks up even the most loving families, and the inevitability of this sad truth is what makes Ozu's best films so moving.

The pace of an Ozu film is set by its conversation rather than by its action or camera movement. The dialogue may have taken Ozu months to write, but onscreen it appears to be spontaneous, and slowly it reveals how bravely each father, mother, and daughter faces unwanted change. Their quiet acts of self-sacrifice remind us of the love that exists in every family, and often make the characters seem so real that one writer has called Ozu "the artist of life as it is."

36
Kurosawa Akira
Japan's Most Widely Admired Film Director

K UROSAWA AKIRA is the one Japanese film director whose movies have been seen around the world. Since 1951, when *Rashomon* won the Grand Prize at the Venice Film Festival, audiences everywhere have admired his movies for being both perceptive and entertaining. Kurosawa's stature is equal to that of Western directors Ingmar Bergman and Federico Fellini.

Kurosawa directed samurai epics, crime thrillers, literary adaptations, and films of social realism. Not all of his thirty movies were successes, but at least a half dozen are among the finest ever made. One, *Seven Samurai*, is thought by many to be the greatest Japanese film of all time.

Kurosawa (1910–1998) elevated the cliché-filled samurai swordfight movie to an art form. Eleven of his films take place before Japan's modernization, and viewers gain a deep appreciation of how rigid the class divisions used to be, and the extraordinary mental and physical alertness of the best samurai.

Kurosawa was born on March 23, 1910, in Tokyo, the youngest of eight children. His father was a retired army officer who taught physical education at a military school. Though a descendant of samurai and a strict disciplinarian, he took his family to see the silent movies of the day. Kurosawa's mother was the daughter of a merchant. A gentle woman, she was so stoic that once, even when she severely burned her hands carrying a flaming tempura pot out of her house, she did not cry.

Unlike his mother, young Kurosawa cried so often that classmates called him "Mr. Gumdrop" for the size of his tears. Yet by fifth grade he was class president, with an assured but friendly manner.

Kurosawa attained a high rank in kendo, fencing with a wooden sword. He walked over an hour to take lessons before school. Years later Kurosawa recalled the sounds of those morning walks: the wind chime peddler, the bells of monks, the tofu seller's bugle.

An art teacher recognized Kurosawa's talent and invited him and several other boys to his home each Sunday to borrow and discuss art books. Kurosawa's father encouraged his son's interest, and bought him a set of oil paints when he was a teenager. After graduating from high school, Kurosawa attended a school of European-style painting, and some of his works were shown at exhibitions.

In 1923, after the severe earthquake that leveled and burned Tokyo, Kurosawa accompanied his older brother Heigo on a walk. If Kurosawa turned away from a corpse, Heigo said, "Akira, look carefully." Later Heigo explained; "If you shut your eyes to a frightening sight, you end up being frightened. If you look at everything straight on, there is nothing to be afraid of."

Heigo introduced his younger brother to Russian literature and foreign films. They walked several extra miles a day and spent the streetcar money they saved buying second-hand novels by Tolstoy, Turgenev, and especially Dostoyevsky, who remained Kurosawa's favorite author all his life. "Ordinary people turn their eyes away from tragedy," Kurosawa once said, but Dostoyevsky "looks straight into it and suffers with the victims." The brothers also saw over a hundred silent movies from America and Europe. Heigo worked as a *benshi*, a narrator of silent films. A *benshi* provided commentary as well as dialogue, and Heigo developed a loyal following.

In 1933 Heigo led a strike to protest the introduction of movies with sound, became depressed when the strike failed, and commited suicide. Another brother had died while serving in the military, and for this reason Kurosawa was never drafted during World War II. Army policy was that one death in a family was enough.

Kurosawa was suddenly the only son in his family, and felt duty bound to make a good living. He drew illustrations for women's magazines and painted visual aids for use in cooking schools, but try as he might, he could not sell any of his oil paintings.

In 1935 the Toho film studio advertised for assistant directors. Applicants had to submit an essay on the faults in Japanese films, and later write a scenario about a laborer in love with a dancer. Kurosawa drew on years of talks with his brother to write the essay, then used his painter's eye to write a script that contrasted the worker's dark factory with the dancer's pink dressing room. Out of five hundred applicants, the studio hired him and four others.

Kurosawa was tall, lean, and had large, powerful hands; a reporter once described him as having the face of a professor and the body of a handyman. He almost quit during his first year because he had been assigned to a director with little talent who treated him as an errand boy. In 1937, however, he began working for Yamamoto Kajiro, a noted director who was an excellent teacher and enjoyed the company of his assistants. Work became fun, and Kurosawa grew ambitious to direct.

During the next four years Kurosawa rose from third assistant to chief assistant director as he learned about every aspect of film production. He built props, designed sets, supervised costumes, set up cameras and microphones, appeared as an extra, developed film, dubbed music, and balanced books. By

1941 Yamamoto called Kurosawa "my other self" and let him direct scenes on his own. Yamamoto's advice was "If you drag an actor by force to where you want him, he can only get halfway there. Push him in the direction *he* wants to go, and make him do twice as much as he was thinking of doing."

During World War II it was difficult to get scripts filmed, but when the novel *Sugata Sanshiro* appeared in 1943, Kurosawa knew immediately that it would appeal to the military. He had his studio buy the rights to the book on its first day of publication, and wrote a screenplay within weeks. Both the novel and the film are about the spiritual education of Sugata, a young judo champion in the 1880s, when there was a bitter rivalry between the followers of jujutsu and the students of its more modern form, judo.

Much of Kurosawa's directing style is already apparent in this first film. In one judo match Kurosawa uses both fast cuts and slow motion. In another fight, filmed at night, a full minute of stillness is followed by lightning-quick action.

At the beginning of the film Kurosawa shows the passage of time vividly when the hero loses his clogs. In a quick montage we see the clogs rained on, chewed by a puppy, hung on a fence, and, finally, floating down a river into the sea. Kurosawa also showed the advance of time by using a "wipe," a moving line that allows the new scene to literally wipe the old one off the screen.

When *Sugata Sanshiro* was finished, an army censor criticized a scene where the hero meets a young woman outside a Shinto shrine as "too American." Kurosawa, who has a short temper, recalled that he nearly stood up and said, "Bastard! Go to hell! Eat this chair!" Fortunately Ozu Yasujiro (see chapter thirty-five) served on the censorship committee, praised the film, and persuaded his colleagues to release it. Within weeks critics agreed with Ozu that Kurosawa's movie was a promising debut.

In 1944 Kurosawa made *The Most Beautiful*, a docudrama about girls who contribute to the war effort by working long hours in a lens factory. To make his starlets act more like factory hands, Kurosawa had the young women work in a real lens factory and live in a girl's dormitory. He also had the actresses run several miles a day to make them tired.

The star, Yaguchi Yoko, had a number of heated arguments with Kurosawa about the actresses' harsh routine. Kurosawa admired her spirit, and when the film was finished asked her to marry him. They married in Tokyo on February 15, 1945, with air raid sirens wailing all through the wedding. Later they had one son and one daughter.

Between 1946 and 1949 Kurosawa made five movies. Though all have powerful scenes, the best film of the period is *Drunken Angel*, released in 1948. "I wanted to point out how foolish the gangsters' way of living is," Kurosawa recalled. In spite of this noble aim, the film is dominated by the magnetic personality of the young criminal, played by actor Mifune Toshio.

Mifune (1920–1997), who starred in sixteen of Kurosawa's films, became an actor by accident. In 1946 the handsome air force veteran applied for a job as an assistant cameraman, but by mistake the studio sent him to an acting audition. Not realizing what had happened, Mifune was insulted when he was asked to act drunk, and became rather menacing. Kurosawa spotted his talent and intensity immediately. He later wrote; "The speed with which [Mifune] expressed himself was astounding . . . he said with a single action what took ordinary actors three separate movements to express."

Mifune won immediate fame playing a gangster who reevaluates his life after a doctor informs him that he has tuberculosis. The alcoholic doctor (the drunken angel) is played by another of Kurosawa's favorite actors, Shimura Takashi (1905–1982). Calm, strong, and humble, Shimura appears in twenty-one of Kurosawa's films. In many, Shimura plays an experienced teacher, while Mifune plays an impatient pupil. In one of *Drunken Angel*'s memorable scenes, Mifune proudly tells Shimura that gangsters have their own moral code. The doctor merely rubs his fingers in the universal sign for money, instantly destroying the young man's delusion.

Rashomon, filmed in 1950, was the first Japanese movie to win the attention of the West, winning first place at the Venice Film Festival in 1951 and the Academy Award for Best Foreign Film the following year. The movie is based on two short stories by the great writer Akutagawa Ryunosuke.

In the twelfth century, in a forest near Kyoto, a woman is raped, her husband is stabbed to death, a bandit is captured, and a dagger is missing. Everyone involved talks to an investigator who never appears onscreen, and the audience must make its own judgment about each person's testimony. In flashbacks, four people give deeply conflicting versions of what happened, and each describes himself in the best possible light. A priest at the Rashomon gate concludes; "Because men are weak, they lie, to deceive themselves."

At first audiences treat the movie as a mystery and try to figure out who is telling the truth. But viewers later see that the point of *Rashomon* is that one can never know the truth with certainty. Even our memories are warped by our inability to be honest with ourselves.

Critics praised the film's striking use of light and shadow, and also admired Kurosawa's ability to tell the same story four times without boring the audience. He did this by using extremely quick shots, and through unusual combinations of close-ups and long shots.

After a day of shooting, Kurosawa typically spent an hour or two editing, and, if possible, he shot a film chronologically. This is unusual in the movie business, but Kurosawa liked to see how a film looked as it progressed, and make adjustments as needed.

The awards for *Rashomon* could not have come at a better time. *The Idiot*, Kurosawa's adaptation of Dostoyevsky's novel, was both a commercial and critical failure, and Kurosawa's career was in jeopardy. The three-hour film is far too faithful to the book, with long talks on anarchism, for example, that could have been cut.

Kurosawa's 1952 film *Ikiru* (*To Live*), is one of his finest. It stars Shimura Takashi as Watanabe, a city bureaucrat so faceless, his subordinates call him "the mummy." As the film begins, Watanabe learns that he has stomach cancer, and just a few months to live. Estranged from his only son, he seeks pleasure at first. He plays pinball, drinks at bars, watches a striptease, and hires a prostitute. Finally Watanabe decides to do something useful. He returns to his office and rescues a previously ignored petition by housewives asking the city to drain a vacant lot and build a park.

At this point Kurosawa could have done the conventional thing and shown Watanabe working hard to build the park. Instead, he devotes the last third of the film to Watanabe's funeral, five months later. At the service, city officials take credit for the park that Watanabe pushed through single-handedly.

One by one mourners (through flashbacks) contradict the bureaucrats. We see the deputy mayor saying, "We've no time for your project just now," and Watanabe bowing low but asking again, "Will you please reconsider?" We also see hoodlums threaten Watanabe because they want to open a bar at the park site. "Don't you value your life?" they ask. Watanabe just smiles. He has never valued his life so highly as he does then. Because his life has a purpose, he is not afraid to die.

Ikiru was cowritten by Oguni Hideo, who also cowrote the masterpieces *Seven Samurai*, *High and Low*, *Red Beard*, and *Ran*. "I do not trust myself to write a script alone," Kurosawa once confessed, "I need people who can give me perspective."

In *Ikiru* actor Shimura plays the bureaucrat who is sick, sad, and, at first, confused. In *Seven Samurai*, Kurosawa's greatest film, the versatile Shimura plays Kambei, a warrior who is a natural leader because he has the calm that comes from great strength. Released in 1954, *Seven Samurai* is set in the war-ravaged sixteenth century, and begins when farmers learn that their village is about to be raided by forty bandits on horseback. To protect their women and crops, the farmers decide to hire samurai to defend them.

Several farmers go to town to look for unemployed samurai, but only when they see Kambei rescue a kidnapped child unarmed do they feel that they have found a man worth hiring. To fight forty bandits Kambei decides that he needs a total of seven men, including himself, but "it's not easy to find seven reliable samurai, especially when the reward is just meals—and the fun of it." Kambei recruits his warriors one at a time, allowing us to get to know each one. A teenage samurai wants to fight his first battle. A middle-aged warrior, Shichiroji, is an old friend. A fourth man tells Kambei, "I work because your character fascinates me." A fifth warrior joins because he is tired of chopping wood for money. The sixth samurai, Kyuzo, is a superb swordsman looking for an opportunity to improve his skill.

Kikuchiyo, the seventh warrior, is played by Mifune. At first the other six men ignore him, because although he claims to be a samurai, he does not have upper-class manners. Kikuchiyo follows them anyway, and they finally accept him because of his ability to get along with the farmers while training them for combat.

A single spear alerts Kikuchiyo to the fact that the farmers have a hidden storehouse of weapons and armor they have taken from wounded samurai on the run. The sight of the stolen armor angers the other six samurai, but Kikuchiyo defends the farmers.

> They hunt the wounded and the defeated. Farmers are miserly, craven, mean, stupid, murderous! But then, who made animals out of them? You did. All of you damned samurai! . . .
>
> Each time you fight you burn villages, destroy the fields, take away the food, rape the women, and enslave the men. And kill them when they resist. You hear me—you damned samurai!

As Kikuchiyo falls to his knees and sobs, Kambei gently asks, "You're a farmer's son, aren't you?"

Kambei's strategy is to kill the bandits one or two at a time. At a gap in a bamboo-spiked fence that surrounds the hamlet, the farmers, armed with spears, form a human gate that closes as soon as one or two bandits ride into the village. Then the samurai (or the farmers) kill the unfortunate bandits who are trapped inside.

In one macabre shot, an old woman walks toward a bandit who has been taken prisoner. She is carrying a hoe and is about to avenge the death of her son. In quick battle scenes we see horses galloping, mud flying, close-ups of pounding hooves, and dying men falling off their horses in slow motion. The slow-motion death is a cliché today, but its origin is credited to this 1954 film.

Viewers are close to the action. *Seven Samurai* was one of the first movies to use telephoto lenses, and Kurosawa also kept three cameras running simultaneously, a technique he continued to use in all of his subsequent movies. Using three cameras wastes a lot of film—over ninety percent ends up on the cutting room floor—but fewer takes are needed when a scene is filmed from all sides, and actors are more natural because they don't know which camera to play to.

On the set Kurosawa shuttled from one camera to the next, supervising everything. He called actors by the names of their characters, and gently guided them through a dozen rehearsals before each scene. He offered suggestions rather than commands.

Three hours into *Seven Samurai*, five samurai fight the last thirteen thieves in a driving rainstorm. "I like extremes because I find them most alive," Kurosawa once said, "I like hot summers, cold winters, heavy rains and snows."

The samurai kill each bandit, but not before the chief bandit shoots Kikuchiyo, whose bravery is useless against bullets. Only three of the seven samurai survive: the leader Kambei, his old friend, and the teenager, who managed to lose his virginity and to kill his first man in battle the same morning.

In the movie's last scene Kambei looks at the graves of his fallen comrades, then watches the farmers sing and plant seedlings to the beat of a drum. Realizing that while the demand for warriors is fleeting, the need for farmers is eternal, he says to his old friend, "The farmers are the winners, not us."

Seven Samurai was a box office success both in Japan and abroad and won the Academy Award for Best Foreign Film in 1955. Even today many students of film agree with critic Rick Lyman that "with its scope, its emotional power, its moral underpinnings and the sheer breathless way that it holds its audience, *Seven Samurai* is probably the greatest action film ever made."

Three years later, in 1957, Kurosawa released *Throne of Blood*, an adaptation of Shakespeare's *Macbeth* set in medieval Japan. The film is admired by many for its striking visual effects. Huge flocks of crows invade the castle, and real arrows fly only a foot from actor Mifune's head. But many critics contend that the characters are stiff and agree with author David Desser that, lacking a substitute for Shakespeare's lines, "Kurosawa has borrowed the bones of tragedy without the heart."

To make the film, Kurosawa constructed a castle so historically accurate that it was built with wooden pegs instead of nails. He used expensive lacquer dishes for banquet scenes and once waited an entire week for the right cloud formation. Because of his perfectionism, Japanese reporters nicknamed Kurosawa "the emperor." His staff, however, called him *Sensei*, which means "teacher."

In 1958 Kurosawa filmed *The Hidden Fortress*. A gentle parody of the typical samurai action movie, it was also Kurosawa's first film to use wide screen photography. Set like *Seven Samurai* during the wars of the sixteenth century, the movie is about two peasants who help rescue a teenage princess. The two men are greedy, cowardly, and quarrelsome, yet remain friends. Years later American director George Lucas acknowledged using them as models for the robots R2-D2 and C3PO in *Star Wars*, another movie about a hidden fortress and the rescue of a princess.

In Kurosawa's 1961 movie *Yojimbo* (*Bodyguard*), the hero is Sanjuro, an unemployed samurai who has run out of money. Played by Mifune, he is gruff, unshaven, and usually scratching himself or chewing on a toothpick. When he walks into a dusty village at the start of the film, a dog trots by with a human hand in its mouth. The town is controlled by a sake brewer who runs a prostitution ring, and his rival, a silk seller who runs a gambling den. Both men are protected by enormous ugly thugs.

Working as a bodyguard, first for one side, then for the other, Sanjuro manages to start a war between the two evil merchants that leaves most of the village dead. "Now it will be quiet in this town," Sanjuro says. As he leaves, mambo music matches his bouncy, swaggering walk. Though *Yojimbo* lacks the depth of *Seven Samurai*, it was Kurosawa's biggest box office hit. Two years later it was the model for *A Fistful of Dollars*, Clint Eastwood's first film.

The New York Times called Kurosawa's 1963 movie *High and Low* "one of the best detective thrillers ever filmed." Set in modern Yokohama and loosely based on Ed McBain's novel *King's Ransom*, the movie consists of three distinct parts: a morality play, a police investigation, and a tour of Yokohama's underworld.

The morality play takes place in the home of Gondo, played by Mifune, a successful shoe company executive who is about to spend his life savings to buy a controlling interest in his firm. At this point a young criminal attempts to kidnap Gondo's son but grabs the chauffeur's boy by mistake. The kidnapper telephones Gondo and demands a ransom of thirty million yen, and this presents Gondo with a terrible dilemma: must he sacrifice his career and everything he has for another man's son?

In *King's Ransom* the businessman refuses to pay a cent; in the film Gondo also at first angrily refuses to help. Gradually the pleas of his wife, the police, and the chauffeur make him realize that he cannot let the little boy die.

For a full hour the movie has been a riveting piece of theater, nearly all of it performed on a single set. Now the film shifts gears quickly. A bullet train whizzes by. Inside, in quick scenes that required nine cameras to film, Gondo, as planned, sees the boy on a riverbank, then throws two briefcases filled with cash out the train's bathroom window. The satchels contain hidden powder that will cause an incriminating smell if they are thrown in water, or make pink smoke if they are burned.

Once the boy is freed, the investigation begins in earnest. The meticulous detectives check out pay phones, tire tracks, and pictures the little boy has drawn. We see jumpy eight-millimeter film shot from the front and back of the train. A car stolen near the riverbank leads to the home of the kidnapper's accomplices, but they have died from taking heroin too pure.

Pink smoke lures the police to the kidnapper, but instead of arresting him right away, the detectives decide to prove that he murdered his accomplices. As the third part of the movie begins, the police follow the kidnapper on a leisurely tour through Yokohama's seedy nighttime honky-tonks.

With a saxophone, a bass guitar, and rockabilly music in the background, Kurosawa shows us a port city's underworld. Clubs are filled with prostitutes, Japanese sailors, and white and black American GIs. Alleyways are lined with drug addicts. The pursuit of the kidnapper slows to a snail's pace, but the streets are so fascinating that audiences do not care.

Toward the end of the movie, Gondo, with no money left, has to auction off his house and possessions. "You can't pay a kidnapper and not pay us," his banker tells him. Before long, however, the kidnapper is caught and sentenced to death, and Gondo gets his money back and buys a smaller shoe company. In the film's last scene the kidnapper asks to see Gondo, and we learn his motive: envy. "Your house [on a hilltop] looked like Heaven, high up there. That's how I began to hate you."

Ed McBain was pleased with the many changes Kurosawa made in filming the novel, including the bullet train, the heroin deaths, Mrs. Gondo's compassion, and the kidnapper's envy. Brendan Gill, in a review for *The New Yorker*, concluded: "*High and Low* lasts nearly two and a half hours, but I, who heartily dislike long pictures, am unable to think of a scene I'd be willing to do without."

Red Beard, completed in 1965, is another one of Kurosawa's finest films. Set in an early-nineteenth-century hospital that has "the smell of the poor," the movie tells the story of Yasumoto, a top graduate of a new school of Western medicine. Yasumoto had expected to be appointed one of the shogun's personal physicians, but instead is assigned to a public clinic. Angry, and hoping to leave as soon as possible, he breaks the hospital's rules and refuses even to wear a uniform.

Soon, however, the intern is deeply impressed by the hospital director, nicknamed Red Beard and played by Mifune. Red Beard is gruff, but totally dedicated to his patients. Shamed by his example, Yasumoto stops behaving arrogantly and learns that there is more to the art of healing than using new techniques. At the end of the film Yasumoto passes up a new opportunity to serve the shogun, and stays at the clinic.

To shoot the film, Kurosawa built an entire nineteenth-century village. He used lumber taken from old farmhouses, and had the hospital futons slept in for six months.

Japanese critics hailed *Red Beard* as a masterpiece. Western critics were cooler; the movie is three hours long. Viewers with patience will find the Japanese opinion is fully justified.

Red Beard may be Kurosawa's most idealistic movie, but it was always important to him that young people not give way to cynicism. "Do you know who I make my pictures for?" Kurosawa once asked. "I make them for young Japanese, those now in their twenties . . . they have to have something to believe in."

By the mid-1960s, television viewing had reduced the size of movie audiences, and studios were more cautious about authorizing films with big budgets or unorthodox themes. In the first half of his career Kurosawa directed twenty-three movies in twenty-three years. In the next three decades he directed only seven.

Even he and Mifune parted ways. During the two years it took Kurosawa to make *Red Beard*, Mifune could not work anywhere else because he had grown a beard. He lost a chance to star in a televison series, and his debts mounted. One day the great actor and director quarreled, and Kurosawa never hired Mifune again.

Twenty years later critic Donald Richie wrote; "Mifune has appeared in almost 120 movies by now, yet only in the sixteen Kurosawa films is he a fine actor." Mifune agreed: "There is nothing of note I have done without Kurosawa, and I am not proud of any of my pictures except those which I have done with him."

In 1967, 20th Century-Fox asked Kurosawa to direct the Japanese scenes in *Tora! Tora! Tora!*, the movie about the attack on Pearl Harbor. Fox promised Kurosawa the authority to make the final cut, then rewrote his script.

Rather than quit, Kurosawa concluded that for legal reasons it would be better to be fired. To provoke Fox into sacking him, he shot entire scenes, declared the set had to be another color, and shot them again. To stay within its budget, Fox dismissed Kurosawa, accusing him of excessive perfectionism and decaying mental health.

Unable to get financing from a Japanese or an American studio, Kurosawa formed a small company with three other directors. They raised $1 million to make *Dodes'kaden*, Kurosawa's first color film.

Shot in just one month in 1970, the movie takes place in a shantytown at a Tokyo garbage dump. The sets are like bright paintings, with loud pinks and garish greens and yellows. The title of the movie is the sound a retarded boy makes when he pretends to be a trolley car driver, *"dodes'kaden"* being comparable to "clickety-clack." Like almost everyone else at the dump, the boy is lost in a world of illusion.

But by 1970 there were no longer any Japanese living in shantytowns, and it was hard for the public to see the point of the film. The movie lost money, and was also panned by Western critics. Kurosawa now felt a triple frustration. He could not get financing from a Japanese studio, he could not secure artistic freedom from a Hollywood studio, and he learned from shooting *Dodes'kaden* that he was unsuccessful at making low-budget films.

On December 22, 1971, a maid found Kurosawa lying unconscious in a half-filled bathtub with twenty-two razor blade slashes in his neck, elbows, wrists, and hands. He had attempted suicide.

As letters and telegrams poured in from all over the world, "I realized I had committed a terrible error," Kurosawa said later. Doctors also diagnosed a severe gallstone condition, which they corrected through surgery. "I didn't realize until after the surgery that I had been in pain for years," Kurosawa told a reporter. "I'm sure it had been affecting my spirits."

The suicide attempt only worsened Kurosawa's reputation at Japanese studios. Fortunately Mosfilm, an agency of the Soviet Union, offered to finance a movie if Kurosawa would make the picture in Russia. The Soviets wanted to interest Japanese investors in their enormous country, and were delighted when Kurosawa suggested that he film explorer Vladimir Arseniev's memoirs, which he had enjoyed reading as a young man.

Arseniev, a captain in the Russian army, was deep in the forest in 1902 mapping Siberia's border with Manchuria when he met a gentle old Mongolian hunter named Dersu Uzala, who agreed to be his guide. Kurosawa's film, *Dersu Uzala*, is about their friendship.

Dersu is in tune with everything in the forest. He talks to animals and to the wind, and, like a rural Sherlock Holmes, can determine a man's age and nationality just from looking at his footprints. He is also a superb marksman.

In the film's most powerful scene, Dersu and Captain Arseniev are exploring a lake, when a blizzard blows in and covers their tracks. Not only are they lost, but it is dusk and they have no shelter from the arctic wind. In a desperate race against time they try to cut enough marsh grass to make a haystack and burrow in before nightfall. As precious minutes tick by, the sky grows darker and the wind howls. Nature has never seemed more terrifying.

Dersu Uzala was a box office hit both in Japan and the Soviet Union, and won the Academy Award for Best Foreign Film in 1976. Yet Kurosawa was still unable to raise money in Japan. To make ends meet he appeared in two television commercials for Suntory whiskey. He also painted over two hundred pictures of scenes from his next two films, *Kagemusha* (Shadow Warrior), and *Ran* (Chaos), a loose adaptation of Shakespeare's *King Lear*. Using watercolors and pastels, Kurosawa painted castles, battles, horses, samurai, suits of armor, and ladies' kimonos.

Because *Ran* required 250 horses, 1,400 extras, and 1,400 suits of armor, Japanese studios hesitated to finance such an expensive picture. Kurosawa decided instead to film the less costly *Kagemusha* as a dress rehearsal for *Ran*. He would make *Kagemusha* to prove that there was still a market for big-budget samurai movies.

The American directors George Lucas and Francis Ford Coppola were shocked by Kurosawa's financial difficulties, and convinced 20th Century-Fox to buy the foreign rights to *Kagemusha* for $1.5 million. Toho agreed to risk $4.5 million, so by 1979 Kurosawa was finally directing again.

Actor Nakadai Tatsuya plays two roles in *Kagemusha*: Lord Takeda and a thief who has been spared execution because he looks like Lord Takeda and can be used to deceive the enemy. When Lord Takeda dies, the thief helps the weak clan keep the news secret. His mastery of the lord's gestures convinces enemy warriors, and even the lord's grandson, that Takeda is still alive. But the thief cannot fool the lord's horse, and when it throws him, his deception is exposed.

At the end of the movie, the lord's son has foolishly gone to war. We never see the battle—only the war's dreadful aftermath in slow motion: dead bodies, stunned faces, wounded horses. To film the horses, Kurosawa had two hundred people simultaneously inject the animals with tranquilizers. Then he filmed the horses stumbling as they fell down and struggled and failed to get up. Despite this powerful image of defeat, the film is not as moving as it could have been because actor Nakadai lacks the emotional intensity that Mifune always brought to the screen.

Kagemusha was a commercial and critical success, but it would still take several years before Kurosawa could raise enough money—$12 million—for his 1985 film *Ran*. Set in the sixteenth century, *Ran* begins when Hidetora, a seventy-five-year-old warlord (played by Nakadai) retires and grants "total authority" to his eldest son, Taro. The second son, Jiro, applauds the action, but Saburo, the youngest son and the only one who really loves his father, tells Hidetora frankly that his action will lead to war among the brothers. As in *King Lear*, the father is enraged by his youngest child's candor and banishes him from the kingdom.

Lady Kaede, Taro's beautiful wife whose own family was killed by Hidetora's army long before, insists that old Hidetora sign an oath in blood that he and his thirty remaining warriors will obey Taro in all matters. Hidetora signs the document but leaves his son's castle in disgust. Soon he and his men take refuge in what was once young Saburo's castle, but Taro and Jiro mount a joint attack and burn their father's new fortress.

The battle takes place in silence, except for a mournful orchestral track. We see an injured man holding his severed arm, a horseman with an arrow in his eye, and ladies of the court stabbing one another to death to avoid capture by strange men. We also watch one of Jiro's men treacherously shoot Taro in the back.

Hidetora leaves the burning castle in a daze. Wandering aimlessly, he meets victims of his youthful cruelty such as Tsurumaru, whose eyes he once gouged out. But as critic Pauline Kael observed in *The New Yorker*, the actor Nakadai [Hidetora] "isn't a towering figure," and "doesn't seem capable of the bloodlust he must have had." Again, the strong presence of Mifune is sorely missed.

It is Lady Kaede who steals the show. "As played by Harada Mieko," Vincent Canby wrote in *The New York Times*, "Lady Kaede is so supremely, breathtakingly evil that her audacity is exhilarating." After Taro's death she angrily accuses Jiro of killing her husband, puts a knife to his throat, and slowly draws tiny droplets of blood. Then she drops the knife, licks his blood, and kisses him passionately. It is one of the greatest seductions in the history of film, and by the time it is over, Jiro has agreed to kill his wife and make Lady Kaede his queen.

Lady Kaede encourages her new husband to assassinate his younger brother, Saburo, and this murder drives Hidetora to insanity and death. Hidetora's court jester cries out in despair, "Are there no gods, no Buddha? . . . Are you so bored up there that you crush us like ants? Is it such fun to see men weep?"

Saburo's general cuts him short: "Enough! It is the gods who weep. They see us killing each other over and over since time began. They can't save us from ourselves."

Lady Kaede goads Jiro into going to war one more time. As Jiro's castle goes up in flames, a loyal general angrily tells Lady Kaede that her vanity has destroyed the entire clan. "Vanity?" replies Lady Kaede calmly. "I wanted to avenge my [childhood] family. I wanted this castle to burn. I have done all that

I set out to do." The outraged general instantly cuts her head off, and a fountain of blood splatters the wall behind her.

Ran was a critical and box office success around the world, not only because ambition and betrayal are universal themes, but also because of the sheer pageantry of the battles. In feudal Japan, warriors wore flags attached to the back of their armor. In *Ran* five armies each have different hues, so every battle is aflame with color. *Ran* won the Academy Award for Best Costume Design in 1986, and Kurosawa was also nominated for Best Director. (The winner that year was Sydney Pollack, director of *Out of Africa*.)

Kurosawa had worked on *Ran* for ten hard years. Now that it was finished, he became a happier and more relaxed man, according to his son and his crew. His next movie, *Akira Kurosawa's Dreams*, released in 1990, was financed by director Steven Spielberg. There are eight dreams in the film, some of which date back to Kurosawa's childhood. Half of them are slow and gloomy nightmares, but several are enchanting.

In one vision, an art student steps into a Van Gogh painting, "The Bridge at Arles," which suddenly comes to life. As the young man walks from one painting to the next, he finally meets Van Gogh himself, painting in a wheat field. In a surprising bit of casting, director Martin Scorsese played the part of Van Gogh.

Kurosawa's next film, *Rhapsody in August*, was his first movie financed entirely by Japanese studios in twenty-six years. Released in 1991, the film is about the reconciliation of two branches of a family long divided between America and Japan. While four Japanese adults visit a dying uncle in Hawaii, their teenage children spend the summer at their grandmother's farm outside Nagasaki.

The grandfather had been killed by the atomic bomb in Nagasaki in 1945. The teenagers visit the rebuilt city, see the Peace Park, and look at a misshapen jungle gym melted by the nuclear blast. They are modern kids with informal manners, and wear American T-shirts that say "Brooklyn" and "USC."

After the parents return from Hawaii, a half-Japanese cousin named Clark arrives to visit the grandmother. Clark, played by Richard Gere, apologizes to her for the bombing of Nagasaki. Since the movie makes no mention of the Japanese aggression that led to the bombing, the scene irritated many critics, including Vincent Canby of *The New York Times*, who wrote, "If Clark can apologize for Nagasaki, why can't Granny apologize for Pearl Harbor?"

To be fair, the grandmother feels no resentment toward America, and the film is as much about the teenagers' appreciation of her traditional way of life as it is about the bomb. The reunion between the American and Japanese cousins is a happy occasion.

Kurosawa once said, "When I die, I'd prefer to just drop dead on the set." Instead, he lived to be eighty-eight, dying of a stroke on September 6, 1998. Thirty-five thousand fans and friends attended his memorial service. In America director Steven Spielberg called him "the pictorial Shakespeare of our time."

"I have lived many whole lifetimes with the films I have made," Kurosawa once wrote, "and have experienced a different life-style with each one." For most of his career, he was free to make whatever sort of film he wanted, whether it was an adaptation of a Dostoyevsky novel or a reenactment of a childhood nightmare. Yet out of thirty films, not one is a piece of fluff.

"From the very beginning," Kurosawa's mentor, Yamamoto Kajiro, recalled, "Kurosawa was completely engrossed in separating what is real from what is false." In *Ikiru*, city officials gradually realize that they have falsely taken credit for building a park. In *Red Beard*, the young doctor discovers the vanity behind his ambition to be the shogun's physician. In *Ran*, Lord Hidetora sees how cruel he was as a young man, and how foolish as an old man. Kurosawa was intolerant of illusion and forced both his characters and the audience to see things as they truly are.

Like Tolstoy, whom he admired as a youth, Kurosawa was a moralist at heart. But just as Tolstoy's artistry sometimes ran counter to his ideology, permitting Anna Karenina to remain a sympathetic character in spite of her adulterous affair, so Kurosawa let us admire villains such as the young gangster in *Drunken Angel* and Lady Kaede in *Ran*. Both artists were too truthful and saw the world too clearly to let a moral stand kill a good story. That is why Tolstoy makes the printed page come alive, and Kurosawa brings life to the screen.

37
Oh Sadaharu
and Ueshiba Morihei
*Japan's Home Run King
and His Teacher, the Founder of Aikido*

ONE OF THE few Japanese widely known in the United States is Oh Sadaharu, considered Japan's greatest baseball player ever. Oh hit 868 home runs during his career, 113 more than Hank Aaron, America's greatest power hitter, and 154 more than Babe Ruth, both of whom, of course, played baseball under different conditions.

As a youth, Oh (b. 1940) led his high school baseball team to a national championship, but his first three years with the Tokyo Giants were lackluster. Then in 1962 he became a student of Ueshiba Morihei, the founder of aikido, sometimes called "the martial art of peace." Oh soon developed a new batting stance that gave him unsurpassed power.

Ueshiba (1883–1969) had spent decades learning jujutsu (the forerunner of judo) and kendo (fencing with wooden swords) before he created a new, less violent, and more spiritual martial art called aikido (EYE-key-doe), which means "the path for harmony of physical and spiritual energy."

Studying aikido, Oh learned about balance, timing, and spiritual energy, then adopted a one-legged flamingolike batting stance that improved his hitting immediately. In contrast to his first three years, when Oh batted just .242 and averaged only 12 home runs a year, during the next nineteen years Oh batted .312 and hit an astonishing average of 44 home runs a year, leading the Central League in homers thirteen years in a row.

Ueshiba was seventy-eight when Oh became his student, but films from that era show that he could still take on three young men at a time and send them flying in all directions. As a challenge to Oh, he held up a long wooden sword and asked him to hit it with a bat as hard as he could. Oh swung with all his might. The sword did not move a millimeter. The aikido master had focused the power of his own *ki* (life force), projecting it outward from his arms. In aikido an attacker's momentum is made to work against him. Only a small amount of strength is required. The martial art first gained fame in the 1930s, when women downed men twice their size.

An aikido student learns to avoid an attack the instant it is launched, then deal not with the opponent's hands, but with the direction of his force. Using the opponent's wrist, elbow, or shoulder, she shifts the direction of his attack into a circular motion that swirls gently around her center of gravity, but throws her opponent completely off balance.

Aikido has several dozen basic techniques that can be combined in thousands of different ways. Here is one combination of movements to use if an opponent grabs a wrist:

Step back with the left leg, guide him in that direction, hold his arm while striking his face with your palm, and down him.

Moves like this take practice. They cannot be learned from a book. A first-degree black belt in aikido typically requires about five years of training. The more experienced a student becomes, the slower his opponent's attack appears. To masters of the art, even the fastest attack seems like a slow-motion film.

Although more than a million people study aikido today around the world, some people not familiar with the art think it is just another form of judo. Like aikido, judo ("the path of pliancy"), also uses wristlocks, throws, and pins. But in judo the central principle is "when pushed, pull back; when pulled, push forward." By contrast, aikido's central tenet is "when pushed, pivot and turn; when pulled, enter while circling." Aikido also has no grappling, which is a major part of judo, or kicking, which is an important part of karate. Its aim is not to disable the attacker, but to make him see the futility of continuing the fight.

Aikido's self-defense techniques are not an end in themselves, but a means toward spiritual growth. This is why aikido has no competitive tournaments. The ego a champion develops would only hinder her spiritual growth. Ueshiba was unusually religious and wanted to revive the spiritual side of the martial arts. "One's body is a miniature universe," he said, and through constant training of the body and mind a man or woman's spirit can be in harmony with the universal spirit of love. "Do you think I'm teaching you merely how to twist someone's arm and knock him to the ground?" Ueshiba asked his students, "That's child's play. Aikido deals with the most important issues of life!"

Oh

OH SADAHARU FIRST approached Ueshiba in 1962, seven years before the master's death. He had developed a "hitch" in his batting swing, a slight but habitual backswing that came just at the moment the bat should whip forward to hit the ball. As a result, Oh was still a mediocre hitter after three years in the Central League.

After just four months of studying the principles of aikido—he did not participate in throwing exercises because of the risk of injury—Oh learned to extend his *ki* outward through his bat, and almost overnight became Japan's greatest home-run hitter.

Oh was born in Tokyo on May 10, 1940, the second son of five children. His father was Chinese, but in 1921 he had left his village to become a laborer in Tokyo. After several years he married a Japanese woman and opened a small noodle restaurant, but because he was Chinese he was arrested during World War II, imprisoned for a year, and tortured during questioning.

After the war, during the American occupation, the Oh family had bigger food rations than their neighbors because as Chinese they were classified as Allies. This may be one reason Oh grew to be five feet ten inches (175 cm) tall, quite the exception at the time.

In school Oh learned some English, how to use an abacus, and competed in the high jump and the shot put. After school he played baseball with bats carved from tree limbs and balls made of wound-up string inside strips of cloth.

Baseball came to Japan in 1873, when an American professor introduced the game to his students. The Japanese took to the sport immediately because they love playing as a group. By 1915 there was a nationwide tournament of high school teams. Business tycoons formed a professional league in 1936. Since 1950 there have been six teams in the Central League, six teams in the Pacific League, and a "Japan Series" between the two league champions.

At fourteen Oh was big, muscular, and good enough to pitch for his brother's team of medical students. He also won soda each time his neighborhood team beat the workers at a bottling factory.

One day in 1954 Arakawa Hiroshi, an outfielder for the Tokyo-based Mainichi Orions, saw Oh playing baseball in a park and walked up to him between innings. "How come you pitch left-handed and bat right-handed?" he asked. "Why don't you try to bat left-handed the next time you come up?" Until then it had never occurred to Oh to bat left-handed because he had never seen anyone do it, but he hit a double on his first try and never looked back.

Oh's father wanted his son to be an engineer, but Oh failed an engineering high school's entrance exam by one point and went to Waseda High School instead. Waseda was a major baseball power, and in Japan, high school baseball is even more popular than high school football is in Texas. Every August the best teams from each of Japan's forty-seven prefectures compete in a playoff at Koshien Stadium in Osaka. This tournament, known as *Koshien*, is nationally televised and earns even higher ratings than the Japan Series.

High school players practice every day of the year, with just one week off for the New Year. Freshmen do laundry and groundskeeping chores, and are punished when they make mistakes in conduct or on the field. Waseda's slogan when Oh was a student is still typical: "The error of one is the error of all." If someone made a mistake, freshmen formed two lines, face-to-face, and hit each other hard. Even today Oh defends the practice as a way to build a sense of shared responsibility. A player who causes his teammates pain, he says, resolves never to make the same mistake again.

In the 1957 *Koshien* tournament Oh had painful blisters on his fingers, but pitched four straight games anyway and led his team to a national championship. Despite this triumph, Oh was not allowed to compete in another tournament a few months later because he was considered Chinese, and the games were for Japanese players only.

After graduating in 1958, Oh signed with the Giants, his favorite team, and received a bonus of about $300,000 in today's money. The Giants were more interested in Oh's hitting than pitching, and made him a first baseman so that he could play every day.

Teams in Japan are named for corporations, not cities. The Tokyo-based Giants, for example, are owned by the *Yomiuri Shimbun* newspaper, so the team is known as the Yomiuri Giants. The Hanshin Tigers of Osaka are named for a railroad, and the Taiyo Whales of Yokohama took their name from a fish-packing company.

Oh began "spring" training in January 1959. Japanese baseball players train so hard that Americans who have played the sport there say the Japanese don't play ball, they "work ball." Players stay on the field six to nine hours a day, often performing "guts" drills where they catch one hundred fly balls or field three hundred ground balls in a row. Americans feel these exercises create bad habits and increase the risk of injury, but the Japanese believe that only by pushing a player to his limits can he surpass them. "We're smaller," Oh once said, "so we have to practice harder." Even in the heat of summer the Japanese work out several hours before a game. Many become tired, and American players in Japan who pace themselves and skip some of the workouts tend to do better than their teammates in the second half of the season.

Although Oh, whose name means "king" in Japanese, trained unusually hard, his first year in the majors was poor. He struck out so often that fans chanted, *"Oh! Oh! Sanshin Oh!"*—"King! King! Strikeout king!" He hit just 7 home runs during the entire year, and batted a miserable .161.

Oh did better in 1960, hitting 17 home runs and batting .270. He also discovered the nightclubs of the Ginza. Being younger and richer than most of the businessmen who frequented these clubs, he was especially popular with the pretty young hostesses, and found pleasure "in the dark corners of the very best clubs I knew." The following year, however, Oh batted just .253, with only thirteen home runs. For all his promise and hard work, his performance after three years with the Giants was just average.

In 1962 the Giants hired a new batting coach, Arakawa Hiroshi, the man who had told Oh to bat left-handed when he was a teenager. Arakawa teased Oh: "A real batsman in the Ginza, eh? Maybe you left your big stick in one of those clubs!" Four days later he said, "If you really want to make it as a pro, you will do exactly as I say for three years." Oh nodded, and his night life was over.

Arakawa had studied aikido for two years, and took Oh to his dojo (training hall) to meet Ueshiba. Ueshiba knew little about baseball, but understood that the contest between a pitcher and a batter is similar to a duel between warriors. "Teach him to wait," Ueshiba said.

Oh soon became more patient about waiting for the right pitch. He stopped swinging at balls outside the strike zone, struck out less often, and drew so many walks that, starting in 1962, he led the Central League in walks eighteen years in a row.

A more important benefit Oh received from aikido was an improved sense of balance. Arakawa had Oh experiment with a one-legged batting stance in which he stood on his left leg and raised his right knee almost up to his belt. The purpose of this new stance was to get rid of the hitch in Oh's swing. A backswing on one leg was impossible because he would fall over backward. But to stay balanced on one leg was a problem.

Aikido teaches that the center of one's energy is at a point two fingers below the navel. Oh discovered that "if I located my energy in this part of my body, I was better balanced than if I located it elsewhere."

One day in June 1962, before a game against the Taiyo (Yokohama) Whales, Arakawa demonstrated the stance to Oh again and said, "I order you to do it." Oh was dubious. But in his first two times at bat he hit a single and a home run. "I had reached a point," Oh recalled, "where aikido became absolutely necessary rather than merely complementary to what I did."

Each night after a game, Oh went to Arakawa's house and practiced swinging a bat in front of a full-length mirror. He wore only his shorts so that Arakawa could observe his muscles. He learned to focus his *ki* by imagining that an iron bar ran from his left knee, down through the one leg, and into the ground. Later he realized that if he held the bat high and tipped it toward the pitcher, the bat became an extension of the iron bar. His *ki* flowed through his bat.

Before long Oh could hold his flamingo stance for a full minute. At the dojo, students pushed and pulled him to test his balance. Oh also learned to use the pivot of his hips, so that when his right foot came down his power exploded as he uncoiled. Like a golfer, Oh would downswing into the ball, meet it with a level hit, and finish with an upward follow-through.

Within weeks Oh's hitting improved dramatically. He hit twenty-eight home runs in the second half of the season, leading the league with a total of 38. He also raised his batting average slightly, to .272. Arakawa permitted Oh to go to the Ginza again, but not every night.

At the dojo during the winter Oh practiced grips and hand twists with a wooden sword, though Arakawa forbade any combat. He also learned to stay on one leg comfortably for over three minutes. In a moment of prophecy Arakawa told him, "Set your mind on Babe Ruth. You are going to beat [his home run record]. You have the body and spirit that will enable you to play until you're forty."

Oh's stance was so difficult that he had to practice it every day, but he enjoyed the work. "My heart was on fire for baseball," he once wrote, "the ball coming toward me was a rabbit, and I was a wolf waiting to devour it." Oh hit 40 home runs in 1963, and raised his batting average to an admirable .305.

The 1964 season was the second-best of Oh's career. He batted .320 and hit 55 home runs, which is still the Japanese record for a season. Even in the United States, fewer than a dozen men have hit 55 home runs in a year. How comparable are records in America and Japan? Oh is the first to say that he would not have done as well in America because the pitching is faster and the fences are typically thirty feet (nine meters) farther away from home plate.

On the other hand, it is usually easier to hit home runs against fastballs than curveballs, and Japanese pitchers, though slower, have more control than Americans do. Japanese teams also play only 130 games in a season (140 before 1969), while American teams play 162. In addition, the foul pole in right field was only three feet (one meter) closer for Oh than it was for Babe Ruth.

In eighty-two exhibition games against American teams, Oh hit 21 home runs. Some were against Hall of Fame pitchers, including Bob Gibson, Steve Carlton, Tom Seaver, and Jim Palmer. Slugger Frank Howard said, "You can kiss my ass if he wouldn't have hit 30 or 35 home runs a year [in the majors]."

Following Oh in the Giants' lineup was another great hitter, Nagashima Shigeo. Nagashima hit only two thirds of the home runs per year that Oh did, but was much more popular with the fans. He won six batting titles and was a tremendous hitter in pressure situations. He had charisma, and his ancestry was pure Japanese. Oh and Nagashima played together for sixteen years, yet never once spent a social evening together. The college-educated Nagashima probably regarded Oh as unsophisticated; Oh felt Nagashima was a ham on the field, making routine plays look spectacular.

But Oh and Nagashima never quarreled. They worked together as professionals, and their back-to-back hitting was devastating. The press called it the "O-N cannon." The Giants won the pennant and the Japan Series in 1965, then repeated the performance eight more times. The nine consecutive championships the Giants won between 1965 and 1973 is a world record in professional sports.

In December 1966 Oh married Koyae Kyoko, a fan he first met seven years earlier when she was still a junior high school student. Twelve hundred guests attended the reception, and her wedding kimono cost roughly $40,000 in today's money. They had three daughters in the next five years, and according to Oh "fought a good deal" during the early years of their marriage.

Oh hit an average of 46 home runs a year between 1965 and 1970, and had a career total of 447 homers before he was thirty. He continued to work hard because he was still "hungry for skill."

In 1968 Gene Bacque, an American pitcher for the Hanshin (Osaka) Tigers, threw two beanballs in a row at Oh, something that is simply not done in Japan. A huge fight erupted between the entire teams, and during the melee Bacque's thumb was broken. Oh learned later that Arakawa had done it, using aikido.

The following year Oh visited Ueshiba just before he died. "You have good eyes," Ueshiba told him, meaning that he had the aura of someone who had mastered his art. That mastery was tested, however, when Arakawa resigned from the Giants to manage the Yakult (Tokyo) Swallows in 1971. For the first time, Oh was entirely on his own. With no one to turn to during a slump, Oh suffered. In 1970 he had hit .325 with 47 home runs. In 1971 his average slipped to .276 and he hit "only" 39 home runs, still enough to lead the league.

Arakawa managed the Swallows for a year, and afterward continued to give Oh advice if a slump lasted longer than usual. In 1972 Oh bounced back with 48 home runs, and in 1973 he had the best season of his career, winning a triple crown as he led the league with 51 homers, 114 runs batted in, and a .355 average. In 1974 he won the triple crown again, batting .332 with 49 home runs.

When Hank Aaron surpassed Babe Ruth's career record of 714 home runs in 1974, Oh, just thirty-four, had already hit 634. CBS Television invited Aaron to fly to Tokyo to compete with Oh in a "home run derby," each player hitting twenty slowly pitched balls into fair terriory. Aaron won the contest, ten home runs to nine.

In 1975 Nagashima became manager of the Giants. Because several veterans had retired, the team finished last, and the players gave a bow of apology to their fans on the final day of the season. For the first time in fourteen years Oh did not lead the league in home runs, hitting only 33 as his batting average slipped to .285.

Both Oh and the Giants bounced back in 1976 and 1977. Fulfilling a vow to "be in better shape than even the hungriest rookie," Oh hit .324 during the next two years and led the league again with 49 home runs in 1976 and 50 in 1977. The Giants won two pennants in a row, but lost the Japan Series both years.

Oh hit his 700th home run on July 23, 1976. Arakawa, now a television commentator, interviewed Oh after the game. Later they celebrated with sushi and sake. On October 11, Oh hit home run number 715, surpassing Babe Ruth. He leapt into the air with joy, the only time he ever showed so much emotion on the field. (Never once did he argue with an umpire.) Oh finished the year just 39 home runs behind Hank Aaron's lifetime mark of 755.

As all of Japan looked forward to a new home run record, 1977 became the year of "Oh fever." Stores sold medals, towels, and T-shirts bearing Oh's photograph. As public pressure increased, Oh occasionally met with Arakawa to go over his swing. He also left his house twenty minutes early every morning so that he could sign two hundred autographs for fans waiting outside. After his name he usually added the word *doryoku*, "effort," or *nin*, "constancy."

Finally, on September 3, 1977, in a game against the Yakult (Tokyo) Swallows, Oh hit a sinker ball and belted his 756th home run, a new world record. "It was the moment of purest joy I had ever known as a baseball player," Oh recalled as fifty thousand fans shouted "Banzai!" When the cheering finally subsided, Hank Aaron congratulated him in a telephone call hooked to a loudspeaker.

Oh never compared himself to Aaron, but was still proud of his achievement. "I don't believe I would have reached 756 if I had played in America," he later told writer David Falkner, but "it is baseball's record nevertheless!" By contrast, veteran manager Davey Johnson, who played with Hank Aaron on the Atlanta Braves in 1974 and with Oh on the Yomiuri Giants in 1975 and 1976, thinks Oh would have hit 700 home runs in the United States because he "gets his whole body into it, like a cobra striking."

Oh hit 39 home runs in 1978 and 33 in 1979. In August 1980 his vision suddenly became less sharp, and fastballs seemed extra swift. Worse, Oh felt that "the fire was gone," that he had lost his desire to conquer the pitcher. He still hit 30 home runs that year, but his average slumped to .236. He was forty years old in a young man's game. Oh announced his retirement as a player on November 4. "I consider myself a very lucky man," he said, borrowing a phrase from Lou Gehrig.

During his career, Oh hit 868 home runs, 113 more than Hank Aaron, with 2,012 fewer times at bat (counting walks). His lifetime batting average was .301, and he also won nine Diamond Glove awards for fielding as a first baseman.

The Giants made Oh assistant manager, with duties that included hitting ground balls to infielders, chauffeuring players between hotels and stadiums, and giving advice on hitting. Oh held the job for three years, then became manager of the Giants at the beginning of the 1984 season.

As a traditional Japanese manager, Oh told his coaches to act like "demons" and work their players hour after hour. Many players were tired by midsummer, but Oh felt "the hot weather does in those players who haven't trained hard all along," and more rather than fewer workouts were required.

For three years Oh's Giants failed to win a pennant. They finished third in 1984, third in 1985, and second in 1986. Giants fans, used to victory, became impatient. They criticized Oh for making too many changes in the lineup, for trusting hunches too often, and for using pinch hitters too early in the game. A few players and coaches resented being led by a man half Chinese.

No one disputed Oh's dedication. When his father died in 1985, Oh took just half a day off to attend the funeral, then caught the bullet train to Nagoya to arrive in time for the night game.

On October 24, 1985, on the last day of the season, Randy Bass, an American playing for the Hanshin (Osaka) Tigers, had hit 54 home runs, one short of Oh's record. In the final game, with Oh looking on, Giants pitchers intentionally walked Bass four times with balls that were way outside. Bass never had a chance to tie Oh's record.

Oh denied that he had ordered his pitchers to walk Bass. No doubt a coach did. The fact remains that Oh could have stopped the walks if he had wanted to. Although fans like the power hitting of American players (limited to two per team), Oh, like most Japanese managers, regards them as a nuisance. A future "world series between Japan and the United States is impossible with [non-Asians] on our teams."

When the Giants finally won a pennant in 1987, Oh cried tears of joy. Then they lost to the Seibu (suburban Tokyo) Lions in the Japan Series. The next year they finished second, and after five years without a series championship Oh was obliged to resign.

During the early 1990s Oh started the World Children's Baseball Fair, a charity that brings children from different countries together to play baseball. He turned down several offers to manage other teams out of loyalty to the Giants.

By 1995, however, Oh felt he had been away from professional baseball long enough, and agreed to manage the Daiei Hawks, a team in the Pacific League based in Fukuoka, on the island of Kyushu. Daiei is a supermarket and department store chain.

Perhaps one day Oh will turn the Hawks around, but his first four years as a manager have not been successful. With mediocre pitching, the Hawks finished in fifth place in 1995, sixth (and last) place in 1996, fifth place in 1997, and fourth place in 1998.

No matter how Oh's career as a manager turns out, few would deny that his *doryoku* (effort), *nin* (constancy), and use of aikido made him the greatest player in the history of Japanese baseball.

Ueshiba

OH'S TEACHER, Ueshiba Morihei, the founder of aikido, was born on December 14, 1883, in the town of Tanabe, seventy miles (115 km) south of Osaka. He was the only son in a family of five children. His father was a wealthy farmer and a member of the town council. His mother was deeply religious, and told him stories about local Shinto gods.

At seven Ueshiba began school at a temple. He studied the Chinese classics and Shingon Buddhist visualization, a technique where one thinks of a deity, then tries to merge with the image. He was a frail child, so his father encouraged him to hike in the hills.

When Ueshiba was twelve, he watched helplessly while his father was beaten up several times by thugs who worked for a political opponent. He swore that someday, no matter what it took, he would be strong enough to defeat any attack he encountered. Ironically the martial art of peace began with a boy's anger.

At an abacus academy Ueshiba was so good that he became an instructor by the time he graduated at fifteen. The next year he began work as an auditor at a local tax office, but did not like the job because in his heart he always sided with the taxpayer.

At eighteen Ueshiba opened a small school supply and stationery store in Tokyo with money from his father. He also studied jujutsu at night, but after about nine months contracted beriberi and had to return to Tanabe to recover. In 1902 he married twenty-one-year-old Itokawa Hatsu, a distant relative with a sunny smile whom he had known since childhood. Their marriage was happy, and they had one daughter and three sons, though only one boy reached adulthood.

When war with Russia broke out in 1904, Ueshiba prepared for military service by lifting heavy boulders and running 2½ miles (4 km) a day. Nevertheless the army rejected him because he was only 5 feet 1½ inches (156 cm) tall, and the minimum height was 5 feet 2 inches (157 cm). Determined to enlist, he spent hours hanging from a tree with weights attached to his legs, and after several months was finally a half-inch taller.

In the army he became a man of iron. On long marches he picked up the backpacks of stragglers and still was the first to finish. He was outstanding at fighting with a bayonet. Though he was shipped to Manchuria in 1905, he never saw action because his father had pulled strings to keep him away from battle.

After the war Ueshiba worked on his father's farm and trained so hard in jujutsu that his father converted a barn into a dojo. He earned a license to teach jujutsu in 1908 and also studied kendo. Sometimes he spent an entire day in the mountains practicing cuts with his wooden sword.

Tanabe was an overcrowded town with many rice farmers and fishermen. To make a better living Ueshiba decided to take part in a government plan to settle Hokkaido, the northernmost and least populated of Japan's main islands. He recruited eighty-three other pioneers, and together in the spring of 1912 they sailed to the island's northeast coast, on the Sea of Okhotsk, where bitter winds blow in from Siberia.

For three years grain harvests were poor, and the settlers lived on potatoes, fish, and wild vegetables. Ueshiba cleared land with custom-made tools that were heavier than usual, to make himself stronger. He also chopped trees, uprooted stumps, and constructed buildings and sanitation facilities. By 1915 harvests had improved, and the lumber and dairy businesses were thriving.

One day Ueshiba heard that Takeda Sokaku, one of the three or four best martial artists of his time, was teaching at a nearby inn. He rushed to enroll in his ten-day course, signed up for another ten days, then invited Takeda to his village and built him a house. Takeda was illiterate and ill tempered, and loved to fight and kill outlaws in the "wild north" of rural Hokkaido. He was also the master of a kind of jujutsu known as *daito-ryu*, in which he used timing and breath to focus an almost unlimited amount of *ki* power. Once at a public bath he broke the ribs of six attacking thugs by projecting his *ki* into a wet towel. (The reader can get a quick appreciation of *ki* by projecting energy into his arm so that it becomes difficult to bend.)

For four years Ueshiba rose at three A.M., started a fire to warm Takeda's room, prepared a bath, bathed him, served him breakfast (and dinner), and massaged him several times a day. In return, for an additional fee, he received two hours of private lessons. By 1919, however, Ueshiba had grown tired of serving his arrogant master and perhaps, also, of Hokkaido. When a telegram told him that his father was ill, he decided that it was time to return to Tanabe.

On the way home Ueshiba stopped at Ayabe, one hour northwest of Kyoto, the headquarters of a new religion called Omoto. Its leader was a charismatic man named Deguchi Onisaburo, who saw himself as the instrument of a Shinto god and hoped to establish an era of world peace. At its peak in the 1920s, the movement had two million followers. Ueshiba was impressed by the sect's organic farming and meditation techniques, and after his father died in 1920 he decided to move to Ayabe with his family. Perhaps he was influenced by his father's last words, "Live the way you really want."

His wife was aghast. "What do you mean, the gods are calling you?" she asked. "Are those gods going to pay you a salary?" As an insurance policy, Ueshiba bought a three-year supply of rice.

Ueshiba spent mornings farming organically. In the afternoon he trained a group of bodyguards to protect Deguchi, and also built a dojo to teach the martial arts to other followers of Omoto. In 1922 he started teaching his own martial art, calling it *aiki bujutsu* (martial art for the harmony of physical and spiritual energy). Later he changed the word *bujutsu* (martial art) to *budo* (martial path), and, finally, to just *do* (path) to emphasize aikido's peaceful nature. News of aikido's effectiveness spread to a nearby navy base, and soon officers as well as sailors were taking his classes.

In 1924 Ueshiba accompanied Deguchi as his chief bodyguard on a trip to Inner (Chinese) Mongolia, where Deguchi proclaimed himself the "Rising Sun Dalai Lama" and tried to enlist Mongolians in establishing *shambhala*, heaven on earth. Neither Deguchi nor Ueshiba were aware that they were being used by right-wing Japanese to stir up trouble in China, and the trip ended disastrously when a local warlord put them in chains. They were saved from execution only by the intervention of a Japanese diplomat.

Back home in 1925, Ueshiba defeated a kendo champion by dodging each one of his sword thrusts. He later said that he sensed his opponent's movements before they were executed. After the match he went to a well and washed himself. Suddenly he recalled;

A golden spirit sprang up from the ground and veiled my body. . . . I was able to hear the whispering of the birds, and was clearly aware of the mind of God. . . . I was enlightened: the source of the martial arts is God's love—the spirit of loving protection for all beings. Endless tears of joy streamed down my cheeks.

Ueshiba described his vision in a religious framework. Whatever he experienced, it helped him develop a sixth sense of anticipation that made him an invincible martial artist. From then on, there is no record of anyone ever challenging Ueshiba and succeeding.

In 1925 and 1926 Ueshiba made several trips to Tokyo to teach aikido to wealthy students, including some princes and their bodyguards. Out of respect for the Imperial family, Ueshiba tossed the princes out and away rather than down on their rear ends. In 1927, with Deguchi's blessing, Ueshiba moved to Tokyo to teach full-time. Soon after his arrival he faced forty military cadets at once and sent them all flying. In 1930 he had a visit from Kano Jigoro, the founder of modern judo, who said, "This is the ideal martial art." Kano assigned two of his best students to learn aikido.

The following year Ueshiba opened a permanent dojo and accepted about thirty live-in students, some of them women. They woke at five A.M., kept the dojo spotless, and trained five hours a day. The workouts were so rigorous that they called their home "hell dojo," but one student recalled, "It wasn't hell, it was heaven, because Ueshiba was always with us and the training was so wonderful."

By the mid-1930s Ueshiba was famous. He taught at the Naval Academy, the Military Staff College, the Osaka Police Academy, the Japan Industrial Club, and the offices of the *Asahi Shimbun* newspaper. He also opened new dojos in Tokyo, Osaka, and Kyoto, and posed for three thousand photographs to help illustrate a textbook.

In 1939 Ueshiba was challenged by a huge well-known sumo wrestler named Tenryu. In a rare display of the depth of his *ki* power, Ueshiba pinned him with a single finger. Tenryu later became one of his best pupils.

After Japan attacked the United States in December 1941, Ueshiba had few students. News of war often made him physically ill, and he was particularly angry when the government asked that his organization become part of the Greater Japan Martial Virtue Association. Japan's military leaders, he told his son, "are a bunch of fools who strut about displaying their violence . . . they misrepresent the martial arts as a tool for power struggles . . . and they want to use me toward this end."

Ueshiba refused to let a wartime bureaucracy swallow his martial art of peace, as if his art were just another collection of fighting techniques. To preserve the spiritual quality of aikido, he resigned all of his teaching positions in 1942 and moved to Iwama, a village in the forest 100 miles (160 km) northeast of Tokyo, where he had bought 17 acres (6.6 hectares) of land.

Ueshiba built a small cottage, cleared some land, and resumed farming, which he had missed while living in Tokyo. He built an outdoor dojo, and, more important, an *aiki* shrine honoring forty-three martial deities. When a master carpenter completed the Shinto shrine in 1943, Ueshiba was moved to tears.

After the war ended in 1945, students were still few in number because food was scarce and no one wanted to waste energy on athletic pursuits. In Tokyo thirty families whose homes had been destroyed lived in the main dojo; the last family did not leave until well into the 1950s. Worst of all, the Allied occupation authorities banned every martial art except karate, which they mistakenly considered to be a form of Chinese boxing.

For two and a half years students practiced aikido in secret in the forest at Iwama. Finally, in 1948, the government allowed the Aikikai Foundation, which had run the Tokyo dojo, to resume its activities. While Ueshiba's son, Kisshomaru, took over the administration, Ueshiba remained in Iwama—farming, praying, growing a long beard, and, always, practicing new techniques.

In the 1950s Ueshiba often traveled to new dojos at college and company gymnasiums, and stressed aikido's spiritual side. Sometimes while traveling he refused to board a train if he felt that its electric power was interfering with his *ki*.

Although Ueshiba taught classes at dojos, he did not give a public demonstration of aikido until 1956, when he performed several techniques on the roof of a department store in Tokyo. Soon he gave more demonstrations, but if he saw *yakuza* (gangsters) in the audience, he canceled the show abruptly.

During the 1950s aikido spread to France, where it was seen as a dynamic form of Zen, although in fact aikido has nothing to do with Zen. Aikido also became popular in Hawaii, and in 1961 Ueshiba spent forty days teaching at dojos throughout the state.

In the 1960s, as aikido expanded around the world, Ueshiba sometimes gave talks that were unintelligibly mystical. He taught fewer classes, and in 1968 began suffering from liver cancer. In his last days he declined surgery and refused to be helped to the bathroom. When some of his students tried to help anyway, he literally threw them out the door.

Ueshiba died at home in Iwama on April 26, 1969. He was eighty-five. Since then Ueshiba's portrait has hung prominently in every aikido dojo in the world, and students both begin and end their training with a bow of thanks in his direction.

Selected Bibliography

Chapter 1

Roberts, John G., *Mitsui: Three Centuries of Japanese Business*, New York, Tokyo: Weatherhill, 1973, 1991; Russell, Oland D., *The House of Mitsui*, Boston: Little, Brown, 1939; Morikawa, Hidemasa, *Zaibatsu: The Rise and Fall of Family Enterprise Groups in Japan*, Tokyo: University of Tokyo Press, 1992; Yoshino, M. Y., and Lifson, Thomas B., *The Invisible Link: Japan's Sogo Shosha and the Organization of Trade*, Cambridge, Massachusetts: The MIT Press, 1989; Mitsui Gomei Kaisha, *The House of Mitsui: A Record of Three Centuries*, Tokyo: privately published, 1933; Eli, Max, *Japan Inc.: Global Strategies of Japanese Trading Corporations*, translated from the German by Michael Capone, Tristam Carrington-Windo, and Charles Foot, London: McGraw-Hill, 1990; *General Trading Companies: A Comparative and Historical Study*, edited by Yonekawa Shin'ichi, Tokyo: United Nations University Press, 1990; *The Mitsui Bank: A History of the First 100 Years*, Japan Business History Institute, editors, Tokyo: Mitsui Bank, 1976; Kearns, Robert L., *Zaibatsu America: How Japanese Firms Are Colonizing Vital U.S. Industries*, New York: The Free Press, 1992; Tamaki, Norio, *Japanese Banking: A History 1859–1959*, Cambridge, England: Cambridge University Press, 1995.

Chapter 2

Mishima, Yasuo, *The Mitsubishi: Its Challenge and Strategy*, translated by Emiko Yamaguchi, Greenwich, Connecticut, London: JAI Press Inc., 1989; Wray, William D., *Mitsubishi and the N.Y.K. 1870–1914: Business Strategy in the Japanese Shipping Industry*, Cambridge, Massachusetts: Harvard University Press, 1984; Morikawa, Hidemasa, *Zaibatsu: The Rise and Fall of Family Enterprise Groups in Japan*, Tokyo: University of Tokyo Press, 1992; Hemphill, Elizabeth Anne, *The Least of These: Miki Sawada and Her Children*, New York: Weatherhill, 1980; Young, Alexander K., *The Sogo Shosha: Japan's Multinational Trading Companies*, Tokyo: Charles E. Tuttle Company, 1979; Tsurumi, Yoshi, *Sogoshosha: Engines of Export-Based Growth*, Montreal: L'Institut de Recherches Politiques, 1980; Fukasaku, Yukiko, *Technology and Industrial Development in Pre-war Japan: Mitsubishi Nagasaki Shipyard, 1884–1934*, London: Routledge, 1992; Miyashita, Kenichi, and Russell, David W., *Keiretsu: Inside the Hidden Conglomerates*, New York: McGraw Hill, 1994; Yoshino, M. Y., and Lifson, Thomas B., *The Invisible Link: Japan's Sogo Shosha and the Orga-*

nization of Trade, Cambridge, Massachusetts: The MIT Press, 1989; Rafferty, Kevin, *Inside Japan's Power Houses*, London: Weidenfeld & Nicolson, 1995.

Chapter 3

Kotter, John P., *Matsushita Leadership: Lessons from the 20th Century's Most Remarkable Entrepreneur*, New York: The Free Press, 1997; Gould, Rowland, *The Matsushita Phenomenon*, Tokyo: Diamond Sha, 1970; Matsushita, Konosuke, *Quest for Prosperity: The Life of a Japanese Industrialist*, Tokyo: PHP Institute, 1988; Matsushita, Konosuke, *As I See It*, Tokyo: PHP Institute, 1989; Matsushita, Konosuke, *Not for Bread Alone*, Kyoto: PHP Institute, 1984; *Matsushita Konosuke, His Life and Legacy*, Tokyo: PHP Institute, 1994; Pascale, Richard T., and Athos, Anthony G., *The Art of Japanese Management, Applications for American Executives*, New York: Simon and Schuster, 1981; Kamioka, Kazuyoshi, *Japanese Business Pioneers*, Singapore: Times Books International, 1988; Yamashita, Toshihiko, *The Panasonic Way: From a Chief Executive's Desk*, translated by Frank Baldwin, Tokyo, New York: Kodansha International, 1989; Sheba, Togo, *Konosuke Matsushita, Portrait of a Japanese Business Magnate*, Tokyo: The Rengo Press, 1969; Lardner, James, *Fast Forward: Hollywood, the Japanese and the Onslaught of the VCR*, New York, London: W. W. Norton, 1987.

Chapter 4

Tashima, Kazuo, *My Personal History*, a collection of twenty-six newspaper articles in the (Tokyo) *Nippon Keizai Shimbun* in the summer of 1983, first draft of a translation made by the Office of the Chairman, Minolta Co., Ltd.; Kusumoto, Sam, with Murray, Edmund P., *My Bridge to America: Discovering the New World for Minolta*, New York: E. P. Dutton, 1989; Jacobson, Gary, and Hillkirk, John, *Xerox: American Samurai*, New York: Macmillan, 1986; Condax, Philip, Tano, Masahiro, Hibi, Takashi, and Fujimura, William, *The Evolution of the Japanese Camera*, Rochester, New York: International Museum of Photography at George Eastman House, 1984; Kamioka, Kazuyoshi, *Japanese Business Pioneers*, Union City, California: Heian International, 1988; *Japanese Business Success: The Evolution of a Strategy*, edited by Takeshi Yuzawa, London: Routledge, 1994; *The Canon Handbook*, Tokyo: Canon Inc., Public Relations Dept., 1994.

Chapter 5

Sanders, Sol, *Honda: The Man and His Machines*, Boston: Little, Brown, 1975; *Good Mileage: The High-Performance Business Philosophy of Soichiro Honda*, Tokyo: The NHK Group, NHK Publishing, 1996; Sakiya, Tetsuo, *Honda Motor: The Men, the Management, the Machines*, Tokyo: Kodansha International, 1987; Shook, Robert L., *Honda: An American Success Story*, New York: Prentice Hall, 1988; Mair, Andrew, *Honda's Global Local*

Corporation, London, New York: St. Martin's Press, 1994; Mito, Setsuo, *The Honda Book of Management*, London, Atlantic Highlands, New Jersey: The Athlone Press, 1990; Kazuyoshi, Kamioka, *Japanese Business Pioneers*, Union City, California: Heian International, 1988; Shimokawa, Koichi, *The Japanese Automobile Industry, a Business History*, London, Atlantic Highlands, New Jersey: The Athlone Press, 1990; Gibney, Frank, *Miracle by Design: The Real Reason Behind Japan's Economic Success*, New York: Times Books, 1982; Gelsanliter, David, *Jump Start: Japan Comes to the Heartland*, Tokyo, New York: Kodansha International, 1992; Ramsey, Douglas, *The Corporate Warriors: Six Classic Cases in American Business*, Boston: Houghton Mifflin, 1987.

Chapter 6

Interview with Kobayashi Koji based on written questions from the author, courtesy of NEC's Office of Corporate Communications.

Kobayashi, Koji, *Rising to the Challenge: The Autobiography of Koji Kobayashi*, Tokyo: Harcourt Brace Jovanovich Japan, 1989; Kobayashi, Koji, *The Rise of NEC: How the World's Greatest C&C Company Is Managed*, Cambridge, Massachusetts: Blackwell, 1991; Kobayashi, Koji, *Computers and Communications: A Vision of C&C*, Cambridge, Massachusetts: The MIT Press, 1986; *NEC Corporation: The First 80 Years*, Tokyo: NEC Corporation, 1984; Porter, Michael, and Wells, John, *NEC Corporation*, Boston: Harvard Business School Case Study No. 2-386-129, 1985; Iansiti, Marco, and Lee, Hyungoh, *NEC*, Boston: Harvard Business School Case Study No. 9-693-095, 1993; Forester, Tom, *Silicon Samurai: How Japan Conquered the World's I.T. Industry*, Cambridge, Massachusetts: Blackwell, 1993; *Competitive Edge: The Semiconductor Industry in the U.S. and Japan*, edited by Daniel I. Okimoto, Takuo Sugano, and Franklin B. Weinstein, Stanford, California: Stanford University Press, 1984; Fransman, Martin, *Japan's Computer and Communications Industry: The Evolution of Industrial Giants and Global Competitiveness*, Oxford, Oxford University Press, 1995; Cusumano, Michael, *Japan's Software Factories: A Challenge to U.S. Management*, New York, Oxford: Oxford University Press, 1991; Fransman, Martin, *The Market and Beyond: Information Technology in Japan*, Cambridge, England: Cambridge University Press, 1990.

Chapter 7

Interview with Toyoda Eiji, loosely based on written questions from the author; courtesy of Toyota's Public Affairs Division.

Cusumano, Michael A., *The Japanese Automobile Industry: Technology and Management at Nissan and Toyota*, Cambridge, Massachusetts: Harvard University Press, 1985, 1991; Toyoda, Eiji, *Toyota: Fifty Years in Motion*, Tokyo, New York: Kodansha International,

1985, translated 1987; Womack, James P., Jones, Daniel T., and Roos, Daniel, *The Machine That Changed the World*, New York: HarperCollins, 1990; Togo, Yukiyasu, and Wartman, William, *Against All Odds: The Story of the Toyota Motor Corporation and the Family That Created It*, New York: St. Martin's Press, 1993; *Kanban, Just-in-Time at Toyota*, edited by the Japan Management Assoc., David J. Lu, translator, Cambridge, Massachusetts: Productivity Press, 1989; Ohno, Taiichi, *Toyota Production System: Beyond Large-Scale Production*, Cambridge, Massachusetts: Productivity Press, 1988; Ohno, Taiichi, with Mito, Setsuo, *Just-in-Time for Today and Tomorrow*, translated by Joseph P. Schmelzeis, Jr., Cambridge, Massachusetts: Productivity Press, 1986; Monden, Yasuhiro, *Toyota Production System: An Integrated Approach to Just-in-Time*, Norcross, Georgia: Industrial Engineering and Management Press, 1993; *Engineered in Japan: Japanese Technology-Management Practices*, Liker, Jeffrey, Ettlie, John, and Campbell, John, editors, Oxford: Oxford University Press, 1995; *Toyota: A History of the First 50 Years*, Toyota City, Japan: Toyota Motor Corporation, 1988; Kamiya, Shotaro, with Elliott Thomas, *My Life with Toyota*, Toyota City, Japan: Toyota Motor Sales Company, 1978; Keller, Maryann, *Collision: GM, Toyota, Volkswagen and the Race to Own the 21st Century*, New York: Currency/Doubleday, 1993.

Chapter 8

Morita, Akio, with Reingold, Edwin M. and Shimomura, Mitsuko, *Made in Japan: Akio Morita and Sony*, New York: E. P. Dutton, 1986; Lyons, Nick, *The Sony Vision*, New York: Crown Publishers, 1976; Barnet, Richard J., and Cavanagh, John, *Global Dreams, Imperial Corporations and the New World Order*, New York: Simon & Schuster, 1994; *Genryu (Origin)*, edited by the Sony Corporation, Tokyo: Sony Corporate Communications, 1996; Kamioka, Kazuyoshi, *Japanese Business Pioneers*, Union City, California, Heian International, 1988; Collins, James C., and Porras, Jerry I., *Built to Last: Successful Habits of Visionary Companies*, New York: Harper Business, 1994; Morita, Akio, and Ishihara, Shintaro, *The Japan That Can Say No, as Excerpted from the Congressional Record*, Washington: The Jefferson Educational Foundation, 1990; Lardner, James, *Fast Forward: Hollywood, the Japanese, and the Onslaught of the VCR*, New York, London: W. W. Norton, 1987; Griffin, Nancy, and Masters, Kim, *Hit and Run: How John Peters and Peter Guber Took Sony for a Ride in Hollywood*, New York: Simon and Schuster, 1996; Malnight, Thomas W., and Yoshino, Michael Y., *Sony Corporation: Globalization*, Boston: Harvard Business School Case Services, 1990; Drucker, Peter, editor, *Preparing Tomorrow's Business Leaders Today*, Englewood Cliffs, New Jersey: Prentice-Hall, Inc., 1969.

Chapter 9

The Tale of Genji, Edward G. Seidensticker, translator, New York: Knopf, 1976, 1996; *The Tale of Genji*, Edward G. Seidensticker, translator, New York: Random House Vintage

Books, 1985; *Genji Monogatari*, Suematsu, Kencho, translator, Tokyo: Charles Tuttle, 1974, 1993; Bowring, Richard, *Murasaki Shikibu: Her Diary and Poetic Memoirs*, Princeton, New Jersey: Princeton University Press, 1982; *The Diary of Lady Murasaki*, translated and introduced by Bowring, Richard, London: Penguin Books, 1996; *The Tale of Genji*, Volumes I and II, Waley, Arthur, translator, Boston: Houghton Mifflin, 1935; *The Tale of Genji*, Waley, Arthur, translator, Garden City, New York: Doubleday Anchor Books, Garden City, 1955; Keene, Donald, *Seeds in the Heart: Japanese Literature from Earliest Times to the Late Sixteenth Century*, New York: Henry Holt & Co., 1993; Puette, William J., *The Tale of Genji, a Reader's Guide*, Tokyo: Charles Tuttle & Co., 1993; Morris, Ivan, *The World of the Shining Prince: Court Life in Ancient Japan*, New York: Penguin Books, 1979; Mulhern, Chieko Irie, editor, *Heroic with Grace: Legendary Women of Japan*, Armonk, New York: M. E. Sharpe, Inc., 1991; Keene, Donald, *Travelers of a Hundred Ages*, New York: Henry Holt, 1989; *Genji & Heike: Selections from "The Tale of Genji" and "The Tale of Heike,"* translated, with introductions, by McCullough, Helen Craig Stanford, California: Stanford University Press, 1994; *Ukifune: Love in the Tale of Genji*, New York: Columbia University Press, 1982; *The Ink Dark Moon: Love Poems by Ono no Komachi and Izumi Shikibu*, translated by Hirshfield, Jane, and Aratani, Mariko, New York: Random House Vintage Books, 1990.

Chapter 10

Castile, Rand, *The Way of Tea*, New York, Tokyo: Weatherhill, 1971; Plutschow, Herbert E., *Historical Chanoyu*, Tokyo: Japan Times Ltd., 1986; Hammitzsch, Horst, *Zen in the Art of the Tea Ceremony*, translated from the German by Peter Lemesurier, New York: E. P. Dutton, 1988; *Tea in Japan: Essays on the History of Chanoyu*, edited by Varley, Paul, and Isao, Kumakura, Honolulu: University of Hawaii Press, 1989; *Sources of Japanese Tradition, Vol. I*, compiled by Tsunoda, Ryusaku, de Bary, William Theodore and Keene, Donald, New York: Columbia University Press, 1964; *Warlords, Artists, & Commoners: Japan in the Sixteenth Century*, edited by Elison, George, and Smith, Bardwell L., Honolulu: University of Hawaii Press, 1987; Okakura, Kazuko, *The Book of Tea*, New York, Tokyo: Kodansha International, 1906, 1991; Sadler, Arthur, *Cha-no-yu: The Japanese Tea Ceremony*, Tokyo, Rutland, Vermont: Charles Tuttle, 1934, 1962; Chikamatsu, Shigenori, *Stories from a Tearoom Window*, edited by Mori, Toshiko, translated by Mori, Kozaburo, Tokyo, Rutland, Vermont: Charles Tuttle, 1982; Sen, Soshitsu, *Chado: The Japanese Way of Tea*, New York, Tokyo: Weatherhill/Tankosha, 1979.

Chapter 11

Inoura, Yoshinobu, and Kawatake, Toshio, *The Traditional Theater of Japan*, New York: Weatherhill, 1971; Kincaid, Zoe, *Kabuki: The Popular Stage of Japan*, New York: Benjamin Blom, Inc., 1925, 1965; Bowers, Faubion, *Japanese Theatre*, New York: Hill and Wang,

1952, 1967; Chiyoko, Higuchi, *Her Place in the Sun*, translated by Rhoads, Sharon, Tokyo: The East Publications, 1973; Kominz, Laurence R., *The Stars Who Created Kabuki*, Tokyo, New York: Kodansha, 1997; *Kabuki: Five Classic Plays*, translated by Brandon, James R., Cambridge, Massachusetts: Harvard University Press, 1975; Brandon, James R., Malm, William P., and Shively, Donald H., *Studies in Kabuki: Its Acting, Music, and Historical Context*, Honolulu: East-West Center, The University Press of Hawaii, 1978.

FICTION:

Ariyoshi, Sawako, *Kabuki Dancer*, translated by Brandon, James R., Tokyo, New York: Kodansha International, 1994.

Chapter 12

Hamill, Sam, *The Essential Basho*, Boston: Shambhala Publications, 1998; Matsuo Basho, *The Narrow Road to the Deep North*, translated and with an introduction by Yuasa, Nobuyuki, London: Penguin, 1966; *A Haiku Journey*, translated and introduced by Britton, Dorothy, Tokyo, New York: Kodansha International, 1974, 1990; Matsuo Basho, *The Narrow Road to Oku*, translated by Keene, Donald, Tokyo: Kodansha International, 1996; *On Love and Barley: Haiku of Basho*, translated and with an introduction by Stryk, Lucien, London: Penguin, 1985; Ueda, Makoto, *Matsuo Basho*, New York: Kodansha International, 1990; *The Essential Haiku, Versions of Basho, Buson and Issa*, edited and translated by Haas, Robert, Hopewell, New Jersey: The Ecco Press, 1994; *Sources of Japanese Tradition Vol. I*, Tsunoda, Ryusaku, de Bary, William Theodore, and Keene, Donald, editors, New York: Columbia University Press, 1964; Hamill, Sam, *Basho's Ghost*, Seattle: Broken Moon Press, 1989; Yasuda, Kenneth, *The Japanese Haiku*, Tokyo: Charles Tuttle, 1957, 1985; *Basho and His Interpreters: Selected Hokku with Commentary*, compiled and translated by Ueda, Makoto, Stanford, California: Stanford University Press, 1992; Aitken, Robert, *A Zen Wave: Basho's Haiku and Zen*, New York, Tokyo: Weatherhill, 1978; Downer, Leslie, *On the Narrow Road*, New York: Summit Books, 1989.

Chapter 13

Major Plays of Chikamatsu, translated by Keene, Donald, New York: Columbia University Press, 1961, 1990; Shively, Donald H., *The Love Suicide at Amijima: A Study of the Japanese Domestic Tragedy by Chikamatsu Monzaemon*, Ann Arbor, Michigan: University of Michigan Center for Japanese Studies, 1953, 1991; Gerstle, C. Andrew, *Circles of Fantasy: Convention in the Plays of Chikamatsu*, Cambridge, Massachusetts: Harvard University Press, 1986; Keene, Donald, *The Battles of Coxinga: Chikamatsu's Puppet Play, Its Background and Importance*, London: Taylor's Foreign Press, 1951; Ando, Tsuruo, *Bunraku: The Puppet Theater*, New York: Weatherhill, 1967; Hironaga, Shuzaburo, *Bunraku:*

Japan's Unique Puppet Theater, revised by Warren-Knott, D., Tokyo: Tokyo News Service Ltd., 1964; Bowers, Faubion, *Japanese Theater*, New York: Hermitage House, 1952; Keene, Donald, *World Within Walls: Japanese Literature of the Pre-Modern Era*, New York: Holt, Rinehart and Winston, 1976; *Chushingura: Studies in the Kabuki and Puppet Theater*, edited by Brandon, James R., Honolulu: University of Hawaii Press, 1982; Keene, Donald, *No and Bunraku: Two Forms of Japanese Theater*, New York: Columbia University Press, 1990; Kominz, Laurence R., *The Stars Who Created Kabuki: Their Lives, Loves and Legacy*, Tokyo, New York: Kodansha International, 1997; Nishiyama Matsunosuke, *Edo Culture: Daily Life and Diversions in Urban Japan, 1600–1868*, translated by Groemer, Gerald, Honolulu: University of Hawaii Press, 1997.

Chapter 14

Hokusai, Kondo, Ichitaro, editor, and Grilli, Elise, author of the English text, Rutland, Vermont: Charles Tuttle, 1955; Hillier, J., *Hokusai: Printings, Drawings and Woodcuts*, New York: Phaidon Publishers Inc., 1955; Ripley, Elizabeth, *Hokusai*, Philadelphia: J. B. Lippincott, 1968; Lane, Richard, *Hokusai: Life and Work*, New York: E. P. Dutton, 1989; Forrer, Matthi, editor, *Hokusai: Prints and Drawings*, Munich, Prestel-Verlag, 1991; Forrer, Matthi, editor, *Hokusai*, New York: Rizzoli, 1989; Kobayashi, Tadashi, *Ukiyo-E: An Introduction to Japanese Woodblock Prints*, Tokyo: New York, Kodansha International, 1982; Smith, Henry D., *Hokusai, One Hundred Views of Mt. Fuji*, New York: George Braziller Inc., 1988; *Hokusai Paintings: Selected Essays*, edited by Calza, Gian Carlo, Venice: University of Venice, 1994; *Catalog of the Exhibition of Paintings of Hokusai*, Geneva: Minkoff Reprint, 1901, 1973; Michener, James A., *The Hokusai Sketchbooks: Selections from the Manga*, Tokyo: Charles Tuttle, 1958; Eckstein, Gustav, *Hokusai: Play in Fourteen Scenes*, New York: Harper and Brothers, 1935; Strange, Edward, *The Colour-Prints of Hiroshige*, Geneva: Minkoff Reprint, 1925, 1973.

Chapter 15

SHINTO:

Anesaki, Masaharu, *History of Japanese Religion*, Tokyo: Charles E. Tuttle, 1963; Piggott, Juliet, *Japanese Mythology*, London: Paul Hamlyn, 1969; Picken, Stuart D. B., *Shinto: Japan's Spiritual Roots*, Tokyo, New York: Kodansha International, 1980; Kitagawa, Joseph M., *On Understanding Japanese Religion*, Princeton, New Jersey: Princeton University Press, 1987; Ellwood, Robert, and Pilgrim, Richard, Japanese Religion, A Cultural Perspective, Englewood Cliffs, New Jersey: Prentice-Hall, 1985; Earhart, H. Byron, *Japanese Religion: Unity and Diversity*, Belmont, California: Dickenson Publications, 1982; Ross, Floyd Hiatt, *Shinto: The Way of Japan*, Boston: Beacon Press, 1965; *Nihongi: Chronicles of Japan from the Earliest Times to A.D. 697*, (A.D. 720, translated by Aston, W. G., 1896) Tokyo: Charles Tuttle, 1971; *The Kojiki: Records of Ancient Matters*,

(A.D. 712) translated by Chamberlain, Basil Hall, Tokyo: Charles Tuttle, 1982; Kitabatake, Chikafusa, *A Chronicle of Gods and Sovereigns*, (mid-1300s) translated by Varley, H. Paul, New York: Columbia University Press, 1980; Farris, William Wayne, *Population, Disease and Land in Early Japan*, Cambridge, Massachusetts: Harvard University Press, 1985; Schwade, Arcadio, *Shinto-Bibliography in Western Languges*, Leiden, Netherlands: E. J. Brill, 1986.

PRINCE SHOTOKU AND THE SPREAD OF BUDDHISM:

The Cambridge History of Japan, Vol. I, Ancient Japan, edited by Brown, Delmer M., Cambridge, England: Cambridge University Press, 1993; Anesaki, Masaharu, *Prince Shotoku: The Sage Statesman and His Mahasattva Ideal*, Tokyo: Boonjudo Publishing House, 1948; Anesaki, Masaharu, *A History of Japanese Religion*, Tokyo: Charles Tuttle, 1963; *Sources of Japanese Tradition, Vol. I*, compiled by Tsunoda, Ryusaku, de Bary, William Theodore, and Keene, Donald, New York: Columbia University Press, 1964; Sansom, George, *A History of Japan to 1334*, Stanford, California: Stanford University Press, 1958, 1993; Kidder, J. Edward, *Early Buddhist Japan*, New York: Praeger, 1972; Asakawa, K., *The Early Institutional Life of Japan: A Study in the Reform of 645 A.D.*, New York, Paragon, (1903) 1963.

Chapter 16

Varley, Paul, *Warriors of Japan as Portrayed in the War Tales*, Honolulu: University of Hawaii Press, 1994; *Court and Bakufu in Japan: Essays in Kamakura History*, edited by Mass, Jeffrey P., Stanford, California: Stanford University Press, 1995; Sansom, George, *A History of Japan to 1334*, Stanford, California: Stanford Unversity Press, 1958, 1993; Farris, William Wayne, *Heavenly Warriors: The Evolution of Japan's Military, 500–1300*, Cambridge, Massachusetts: Harvard University Press, 1992; *Heroic with Grace: Legendary Women of Japan*, edited by Mulhern, Chieko Irie, Armonk, New York: M. E. Sharpe, 1991; Morris, Ivan, *The Nobility of Failure: Tragic Heroes in the History of Japan*, New York: Farrar, Straus & Giroux, 1975, 1994; *Yoshitsune: A Fifteenth-Century Chronicle*, translated with an introduction by McCullough, Helen Craig, Stanford, California: Stanford University Press, 1966; Mass, Jeffrey P., *Antiquity and Anachronism in Japanese History*, Stanford, California: Stanford University Press, 1992; Mass, Jeffrey P., *Warrior Government in Early Medieval Japan: A Study of the Kamakura Bakufu, Shugo and Jito*, New Haven, Connecticut: Yale University Press, 1974; *Selections from "The Tale of Genji" and "The Tale of the Heike,"* translated by McCullough, Helen C., Stanford, California: Stanford University Press, 1988.

Chapter 17

Sansom, George, *A History of Japan 1334–1615*, Stanford, California: Stanford University Press, 1961, 1991; McMullin, Neil, *Buddhism and the State in Sixteenth Century*

Japan, Princeton, New Jersey: Princeton University Press, 1984; Elison, George, and Smith, Bardwell L., editors, *Warlords, Artists & Commoners: Japan in the Sixteenth Century*, Honolulu: University of Hawaii Press, 1987; Berry, Mary Elizabeth, *Hideyoshi*, Cambridge, Massachusetts: Harvard University Press, 1990; Hall, John Whitney, Keiji, Nagahara, and Yamamura, Kozo, editors, *Japan Before Tokugawa: Political Consolidation and Economic Growth, 1500 to 1650*, Princeton, New Jersey: Princeton University Press, 1981; Nakane, Chie, and Oishi, Shinzaburo, editors, and Totman, Conrad, translator, *Tokugawa Japan: The Social and Economic Antecedents of Modern Japan*, Tokyo: University of Tokyo Press, 1991; Sugawa, Shigeo, *The Japanese Matchlock: A Story of the Tanegashima*, Tokyo: Dentsu, 1990.

Chapter 18

Berry, Mary Elizabeth, *Hideyoshi*, Cambridge, Massachusetts: Harvard University Press, 1990; Boscaro, Adriana, editor and translator, *101 Letters of Hideyoshi: The Private Correspondence of Toyotomi Hideyoshi*, Tokyo: Sophia University Press, 1975; Dening, Walter, *The Life of Toyotomi Hideyoshi*, Tokyo: Hokuseido Press, 1888, 1955; Sansom, George, *A History of Japan 1334–1615*, Stanford, California: Stanford University Press, 1961, 1991; Elison, George, and Smith, Bardwell L., editors, *Warlords, Artists & Commoners: Japan in the Sixteenth Century*, Honolulu: University of Hawaii Press, 1987; Hall, John Whitney, Keiji, Nagahara, and Yamamura, Kozo, editors, *Japan Before Tokugawa: Political Consolidation and Economic Growth, 1500 to 1650*, Princeton, New Jersey: Princeton University Press, 1981; McMullin, Neil, *Buddhism and the State in Sixteenth Century Japan*, Princeton, New Jersey: Princeton University Press, 1984.

FICTION:

Yoshikawa, Eiji, *Taiko: An Epic Novel of War and Glory in Feudal Japan*, translated by Wilson, William Scott, Tokyo, New York: Kodansha International, 1937, 1992.

Chapter 19

Totman, Conrad, *Tokugawa Ieyasu: Shogun*, Union City, California: Heian International Inc., 1983; Sadler, A. L., *The Maker of Modern Japan: The Life of Tokugawa Ieyasu*, Tokyo: Charles Tuttle, 1937, 1992; Sansom, George, *A History of Japan, 1334–1615*, Stanford, California: Stanford University Press, 1961; Sansom, George, *A History of Japan, 1615–1867*, Stanford, California: Stanford University Press, 1963; Totman, Conrad, *Politics in the Tokugawa Bakufu, 1600–1843*, Cambridge, Massachusetts: Harvard University Press, 1967; *Tokugawa Japan: The Social and Economic Antecedents of Modern Japan*, edited by Nakane, Chie and Oishi, Shinzaburo, Tokyo: University of Tokyo Press, 1991; *Sources of Japanese Tradition, Vol. I*, compiled by Tsunoda, Ryusaku, de Bary, William Theodore, and Keene, Donald, New York: Columbia University Press, 1964; Totman, Conrad, *Early Modern Japan*, Berkeley, California: University of California Press, 1993; *Japan Before Tokugawa: Political Consolidation and Economic Growth, 1500 to 1650*, edited by Hall, John Whitney, Keiji, Nagahara, and Yamamura, Kozo, Princeton, New Jersey: Princeton University Press, 1981; Dunn, Charles J., *Everyday Life in Traditional Japan*, Tokyo: Charles Tuttle, 1969, 1990; Vlastos, Stephen, *Peasant Protests and Uprisings in Tokugawa Japan*, Berkeley, California: University of California Press, 1986.

FICTION:

Clavell, James, *Shōgun*, New York: Dell, 1975, 1986.

Chapter 20

Allyn, John, *The Forty-Seven Ronin Story*, Tokyo, Rutland, Vermont: Charles Tuttle, 1970, 1992; Takeda Izumo II, Miyoshi Shoraku, and Namiki Senryu, *Chushingura (The Treasury of Loyal Retainers)*, translated by Keene, Donald, New York: Columbia University Press, 1971; Mitford, A. B., *Tales of Old Japan*, Tokyo and Rutland, Vermont: Charles Tuttle, 1871, 1991; Statler, Oliver, *Japanese Inn*, Honolulu: University of Hawaii Press, 1961, 1982; Benedict, Ruth, *The Chrysanthemum and the Sword: Patterns of Japanese Culture*, Rutland, Vermont, Tokyo: Charles Tuttle 1946, 1984; *Sources of Japanese Tradition, Vol. I*, compiled by Tsunoda, Ryusaku, de Bary, William Theodore, and Keene, Donald, New York: Columbia University Press, 1964; Nitobe, Inazo, *Bushido, The Soul of Japan*, Tokyo: Charles Tuttle, 1970.

Chapter 21

Iwata, Masakazu, *Okubo Toshimichi: The Bismarck of Japan*, Berkeley: University of California Press, 1964; Beasley, W. G., *The Meiji Restoration*, Stanford, California: Stanford University Press, 1972; Akamatsu, Paul, *Meiji 1868: Revolution and Counter-Revolution in Japan*, translated from the French by Kochan, Miriam, New York: Harper & Row, 1972; *Personality in Japanese History*, edited by Craig, Albert M. and Shively, Donald H., Berkeley: University of California Press, 1970; *The Diary of Kido Takayoshi, Vol I: 1868–1871*, translated by Brown, Sidney Devere, and Hirota, Akiko, Tokyo: University of Tokyo Press, 1983; *Japan in Transistion: From Tokugawa to Meiji*, edited by Jansen, Marius B., and Rozman, Gilbert, Princeton, New Jersey: Princeton University Press, 1986; Yates, Charles L., *Saigo Takamori: The Man Behind the Myth*, London: Kegan Paul International, 1995; Morris, Ivan, *The Nobility of Failure: Tragic Heroes in the History of Japan*, New York: Farrar, Straus & Giroux, 1975; Hamada, Kengi, *Prince Ito*, Tokyo: Sanseido, 1936; Norman, E. Herbert, *Japan's Emergence as a Modern State: Political and Economic Problems of the Meiji Period*, New York: Institute of Pacific Relations, 1940; *Origins of the Modern Japanese*

State: Selected Writings of E. H. Norman, edited by Dower, John W., New York: Pantheon Books, 1975; Craig, Albert M., *Choshu in the Restoration*, Cambridge, Massachusetts: Harvard University Press, 1961; Huber, Thomas M., *The Revolutionary Origins of Modern Japan*, Stanford, California: Stanford University Press, 1981; Hackett, Roger F., *Yamagata Aritomo in the Rise of Modern Japan 1838–1922*, Cambridge, Massachusetts: Harvard University Press, 1971; Totman, Conrad, *The Collapse of the Tokugawa Bakufu 1862–1868*, Honolulu: University of Hawaii Press, 1980; Smith, Thomas C., *Native Sources of Japanese Industrialization, 1750–1920*, Berkeley: University of California Press, 1988.

Chapter 22

Butow, Robert J. C., *Tojo and the Coming of the War*, Princeton: Princeton University Press, 1961; Browne, Courtney, *Tojo: The Last Banzai*, New York: Holt, Rinehart and Winston, 1967; Hoyt, Edwin P., *Warlord: Tojo Against the World*, Lanham, Maryland: Scarborough House, 1993; Togo, Shigenori, *The Cause of Japan*, translated from Japanese and edited by Fumihiko, Togo, and Blakeney, Ben Bruce, New York: Simon & Schuster, 1956; Toland, John, *The Rising Sun: The Decline and Fall of the Japanese Empire 1936–1945*, New York: Random House, 1970; Dower, John W., *War Without Mercy: Race and Power in the Pacific War*, New York: Pantheon, 1986; Shillony, Ben-Ami, *Politics and Culture in Wartime Japan*, Oxford: Clarendon Press, 1981; Edgerton, Robert. B., *Warriors of the Rising Sun: A History of the Japanese Military*, New York: W. W. Norton, 1997; Harries, Meirion, and Harries, Susan, *Soldiers of the Sun: The Rise and Fall of the Imperial Japanese Army*, New York: Random House, 1991; *The Japanese Wartime Empire, 1931–1945*, edited by Duus, Peer, Myers, Ramon H., and Peattie, Mark R., Princeton, New Jersey: Princeton University Press, 1996; Grew, Joseph, *Ten Years in Japan*, New York: Simon and Schuster, 1944; Guillain, Robert, *I Saw Tokyo Burning*, Garden City, New York: Doubleday, 1981, translated from the French by Byron, William; Harris, Sheldon H., *Factories of Death*, London: Routledge, Chapman & Hall, 1994; Daws, Gavan, *Prisoners of the Japanese: POWs of World War II in the Pacific*, New York: William Morrow, 1994; Minear, Richard H., *Victor's Justice: The Tokyo War Crimes Trial*, Tokyo: Charles Tuttle, 1971.

Chapter 23

BOOKS ON YAMAMOTO AND JAPAN'S MILITARY:

Agawa, Hiroyuki, *The Reluctant Admiral: Yamamoto and the Imperial Navy*, Tokyo, New York: Kodansha International, 1969, 1994; Hoyt, Edwin P., *Yamamoto: The Man Who Planned Pearl Harbor*, New York: McGraw-Hill, 1990; Potter, John Deane, *Yamamoto: The Man Who Menaced America*, New York: Viking, 1965; Hoyt, Edwin P., *Three Military Leaders: Togo, Yamamoto, Yamashita*, Tokyo, New York: Kodansha International, 1993; Glines, Carroll, *Attack on Yamamoto*, New York: Orion Books, 1990; Ito, Masanori, with Pineau, Roger, *The*

End of the Imperial Japanese Navy, translated by Kuroda, Andrew, and Pineau, Roger, New York: W. W. Norton, 1956; Toland, John, *The Rising Sun: The Decline and Fall of the Japanese Empire, 1936–1945*, New York: Random House, 1970; Edgerton, Robert B., *Warriors of the Rising Sun: A History of the Japanese Military*, New York: W. W. Norton, 1997; Dull, Paul S., *The Imperial Japanese Navy, 1941–1945*, Annapolis, Maryland: Naval Institute Press, 1978.

BOOKS ON PEARL HARBOR AND MIDWAY:

Prange, Gordon, with Goldstein, Donald and Dillon, Kathrine, *At Dawn We Slept: The Untold Story of Pearl Harbor*, New York: Viking, 1981; Prange, Gordon, with Goldstein, Donald, and Dillon, Kathrine, *Pearl Harbor: The Verdict of History*, New York, McGraw-Hill, 1986; Wohlstetter, *Pearl Harbor: Warning and Decision*, Stanford, California: Stanford University Press, 1962; Morison, Samuel Eliot, *A History of United States Naval Operations in the Pacific, Vol. III, The Rising Sun in the Pacific, 1931–April 1942*, Boston: Little, Brown, 1963; Lord, Walter, *Day of Infamy*, New York: Henry Holt, 1957; Clausen, Henry, and Lee, Bruce, *Pearl Harbor: Final Judgment*, New York: Crown, 1992; Prange, Gordon, with Goldstein, Donald, and Dillon, Kathrine, *Miracle at Midway*, New York, London: Penguin, 1982, 1983; Morison, Samuel Eliot, *History of the United States Naval Operations in World War II, Vol. IV, Coral Sea, Midway and Submarine Actions, May 1942–August 1942*, Boston: Little, Brown, 1964; Lord, Walter, *Incredible Victory*, New York: Harper & Row, 1967; Fuchida, Mitsuo, and Okumiya, Masatake, *Midway*, Annapolis, Maryland: Naval Institute Press, 1955.

Chapter 24

BOOKS ABOUT HIROHITO:

Large, Stephen S., *Emperor Hirohito and Showa Japan: A Political Biography*, London: Routledge, 1992; Mosley, Leonard, *Hirohito: Emperor of Japan*, Englewood Cliffs, New Jersey: Prentice-Hall, 1966; Kawahara, Toshiaki, *Hirohito and His Times: A Japanese Perspective*, Tokyo, New York: Kodansha International, 1990; Behr, Edward, *Hirohito: Behind the Myth*, New York, Villard Books, 1989, Hoyt, Edwin P., *Hirohito: The Emperor and the Man*, New York: Praeger, 1992; Kanroji, Osanaga, *Hirohito: An Intimate Portrait of the Japanese Emperor*, Los Angeles: Gateway Publishers, 1975; Large, Stephen S., *Emperors of the Rising Sun: Three Biographies*, Tokyo, New York: Kodansha International, 1997; Irokawa, Daikichi, *The Age of Hirohito: In Search of Modern Japan*, New York: Free Press, 1995; Bergamini, David, *Japan's Imperial Conspiracy*, New York: William Morrow, 1971.

BOOKS ABOUT TRUMAN'S DECISION TO DROP THE ATOMIC BOMB:

Allen, Thomas B., and Polmar, Norman, *Code-Name Downfall: The Secret Plan to Invade Japan — and Why Truman Dropped the Bomb*, New York: Simon and Schuster, 1995; Maddox, Robert James, *Weapons for Victory: The Hiroshima Decision Fifty Years Later,* Columbia, Missouri: University of Missouri Press, 1995; Skates, John Ray, *The Invasion of Japan: Alternative to the Bomb,* Columbia, South Carolina: University of South Carolina Press, 1994; Alperovitz, Gar, *The Decision to Use the Atomic Bomb and the Architecture of an American Myth,* New York: Knopf, 1995; Feis, Herbert, *Japan Subdued: The Atomic Bomb and the End of the War in the Pacific,* Princeton, New Jersey: Princeton University Press, 1961; Takaki, Ronald, *Hiroshima: Why America Dropped the Bomb,* Boston: Little, Brown, 1995.

BOOKS ABOUT JAPAN'S SURRENDER:

Toland, John, *The Rising Sun: The Decline and Fall of the Japanese Empire, 1936–1945,* New York: Random House, 1970; Butow, Robert J. C., *Japan's Decision to Surrender,* Stanford, California: Stanford University Press, 1954; Togo, Shigenori, *The Cause of Japan,* translated and edited by Togo Fumihiko and Blakeney, Ben Bruce, New York: Simon & Schuster, 1956; Lee, Bruce, *Marching Orders: The Untold Story of World War II,* New York: Crown Publishers, 1995; Harries, Merion, and Harries, Susie, *Soldiers of the Sun: The Rise and Fall of the Imperial Japanese Army,* New York: Random House, 1991; Morison, Samuel Eliot, *The Two-Ocean War: A Short History of the United States Navy in the Second World War,* Boston: Little, Brown, 1963.

Chapter 25

Dower, J. W., *Empire and Aftermath: Yoshida Shigeru and the Japanese Experience 1878–1954,* Cambridge, Massachusetts: Harvard University Press, 1988; Finn, Richard B., *Winners in Peace: MacArthur, Yoshida, and Postwar Japan,* Berkeley: University of California Press, 1992; Yoshida, Shigeru, *The Yoshida Memoirs: The Story of Japan in Crisis,* translated by Yoshida, Kenichi, Boston: Houghton Mifflin, 1962; Yoshida, Shigeru, *Japan's Decisive Century, 1867–1967,* New York: Praeger, 1967; Cohen, Theodore, *Remaking Japan: The American Occupation as New Deal,* New York: The Free Press, 1987; Dower, John W., *Japan in War and Peace: Selected Essays,* New York, New Press, 1993; Chapman, William, *Inventing Japan: The Making of a Postwar Civilization,* New York: Prentice Hall, 1991; Schaller, Michael, *The American Occupation of Japan: The Origins of the Cold War in Asia,* New York: Oxford: Oxford University Press; *Democratizing Japan: The Allied Occupation,* edited by Ward, Robert E., and Yoshikazo, Sakamoto, Honolulu: University of Hawaii Press, 1987; Manchester, William, *American Caesar: Douglas MacArthur 1880–1964,* Boston: Little, Brown, 1978; Schaller, Michael, *Douglas MacArthur: The Far-Eastern General,* New York, Oxford: Oxford University Press, 1989; Inoue, Kyoko, *MacArthur's Japanese Constitution: A Linguistic and Cultural Study of Its Making,* Chicago: University of Chicago Press, 1991; Kawai, Kazuo, *Japan's American Interlude,* Chicago: University of Chicago Press, 1960; Fearey, Robert A., *The Occupation of Japan, Second Phase: 1948–50,* New York: Macmillan, 1950; Ward, Robert E., and Schulman, Frank Joseph, *The*

Allied Occupation of Japan, 1945–52: An Annotated Bibliography of Western-Langauge Materials, Chicago: American Library Association, 1974.

Chapter 26

I am indebted to Ms. Kato Shidzue, who talked with me for three hours at her home in Tokyo.

Hopper, Helen M., *A New Woman of Japan: A Political Biography of Kato Shidzue*, Boulder, Colorado: Westview Press, 1996; Ishimoto, Baroness Shidzue, *Facing Two Ways: The Story of My Life*, Stanford, California: Stanford University Press, (1935) 1984; Beard, Mary R., *The Force of Women in Japanese History*, Washington, D.C.: Public Affairs Press, 1953; *The Occupation of Japan: Educational and Social Reform*, Burkman, Thomas W., editor, Norfolk, Virginia: Gatling Publishing Company, 1982 (chapter on Kato Shidzue by Helen M. Hopper); Robins-Mowry, Dorothy, *The Hidden Sun: Women of Modern Japan*, Boulder, Colorado: Westview Press, 1983; Coleman, Samuel, *Family Planning in Japanese Society: Traditional Birth Control in a Modern Culture*, Princeton, New Jersey: Princeton University Press, 1983; *Women of Japan and Korea: Continuity and Change*, edited by Gelb, Joyce, and Palley, Marian Lief, Philadelphia: Temple University Press, 1994; Totten, George Oakley III, *The Social Democratic Movement in Prewar Japan*, New Haven, Connecticut: Yale University Press, 1966; La Fleur, William A., *Liquid Life, Abortion and Buddhism in Japan*, Princeton, New Jersey: Princeton University Press, 1992; Hodge, Robert W., and Ogawa, Naohiro, *Fertility Change in Contemporary Japan*, Chicago: University of Chicago Press, 1991.

Chapter 27

Schlesinger, Jacob M., *Shadow Shoguns: The Rise and Fall of Japan's Postwar Political Machine*, New York: Simon & Schuster, 1997; Johnson, Chalmers, *Japan: Who Governs? The Rise of the Developmental State*, New York: W. W. Norton, 1995; Masumi, Junnosuke, *Contemporary Politics in Japan*, translated by Lonny E. Carlile, Berkeley: University of California Press, 1995; Curtis, Gerald L., *The Japanese Way of Politics*, New York: Columbia University Press, 1988; *Political Leadership in Contemporary Japan*, edited by Terry Edward MacDougall, Ann Arbor, Michigan: University of Michigan Press, 1982, chapter by Kent E. Calder; Van Wolferen, Karl, *The Enigma of Japanese Power: People and Politics in a Stateless Nation*, New York: Random House, 1990; Tanaka, Kakuei, *Building a New Japan: A Plan for the Japanese Archipelago*, translated by Simul International, Tokyo, The Simul Press, 1974; Reading, Brian, *Japan: The Coming Collapse*, New York: Harper Business, 1992; Woodall, Brian, *Japan Under Construction: Corruption, Politics, and Public Works*, Berkeley: University of California Press, 1996; Ramseyer, J. Mark, and Rosenbluth, Frances McCall, *Japan's Political Marketplace*, Cambridge, Massachusetts: Harvard University Press, 1993; Baerwald, Hans, *Party Politics in Japan*, Boston: Allen & Unwin, 1986; Noonan, John T., Jr., *Bribes*, Berkeley: University of California Press, 1984; Horsley, William, and Buckley, Roger, *Nippon, New Superpower: Japan Since 1945*, London: BBC Books, 1990; Harvey, Robert, *The Undefeated: The Rise, Fall and Rise of Modern Japan*, London: Macmillan, 1994; Hrebenar, Ronald J., *The Japanese Party System: From One-Party Rule to Coalition Government*, Boulder, Colorado: Westview Press, 1986; Ikuda, Tadahide, *Kanryo: Japan's Hidden Government*, Tokyo: NHK Publishing, 1995; Richardson, Bradley, *Japanese Democracy: Power, Coordination, and Performance*, New Haven, Connecticut: Yale University Press, 1997.

Chapter 28

The Autobiography of Yukichi Fukuzawa, revised translation by Kiyooka, Eiichi, New York: Columbia University Press, 1899, 1966; Blacker, Carmen, *The Japanese Enlightenment: A Study of the Writings of Fukuzawa Yukichi*, Cambridge: England, Cambridge University Press, 1964; *Fukuzawa Yukichi's An Encouragement of Learning*, translated, with an introduction, by Dilworth, David A., and Hirano, Umeyo, Tokyo: Sophia University Press, 1969; *Fukuzawa Yukichi on Japanese Women: Selected Works*, translated and edited by Kiyooka, Eiichi, Tokyo: University of Tokyo Press, 1988; Fukuzawa, Yukichi, *An Outline of a Theory of Civilization*, translated by Dilworth, David A., and Hurst, G. Cameron, Tokyo: Sophia University Press, 1973; *Fukuzawa Yukichi on Education: Selected Works*, translated and edited by Eiichi Kiyooka, Tokyo: Tokyo University Press, 1985; Miyamori, Asataro, *A Life of Mr. Fukuzawa*, Tokyo: Maruzen, 1902; Hwang, In K., *The Korean Reform Movement in the 1880's*, Cambridge, Massachusetts: Schenkman Publishing, 1978.

Chapter 29

Yu, Beongcheon, *Natsume Soseki*, New York: Twayne Publishers, 1969; McClellan, Edwin, *Two Japanese Novelists: Soseki and Toson*, Chicago: University of Chicago Press, 1969; Gessel, Van C., *Three Modern Novelists, Soseki, Tanizaki, Kawabata*, Tokyo, New York: Kodansha International, 1993; Keene, Donald, *Dawn to the West: Japanese Literature of the Modern Era, Fiction*, New York: Holt, Rinehart and Winston, 1984; Matsui, Sakuko, *Natsume Soseki as a Critic of English Literature*, Tokyo: Centre for East Asian Cultural Studies, 1975; Masao, Miyoshi, *Accomplices of Silence: The Modern Japanese Novel*, Berkeley: University of California Press, 1974; Soseki, Natsume, *Kokoro and Selected Essays*, novel translated by McClellan, Edwin, essays translated by Rubin, Jay, Lanham, New York, London: Madison Books, 1992; Soseki, Natsume, *Ten Nights of Dream*, translated with an introduction by Ito, Aiko, and Wilson, Graeme, Tokyo: Charles Tuttle, 1974; Turney, Alan, *Soseki's Development as a Novelist until 1907*, Tokyo: The Toyo Bunko, 1985; Soseki, Natsume, *And Then*, translated with an afterword by Field, Norma Moore, Tokyo: University of Tokyo Press, 1978; Ueda, Makoto, *Modern Japanese Writers and the Nature of Literature*, Stanford, California: Stanford University Press, 1976; *The World of Natsume Soseki*, Iijima, Takehisa and Vardaman, James M. editors, Tokyo: Kinseido, 1987.

Chapter 30

Liman, Anthony V., *A Critical Study of the Literary Style of Ibuse Masuji: As Sensitive as Waters*, Lewiston, New York and Queenston, Ontario: The Edwin Mellen Press, 1992; Treat, John Whittier, *Pools of Water, Pillars of Fire: The Literature of Ibuse Masuji*, Seattle: University of Washington Press, 1988; Lewell, John, *Modern Japanese Novelists: A Bio-graphical Dictionary*, New York and Tokyo: Kodansha International, 1993; Treat, John Whittier, *Writing Ground Zero: Japanese Literature and the Atomic Bomb*, Chicago: University of Chicago Press, 1995; *Approaches to the Modern Japanese Novel*, Tsuruta, Kinya, and Swann, Thomas, editors, Tokyo, Sophia University Press, 1976; *Two Stories by Ibuse Masuji*, translated and with a critical biography by Nikao, Kiyoaki, Tokyo: The Hoku-seido Press, 1970; Rimer, J. Thomas, *Modern Japanese Fiction and Its Traditions: An Intro-duction*, Princeton, New Jersey: Princeton University Press, 1978; Keene, Donald, *Dawn to the West: Japanese Literature in the Modern Era*, New York: Holt, Rinehart and Winston, 1984; Lifton, Robert Jay, *Death in Life:* Survivors of Hiroshima, New York: Random House, 1967 (Appendix on "Black Rain"); Bernard, Donald R., *The Life and Times of John Manjiro*, New York: McGraw Hill, 1972.

Chapter 31

I am indebted to the staff of the public library in the city of Onomichi, Hiroshima pre-fecture, for preparing a detailed chronology of Hayashi Fumiko's life.

Keene, Donald, *Dawn to the West: Japanese Literature of the Modern Era*, New York: Holt, Rinehart and Winston, 1984; *To Live and to Write: Selections by Japanese Women Writers, 1913–1938*, edited by Tanaka, Yukiko, Seattle: Seal Press, 1987; *Japanese Women Writers: A Bio-Critical Sourcebook*, edited by Mulhern, Chieko I., Westport, Connecticut: Green-wood Press, 1994; Mamola, Claire Zebroski, *Japanese Women Writers in English Transla-tion, an Annotated Bibliography*, New York: Garland, 1989; Vernon, Victoria V., *Daughters of the Moon: Wish, Will, and Social Constraint in Fiction by Modern Japanese Women*, Berke-ley: University of California Press, 1988; *Approaches to the Modern Short Story*, edited by Swann, Thomas E. and Tsuruta, Kinya, Tokyo: Waseda University Press, 1982; *Japanese Women Writers: Twentieth Century Short Fiction*, translated and edited by Lippit, Noriko Mizuta, and Selden, Kyoko Iriye, Armonk, New York: M. E. Sharpe, Inc., 1991.

Chapter 32

Nathan, John, *Mishima: A Biography*, Boston: Little, Brown, 1974; Stokes, Henry Scott, *The Life and Death of Yukio Mishima*, Tokyo: Charles Tuttle, 1985; Wolfe, Peter, *Yukio Mishima*, New York: Continuum, 1989; Yourcenar, Marguerite, *Mishima: A Vision of the*

Void, translated from the French by Manguel, Alberto in collaboration with the author, New York: Farrar, Straus, Giroux, 1986; Ueda, Makoto, *Modern Japanese Writers,* Stanford, California: Stanford University Press, 1976; Napier, Susan J., *Escape from the Wasteland: Romanticism and Realism in the Fiction of Mishima Yukio and Oe Kenzaburo,* Cambridge, Massachusetts: Harvard University Press, 1991; Lifton, Robert J., Shuichi, Kato, and Reich, Michael R., *Six Lives, Six Deaths: Portraits from Modern Japan,* New Haven, Connecticut: Yale University Press, 1979; Kimball, Arthur G., *Crisis in Identity and Contemporary Japanese Novels,* Tokyo, Rutland, Vermont: Charles Tuttle, 1973.

Chapter 33

I am grateful for telephone interviews with Mildred Tahara, associate professor of Japanese literature at the University of Hawaii, and friend and translator of Ariyoshi Sawako.

Selected Works by Ariyoshi Sawako, a forthcoming book compiled, edited, and translated by Tahara, Mildred; *Heroic with Grace: Legendary Women of Japan,* edited by Mulhern, Chieko Irie, Armonk, New York: M. E. Sharpe, Inc. chapter by Tahara, Mildred; Lewell, John, *Modern Japanese Novelists,* New York, Tokyo: Kodansha International, 1993; *Japanese Women Writers: A Bio-Critical Source Book,* edited by Mulhern, Chieko Irie, Westport, Connecticut: Greenwood Press, 1994; Shinya, Arai, *Shoshaman: A Tale of Corporate Japan,* Berkeley: University of California Press, 1991; Allen, Louis, *A Critique of Ariyoshi Sawako: Hanaoka Seishu No Tsuma,* London: British Association for Japanese Studies (Vol. 9), 1984.

Chapter 34

KAWABATA:

Gessel, Van C., *Three Modern Novelists: Soseki, Tanizaki, Kawabata,* Tokyo, New York: Kodansha International, 1993; Keene, Donald, *Dawn to the West: Japanese Literature in the Modern Era,* New York: Holt, Rinehart and Winston, 1984; Petersen, Gwenn Boardman, *The Moon in the Water: Understanding Tanizaki, Kawabata, and Mishima,* Honolulu: The University Press of Hawaii, 1979; Ueda, Makoto, *Modern Japanese Writers and the Nature of Literature,* Stanford, California: Stanford University Press, 1976; Vernon, Victoria V., *Daughters of the Moon,* Berkeley: University of California Press, 1988; Miyoshi, Masao, *Accomplices of Silence: The Modern Japanese Novel,* Berkeley: University of California Press, 1974.

OE:

Napier, Susan J., *Escape from the Wasteland: Romanticism and Realism in the Fiction of Mishima Yukio and Oe Kenzaburo,* Cambridge, Massachusetts: Harvard Univeristy Press, 1991; Wilson, Michiko N., *The Marginal World of Oe Kenzaburo: A Study in Themes and Techniques,* Armonk, New York: M. E. Sharpe, 1986; Oe, Kenzaburo *Teach Us to Outgrow*

Our Madness: Four Short Novels, translated and with an introduction by Nathan, John, New York: Grove Press, Inc., 1977; Lewell, John, *Modern Japanese Novelists: A Biographical Dictionary*, New York, Tokyo: Kodansha International, 1993; Treat, John Whittier, *Writing Ground Zero: Japanese Literature and the Atomic Bomb*, Chicago: University of Chicago Press, 1995; Pollack, David, *Reading Against Culture: Ideology and Narrative in the Japanese Novel*, Ithaca, New York: Cornell University Press, 1992; Oe, Kenzaburo, *Hiroshima Notes*, Tokyo: YMCA Press, 1965; Oe, Kenzaburo, *Japan, the Ambiguous, and Myself: The Nobel Prize Speech and Other Lectures*, Tokyo, New York: Kodansha International, 1995.

Chapter 35

Richie, Donald, *Ozu: His Life and Films*, Berkeley: University of California Press, 1974; Bordwell, David, *Ozu and the Poetics of Cinema*, Princeton, New Jersey: Princeton University Press, 1994; *Yasujiro Ozu: A Critical Anthology*, edited by Gillett, John, and Wilson, David, London: British Film Institute, 1976; Bock, Audie, *Japanese Film Directors*, Tokyo, New York: Kodansha International, 1985; *Reframing Japanese Cinema: Authorship, Genre, History*, edited by Nolletti, Jr., Arthur, and Desser, David, Bloomington, Indiana: Indiana University Press, 1992 (chapters by Kathe Geist and Donald Richie); Schrader, Paul, *Transcendental Style in Film: Ozu, Bresson, Dreyer*, New York: Da Capo, 1988; Richie, Donald, *Japanese Cinema: Film Style and National Character*, Garden City, New York: Doubleday, 1961; Anderson, Joseph, and Richie, Donald, *The Japanese Film: Art and Industry*, Princeton, New Jersey: Princeton University Press, 1959, 1982; Sato, Tadao, *Currents in Japanese Cinema*, translated by Barrett, Gregory, Tokyo, New York: Kodansha International, 1987; Burch, Noel, *To the Distant Observer: Form and Meaning in Japanese Cinema*, revised and edited by Michelson, Annette, Berkeley: University of California Press, 1979; McDonald, Keiko, I., *Cinema East: A Critical Study of Major Japanese Films*, Rutherford, New Jersey: Fairleigh Dickinson University Press, 1983.

Chapter 36

Richie, Donald, *The Films of Akira Kurosawa*, Berkeley: University of California Press, 1984; Kurosawa, Akira, *Something Like an Autobiography*, translated by Bock, Audie, New York: Random House Vintage Books, 1983; Desser, David, *The Samurai Films of Akira Kurosawa*, Ann Arbor, Michigan: Univeristy of Michigan Research Press, 1981; Erens, Patricia, *Akira Kurosawa: A Guide to References and Resources*, Boston: G. K. Hall, 1979; Prince, Stephen, *The Warrior's Camera: The Cinema of Akira Kurosawa*, Princeton, New Jersey: Princeton University Press, 1991; Bock, Audie, *Japanese Film Directors*, Tokyo, New York: Kodansha International, 1978; Mellen, Joan, *Voices from the Japanese Cinema*, New York: Liveright, 1975; Burch, Noel, *To the Distant Observer: Form and Meaning in the Japanese Cinema*, Berkeley: University of California Press, 1979; *Perspectives on Akira Kurosawa*, New York: Goodwin,

James, editor, G. K. Hall, 1994; Kurosawa, Akira, *Seven Samurai and Other Screenplays*, translated by Richie, Donald, and Niki, Hisae, London: Faber and Faber, 1992; Kurosawa, Akira, and Hasimoto, Shinobu, *Rashomon: A Film by Akira Kurosawa*, edited by Donald Richie, New York, Grove Press, 1969; Richie, Donald, *Different People: Pictures of Some Japanese*, Tokyo, New York: Kodansha International, 1987.

Chapter 37

OH AND JAPANESE BASEBALL:

Oh, Sadaharu, and Falkner, David, *Sadaharu Oh: A Zen Way of Baseball*, New York: Random House Vintage, 1985; Whiting, Robert, *You Gotta Have Wa*, New York: Vintage, 1990; Maitland, Brian, *Japanese Baseball: A Fan's Guide*, Tokyo: Charles Tuttle, 1991; Whiting, Robert, *The Chrysanthemum and the Bat: Baseball Samurai Style*, New York: Dodd Mead, 1977; Obojski, Robert, *The Rise of Japanese Baseball Power*, Radnor, Pennsylvania: Chilton Books, 1975; Cromartie, Warren, with Whiting, Robert, *Slugging It Out in Japan: An American Major Leaguer in the Tokyo Outfield*, Tokyo, New York: Kodansha International, 1991.

UESHIBA AND AIKIDO:

Stevens, John, *Abundant Peace: The Biography of Morihei Ueshiba, Founder of Aikido*, Boston: Shambhala, 1987; Ueshiba, Kisshomaru, *The Spirit of Aikido*, translated by Taitetsu, Unno, Tokyo, New York: Kodansha International, 1984; Saotome, Mitsugi, *Aikido and the Harmony of Nature*, Boston: Shambhala, 1993; Stevens, John, *Three Budo Masters*, Tokyo, New York: Kodansha International, 1995; Stevens, John, and Shirata, Rinjiro, *Aikido: The Way of Harmony*, Boston: Shambhala, 1984; Ueshiba, Morihei, *Budo: Teaching of the Founder of Aikido*, Tokyo, New York: Kodansha International, 1938, 1991; Ueshiba, Morihei, *Budo Training in Aikido*, Tokyo, New York: Kodansha International, 1933, 1997; Ueshiba, Kisshomaru, *Aikido*, Tokyo: Hozansha Publications, 1985; Westbrook, A., and Ratti, O., *Aikido and the Dynamic Sphere: An Illustrated Introduction*, Tokyo: Charles Tuttle, 1982; Stevens, John, *The Shambhala Guide to Aikido*, Boston: Shambhala, 1996; O'Connor, Greg, *The Aikido Student Handbook*, Berkeley: Frog, Ltd., 1993.

Acknowledgment of Permissions

In the chapter on Murasaki, grateful acknowledgment is made to Alfred A. Knopf, Inc., for permission to quote from *The Tale of Genji*, translated by Edward G. Seidensticker, Copyright © 1976, and to Vintage Books for permission to use a poem by Izumi Shikibu from *The Ink Dark Moon: Love Poems by Ono no Komachi and Izumi Shikibu*, translated by Jane Hirshfield and Aratani Mariko, Copyright © 1986.

In the chapter on Sen no Rikyu, grateful acknowledgment is made to the University of Hawaii Press for permission to use a poem by Fujiwara Ietaka from *Warlords, Artists and Commoners: Japan in the Sixteenth Century*, edited by George Ellison and Bardwell J. Smith, Copyright © 1981.

In the chapter on Basho, grateful acknowledgment is made to Penguin Books, Ltd. (London), for permission to quote from *On Love and Barley*, translated by Lucien Stryk, Copyright © 1985 (the 2nd, 4th, 11th, 14th, and 18th haiku in the chapter), and also for permission to quote from *Narrow Road to the Interior*, translated by Yuasa Nobuyuki, Copyright © 1966 (the 12th and 13th haiku in the chapter).

Grateful acknowledgment is also made to Kodansha International, Ltd. for permission to quote from *Matsuo Basho* by Makoto Ueda, Copyright © 1982 (the 3rd, 9th, 10th, and 22nd haiku in the chapter), and also for permission to quote from *A Haiku Journey*, translated by Dorothy Britton, Copyright © 1974 (the 17th, 19th, 20th, and 21st haiku in the chapter).

Grateful acknowledgment is made to Charles E. Tuttle & Company, Inc., for permission to quote from *The Japanese Haiku* by Kenneth Yasuda, Copyright © 1957 (the 5th and 6th haiku in the chapter).

Grateful acknowledgment is also made to Shambhala Publications Inc. (Boston), for permission to quote from *The Essential Basho* by Sam Hamill, Copyright © 1998 (the 15th poem in the chapter).

In addition, grateful acknowledgment is made to the Columbia University Press for permission to quote a haiku from the collection of Yamazaki Sokan from *Sources of Japanese Tradition, Volume 1*, edited by Ryusaku Tsunoda, William Theodore deBary, and Donald Keene, Copyright © 1965 (the 1st haiku of the chapter.)

And grateful acknowledgment is made to writer Misuzu Bergman for permission to use her unpublished translations of the 7th, 8th, and 16th haiku in this chapter.

In the chapter on Chikamatsu, grateful acknowledgment is made to the Columbia University Press for permission to quote from *Major Plays by Chikamatsu*, translated by Donald Keene, Copyright © 1961.

And in the chapter on Hayashi Fumiko, grateful acknowledgment is made to the Seal Press (Seattle) for permission to quote from *To Live and To Write: Selections by Japanese Women Writers, 1913–1918*, edited by Yukiko Tanaka and translated by Elizabeth Hanson, Copyright © 1987.

PHOTO CREDITS

Page 3: Courtesy of the Mitsui Research Institute for Social Economic History.

Page 12: Courtesy of the Mitsubishi Public Affairs Committee.

Page 24: Courtesy of the Matsushita Electric Corporation of America.

Page 34: Courtesy of the Minolta Corporation.

Page 43: Courtesy of the Honda Motor Co., Ltd.

Page 49: Courtesy of NEC USA Inc.

Page 58: Courtesy of the Toyota Motor Company.

Page 67: Courtesy of the Sony Corporation of America.

Page 85: Courtesy of Fushinan temple.

Page 94: Courtesy of the Kyoto University Library.

Page 130: Courtesy of Jingoji temple (top), Anyō-in temple (center), and Akama Jingu shrine (bottom).

Page 140: Courtesy of Chōkōji temple.

Page 154: Courtesy of Rinnōji temple.

Page 216: Courtesy of Katoh Taki.

Page 264: Courtesy of the Onomichi Public Library.

Page 303: Courtesy of the Film Stills Archive of the Museum of Modern Art.

Page 314: Courtesy of the Film Stills Archive of the Museum of Modern Art.

Index

About the Author

Mark Weston has been a lawyer for ABC Television and a journalist for ABC News. His first book, *The Land and People of Pakistan*, was written for young adults and published by HarperCollins in 1992. He has also written articles for *The Washington Post* and *The Los Angeles Times*, and a one-character play about George Orwell, *The Last Man in Europe*.

Weston grew up in Armonk, New York, and graduated from Brown University and the University of Texas Law School. He also spent a year at the London School of Economics. In 1992 he won enough money on TV's *Jeopardy!* to start a company that made geographical jigsaw puzzles for children. After selling the firm to a larger puzzle company in 1994, Weston began writing *Giants of Japan*. In 1995 he lived with a Japanese family just outside Tokyo.